# *CAD APPLICATIONS: ARCHITECTURAL*

Fitz Memorial Library
Endicott College
Beverly, Massachusetts 01915

# *CAD APPLICATIONS: ARCHITECTURAL*

## David L. Goetsch
**OKALOOSA–WALTON JUNIOR COLLEGE**

Fitz Memorial Library
Endicott College
Beverly, Massachusetts 01915

 **DELMAR PUBLISHERS INC.**®

*Dedication*
*To our good friends and Savannah's godparents—*
*Sharon and Jim*

*Delmar Staff*
    Administrative Editor: Mark Huth
    Production Editor: Ruth East

For information, address Delmar Publishers Inc.
2 Computer Drive West, Box 15–015
Albany, New York 12212–5015

COPYRIGHT © 1986
BY DELMAR PUBLISHERS INC.

All rights reserved. No part of this work covered by
the copyright hereon may be reproduced or used in any form or
by any means—graphic, electronic, or mechanical, including
photocopying, recording, taping, or information storage
and retrieval systems—without written permission of the
publisher.

Printed in the United States of America
Published simultaneously in Canada
by Nelson Canada,
A division of International Thomson Limited

10 9 8 7 6 5 4 3 2 1

**Library of Congress Cataloging-in-Publication Data**
Goetsch, David L.
    CAD applications, architectural.
    1. Architecture—Data processing. 2. Architectural
drawing—Data processing. 3. Computer-aided design.
I. Title. II. Title: C.A.D. applications, architectural.
NA2728.G64  1986    720′.28′40285    85-25221
ISBN 0-8273-2633-5 (Instructor's Guide)
ISBN 0-8273-2632-7 (pbk.)

NA
2728
.G64
1986

# Contents

|  |  |  |
|---|---|---|
|  | **PREFACE** | vii |
| **CHAPTER 1** | **INTRODUCTION** | 1 |

Use the Text as a Supplement • Learn CAD Fundamentals • Learn to Operate Your CAD System • Establish the Learning Sequence • Complete the Application Chapters • Complete the Advanced Application Project

| **CHAPTER 2** | **OVERVIEW OF CAD** | 3 |
|---|---|---|

The Concept • Evolution of Drafting • CAD Systems • CAD Hardware • CAD Software • Making Drawings on a CAD System • Generic CAD Commands and Functions

| **CHAPTER 3** | **FLOOR PLANS** | 19 |
|---|---|---|

Definition, Purpose, and Contents • Special Symbols Needed • CAD Commands and Functions Used • Procedures for Preparing the Plan • Review Questions • Application Projects

| **CHAPTER 4** | **CONSTRUCTION DETAILS** | 41 |
|---|---|---|

Definition, Purpose, and Contents • Special Symbols Needed • CAD Commands and Functions Used • Procedures for Preparing the Details • Review Questions • Application Projects

| **CHAPTER 5** | **ELEVATIONS** | 63 |
|---|---|---|

Definition, Purpose, and Contents • Special Symbols Needed • CAD Commands and Functions Used • Procedures for Preparing the Elevation • Review Questions • Application Projects

| **CHAPTER 6** | **FOUNDATION PLANS** | 77 |
|---|---|---|

Definition, Purpose, and Contents • Special Symbols Needed • CAD Commands and Functions Used • Procedures for Preparing the Plan • Review Questions • Application Projects

**CHAPTER 7   PLUMBING, ELECTRICAL, AND HVAC PLANS**  **93**

Definition, Purpose, and Contents • Special Symbols Needed • CAD Commands and Functions Used • Procedures for Preparing the Plan • Review Questions • Application Projects

**CHAPTER 8   PLOT PLANS**  **109**

Definition, Purpose, and Contents • Special Symbols Needed • CAD Commands and Functions Used • Procedures for Preparing the Plan • Review Questions • Application Projects

**CHAPTER 9   STRUCTURAL ENGINEERING DRAWINGS**  **125**

Definition, Purpose, and Contents • Special Symbols Needed • CAD Commands and Functions Used • Procedures for Preparing the Drawing • Review Questions • Application Projects

**CHAPTER 10   STRUCTURAL SHOP AND PLACEMENT DRAWINGS**  **149**

Definition, Purpose, and Contents • Special Symbols Needed • CAD Commands and Functions Used • Procedures for Preparing the Drawing • Review Questions • Application Projects

**APPENDIX A   ADVANCED APPLICATION PROJECTS**  **173**

**APPENDIX B   DESIGN DATA**  **183**

# Preface

This text is designed for use in courses such as architectural drafting; construction drafting; structural drafting; and residential design, planning, and drafting. It is appropriate for use in such courses offered in comprehensive high schools, area vocational schools, technical schools, community colleges, trade and technical schools, and at the freshman and sophomore levels in universities.

## PREREQUISITES

This text was designed primarily as a supplement to be used in a course on architectural drafting. Ideally, students using this book will have completed an introduction to CAD and will be enrolled in an architectural drafting course. This book does not attempt to teach architectural drafting. Rather, it is especially designed to help students studying architectural drafting learn how to produce architectural drawings on a CAD system. Before a student attempts to produce an architectural drawing using this book—say a floor plan—he or she should already know how to produce the floor plan manually. The student should also be familiar with the operation of the CAD system that will be used.

To soften this requirement, *CAD Applications: Architectural* has two special features: Chapter 2 provides a comprehensive overview of CAD for students who need a refresher and Appendix B contains a summary of commonly used design information for architectural drafting. These special features will allow students who might need a refresher in both CAD and architectural drafting to use the book without having to retake courses in these areas.

## INNOVATIONS

This book was especially designed to help students and teachers solve several problems that have grown out of the slow but steady move away from manual drafting to CAD. These problems include:

1. Because the world of drafting is in a state of transition, students must still learn and teachers must still teach both manual drafting and CAD.
2. Students must enter the work force with dual skills—manual and CAD.
3. Students must learn both system-specific skills on a given CAD system and broad skills that apply to all CAD systems.

*CAD Applications: Architectural* discusses all these problems. It allows teachers to continue to teach their normal architectural design and drafting courses requiring the students to use manual techniques. Then, when students know the fundamentals of architectural design and can produce architectural plans manually, this text helps them learn how to produce the same types of plans on a CAD system—any CAD system. This text allows students to enter the work force fully prepared for a world of drafting that is undergoing a transition. If they still need manual skills, they will have them. When— not if, but when—they need CAD skills, they will have those too.

This book speaks to the third problem in a unique way. In each "drawing chapter," the generic names for the commands used to create the drawings are listed. Before students can begin the application projects for the chapter, they are required to match these generic commands with their corresponding commands on the CAD system employed. Students then use the actual command names in completing the application projects. This type of approach has proven very successful in my CAD program at Okaloosa-Walton Junior College where students have been using it for five years. We have had students who learned to use three different types and models of CAD systems before graduation. The specific names for such generic commands as LINE, EDIT, MOVE, ZOOM-IN, and so forth are different on each system. Using the approach in this book allows my students to become very versatile and improves their ability to adapt quickly to any CAD system they may have to use on the job. By completing activities such as those set forth in this book, students quickly learn that although every CAD system has its own specific names for the commands and functions used in producing drawings there is a set of generic commands and functions common to most systems. Once they learn these generic commands and functions, they can quickly pick up the corresponding commands and functions on any CAD system.

## MAJOR FEATURES

### Comprehensive Contents

The Contents was designed to give teachers and students an easy to follow road map for locating material in the text. In addition to the chapter titles, the Contents contains a breakdown of the major topical headings for each chapter.

### Review Material

Review material on CAD and architectural design is included for students who may need a refresher in these areas. Chapter 2 provides a comprehensive overview of CAD. Appendix B contains frequently called for design data.

### Standard Chapter Format

Chapters 3 through 10 are the "drawing" chapters. Each of these chapters uses the same format. Each begins with a definition, purpose, and contents section for the type of architectural plan in question (e.g., floor plans, foundation plans, elevations). The next section covers the graphic symbols needed to complete the drawings for the chapter and necessary steps to undertake if these symbols are not contained in the symbols library of the CAD system used.

The next section is an explanation of the *generic* commands and functions that will be used in producing the subject drawings on a CAD system. This section is followed by a step-by-step, illustrated example of how a given drawing is produced on a CAD system.

The next section is a comprehensive question-and-answer review of the chapter that is to be completed before beginning the application projects for the chapter. Finally, each chapter concludes with a set of realistic application projects that students complete on the CAD system or systems available to them.

One of the risks of using a standard format is that it builds in a certain amount of redundancy. For example, the commands used for creating drawings are listed in each chapter, and they don't really vary a great deal from chapter to chapter. However, this redundancy serves two positive purposes with regard to teaching and learning: 1) by continuously repeating these commands in each chapter, students are assured of knowing them well by the time they complete the text, and 2) the standard format allows teachers flexibility in marrying this text to their existing architectural drafting courses. The redundancy allows teachers to assign the chapters in *any* order; it is not necessary to begin at the beginning and proceed through in sequence.

An additional advantage of the standard chapter format for drawing chapters is that teachers can begin one group of students on the floor plan chapter, another on elevations, another on foundations, and so forth. This has proven to be a boon to classroom management in my CAD classes at Okaloosa-Walton Junior College. It allows me to assign projects to groups of students so they learn to work as a team as they will have to on the job.

### *Heavily Illustrated*

Each chapter has been heavily illustrated so that students become used to seeing drawings prepared on a variety of CAD systems and are not overcome by the high text-to-illustration ratio that students so often dislike in drafting textbooks. All concepts and procedures presented have at least one drawing or photograph—and frequently several—to illustrate them visually.

### *Extensive Application Projects*

Chapters 3 through 10 are the drawing chapters, and together they contain over 150 realistic application projects that can be completed on any CAD system. Most of the activities involve residential dwellings. However, numerous commercial projects have been included to expand the student's skills in this area. In addition, several of the projects are actual architect's sketches that represent real world projects. This book contains not just a copious amount of application work but also a wide variety.

To provide for the especially talented and motivated student, Appendix A contains a major final application project in which students are required to reconstruct an entire set of architectural plans from a given set that contains all of the essential elements of a typical set of architectural plans.

### *Simply Written*

*CAD Applications: Architectural* is written in a straightforward, simple, conversational style. Students often find the language of drafting books verbose, abstract, and complicated; consequently, they are turned off by them. Even when a concept is complicated—as many drafting concepts are—the explanation of it doesn't have to be. This text was written to communicate plainly and simply; therefore, students can concentrate on what they are learning rather than on unscrambling overly complicated explanations.

### *Instructive Introduction*

The Introduction to this text explains the recommended approach to using it for best results. Teachers and students are free to use the book in any way that fits into their teaching or learning pattern. However, the suggestions in the Introduction may be helpful for students and teachers who do not already have a plan formulated. They are based on successes and failures accomplished in my CAD classes at Okaloosa-Walton Junior College over the past five years.

## ACKNOWLEDGMENTS

The author wishes to acknowledge the efforts of several people without whose assistance this project could not have been completed in a timely manner. Thanks to Mark Huth, Administrative Editor at Delmar Publishers, for having the foresight to recognize the need for a book to help bridge the transitional gap from manual drafting to CAD. Thanks to Ray Adams, Susan Wilkinson, Robert Rosen, Jeff Bruechart, and Ray Rickman for assisting with the illustrations.

Special thanks to Jim Vandervest, Professor of CAD at Gulf Coast Community College, for providing the special advanced application project in Appendix A and several other CAD-produced drawings. Jim and Gulf Coast Community College have one of the best CAD training programs in the country.

The author also wishes to express his appreciation to Delmar Publishers Inc. for the use of the following illustrations: Figures 3–1, 9–2, 9–5, 10–6, 11–9, 14–1, 14–3, 14–4, 14–5, 15–8, 15–11, 16–12, and 17–2 from *Structural Drafting* (Goetsch); Figures 2–5, 2–8, 2–12, and 3–1 from *Drafting for Trades and Industry: Architectural* (Nelson); and figures from pages 14, 40, 45, 47, and 49 from *Drafting for Trades and Industry: Civil* (Nelson).

## ABOUT THE AUTHOR

Dr. David L. Goetsch is Director of Technical Education and Professor of Computer-Aided Design and Drafting at Okaloosa-Walton Junior College in Niceville, Florida. Dr. Goetsch was one of the pioneers of CAD training in this country. His involvement with CAD began in 1973 in industry. When he entered education full time in 1976, he immediately moved to convert his manual drafting program to a CAD program.

Dr. Goetsch has written numerous books on CAD, is a nationally recognized speaker on CAD instruction, and frequently presents seminars and workshops on CAD for teachers and practitioners at national conferences of such organizations as the American Institute of Design and Drafting and the National Computer Graphics Association.

In October 1984, Dr. Goetsch's CAD program was selected as a winner of the prestigious "Secretary's Award," which is presented each year by the U.S. Secretary of Education to the top ten vocational programs in the country. Dr. Goetsch's teaching awards include Teacher of the Year honors in 1976, 1981, 1982, and 1983.

# chapter 1
# Introduction

*CAD Applications: Architectural* is designed to help architectural drafting students learn how to produce architectural plans on a CAD system or systems. It is not designed to teach architectural drafting and does not attempt to. This approach, as set forth in this text, has been used successfully for over five years in a national award-winning drafting and design program. This chapter sets forth the recommended teaching/learning approach that will help ensure positive results.

## USE THE TEXT AS A SUPPLEMENT

*CAD Applications: Architectural* will be most effective if used as a supplemental text in an established architectural drafting course or program. Ideally, students should have completed an introduction to CAD and a complete set of manually prepared architectural plans before attempting the activities in this book.

This approach offers two advantages: 1) It ensures that students learn to produce architectural plans manually (This is important. Students still need manual drafting skills and they will for some time to come) and 2) it shortens the amount of time required for students to learn how to produce architectural plans on a CAD system. Experience has shown that students who already know how to prepare architectural plans manually learn how to produce them on a CAD system much faster than students who are trying to learn both CAD and architectural drafting concurrently.

## LEARN CAD FUNDAMENTALS

Before attempting to use this book as a supplemental text, students should learn the fundamentals of CAD. The fundamentals include the terminology, concepts, principles, and theories one would expect to learn in an introductory CAD course. Students who have not learned the fundamentals of CAD should study Chapter 2 carefully before proceeding to the application chapters (Chapters 3 through 10). Chapter 2 provides a comprehensive overview of CAD that can be used for initial study or for a refresher.

## LEARN TO OPERATE YOUR CAD SYSTEM

Before attempting to use this book, students should learn how to operate the CAD system or systems they will use in completing the application projects. Students should be able to perform all of the following tasks on their CAD systems:

1. System start-up.
2. Logging on to the system.
3. File retrieval.
4. Keying.
5. Cursor control.
6. Menu manipulation.
7. Command activation.
8. Input, modification, manipulation, and facilitation of data.
9. Loading the plotter.
10. Specifying plotting requirements and limits.
11. Output of data.

## ESTABLISH THE LEARNING SEQUENCE

Chapters 3 through 10 deal with the most common components of a typical set of architectural plans: the plot plan, foundation plan, floor plan, elevations, construction details, and mechanical plans. Chapter 9 deals with structural engineering drawings. Chapter 10 deals with structural shop drawings.

All of these chapters share a common format so that it is not necessary to begin with Chapter 3 and proceed through in order. Instructors will achieve the best results by proceeding through the chapters in the same order used for teaching manual architectural drafting.

## COMPLETE THE APPLICATION CHAPTERS

Chapters 3 through 10 should be completed as follows for best results:

1. Read the definition, purpose, and contents section carefully to acquaint yourself with the plan in question. Make a mental note of the required contents of the plan or the rule of thumb to be used in deciding on the content.
2. Compare the graphic symbols required with those available in the symbols library of your CAD system and make a mental note of any missing symbols.
3. Examine the list of generic commands that will be used in producing the subject plan and determine the actual name for each command on your CAD system.
4. Read each step in the sample procedures section and make a list of the actual commands on your CAD system that would be used in accomplishing each step in the procedure.
5. Complete the chapter review.
6. Complete all application projects assigned by the instructor according to the directions provided. SAVE all completed projects and PLOT a hard copy of all completed projects.

## COMPLETE THE ADVANCED APPLICATION PROJECT

Appendix A contains a major advanced application project. Once the assigned application projects for each chapter have been completed, do the corresponding part of the advanced project in Appendix A. This project should be SAVED and PLOTTED, and a copy should be kept as part of the student's portfolio of work samples to be used during job searching.

# chapter 2
# Overview of CAD

This chapter provides a brief overview of CAD. For students who have already had an introductory course in CAD, it will provide a comprehensive review. For students who have not studied CAD, it will provide enough information to allow the activities in this book to be pursued. However, this chapter should not be used in place of or instead of a CAD course. There is not sufficient space in just one chapter to cover the topic in the depth needed. Students who complete the activities in this book without having completed at least an introductory course in CAD should arrange to take such a course as soon as possible.

## THE CONCEPT

Computer-aided drafting, as a concept, had its birth in the 1960s when the most well-established computer company—IBM—released the first CAD system produced for the commercial market. CAD represents a radical departure from the many other time- and work-saving innovations that preceded it.

Anyone who has been associated with drafting for the last twenty years could list many of these innovations. They include the T-square, the parallel bar, the adjustable triangle, the drafting machine, templates, the electric eraser, and numerous media advances such as sepias and polyester film. All of these innovations—and the many others not named—were *manual* tools to improve *manual* drafting techniques. CAD, on the other hand, represents *automation* in drafting.

### CAD Defined

In order to understand the definition of CAD, one must first understand the definition of drafting. In order to understand the definition of drafting, one must begin with the design process because the need for the occupation of drafting is rooted in the design process.

The design process is a systematic, five-step approach to solving problems or meeting needs, Figure 2–1. It is the process engineers, architects, and designers go through in designing every kind of structure from the smallest house to the largest skyscraper. Drafting is the process through which the design process is documented. That documen-

# CAD Applications: Architectural

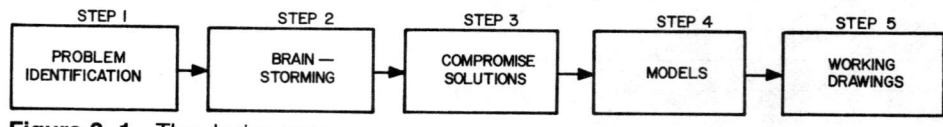

**Figure 2–1**  The design process.

tation might take the form of sketches, preliminary drawings, working drawings, door and window schedules, bills of material, and numerous types of calculation records.

If one understands that drafting means documenting the design process, it is easy to understand that computer-aided drafting means using a computer and various peripheral devices to document the design process.

## *EVOLUTION OF DRAFTING*

Drafting has been in evidence almost since the beginning of time. Many of the world's greatest wonders—the pyramids, the Parthenon, the hanging gardens of Babylon—were the result of detailed designs carefully documented by drafters. Over the years, the tools and techniques of drafting have evolved continually.

Since the days of lapboards and T-squares, the tools and techniques of drafting have undergone numerous advances. Figures 2–2 through 2–11 on pages 4 through 8 show some of the many developments in manual drafting that preceded CAD. Figure 2–12 on page 9 is an example of the type of modern CAD hardware that is replacing the manual tools of the past.

The hardware configuration in Figure 2–12 consists of a processor, a keyboard, a graphics terminal, a menu on a graphics tablet with a puck, and a plotter.

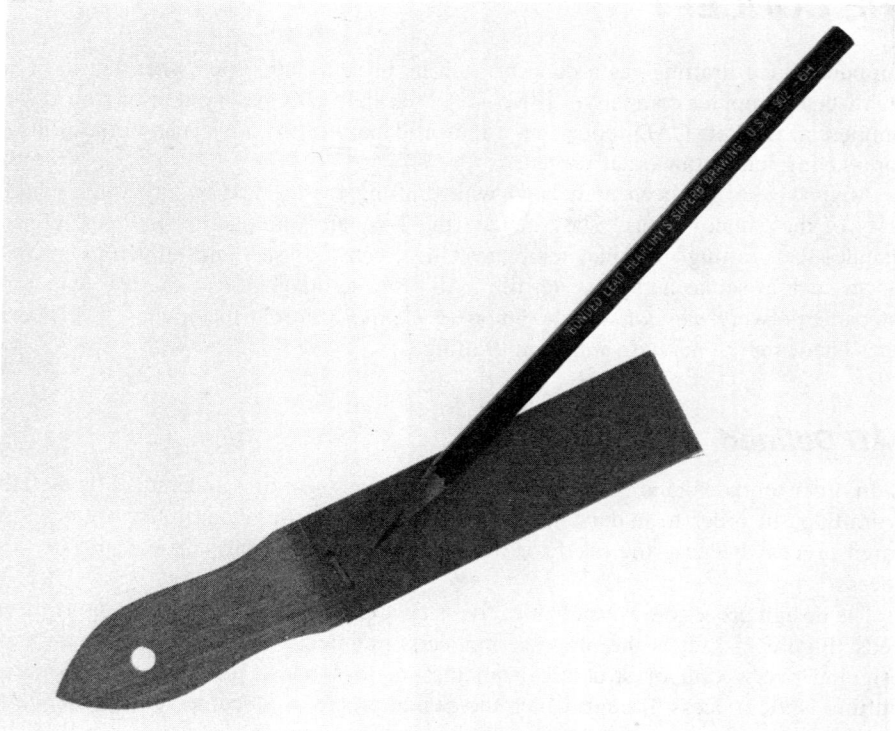

**Figure 2–2**  Manual pencil pointer and pencil. *(Courtesy of Hearlihy & Co.)*

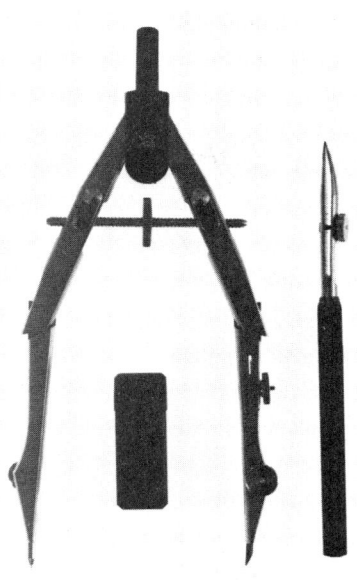

**Figure 2–3** Manual compass and ruling pen. *(Courtesy of Hearlihy & Co.)*

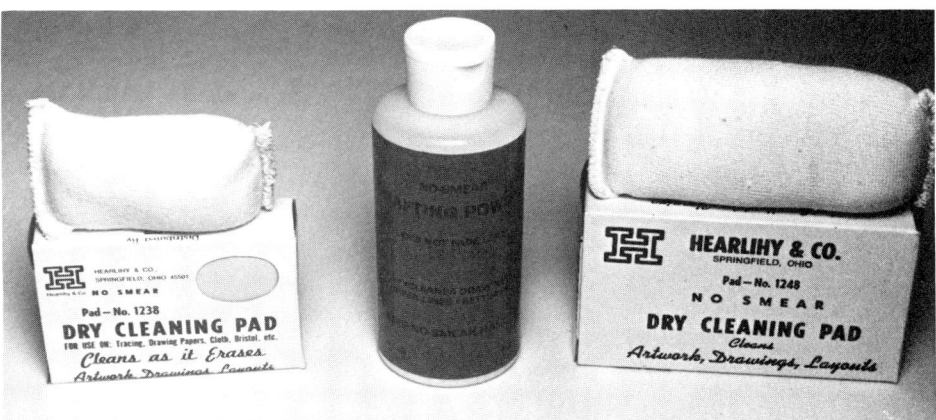

**Figure 2–4** Manual dry cleaning pads. *(Courtesy of Hearlihy & Co.)*

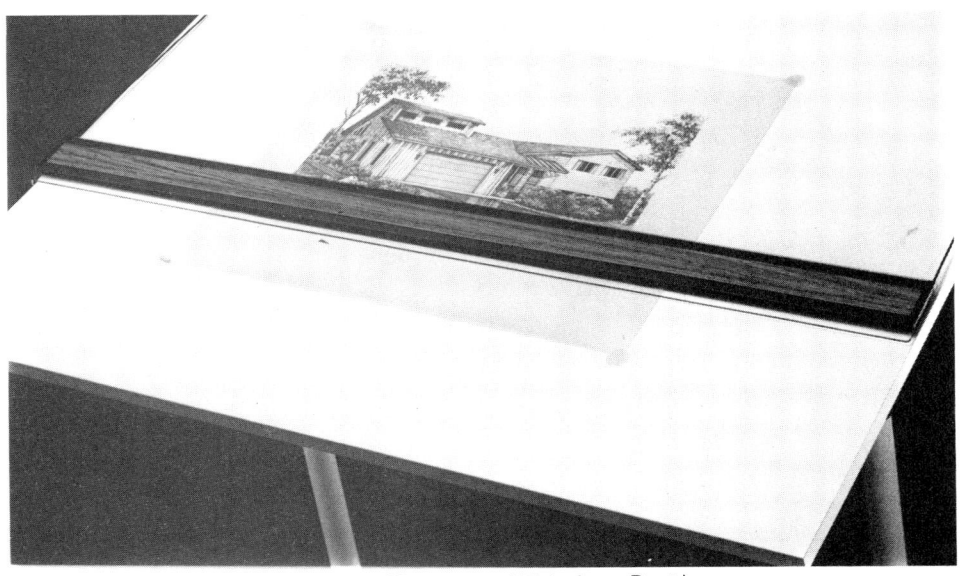

**Figure 2–5** Manual parallel bar. *(Courtesy of Teledyne Post.)*

**6** | CAD Applications: Architectural

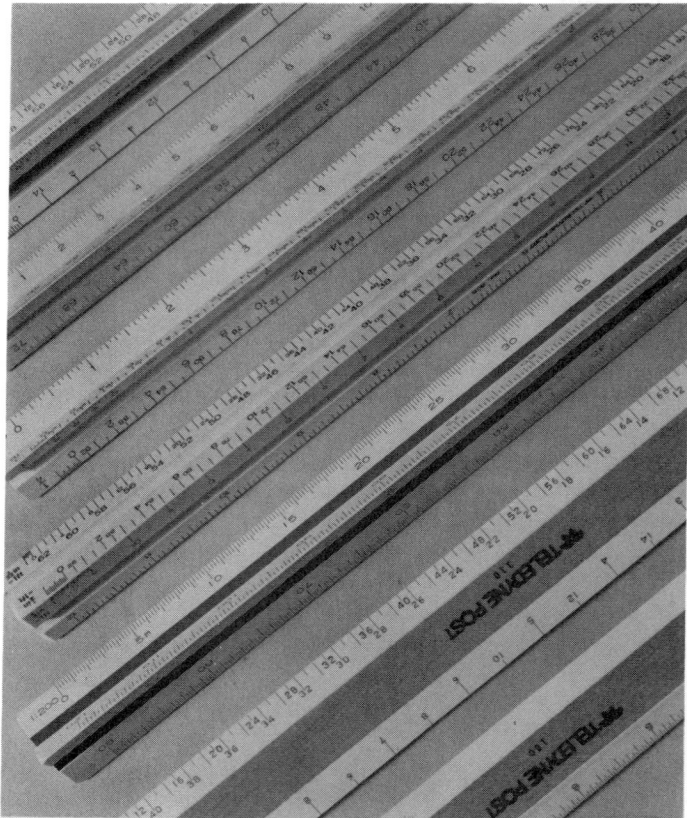

**Figure 2–6** Manual scales. *(Courtesy of Teledyne Post.)*

**Figure 2–7** Manual electric eraser. *(Courtesy of Teledyne Post.)*

Chapter 2 Overview of CAD | 7

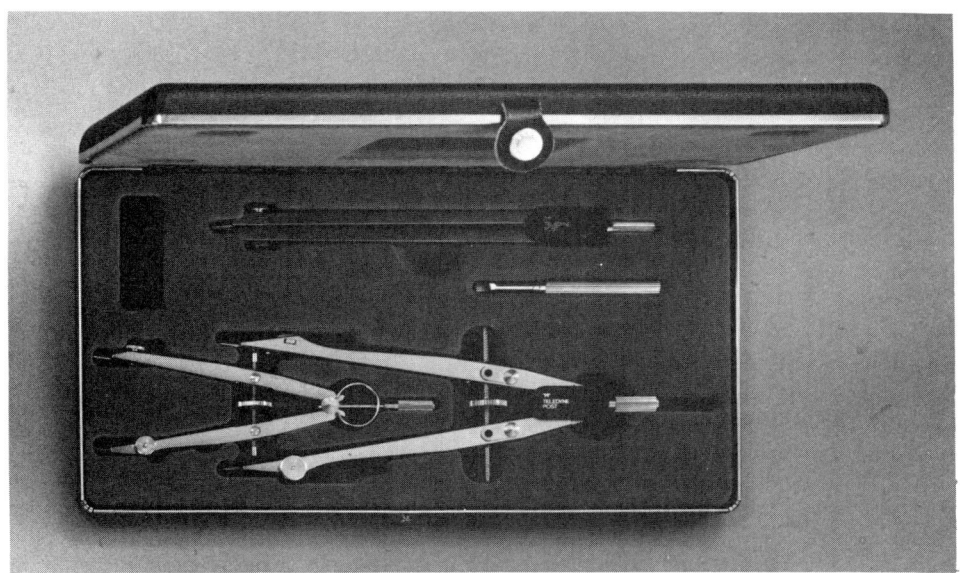

**Figure 2–8** Manual instrument set. *(Courtesy of Teledyne Post.)*

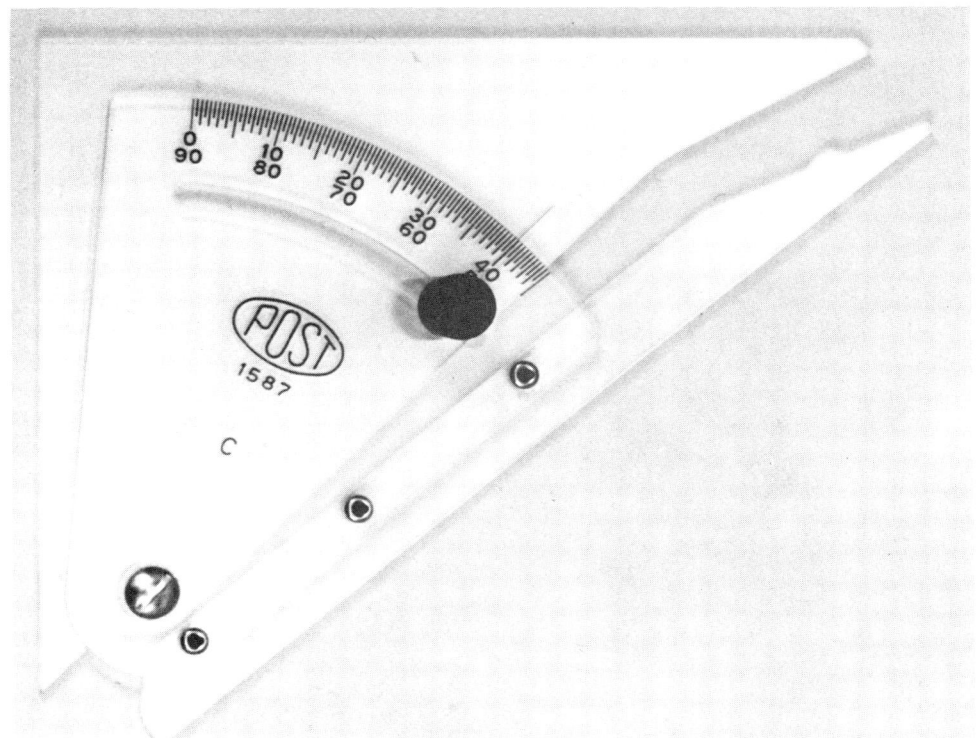

**Figure 2–9** Manual adjustable triangle. *(Courtesy of Teledyne Post.)*

**8** | CAD Applications: Architectural

**Figure 2–10** Manual triangles. *(Courtesy of Teledyne Post.)*

**Figure 2-11** Manual inking set *(Courtesy of K & E Company).*

**Figure 2-12** Modern CAD system. (*Courtesy of Bausch & Lomb/Houston Instrument.*)

## CAD SYSTEMS

The term *CAD system* is used frequently and, often, improperly. Many people look at a hardware configuration and call it a CAD system. This is a convenient but technically incorrect use of the term.

A CAD system actually consists of three components, Figure 2-13:

1. The hardware.
2. The software.
3. The users.

Hardware is what one sees when looking at a configuration—the machines. Software consists of computer programs and various types of written documentation that accompany programs. Users are the people who operate CAD systems and *think* for the systems. CAD system is a much more convenient term for day-to-day conversation than the cumbersome phrase "hardware configuration with software and users." It is correct to use the term when referring to just a configuration, provided you understand the difference.

## CAD HARDWARE

The hardware that makes up a typical configuration for a modern CAD system includes:

1. A processor.
2. A disk drive unit.
3. A keyboard.
4. A graphics terminal and sometimes a separate text terminal.
5. A graphics tablet and/or digitizer.
6. A plotter.

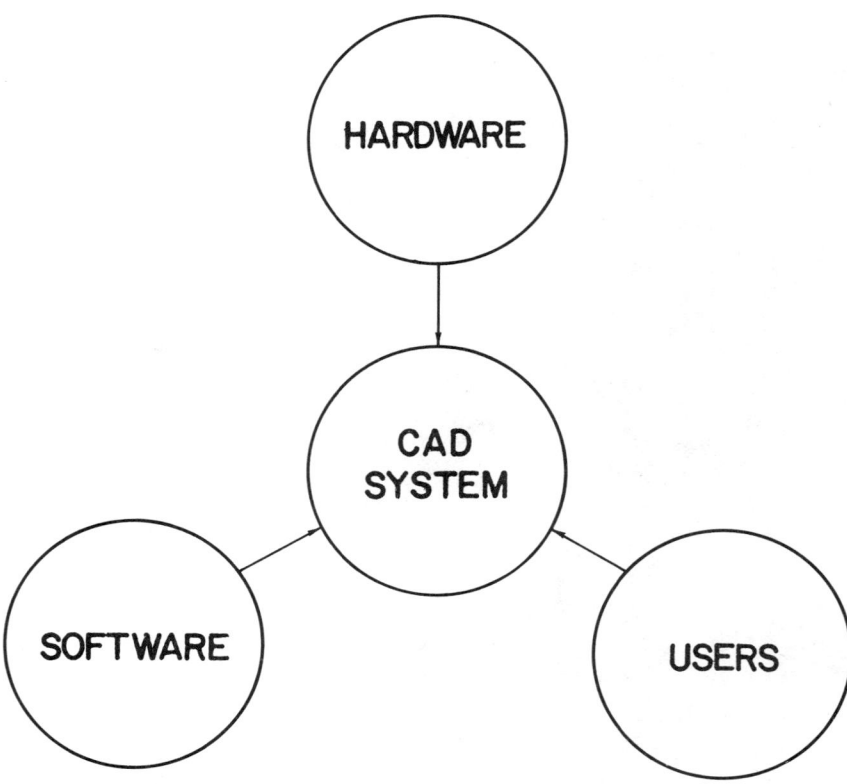

**Figure 2–13** Components of a CAD system.

All hardware components, except the processor, are referred to as input, output, or input/output devices. These devices are sometimes collectively known by the term *peripherals*.

An input device is a peripheral device used for getting data into the system in a computer-useable form. An output device is a peripheral device for getting data out of the system in human-useable form. Input/output devices are peripherals capable of performing both operations. The processor is not called an input, output, input/output, or peripheral device because it is the computer in a CAD system. It is the device into which and out of which data is put or taken. The processor is the "brains" of the CAD system.

In many systems, such as the one shown in Figure 2–14, the graphics terminal, keyboard, and disk drive are all one unit. The graphics tablet for the system in Figure 2–14 can be seen to the left of the graphics terminal.

Figure 2–15 contains a range of digitizers that can be interfaced, or connected, as needed to meet the drawing size requirements of an individual architectural drafting setting. Figures 2–16 and 2–17 contain examples of the various sizes of pen plotters that might be part of a CAD system used in an architectural drafting setting. Figure 2–16 is a small desk top single pen plotter that can plot on A- and B-size media.

Figure 2–17 contains a wide range of pen plotters that can be interfaced as needed to meet the drawing size requirements of individual architectural drafting settings.

**Figure 2-14** Graphics display, disk drive, and keyboard of a modern CAD system. *(Courtesy of Bausch & Lomb/Houston Instrument.)*

**Figure 2–15** Digitizers. *(Courtesy of Bausch & Lomb/Houston Instrument.)*

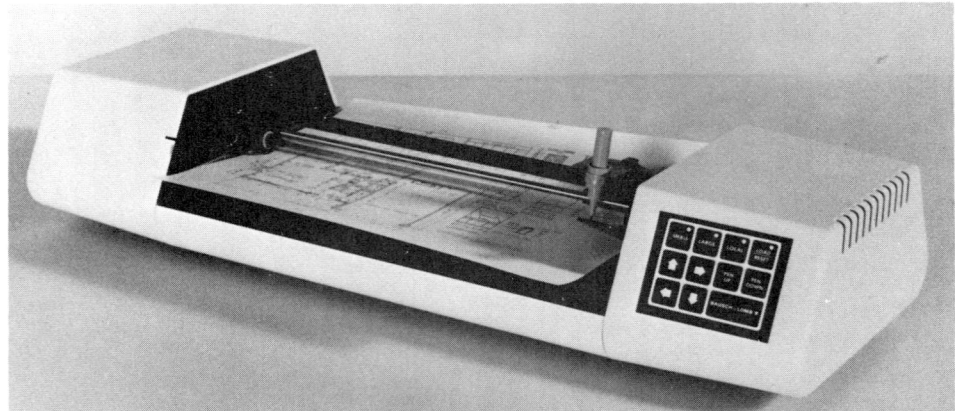

**Figure 2–16** Pen plotter. *(Courtesy of Bausch & Lomb/Houston Instrument.)*

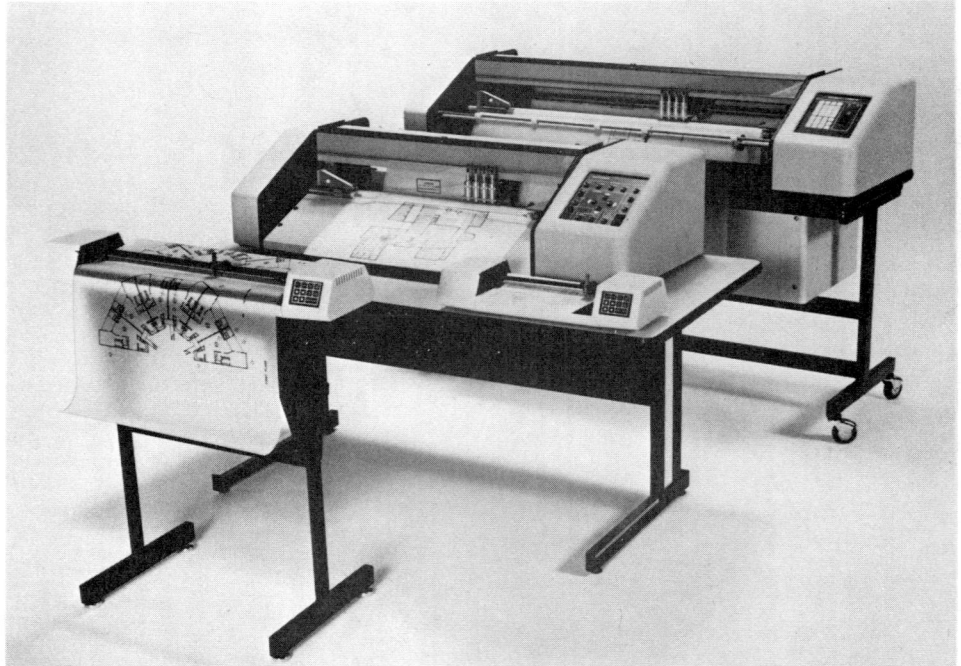

**Figure 2–17** Pen plotters. *(Courtesy of Bausch & Lomb/Houston Instrument.)*

## CAD SOFTWARE

There are three types of software used in CAD: operational, applications, and user-defined, Figure 2–18. Operational software is the software that allows the system to perform such basic functions as accepting data, storing data, and operating peripheral devices.

Applications software is software especially designed to perform graphic and drafting tasks relating to general drafting or to specific drafting applications such as architectural drafting. Applications software for architectural drafting gives CAD systems the ability to produce plot plans, foundation plans, floor plans, construction details, elevations, schedules, and all of the other types of documentation intrinsic to architectural drafting.

User-defined software gives CAD systems the ability to accept on-site creation and modification by users. Some systems have this capability and others don't. It is an important capability for CAD systems used in an architectural setting, especially in the

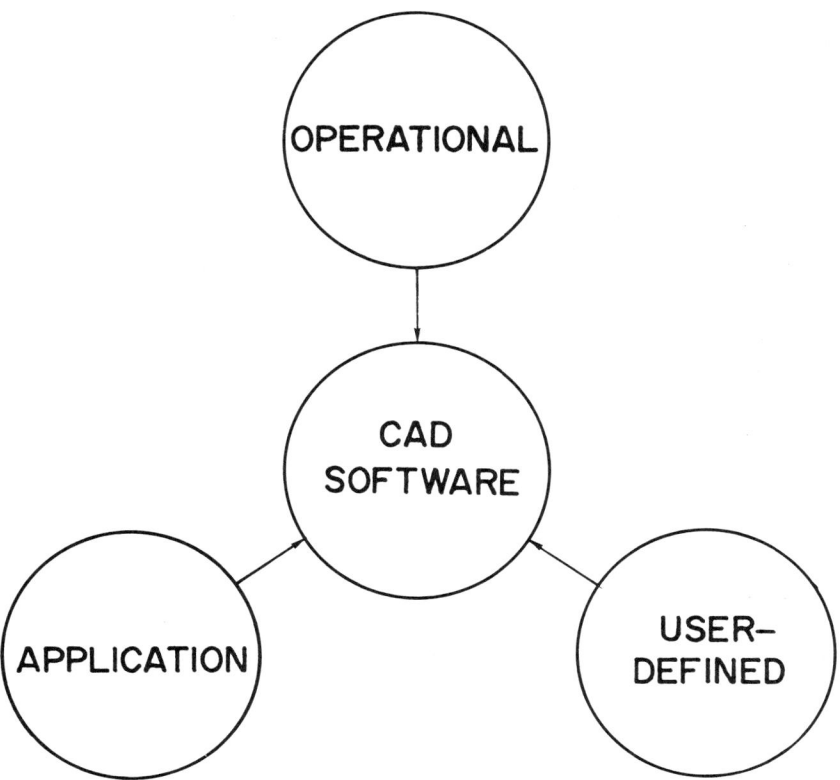

**Figure 2–18** Types of software in CAD.

area of symbol creation. CAD systems that allow users to define symbols, add them to a symbols library, and call them up as needed, rather than having to recreate them every time, offer significant time-saving opportunities to users.

## MAKING DRAWINGS ON A CAD SYSTEM

Making drawings on a CAD is a lot like making a drawing by telling someone else to do it. Suppose you wished to draw a floor plan, but both of your hands were in casts. Your solution would be to tell another drafter what you want and have it drawn. This, however, presents you with the same two problems you will encounter in trying to produce drawings on a CAD system:

1. The other drafter cannot read your mind. You must tell the other drafter *exactly* what to do.
2. You are limited because you can only tell the other drafter to perform tasks he or she already knows how to perform (has in memory).

This is what it is like using a CAD system. A CAD system must be told exactly what to do and can perform only those tasks it has been programmed to perform. This brings to mind two critical questions about using a CAD system:

1. How does a user know what tasks a CAD system has been programmed to perform?
2. How does a user tell a CAD system to perform these tasks?

Every type of documentation required in architectural drafting is composed of graphic and alphanumeric data. Graphic data are such things as points, lines, planes, and the various geometric characters made up of points, lines, and planes (e.g., circles, ellipses, triangles, rectangles, arcs, arrowheads). Alphanumeric data consist of letters, numbers, and special characters or, in other words, keyboard characters.

**14** | CAD Applications: Architectural

**Figure 2–19** CAD system with tablet-mounted menu. *(Courtesy of Bausch & Lomb/ Houston Instrument.)*

The graphic capabilities of most CAD systems are readily visible on function menus. There are several different types of function menus, but most CAD systems have either a tablet-mounted menu or a screen-mounted menu. Tablet-mounted menus, such as the one in Figure 2–19, are plastic or paper overlays attached to graphics tablets. Annotated positions on the overlay match electronic positions in the processor's memory. Each annotated position on the overlay represents a capability the system has been programmed for (e.g., draw a line, draw a circle, erase, edit).

Screen-mounted menus, such as the one in Figure 2–20, appear on the display of the graphics or text terminal, depending on the makeup of the hardware configuration. In either case, users can quickly learn the capabilities of a given CAD system by examining its function menus.

**Figure 2–20** CAD system with screen-mounted menu. *(Courtesy of Arrigoni Technology, Inc.)*

As to the second question, users tell a system to perform certain drafting tasks by activating menu positions using a variety of input devices such as light pens, pucks, or keyboards or by typing in the desired command. It is usually much faster and more convenient to simply activate a menu location than to type in a command.

Another important ingredient in the process is the *cursor*. The cursor is a small electronic crosshair that appears on the graphics display when a CAD system is in use. It is an important device used for locating and identifying data displayed on the graphics terminal. If a user wishes to draw a circle, the cursor is used to tell the CAD system where. If the user wishes to erase a line, the cursor is used to tell the CAD system which line.

The cursor can be manipulated using a variety of processes and devices. Some systems have horizontal and vertical thumbwheels for moving the cursor. Other systems use a joystick. Probably the most common method is to use either a light pen or a puck in conjunction with a graphics tablet. The positions on the tablet match positions on the screen. By moving the light pen or puck over the surface of the tablet, electronic impulses are sent to the processor and, in turn, to the screen. In this way, the cursor can be moved as needed.

There are almost as many different names for the various commands and functions that CAD systems are programmed to handle as there are CAD systems. However, in spite of the multiplicity of names and systems, these capabilities can be generalized and given generic names. It's a lot like deciding what you want a drafting student to learn in a fundamentals course. To simplify matters even further, the generic names can be simplified. To understand this concept, ask yourself this question: "What do I need to know how to do in order to draw an architectural plan?"

## GENERIC CAD COMMANDS AND FUNCTIONS

There are three functions to be concerned with. They already have been spoken about briefly: *cursor manipulation, digitizing, and keying.* All of these functions are intrinsic to CAD and must be done at different times in the operation of a CAD system.

Cursor manipulation, as explained in the preceding section, involves moving the cursor around on the graphics display. This is done for a variety of reasons. The cursor can be used to locate and identify data. It can also be used for selecting options displayed on screen-mounted menus, although this is not a common use on modern CAD systems.

Digitizing is the process through which graphic data are converted into digital data so that the computer can accept them. A digitizer, as shown in Figure 2–15, resembles a traditional drafting table. However, it is considerably more. It is an electromechanical device that can be used for converting all of the graphic data on a drawing into X–Y or X–Y–Z coordinates for storage in memory.

Keying is self-explanatory. It involves entering data or giving commands by pressing the appropriate keys on a special keyboard. Keyboards for most CAD systems contain not only the normal typewriter keys but also many special auxiliary keys especially designed to speed the drafting process.

The basic commands needed in any CAD system can be placed in seven general categories:

1. Graphic creation commands.
2. Manipulation commands.
3. Size specification commands.
4. Output commands.
5. Text creation commands.
6. Modification commands.
7. Facilitation commands.

*Graphics creation commands* are those that allow users to create data such as points, lines, planes, and the various geometric characters found on any architectural drawing.

The generic names for commands typically found in this category include:

    POINT
    SOLID LINE
    HIDDEN LINE
    CONSTRUCTION LINE
    CENTER LINE
    RECTANGLE
    CIRCLE
    ARC
    IRREGULAR CURVE
    ELLIPSE
    POLGYON
    GRID
    XYPT
    POLAR
    LINE WEIGHT
    FILLET
    CHAMFER
    LEADERS
    RECT
    HATCH

*Manipulation commands* offer one of the greatest advantages of CAD over manual drafting. They give users almost infinite capabilities for manipulating data that have been input. Manipulation commands, coupled with modification commands, make corrections and revisions—both time-consuming, cost-ineffective tasks in manual drafting—relatively simple and easy. The generic names for commands typically found in this category include:

    MOVE
    COPY
    ROTATE
    SCALE
    ZOOM
    PAN
    MIRROR

*Size specification commands* allow users to indicate the size of the data created. The generic names for commands typically found in this category include:

    AUTOMATIC DIMENSION
    DIMENSION
    TOLERANCE
    CALC AREA

*Output commands* are those commands that allow users to take data out of the system in a human-useable form such as a drawing or a printout. The generic names for commands that are typically found in this category include:

    PLOT
    PRINT

*Text creation commands* are those that allow users to create all of the alphanumeric data needed on a piece of documentation. The generic name for the command typically used in this category is:

    TEXT

*Modification commands* are those that allow users to correct errors, make revisions, or change their minds. These commands allow users to perform the same type of tasks performed by manual drafters with erasers—and, of course, much more. The generic names for commands typically found in this category include:

    EDIT
    DELETE
    REDRAW
    CLIP

*Facilitation commands* are those that allow users to manage, control, and store data. The generic names for commands typically found in this category are:

    SAVE
    FILE
    SYMBOL LIBRARY
    LAYER
    QUIT
    DEFAULT

By activating commands such as those outlined above and responding to their corresponding "prompts," users can create all of the various types of documentation needed in architectural drafting. A *prompt* is a question or statement the computer has been programmed to ask a user for clarification during the drafting process. The questions are the same type that a drafter would ask you if you were instructing him or her in drawing a plan.

For example, if you activate the CIRCLE command, the following prompt might be displayed on the screen:

    "LOCATE CIRCLE'S CENTERPOINT"

The user would respond by moving the cursor to the point on the display where the centerpoint is to be and pressing the activation key on the puck, keyboard, or light pen. The computer would then display a prompt such as:

    "INDICATE CIRCLE'S DIAMETER"

The user would respond by typing the desired diameter and pressing the activation key (usually the ENTER or RETURN key). The circle would immediately appear on the graphics display in the desired location.

# chapter 3
# Floor Plans

## DEFINITION, PURPOSE, AND CONTENTS

The floor plan is the heart of a set of architectural plans. It is frequently drawn first and then used as the basis for drawing other plans such as the electrical, plumbing, and heating-ventilation-air conditioning (HVAC) plans. A floor plan is a plan view in section used to show the overall layout of the building, interior and exterior walls, windows, doors, dimensions, and all fixed features.

The floor plan is the basic tool for communicating the design and space and room planning concepts to both lay and tradespeople. It is the most used component in a complete set of architectural plans. Typical contents include:

- exterior walls
- interior walls
- doors and swing symbols
- windows
- fixed cabinets
- built-in appliances
- fixed features
- fireplaces
- stairs
- walkways
- patios and decks
- door and window schedules (may appear on a separate sheet)
- dimensions
- scale notation

Figures 3–1 to 3–4 on pages 20 through 22 are examples of floor plans produced on modern CAD systems. Figure 3–1 is a floor plan for the south lobby of a commercial building. Figure 3–2 is a floor plan for the north lobby of the same commercial building. Figure 3–3 is the second floor plan of a steel and concrete commercial building. Figure 3–4 is a floor plan for a typical residential dwelling. Figure 3–5 on page 22 is an example of a door schedule that might accompany the floor plan for a residential dwelling.

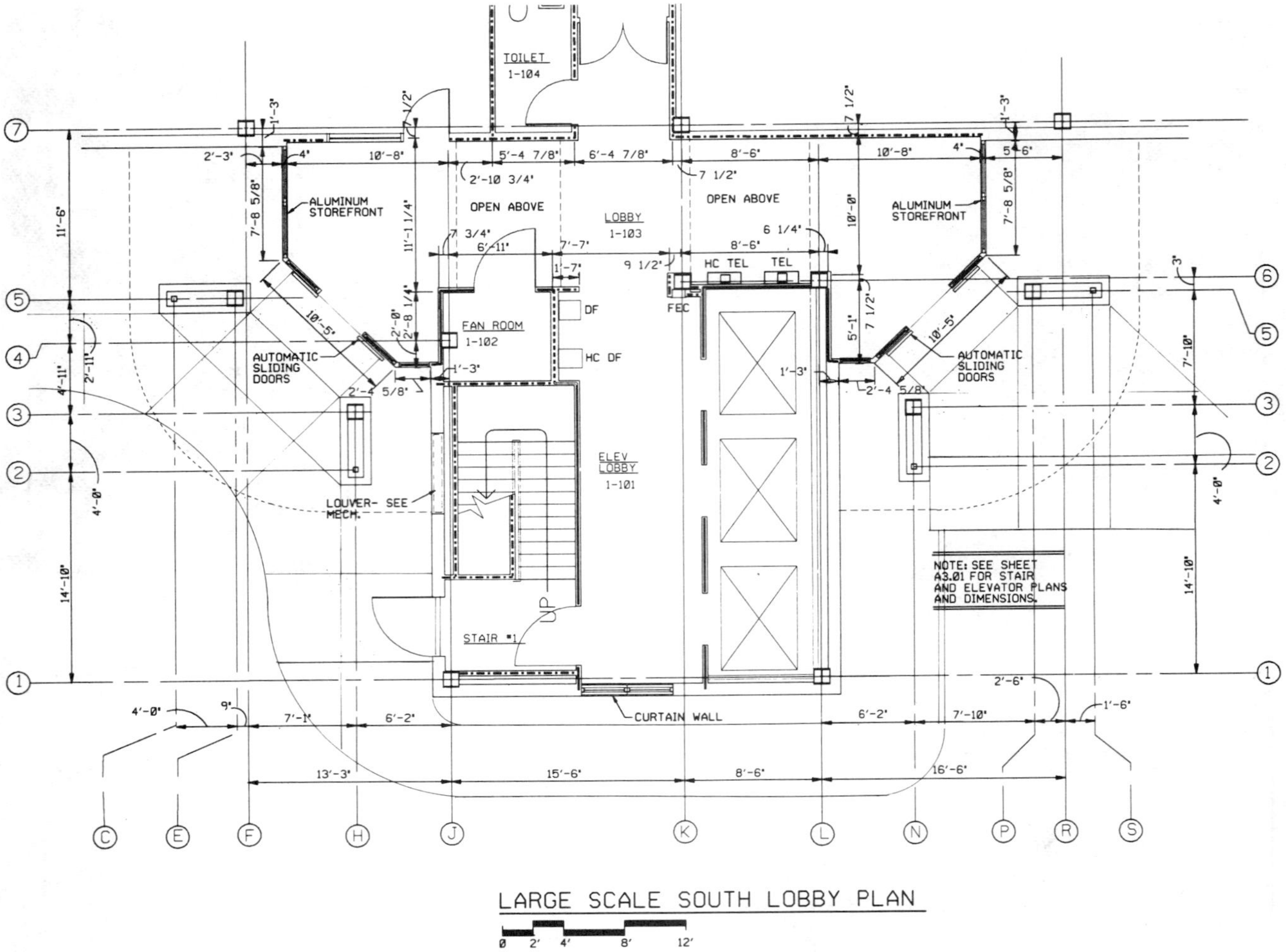

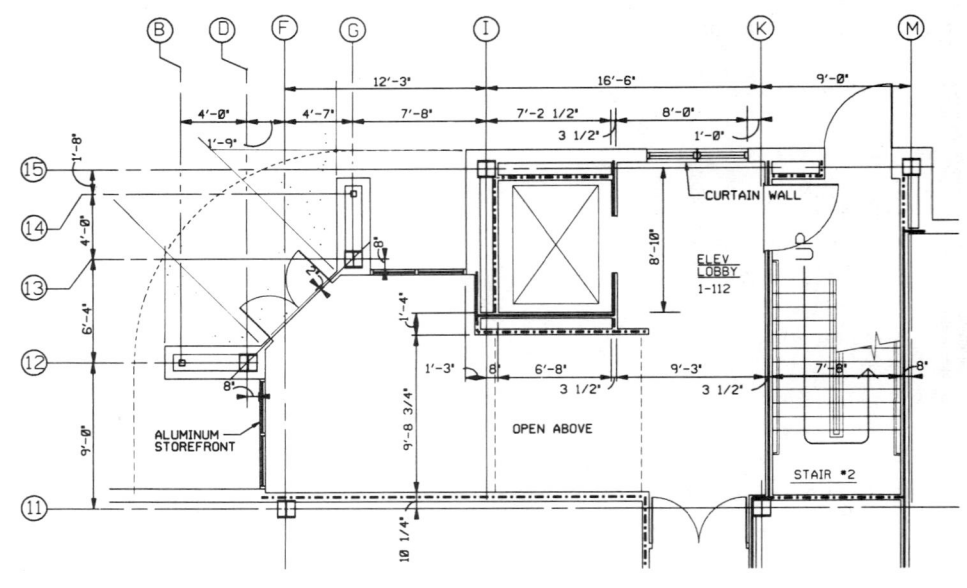

**Figure 3–1** Partial commercial floor plan. *(Courtesy of Intergraph Corporation.)*

**Figure 3–2** Partial commercial floor plan. *(Courtesy of Intergraph Corporation.)*

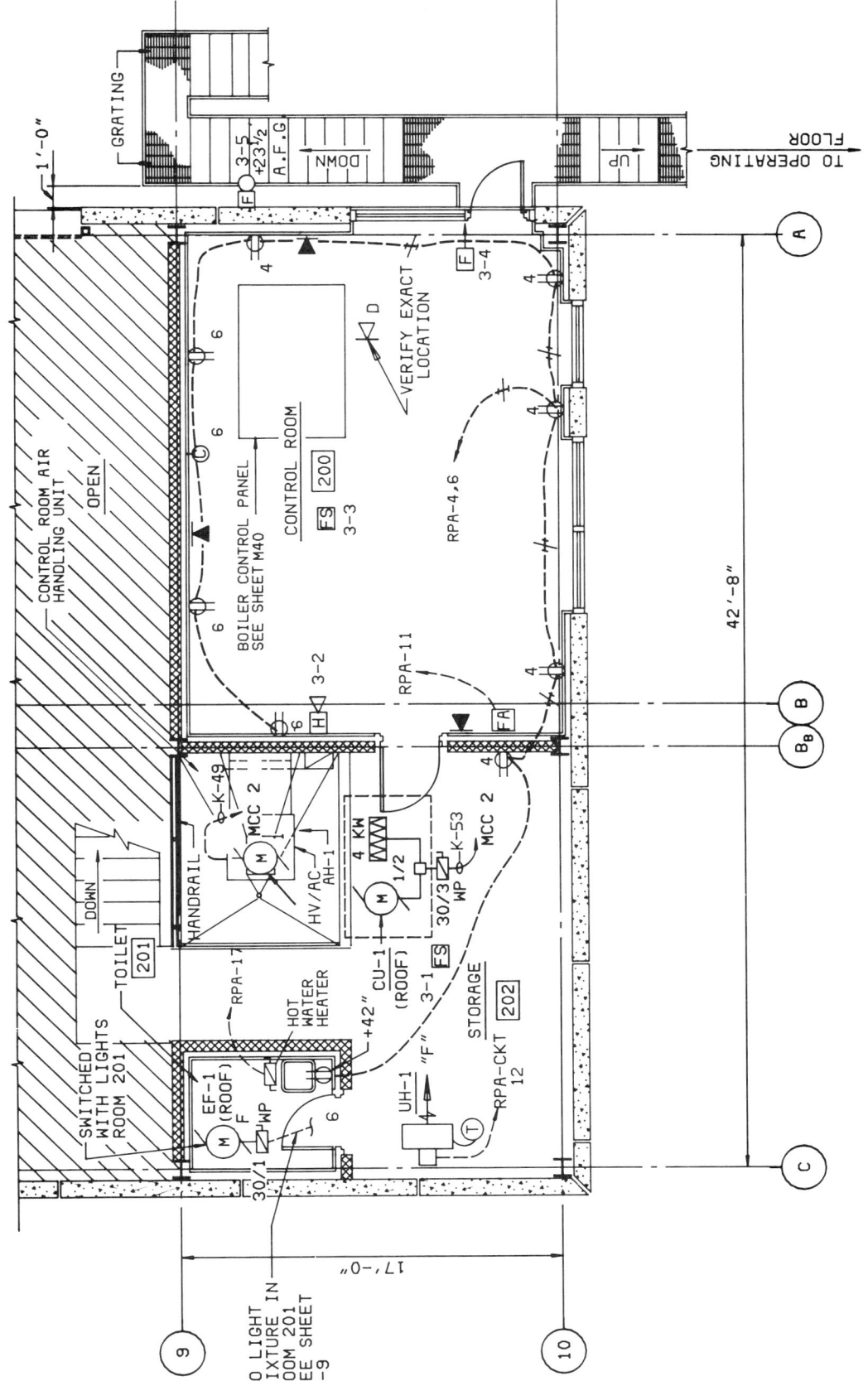

**Figure 3-3** Second floor plan for a commercial building. *(Courtesy of Rust Engineering Company.)*

**22** | CAD Applications: Architectural

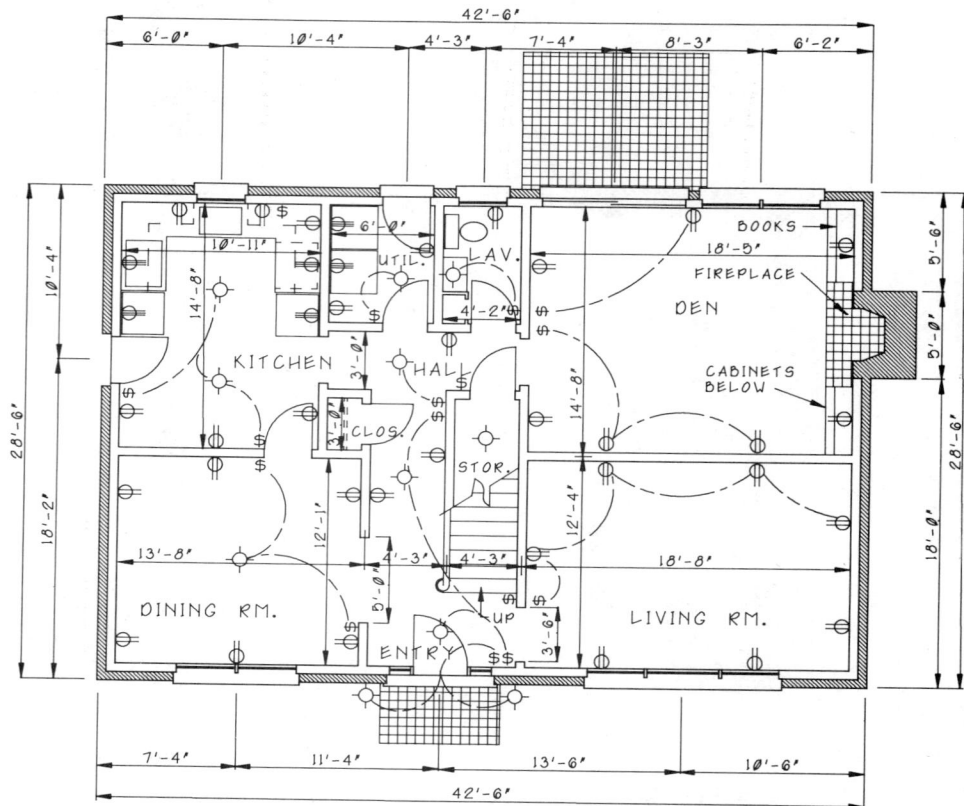

**Figure 3–4** Floor plan for a residential dwelling. *(Courtesy of Bausch & Lomb/Houston Instrument.)*

| DOOR SCHEDULE ||||||
|---|---|---|---|---|---|
| MARK | QUANTITY | SIZE | TYPE | MATERIAL | REMARKS |
| A | 1 | 3'-0"x6'-8"x1 3/4" | See Elev. | Pine | Paint |
| B | 8 | 2'-6"x6'-8"x1 3/8" | Flush | Birch | Hollow Core |
| C | 3 | 2'-6"x6'-8"x1 3/8" | Louvered | Pine | |
| D | 1 | 2'-6"x6'-8"x1 3/4" | 10 Lights | Pine | |
| E | 3 | 5'-0"x6'-8"x1 3/8" | Folding | Pine | Louvered |
| F | 1 | 2'-0"x6'-8"x1 3/8" | Flush | Birch | Hollow Core |
| G | 1 | 2'-6"x6'-8"x1 3/4" | Lights | Pine | See rear Elevation |

**Figure 3–5** Door schedule.

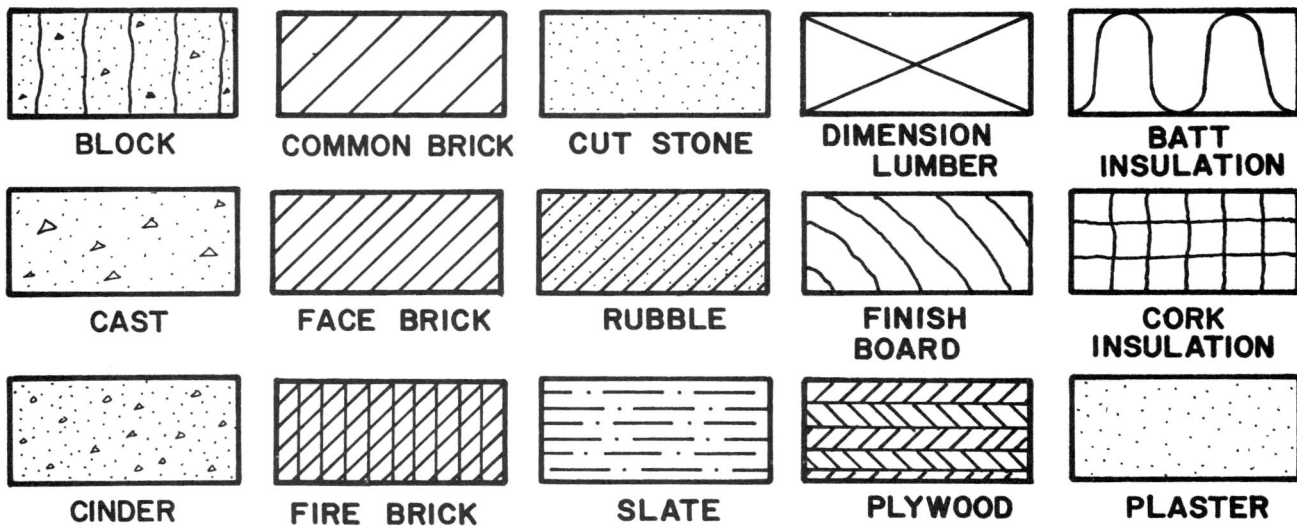

**Figure 3–6** Floor plan symbols.

## SPECIAL SYMBOLS NEEDED

There are several special graphic symbols used in producing floor plans on a CAD system. These symbols apply to both residential and commercial plans. Those most frequently used are shown in Figure 3–6. Examine the symbols library of your CAD system to determine which of these symbols it contains. If the symbols library does not contain a particular symbol, you have two options:

1. Create the symbol and add it to the symbols library. This can be done only on those CAD systems that are programmed to accept user-defined symbols.
2. Construct the symbols on the drawing as they are needed, using the appropriate geometric characters and commands. For example, the "slate" symbol can be made using the POINT and SOLID LINES commands. The "finish board" symbol can be made using the IRREGULAR CURVE or SPLINE command.

## CAD COMMANDS AND FUNCTIONS USED

There are several different commands and manipulation functions used in constructing a floor plan on a CAD system. The commands are basically the same for residential and commercial plans. Most CAD systems have these commands and functions. However, they are often given different names on different systems (see Chapter 1).

The generic commands and functions used to produce a floor plan on a CAD system are listed in the Commands and Functions chart. Before attempting the drawing activities in this chapter, match these generic commands and functions with their corresponding commands and functions on your CAD system.

## COMMANDS AND FUNCTIONS

**Graphic Creation Commands**

____ Point
____ Solid Line
____ Hidden Line
____ Construction Line
____ Dashed Line
____ Center Line
____ Rectangle
____ Circle
____ Arc
____ Irregular Curve
____ Ellipse
____ Polygon
____ Grid
____ Xypt
____ Polar
____ Line Weight
____ Fillet
____ Chamfer
____ Leaders
____ Rect
____ Hatch

**Manipulation Commands**

____ Move
____ Copy
____ Rotate
____ Scale
____ Zoom
____ Pan
____ Mirror

**Size Specification Commands**

____ Auto. Dimension
____ Dimension
____ Tolerance
____ Calc. Area

**Output Commands**

____ Plot
____ Print (Screen Dump)

**Text Creation Commands**

____ Text

**Modification Commands**

____ Edit
____ Delete
____ Redraw
____ Clip
____ Erase

**Facilitation Commands**

____ Save
____ File
____ Symbol Library
____ Layer
____ Quit
____ Default

## PROCEDURES FOR PREPARING THE PLAN

What follows is an illustrated, step-by-step description of how such a plan is produced on a CAD system. The floor plan used to illustrate these procedures is for a residential dwelling. However, the procedures described also apply when preparing commercial floor plans.

■ *Step 1*

Log-on to the system and create a file called FLRABC. Substitute your initials for the ABC. Decide what size of paper you will plot the completed floor plan on.

■ *Step 2*

Lay out the exterior and interior walls using the CONSTRUCTION LINES function if it is available. If not, use the SOLID LINES function. Make sure that any walls that will contain pipes for plumbing are thickened to either 6″ or 8″ (either a 6″ sole plate or two abutting 4″ sole plates), Figure 3–7.

■ *Step 3*

Add windows, door openings in the walls, and door symbols to indicate the direction of swing or opening. Once you are satisfied with what you have produced so far, convert all construction lines to solid lines, Figure 3–8.

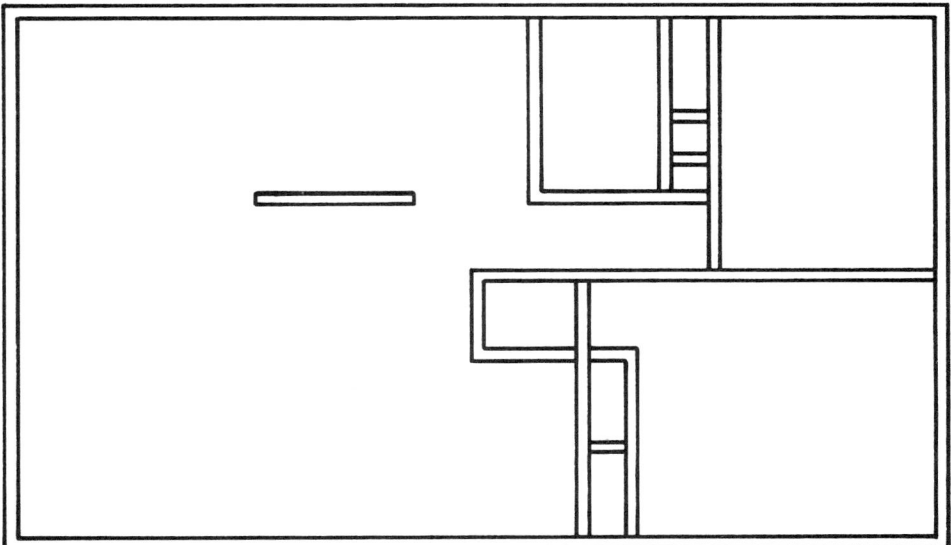

**Figure 3–7** Illustration for Step 2.

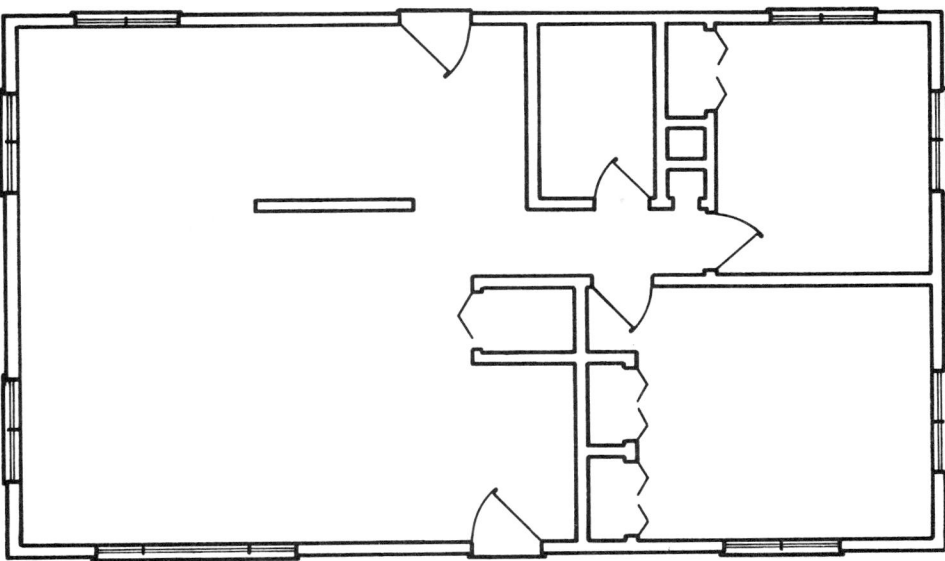

**Figure 3–8** Illustration for Step 3.

■ *Step 4*

While still in the SOLID LINES mode, add all cabinets, appliances, and fixtures. Use the CIRCLE function to label doors with letters and windows with numbers. Switch to the DIMENSION mode and add all necessary dimensions. Switch to the TEXT mode and add door and window labels in the circles and room designations, Figure 3–9.

With the floor plan completed, you are ready to produce the door and window schedules to accompany it. The schedules are handy summaries that list the various types of windows or doors used in the house and the quantity, size, and material information. An additional column is normally provided for miscellaneous comments. Figure 3–5 contains an example of a completed door schedule. The same format may be used for window schedules.

Door and window schedules are developed according to the same procedures. What follows is an illustrated, step-by-step description of how a door or window schedule is produced on a CAD system.

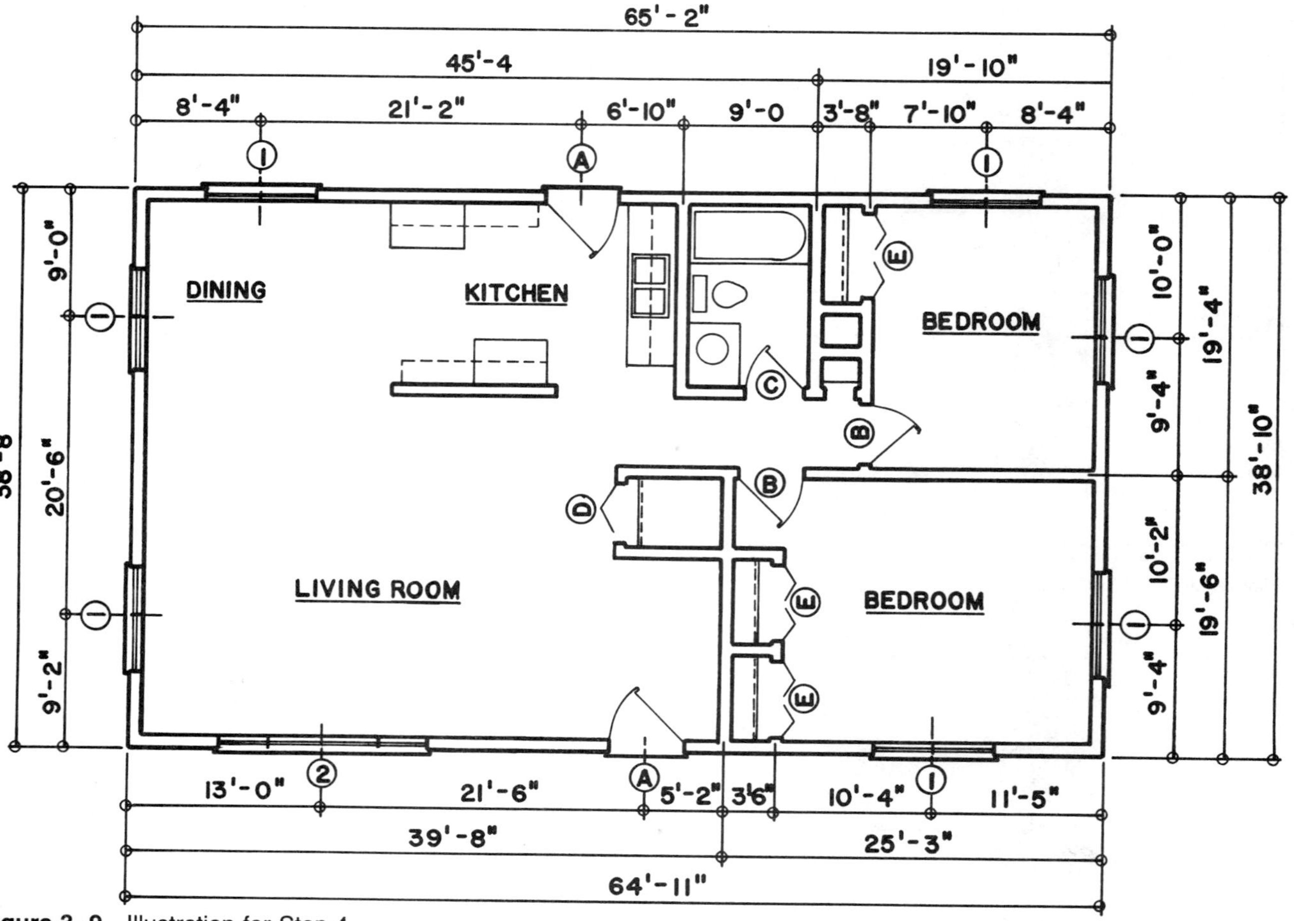

**26** | CAD Applications: Architectural

**Figure 3–9** Illustration for Step 4.

### ■ Step 1
Log-on to the system and create a drawing designation called DRABC or WNABC, depending on whether you plan to do a door or a window schedule.

### ■ Step 2
Lay out the chart using the CONSTRUCTION LINES function if it is available and the SOLID LINES function if it is not. Make the rows at least ⅜″ wide and use the following specifications for columns: MARK—½″ wide; QUANTITY—¾″ wide; SIZE—2″ wide; TYPE—1″ wide; MATERIAL—1½″ wide; and REMARKS—1½″ wide. When you are satisfied with the chart's layout, convert all construction lines to hidden lines, Figure 3–10.

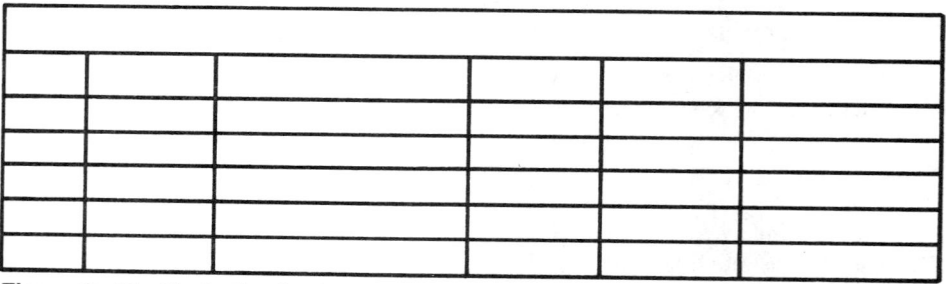

**Figure 3–10** Illustration for Step 2 (window schedule).

■ *Step 3*

Switch to the TEXT mode and add the chart and column titles. For the chart title, use only the word *schedule* so that you can use the chart for either window or door schedules, Figure 3–11. At this point, save the chart using the SAVE function. This will allow you to reuse the basic chart each time it is needed without having to redo it. All that will be necessary for future use is to call up the saved chart and fill in the missing text.

| | | SCHEDULE | | | |
|---|---|---|---|---|---|
| MARK | QUANTITY | SIZE | TYPE | MATERIAL | REMARKS |
| | | | | | |
| | | | | | |
| | | | | | |
| | | | | | |
| | | | | | |

**Figure 3–11** Illustration for Step 3 (window schedule).

■ *Step 4*

Call up the saved chart and display it on the graphics terminal. Switch to the TEXT mode and complete each column. In this case, the chart title would be completed as "Door Schedule," Figure 3–12.

| | | DOOR SCHEDULE | | | |
|---|---|---|---|---|---|
| MARK | QUANTITY | SIZE | TYPE | MATERIAL | REMARKS |
| A | 2 | 3'-0" x 6'-8" x 1 3/4" | EXTERIOR | BIRCH | INSULATED |
| B | 2 | 2'-8" x 6'-8" x 1 3/8" | FLUSH | BIRCH | HOLLOW CORE |
| C | 1 | 2'-6" x 6'-8" x 1 3/8" | FLUSH | BIRCH | HOLLOW CORE |
| D | 1 | 3'-0" x 6'-8" x 1 3/8" | FOLDING | BIRCH | ———— |
| E | 3 | 4'-0" x 6'-8" x 1 3/8" | FOLDING | BIRCH | ———— |

**Figure 3–12** Illustration for Step 4 (window schedule).

## REVIEW QUESTIONS

The following questions are provided as a review of Chapter 3 and should be completed before attempting the application projects for the chapter. Write your answers in the spaces and blanks provided.

1. Define "floor plan."

2. List two ways a floor plan might be used.

3. Sketch the symbols for the following:
   Batt insulation—

   Cork insulation—

   Dimension lumber—

Plywood—

Plaster—

4. List five items that might be included on a typical floor plan.

5. Explain the steps you would use to create the "batt insulation" symbol on a drawing if it is not contained in the symbols library.

6. Explain the steps you would use to create the "finish board" symbol on a drawing if it is not contained in the symbols library.

7. Explain the steps you would use on your CAD system to correct the spelling errors in the following room designation:
   BEDROM NMUBER 1

# APPLICATION PROJECTS

The following applications projects are provided to help you become proficient in producing floor plans on a CAD system. To ensure that you use input, modification, and manipulation functions, you will be required to reconstruct floor plans as shown and make modifications to them. To ensure that you use facilitation and output functions, SAVE each completed floor plan and PLOT it on the size and type of medium specified by your instructor. In reconstructing the given floor plans, you may digitize the plan from the book and use the SCALE function to display the plan in the size of your choice on the graphics terminal, or you may use the room sizes to compute the dimensions and draw the plans from scratch.

**Project 1:** Figure 3–13 is a floor plan for a residential dwelling. Reconstruct the floor plan as shown on your CAD system. From the room sizes given, completely dimension the floor plan. Assign window and door sizes and create a window and door schedule for the house.

**Project 2:** Repeat the instructions in Project 1 for a house that is the mirror image of the one in Figure 3–13.

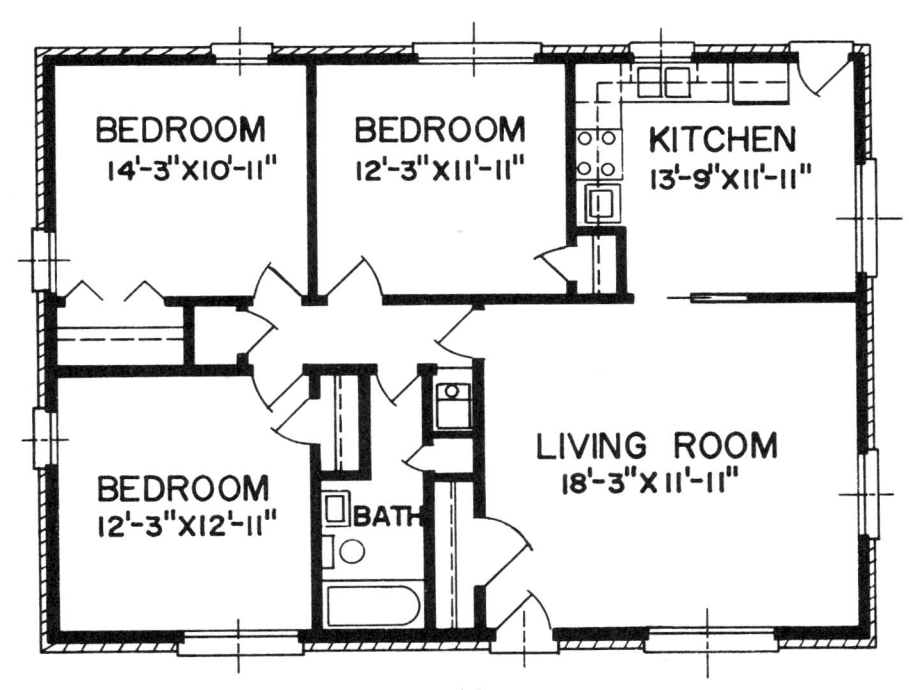

**Figure 3–13** Application projects 1 and 2.

# 30 | CAD Applications: Architectural

**Project 3:**  Figure 3–14 is a floor plan for a residential dwelling. Reconstruct the floor plan as shown on your CAD system. Convert the room sizes into a complete dimension system for the house. Assign door and window sizes and create a door and a window schedule for the house.

**Project 4:**  Repeat the instructions in Project 3 for a house that is the mirror image of the one in Figure 3–14.

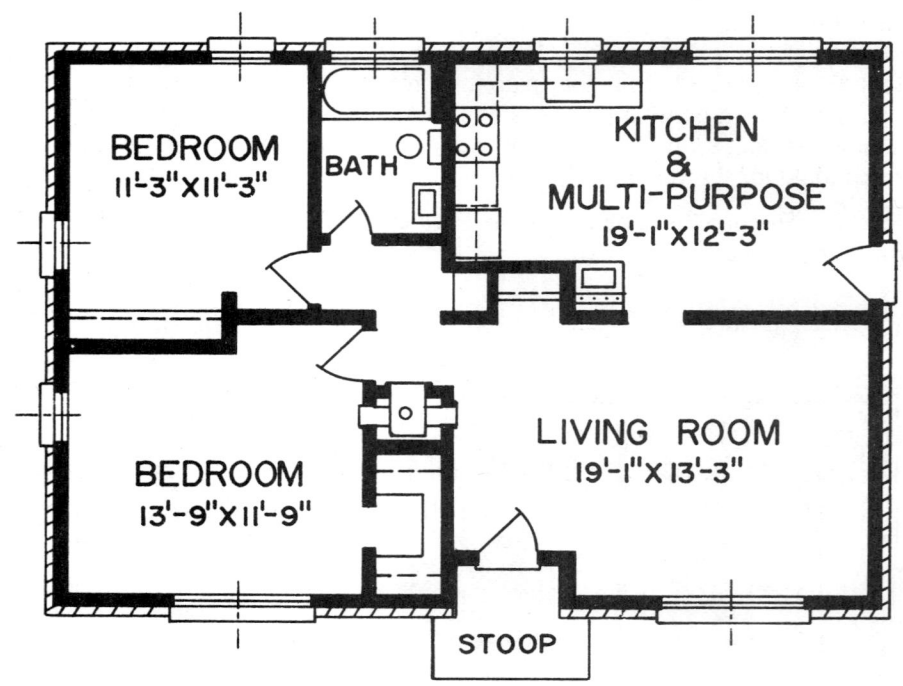

**Figure 3–14**  Application projects 3 and 4.

**Project 5:**  Figure 3–15 is a floor plan for a residential dwelling. Reconstruct the floor plan as shown on your CAD system. Convert the room sizes into a complete dimension system for the house. Assign door and window sizes and create a door and a window schedule for the house.

**Project 6:**  Repeat the instructions in Project 5 for a house that is the mirror image of the one in Figure 3–15.

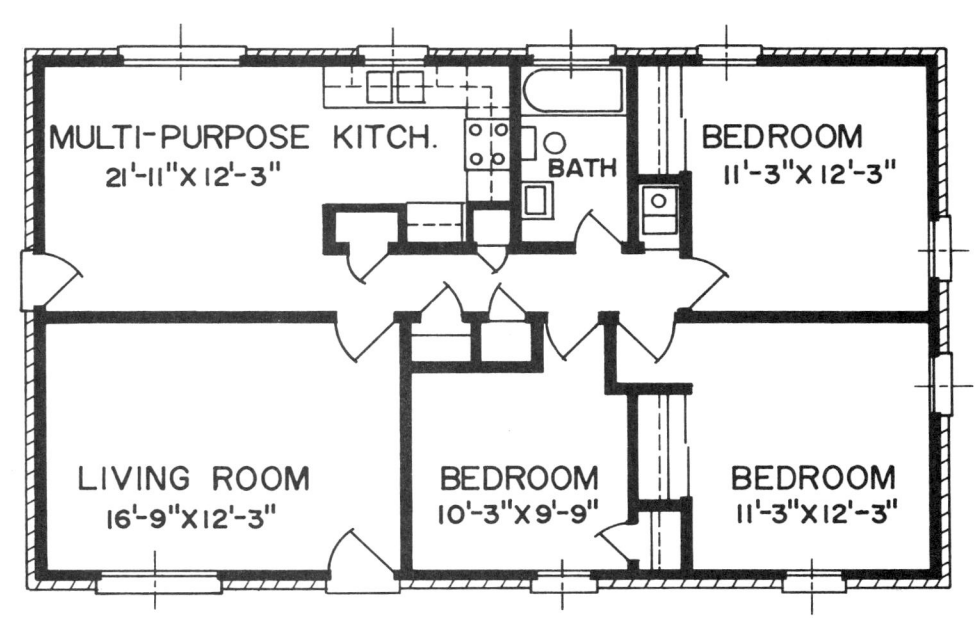

**Figure 3–15** Application projects 5 and 6.

**Project 7:** Figure 3–16 is a floor plan for a residential dwelling. Reconstruct the floor plan as shown on your CAD system. Convert the room sizes into a complete dimension system for the house. Assign door and window sizes and create a door and a window schedule for the house.

**Project 8:** Repeat the instruction in Project 7 for a house that is the mirror image of the one in Figure 3–16.

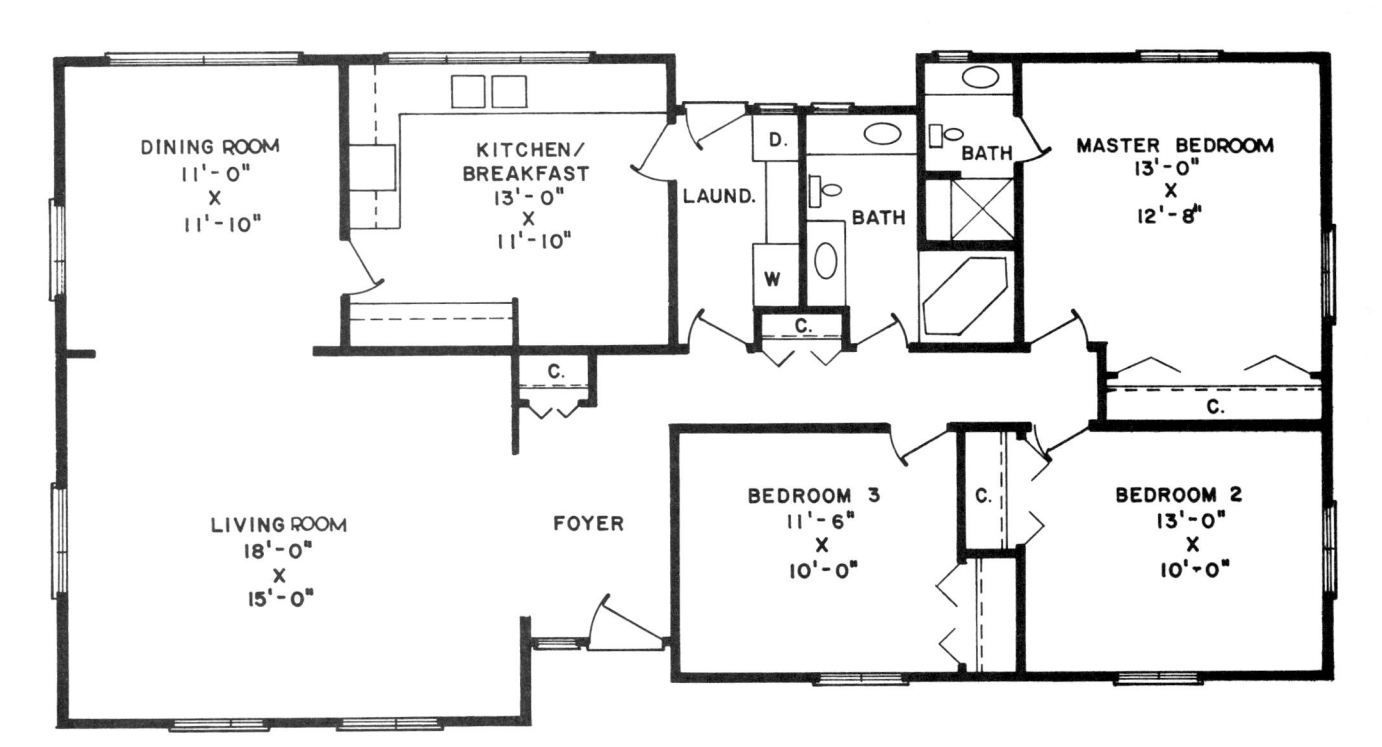

**Figure 3–16** Application projects 7 and 8.

**Project 9:** Figure 3–17 is a floor plan for a residential dwelling. Reconstruct the floor plan as shown on your CAD system. Convert the room sizes into a complete dimension system for the house. Assign door and window sizes and create a door and a window schedule for the house.

**Project 10:** Repeat the instructions in Project 9 for a house that is the mirror image of the one in Figure 3–17.

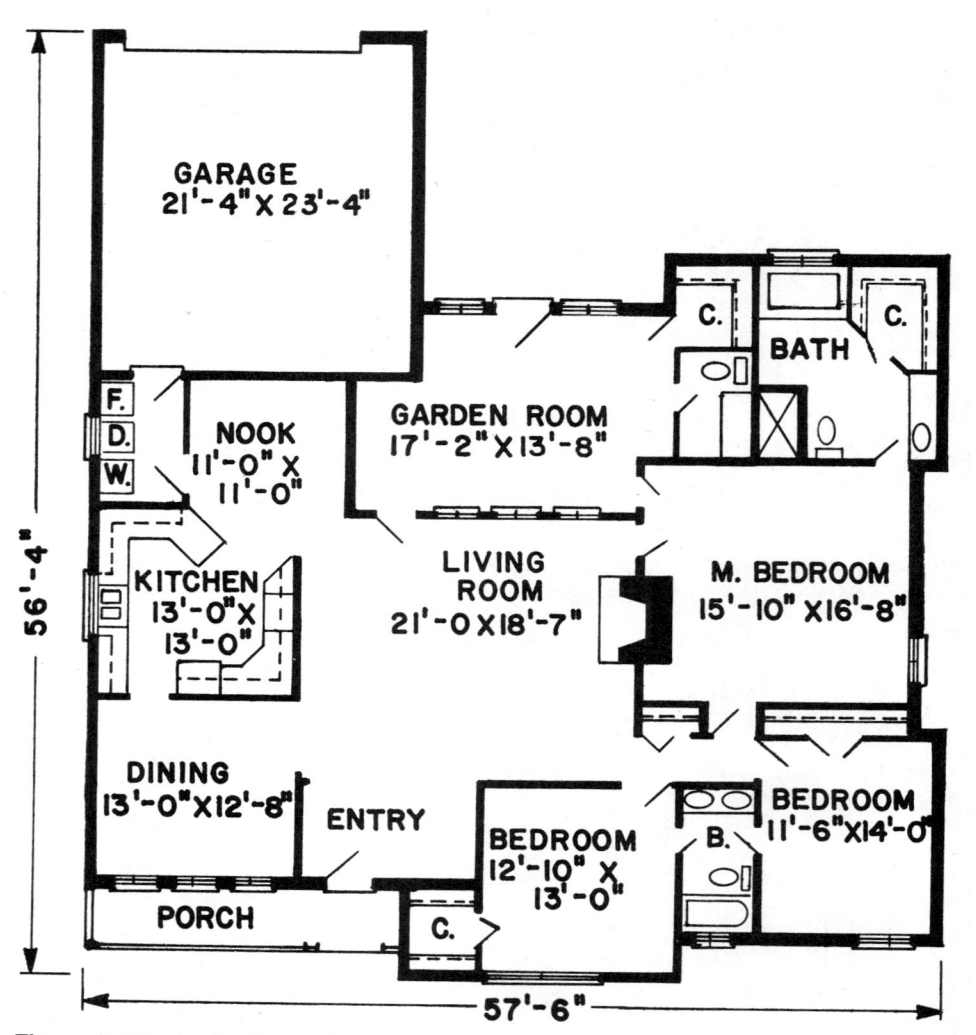

**Figure 3–17** Application projects 9 and 10.

**Project 11:** Figure 3–18 is a floor plan for a residential dwelling. Reconstruct the floor plan as shown on your CAD system. Convert the room sizes into a complete dimension system for the house. Assign door and window sizes and create a door and a window schedule for the house.

**Project 12:** Repeat the instructions in Project 11 for a house that is the mirror image of the one in Figure 3–18.

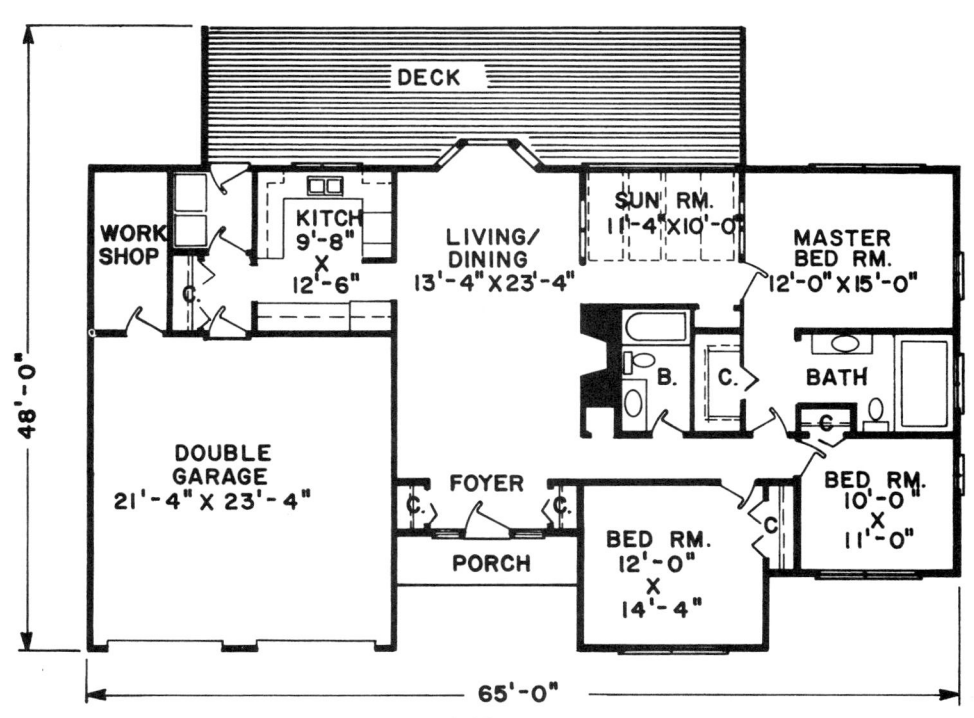

**Figure 3–18** Application projects 11 and 12.

**Project 13:** Figure 3–19 is a floor plan for a residential dwelling. Reconstruct the floor plan as shown on your CAD system. Convert the room sizes into a complete dimension system for the house. Assign door and window sizes and create a door and a window schedule for the house.

**Project 14:** Repeat the instructions in Project 13 for a house that is the mirror image of the one in Figure 3–19.

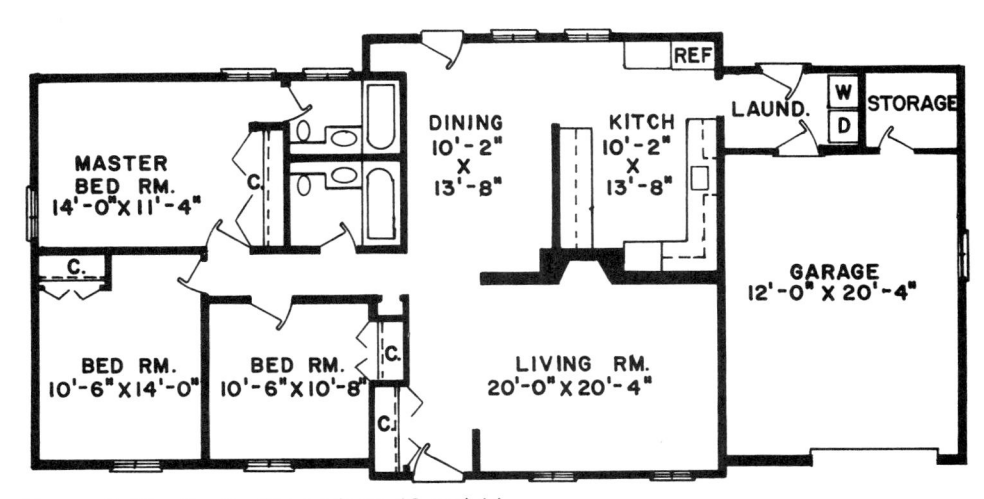

**Figure 3–19** Application projects 13 and 14.

**Project 15:** Figure 3–20 is a floor plan for a residential dwelling. Reconstruct the floor plan as shown on your CAD system. Convert the room sizes into a complete dimension system for the house. Assign door and window sizes and create a door and a window schedule for the house.

**Project 16:** Repeat the instructions in Project 15 for a house that is the mirror image of the one in Figure 3–20.

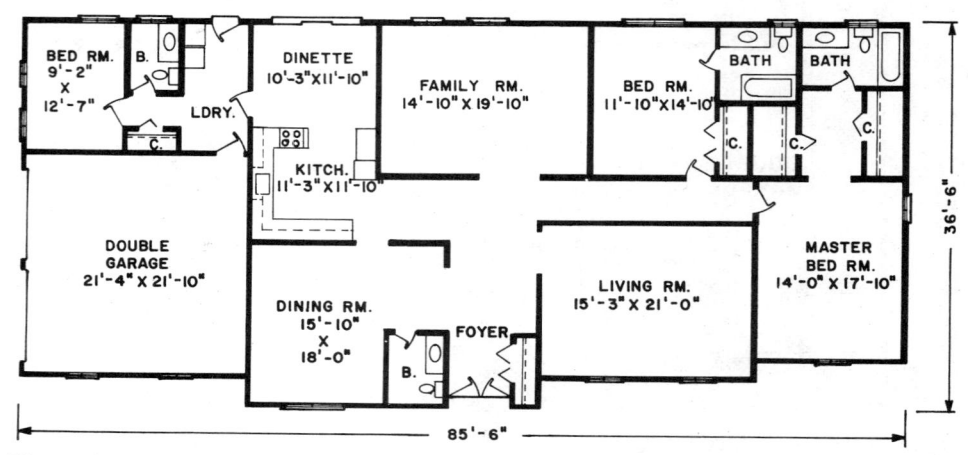

**Figure 3–20** Application projects 15 and 16.

**Project 17:** Figure 3–21 is a floor plan for a residential dwelling. Reconstruct the floor plan as shown on your CAD system. Convert the room sizes into a complete dimension system for the house. Assign door and window sizes and create a door and a window schedule for the house.

**Project 18:** Repeat the instructions in Project 17 for a house that is the mirror image of the one in Figure 3–21.

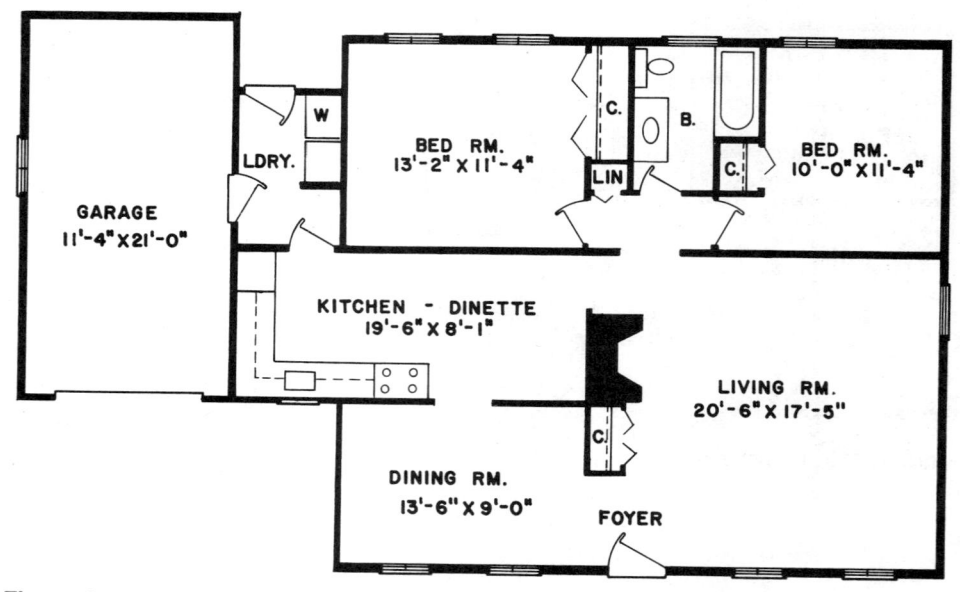

**Figure 3–21** Application projects 17 and 18.

**Project 19:** Figure 3–22 is a floor plan for a residential dwelling. Reconstruct the floor plan as shown on your CAD system. Convert the room sizes into a complete dimension system for the house. Assign door and window sizes and create a door and a window schedule for the house.

**Project 20:** Repeat the instructions in Project 19 for a house that is the mirror image of the one in Figure 3–22.

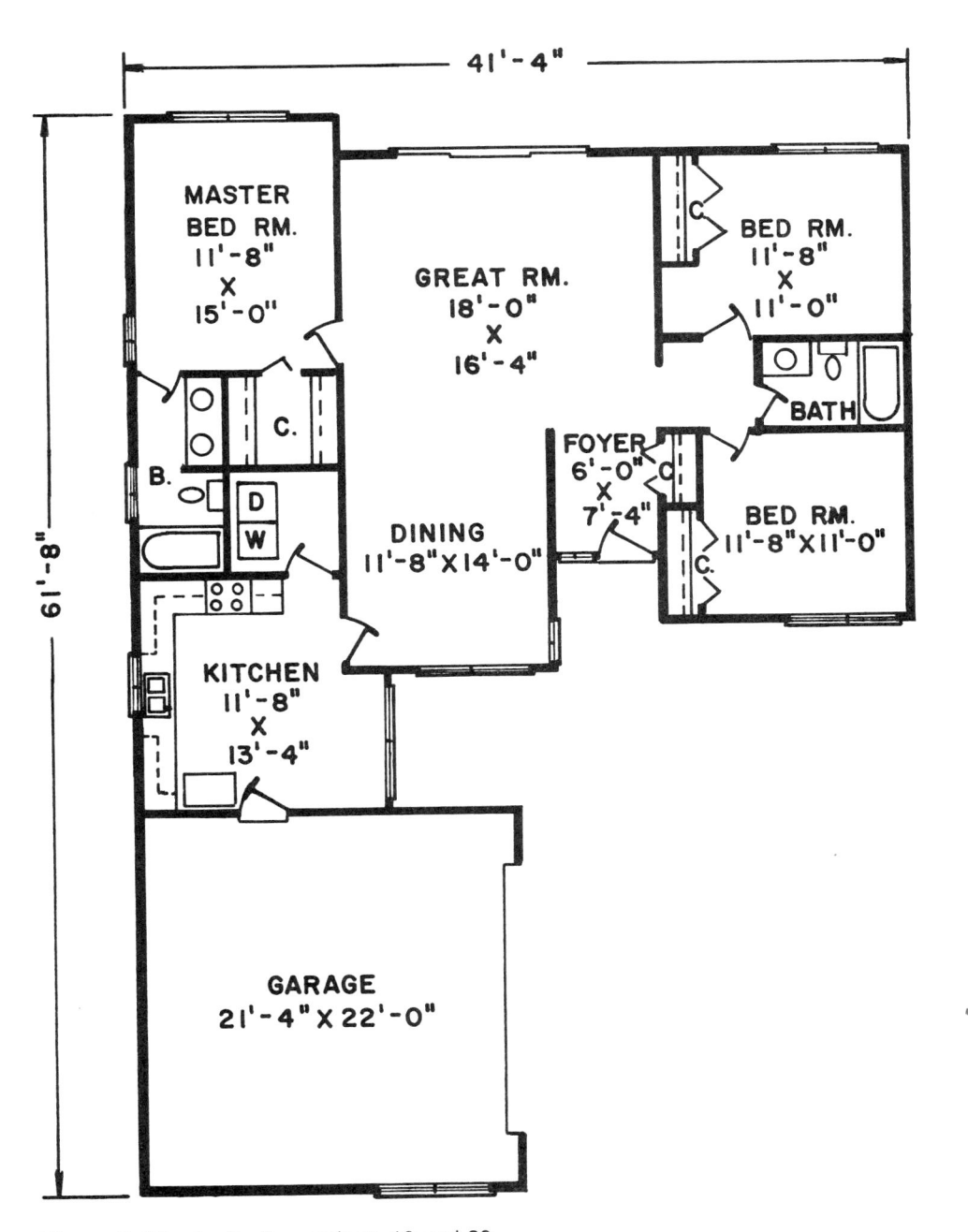

**Figure 3–22** Application projects 19 and 20.

# 36 | CAD Applications: Architectural

**Project 21:** Figure 3–23 is a floor plan for a residential dwelling. Reconstruct the floor plan on your CAD system as shown. Convert the room sizes into a complete dimension system for the house. Assign door and window sizes and create a door and a window schedule for the house.

**Project 22:** Repeat the instructions in Project 21 for a house that is the mirror image of the one in Figure 3–23.

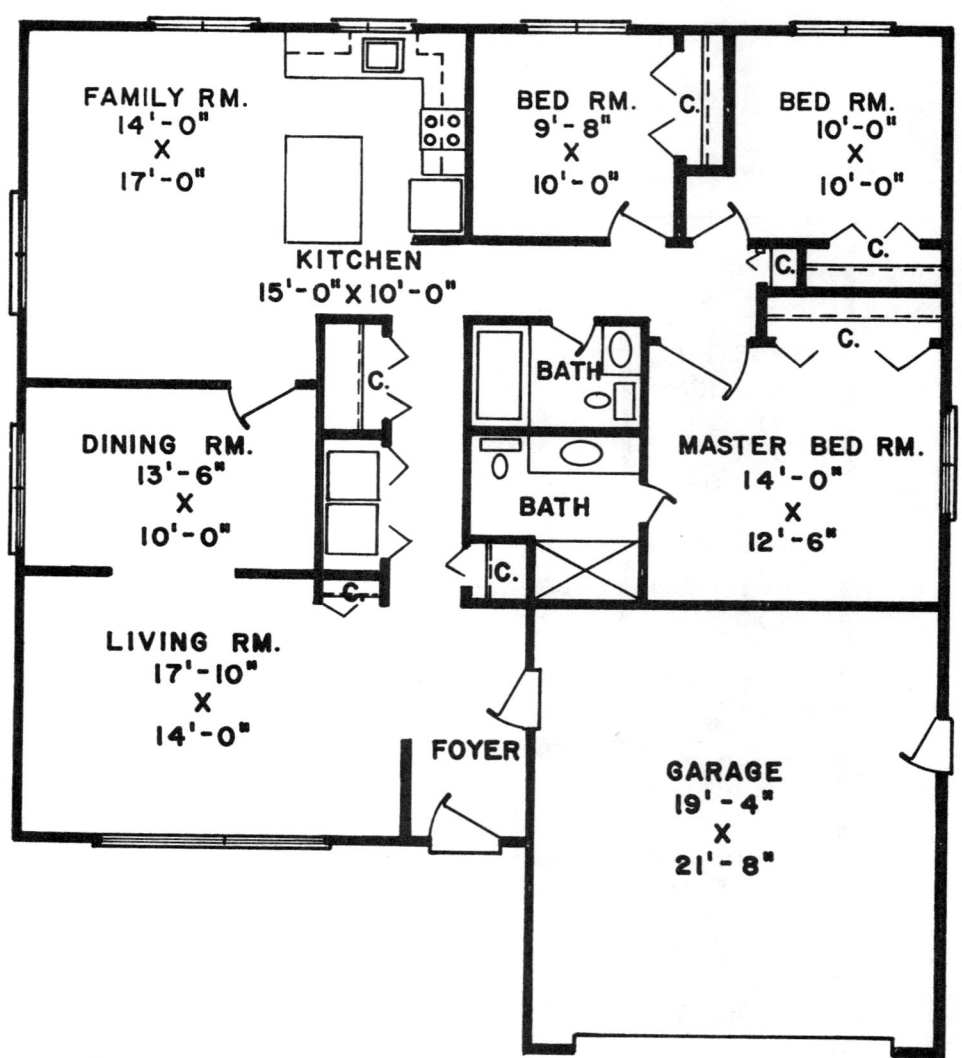

**Figure 3–23** Application projects 21 and 22.

**Project 23:** Figure 3–24 is a floor plan for a residential dwelling. Reconstruct the floor plan on your CAD system as shown. Convert the room sizes into a complete dimension system for the house. Assign door and window sizes and create a door and a window schedule for the house.

**Project 24:** Repeat the instructions in Project 23 for a house that is the mirror image of the one in Figure 3–24.

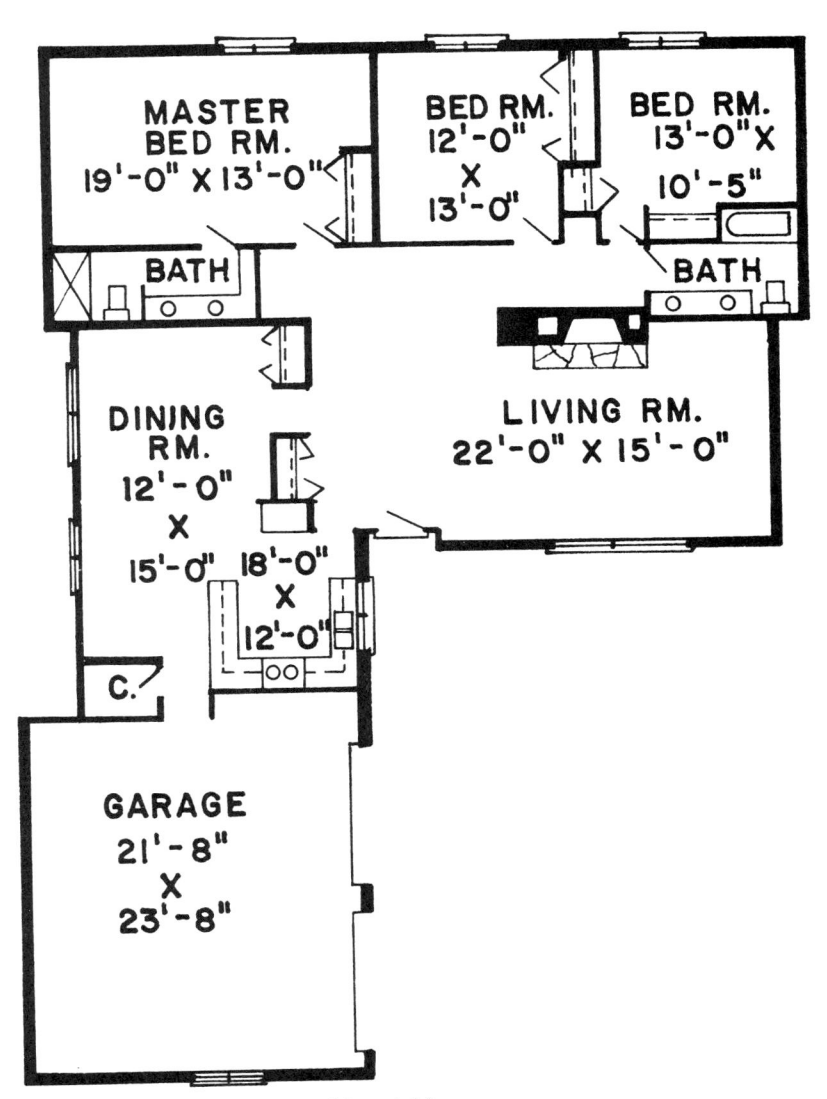

**Figure 3–24** Application projects 23 and 24.

**Project 25:** Figure 3–25 is a floor plan for a residential dwelling. Reconstruct the floor plan on your CAD system as shown. Convert the room sizes into a complete dimension system for the house. Assign door and window sizes and create a door and a window schedule for the house.

**Project 26:** Repeat the instructions in Project 25 for a house that is the mirror image of the one in Figure 3–25.

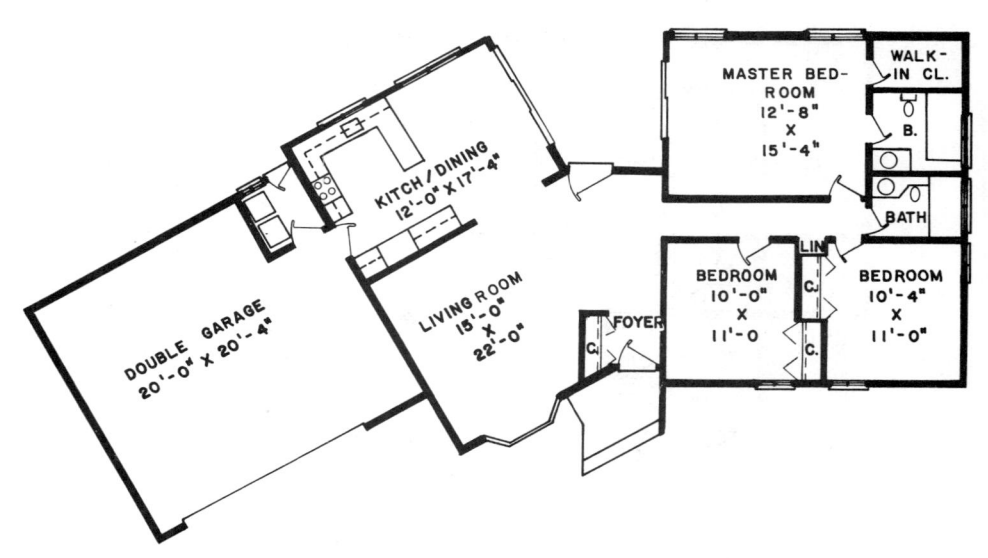

**Figure 3–25** Application projects 25 and 26.

**Project 27:** In some areas of the country, tilt-up construction is popular. Tilt-up construction is a building method in which prefabricated walls are erected on the job site by "tilting" them up, Figure 3–26. This application project will give you experience in dealing with tilt-up wall construction. Figure 3–27 is a floor plan for a light commercial building—a three-unit apartment complex. Reconstruct the floor plan as shown and then do the following:

1. Fill in the interior wall and fixtures for units one and three.
2. Using 10'-0" wide, 4" thick poured concrete wall slabs that are to be tilted-up, create a wall-framing plan for all four walls of the apartment complex.

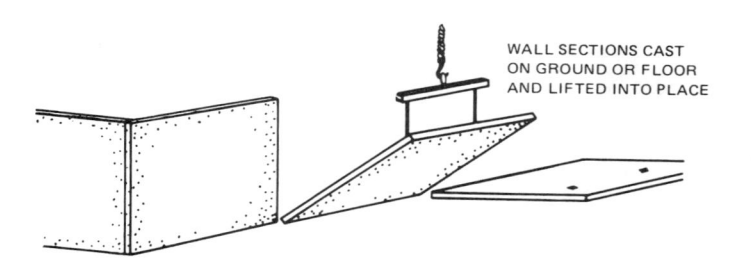

**Figure 3–26** Application project 27.

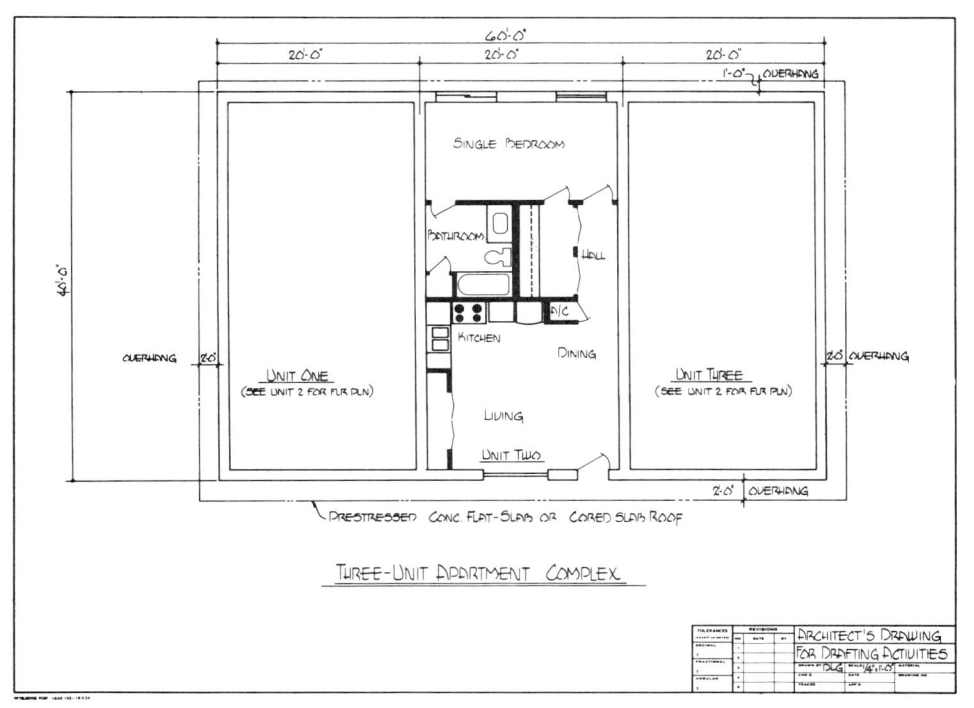

**Figure 3–27** Application project 27.

# chapter 4
# Construction Details

## DEFINITION, PURPOSE, AND CONTENTS

Many different types of construction details are required in a set of architectural plans. There are footing details, cornice details, roof details, curb details, and many other types of details. A construction detail is an orthographic view in section used to clarify situations that cannot be adequately explained on other plans such as floor plans and elevations.

Construction details are used primarily by tradespeople for guidance in actually accomplishing such tasks as digging footing trenches, pouring footings, erecting columns, erecting beams, building foundation walls, building exterior and interior walls, constructing ceilings and roofs, and so forth.

The contents of construction details are dictated by the nature of the project to be built and the perceived needs of the tradespeople who will use them in constructing the project. For example, if a footing detail is to be drawn, the drafter must ask "what information will the tradespeople need?" The answer to this question would be: the grade line; the size of the footing and material, including reinforcement; the foundation wall and material; the floor system makeup; dimensions; notes; and appropriate symbols where needed to communicate material specifications.

There are too many different types of construction details to attempt to list the contents of each. In deciding what information to include in a construction detail, try to put yourself in the place of the tradespeople who will use it in constructing what it represents.

Figures 4–1 through 4–6 on pages 42 through 46 contain examples of some of the many different types of construction details found in architectural plans for residential and commercial projects. All of these details were produced on modern CAD systems.

## SPECIAL SYMBOLS NEEDED

There are several different graphic symbols used in producing construction details on a CAD system. Those most frequently used are shown in Figure 4–7 on page 47. Examine the symbols library of your CAD system to determine which of these symbols it contains. If the symbols library does not contain a particular symbol, you have two options:

**42** | CAD Applications: Architectural

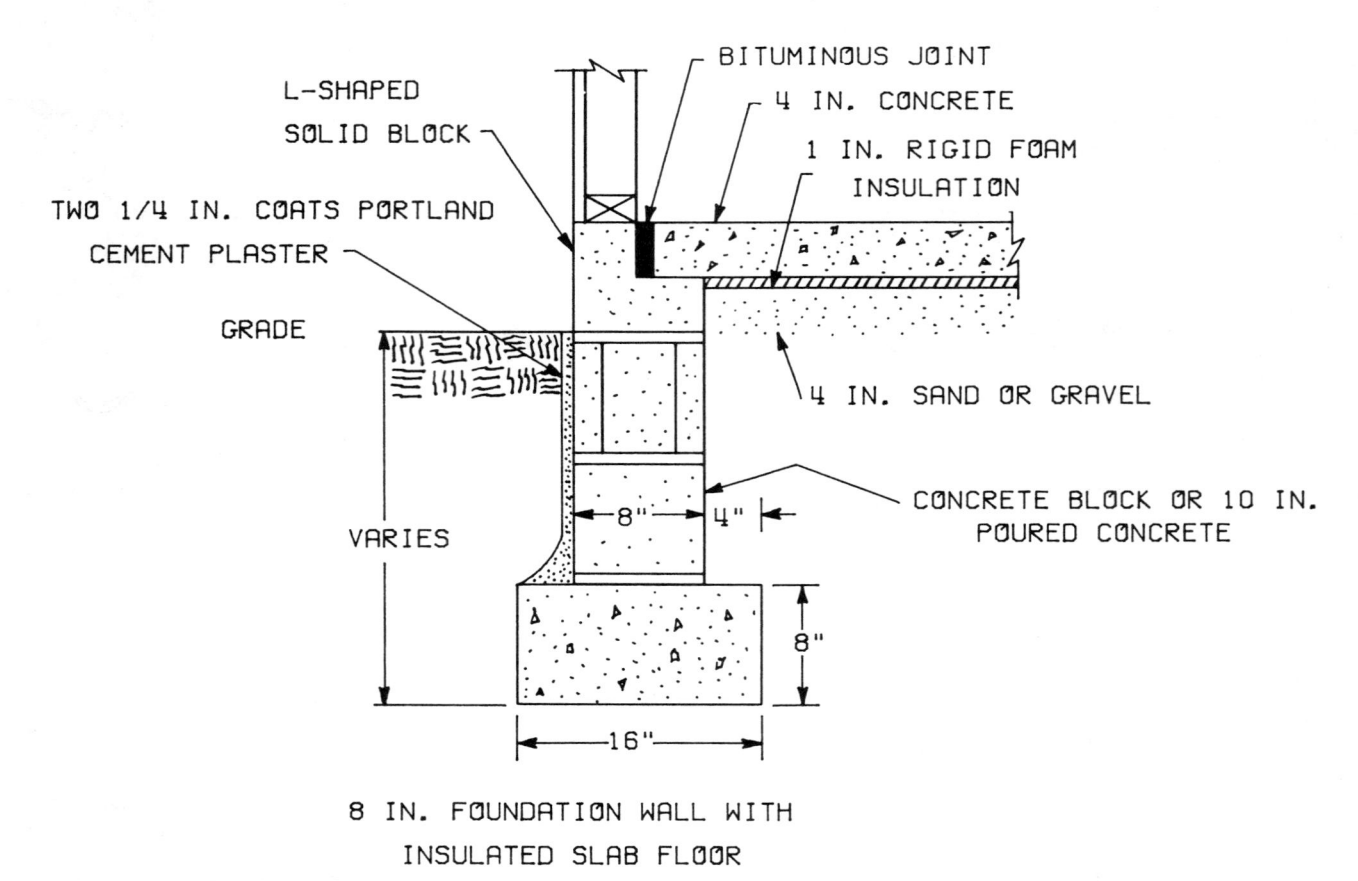

**Figure 4–1** Residential foundation detail.

1. Create the symbol and add it to the symbols library. This can only be done on those CAD systems that are programmed to allow for the creation of user-defined symbols.
2. Construct the symbols as they are needed on the drawing, using the appropriate geometric characters and commands. For example, the "batt insulation" symbol can be made using the "irregular curve" or "spline" command.

## CAD COMMANDS AND FUNCTIONS USED

There are several different commands and manipulation functions used in producing construction details on a CAD system. Most CAD systems have these functions and commands, but they are often given different names on different systems (see Chapter 1).

The generic commands and functions used to produce construction details on a CAD system are listed in the Commands and Functions chart. Before attempting the application projects in this chapter, match the generic commands and functions listed in the chart with their corresponding commands and functions on your CAD system.

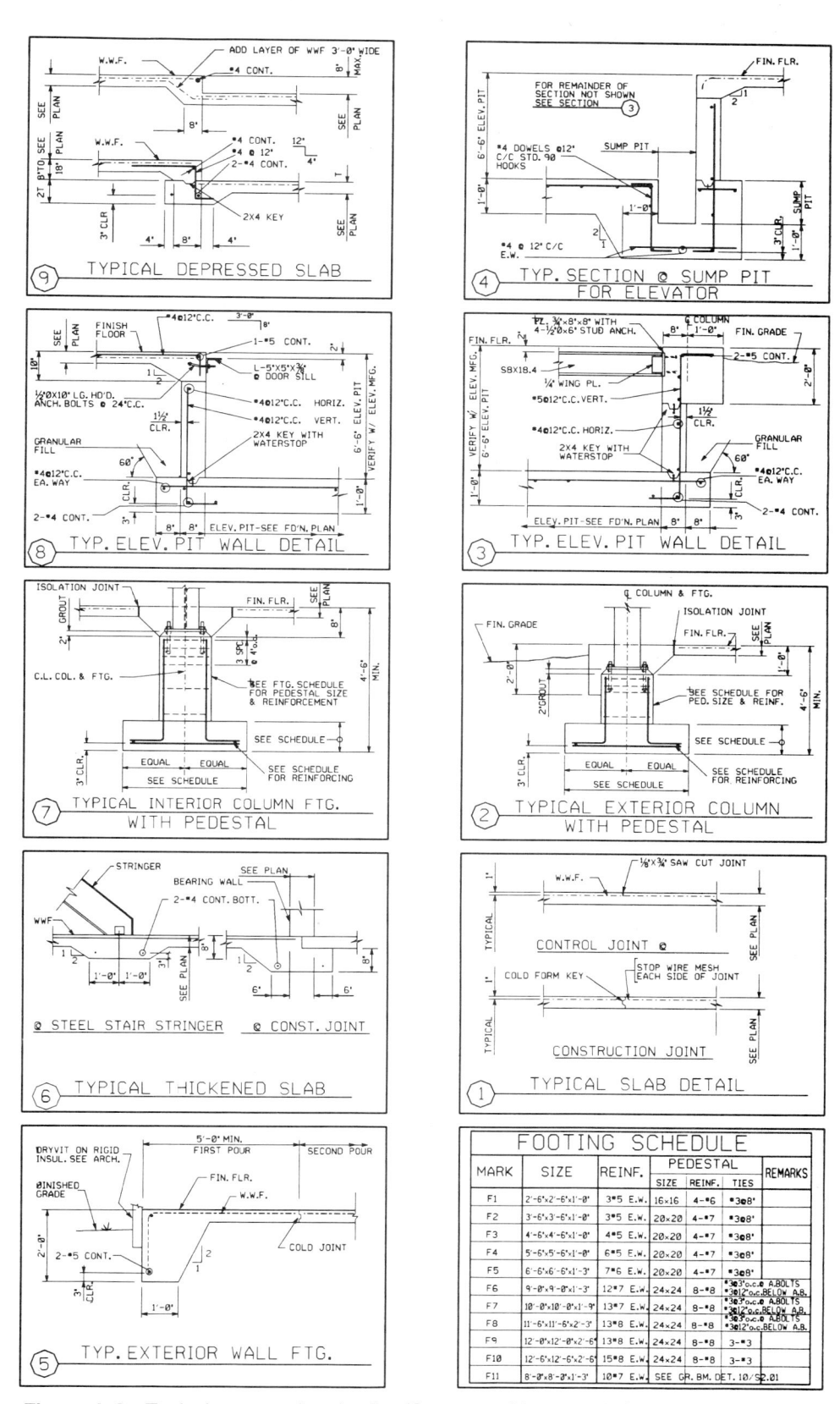

**Figure 4–2** Typical construction details. *(Courtesy of Intergraph Corporation.)*

**44** | CAD Applications: Architectural

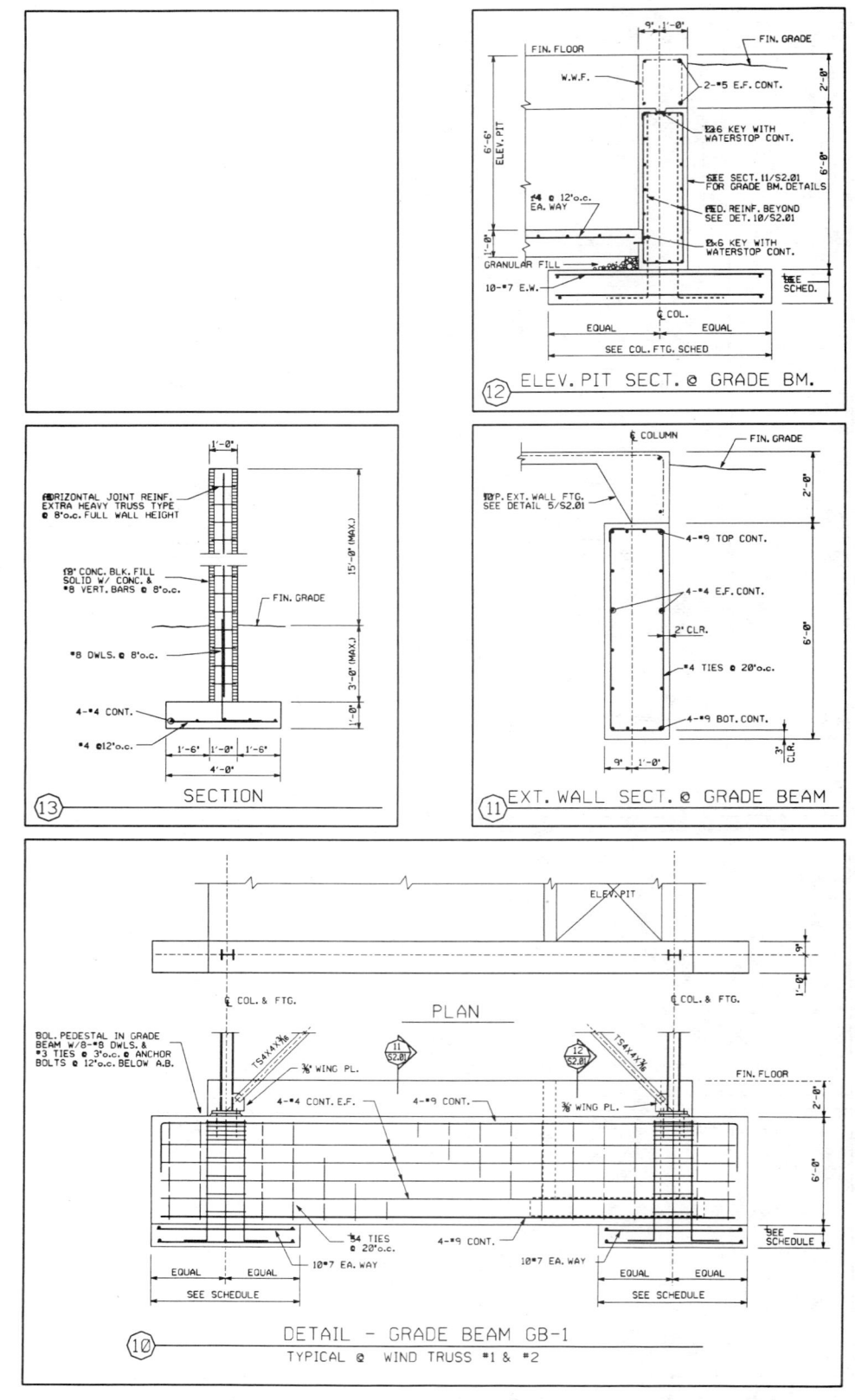

**Figure 4–3** Commercial construction details. *(Courtesy of Intergraph Corporation.)*

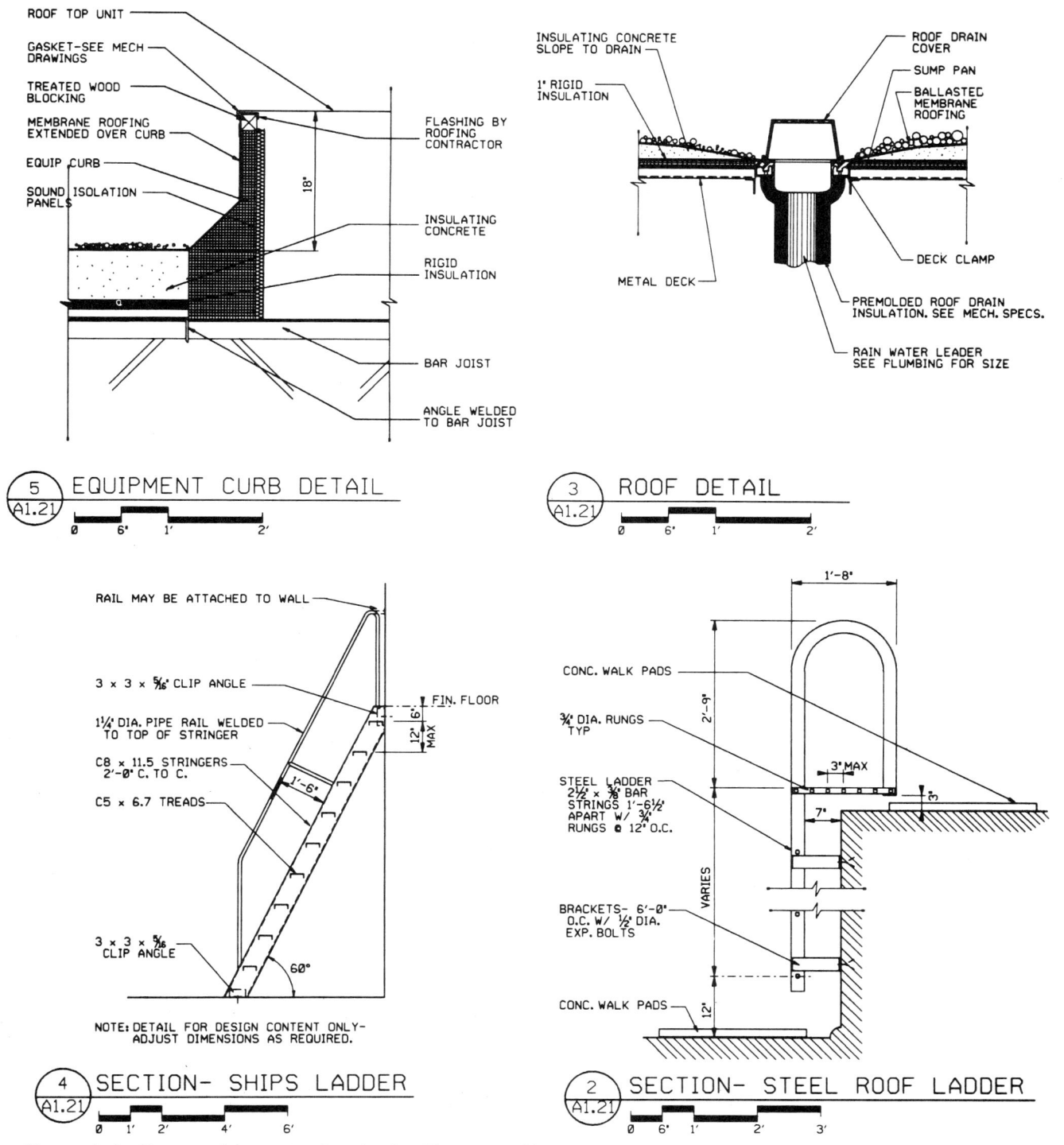

**Figure 4–4** Commercial construction details. *(Courtesy of Intergraph Corporation.)*

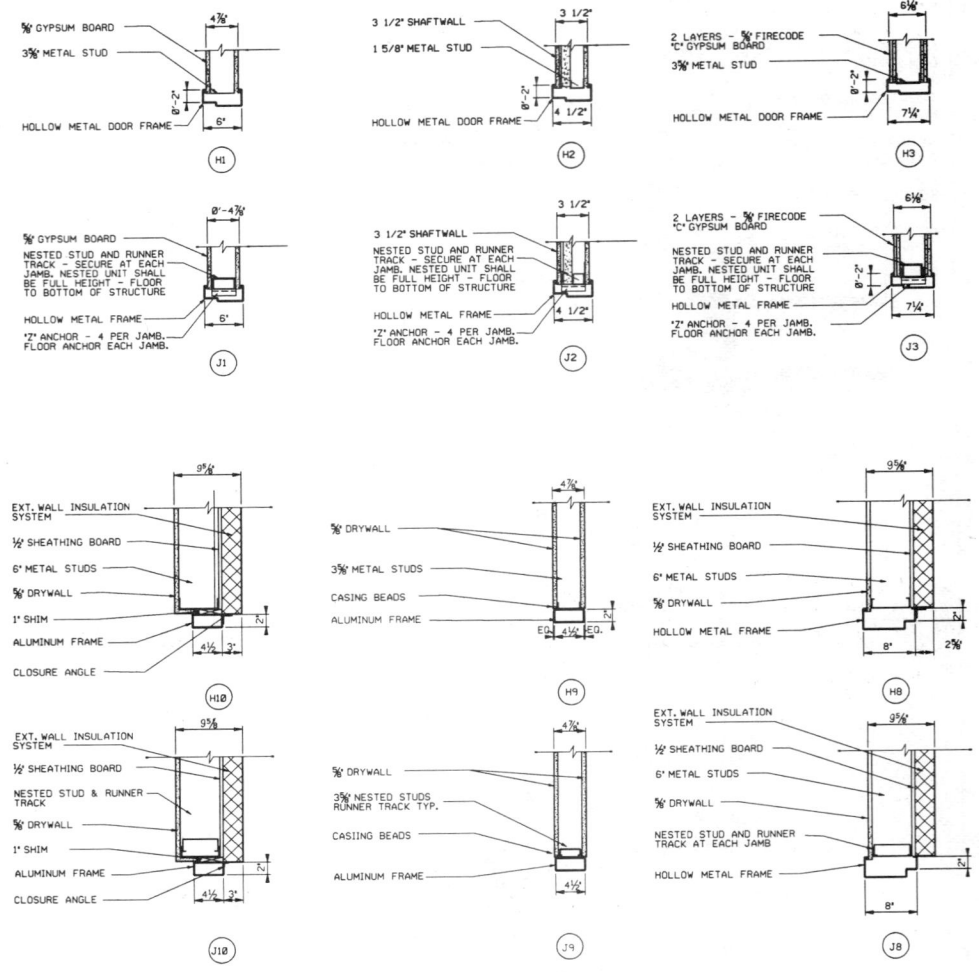

**Figure 4–5** Wall details. *(Courtesy of Intergraph Corporation.)*

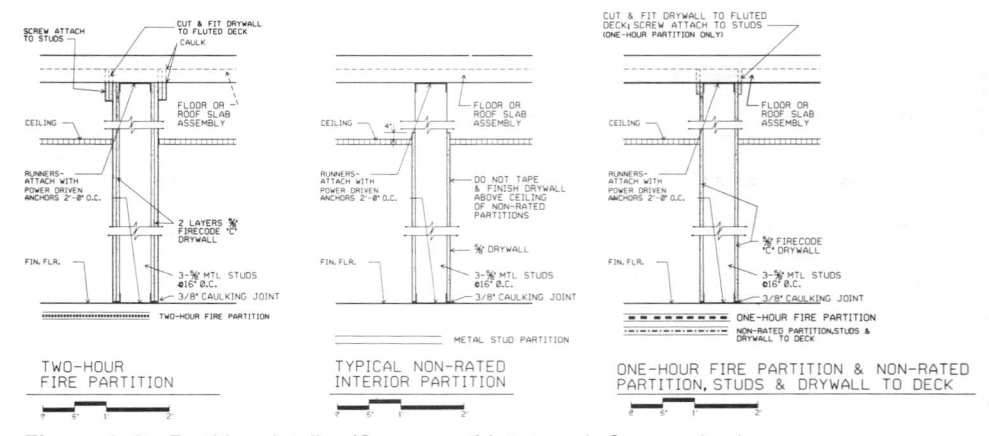

**Figure 4–6** Partition details. *(Courtesy of Intergraph Corporation.)*

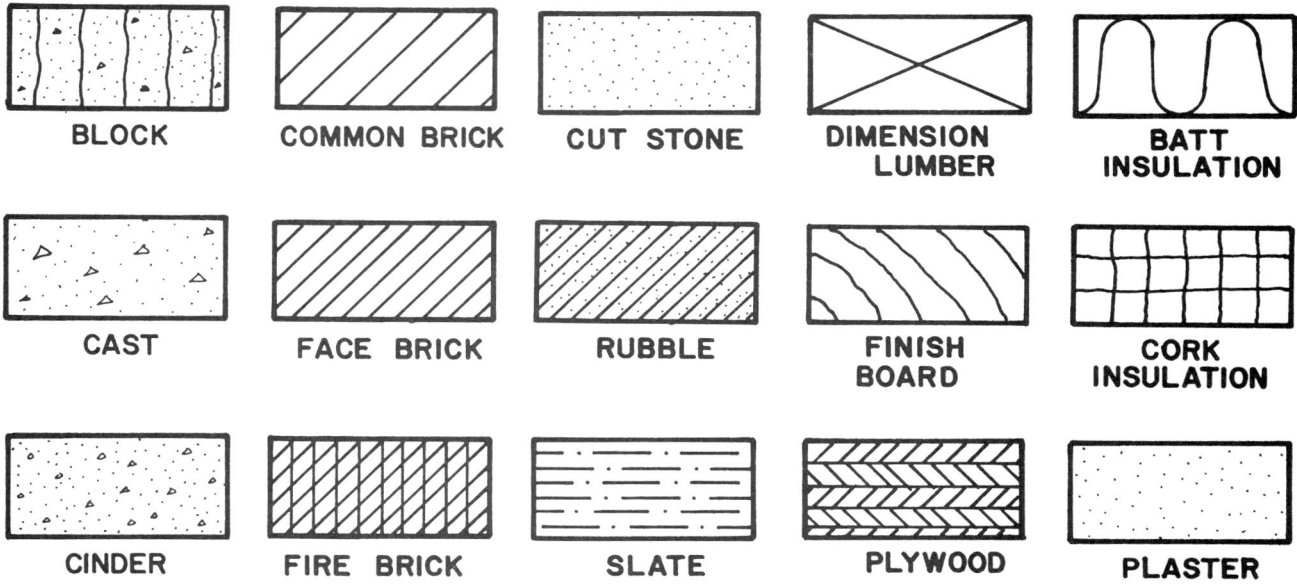

**Figure 4-7** Symbols for construction details.

## COMMANDS AND FUNCTIONS

**Graphic Creation Commands**

- ✓ Point
- ✓ Solid Line
- ✓ Hidden Line
- ✓ Construction Line
- ✓ Dashed Line
- ✓ Center Line
- ✓ Rectangle
- ✓ Circle
- ✓ Arc
- ✓ Irregular Curve
- ✓ Ellipse
- ___ Polygon
- ___ Grid
- ___ XYPT
- ___ Polar
- ___ Line Weight
- ___ Fillet
- ___ Chamfer
- ___ Leaders
- ___ Rect.
- ___ Hatch

**Manipulation Commands**

- ✓ Move
- ✓ Copy
- ✓ Rotate
- ✓ Scale
- ✓ Zoom
- ✓ Pan
- ___ Mirror

**Size Specification Commands**

- ✓ Auto. Dimension
- ___ Dimension
- ___ Tolerance
- ___ Calc. Area

**Output Commands**

- ✓ Plot
- ___ Print (Screen Dump)

**Text Creation Commands**

- ✓ Text

**Modification Commands**

- ✓ Edit
- ✓ Delete
- ✓ Redraw
- ___ Clip
- ✓ Erase

**Facilitation Commands**

- ✓ Save
- ✓ File
- ✓ Symbol Library
- ___ Layer
- ___ Quit
- ___ Default

## PROCEDURES FOR PREPARING THE DETAILS

What follows is an illustrated, step-by-step description of how a construction detail is produced on a CAD system. The detail selected as the example is a typical wall detail for a residential dwelling. However, the procedures that follow can be used to produce any of the many types of construction details.

### ■ Step 1

Log-on to the system and create a drawing designation called DETABC. Substitute your initials for the ABC. Decide what size of medium the completed detail will be plotted on.

### ■ Step 2

Lay out the overall profile of the detail using the CONSTRUCTION LINES function if it is available and SOLID LINES if it is not. Begin at the bottom of the footing and build upwards as the tradespeople would build the house, Figure 4-8.

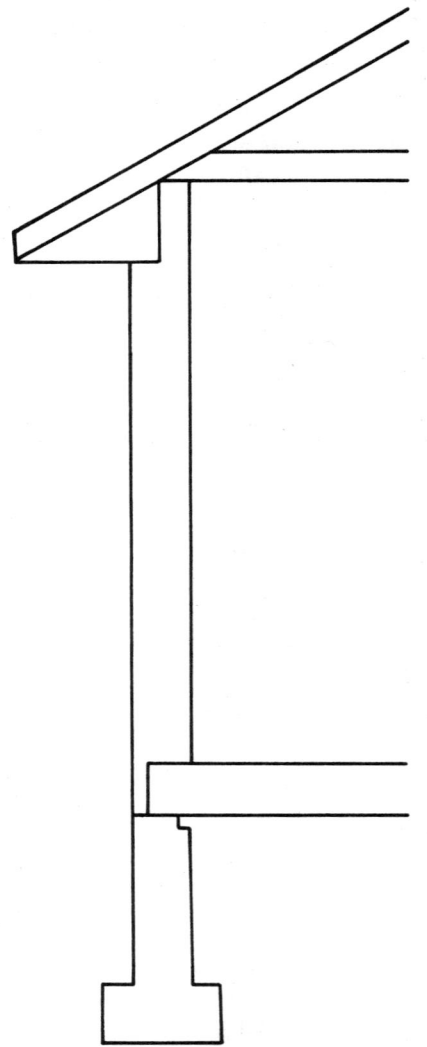

**Figure 4-8** Illustration for Step 2.

■ *Step 3*

Convert the construction lines from Step 2 into solid lines. Add the symbols for the footing, brick siding, and dimension lumber. Switch to the SOLID LINES mode and create a line to represent grade, Figure 4–9.

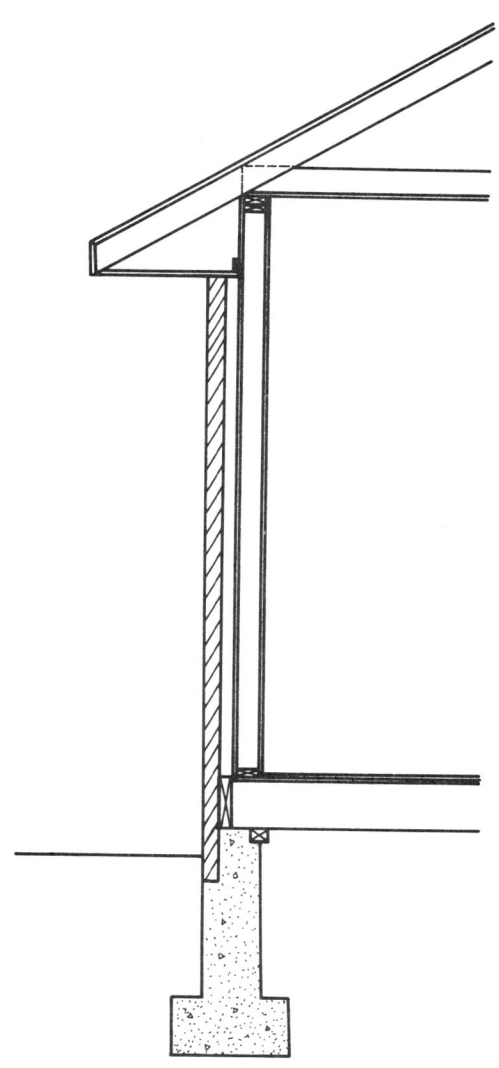

**Figure 4–9** Illustration for Step 3.

■ *Step 4*

Switch to the DIMENSION mode and add the dimensions for the overhand, crawl space, and floor-to-ceiling. Call out the descriptions for the drywall, plywood subflooring, shingles, and floor joists. Switch to the TEXT mode and add all remaining notation to complete the detail, Figure 4–10.

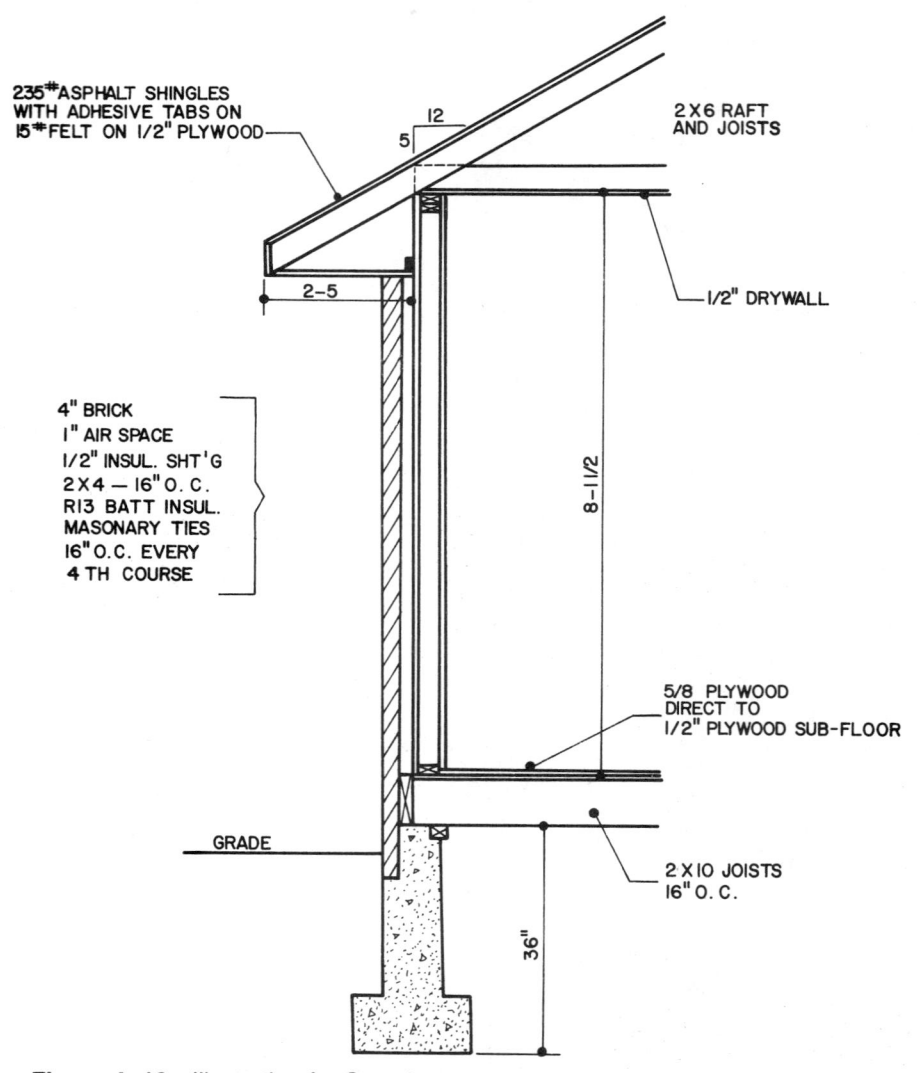

**Figure 4–10**   Illustration for Step 4.

# REVIEW QUESTIONS

The following questions are provided as a review of Chapter 4 and should be completed before attempting the application projects for the chapter. Write your answers in the spaces and blanks provided.

1. Define "construction detail."

2. Name four different types of construction details that might be found in a set of architectural plans.

3. List three ways construction details might be used:

4. Sketch the symbols for the following:
   Batt insulation—

   Cork insulation—

   Plaster—

5. What is your CAD system's command for the generic command POINT?

6. What is your CAD systems command for the generic command SAVE?

7. What is your CAD system's command for the generic command DELETE?

8. Explain the steps you would use on your CAD system to create the "batt insulation" symbol on a drawing if it is not contained in the symbols library.

9. Explain the steps you would use on your CAD system to create the "cork insulation" symbol on a drawing if it is not contained in the symbols library.

10. Explain the steps you would use on your CAD system to create the "dimension lumber" symbol on a drawing if it is not contained in the symbols library.

# APPLICATION PROJECTS

The following application projects are provided to help you become proficient in producing construction details on a CAD system. To ensure that you use input, modification, and manipulation functions, you will be required to reconstruct projects as shown and make modifications to them. To ensure that you use facilitation and output functions, SAVE each completed project and PLOT it on the size and type of medium specified by your instructor.

**Project 1:** Figure 4–11 is a construction detail for an 8″ block partition wall. Reconstruct the detail on your CAD as shown.

**Project 2:** Using Figure 4–11 as a guide, construct a similar partition detail for a 12″ concrete block wall. Adjust all dimensions proportionally.

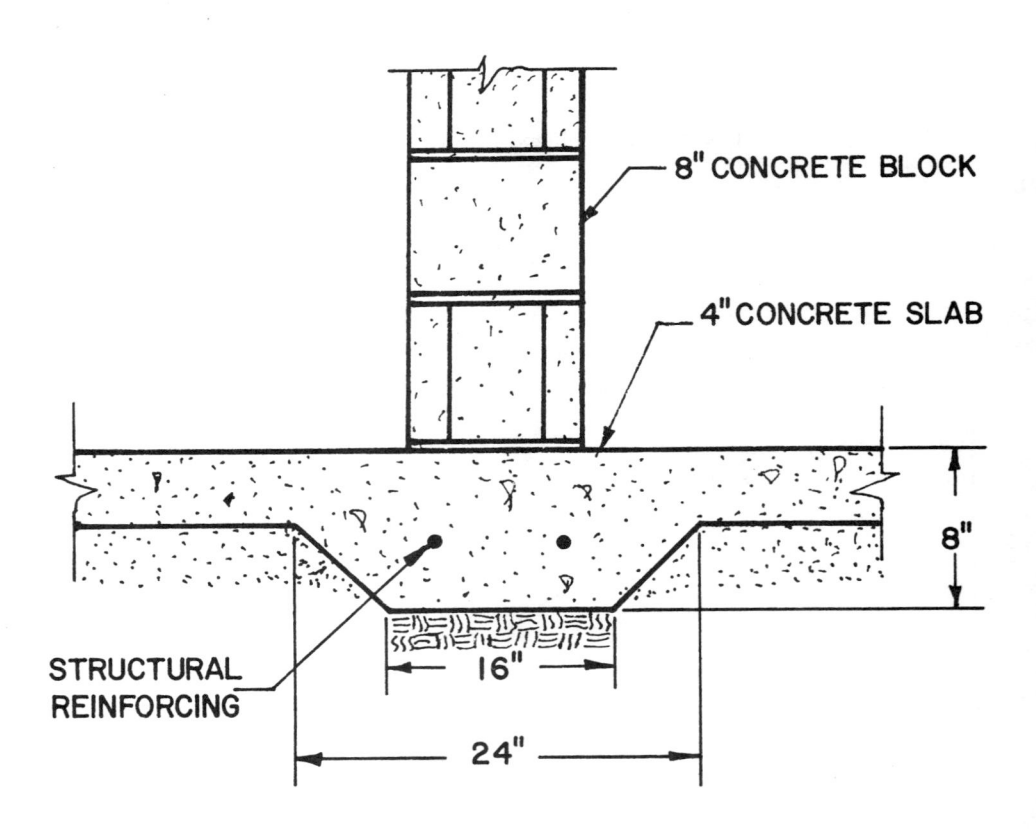

PARTITION WALL DETAIL

**Figure 4–11** Application projects 1 and 2.

**Project 3:** Using Figure 4-12 as a guide, construct a similar partition detail for a 4" wooden stud wall. Adjust all dimensions proportionally.

**Project 4:** Figure 4-12 is a construction detail for a 12" basement wall. Reconstruct the detail on your CAD system as shown.

**Project 5:** Using Figure 4-12 as a guide, construct a similar basement wall detail for an 8" basement wall and adjust all dimensions proportionally.

**Project 6:** Using Figure 4-12 as a guide, construct a basement wall detail that is the mirror image of Figure 4-12.

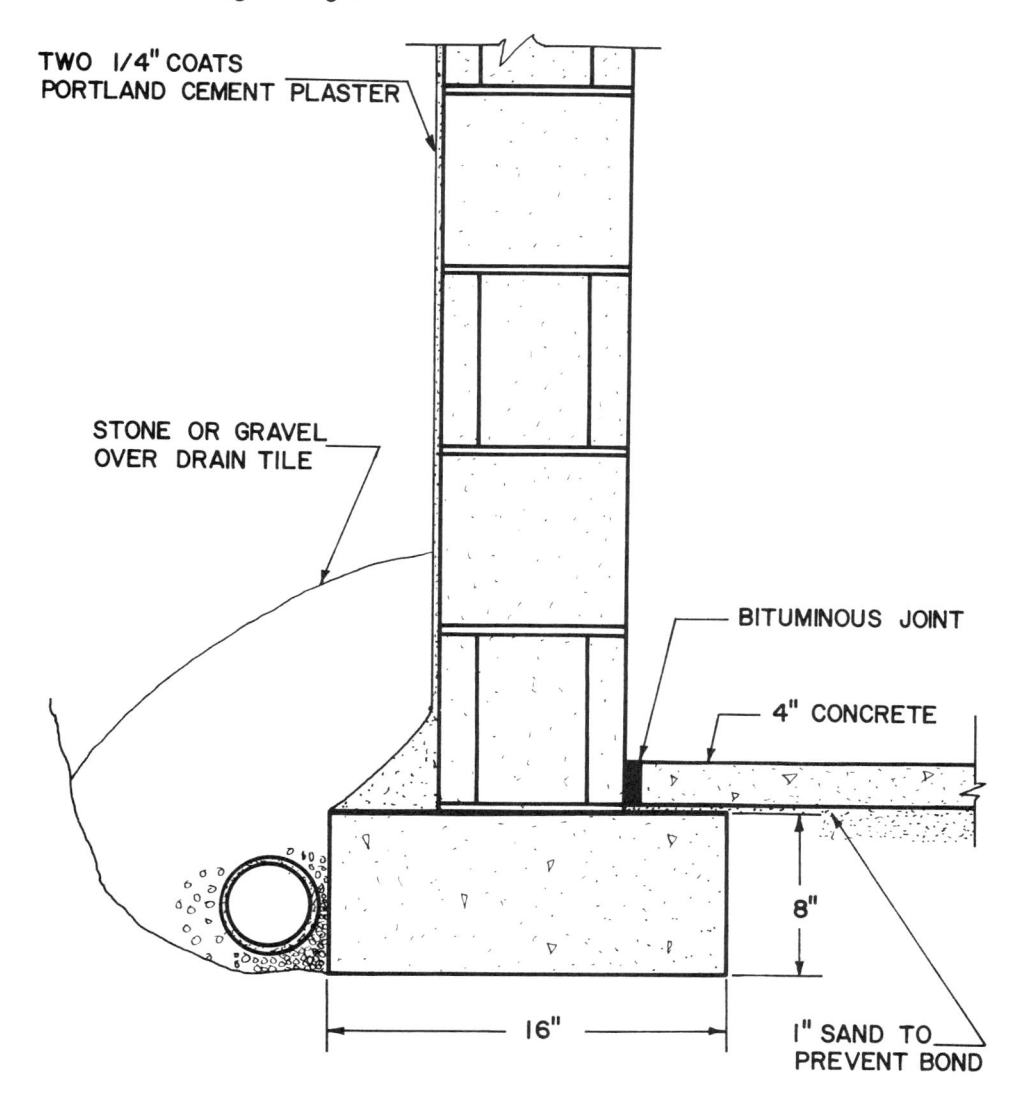

**Figure 4-12** Application projects 3, 4, 5, and 6.

**Project 7:** Figure 4–13 is a construction detail for a residential dwelling with a concrete block foundation and a poured concrete slab floor system. Reconstruct the detail on your CAD system as shown.

**Project 8:** Using Figure 4–13, construct a similar foundation wall detail, but with the following differences:

1. Use 12″ block for the foundation wall and adjust the footing accordingly.
2. Add brick veneer to the outside of the wall.

**Project 9:** Using Figure 4–13 as a guide, construct a foundation wall detail that is the mirror image of Figure 4–13.

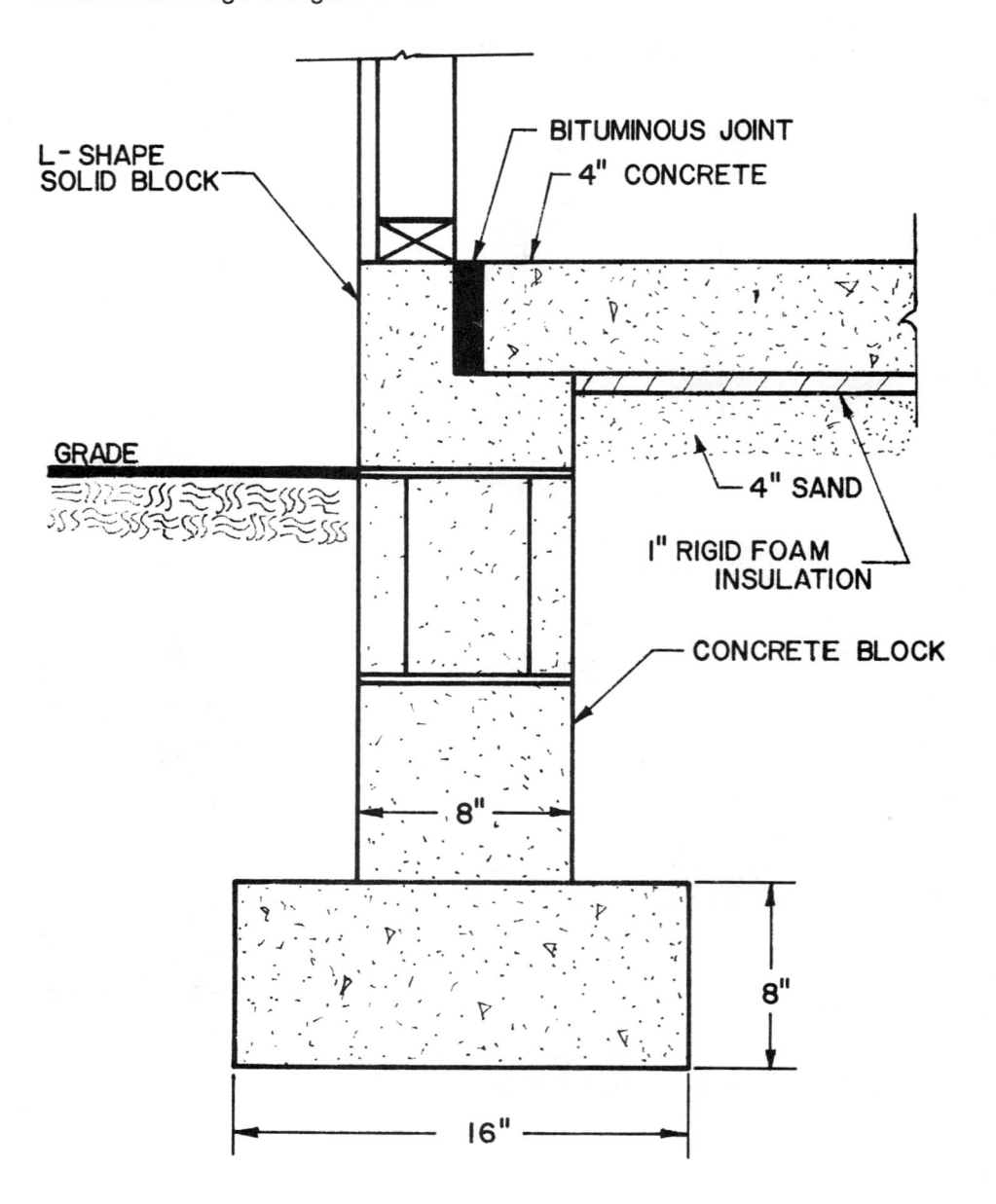

**Figure 4–13** Application projects 7, 8, and 9.

**Project 10:** Figure 4–14 is a construction detail for a 12" concrete block foundation wall. Reconstruct the detail on your CAD system as shown.

**Project 11:** Using Figure 4–14 as a guide, construct a similar foundation wall detail, but with the following differences:

1. Use an 8" foundation wall and run the brick veneer all the way down to the footing.
2. Change the floor joists to 2 × 10s and label them.

**Project 12:** Using Figure 4–14 as a guide, construct a similar foundation wall detail that is the mirror image of 4–14.

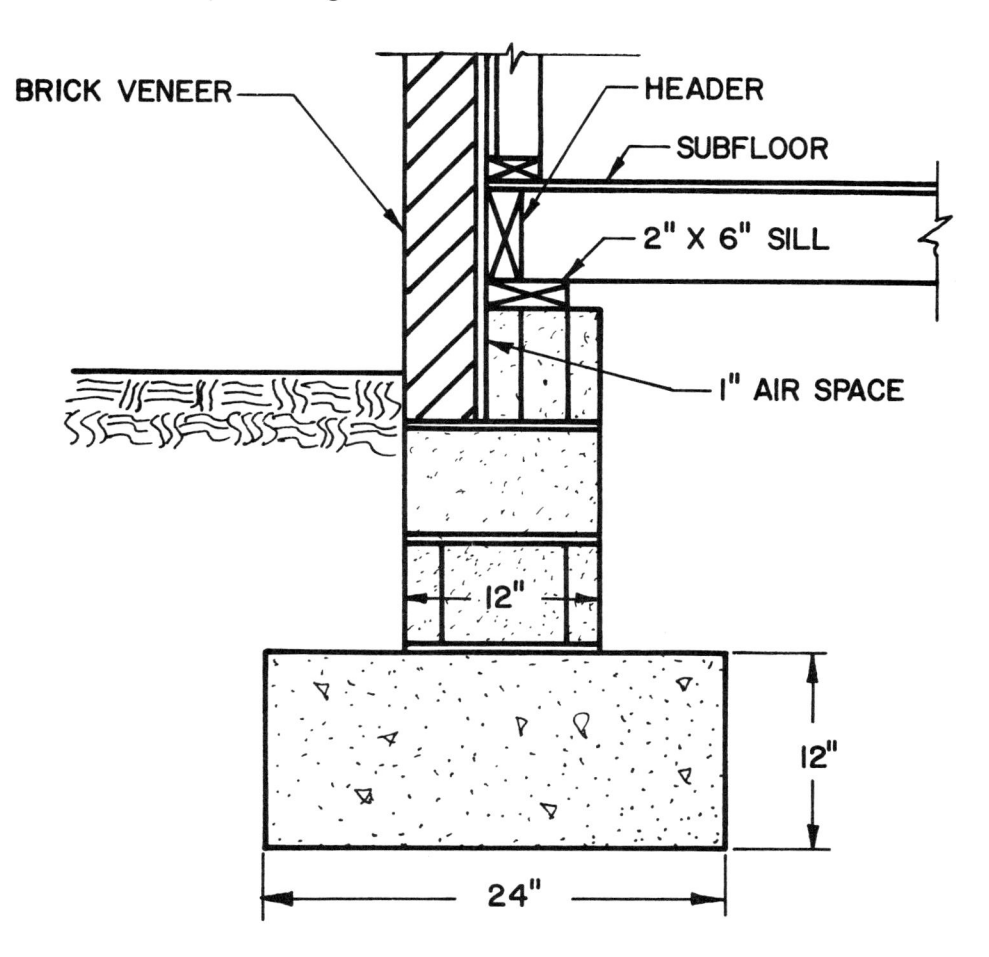

## 12" CONCRETE BLOCK FOUNDATION DETAIL

**Figure 4–14** Application projects 10, 11, and 12.

**Project 13:** Figure 4–15 is a construction detail for a brick and tile foundation system. Reconstruct the detail on your CAD system as shown.

**Project 14:** Using Figure 4–15 as a guide, construct a similar foundation detail, but with the following differences:

1. Use three 10" solid units for the foundation wall.
2. Use wood siding instead of brick.

**Project 15:** Using Figure 4–15 as a guide, construct a foundation detail that is the mirror image of Figure 4–15.

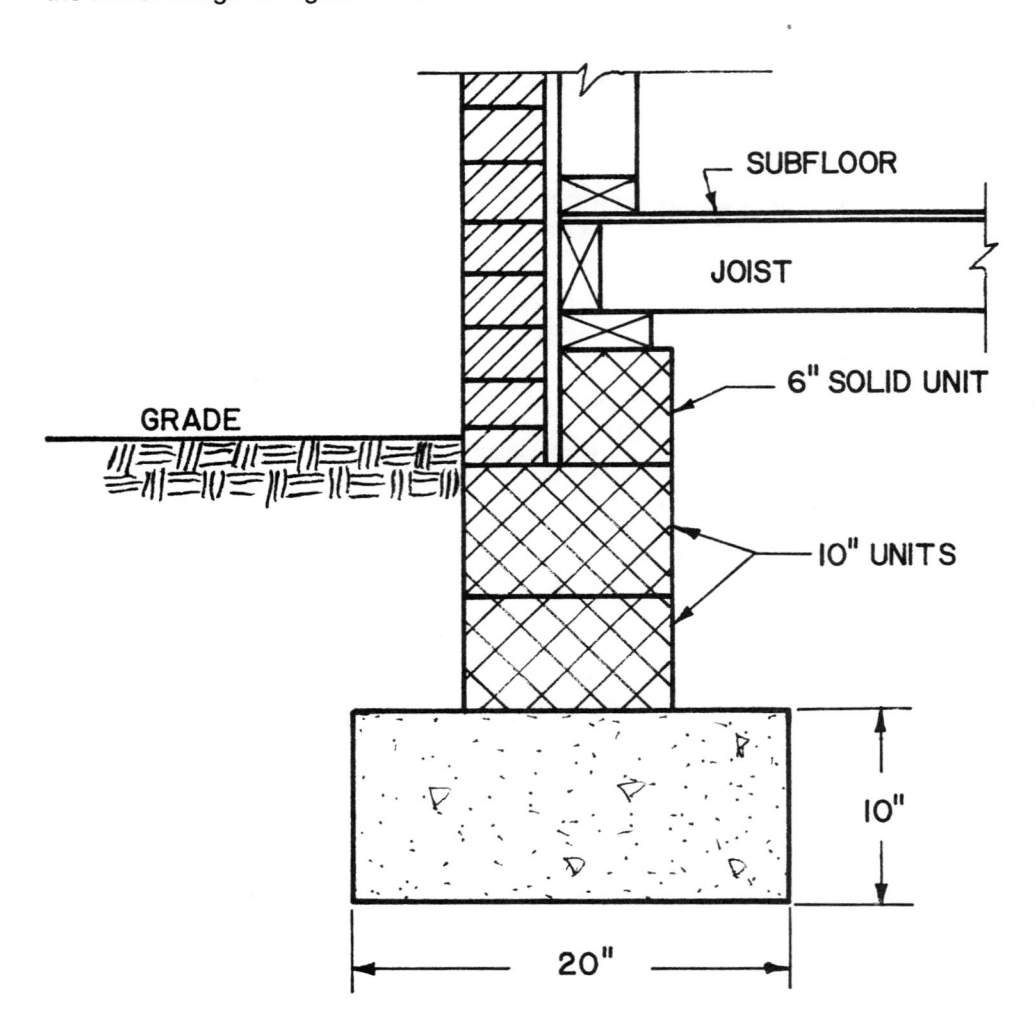

**BRICK AND TILE FOUNDATION DETAIL**

**Figure 4–15** Application projects 13, 14, and 15.

**Project 16:** Figure 4–16 is a construction detail for a masonry wall foundation detail. Reconstruct the detail on your CAD system as shown.

**Project 17:** Using Figure 4–16 as a guide, construct a similar foundation detail, but with the following differences:

1. Decrease the depth of the concrete foundation wall to 16".
2. Increase the width of the foundation wall to 12" and the footing to 24".

**Project 18:** Using Figure 4–16 as a guide, construct a foundation detail that is the mirror image of Figure 4–16.

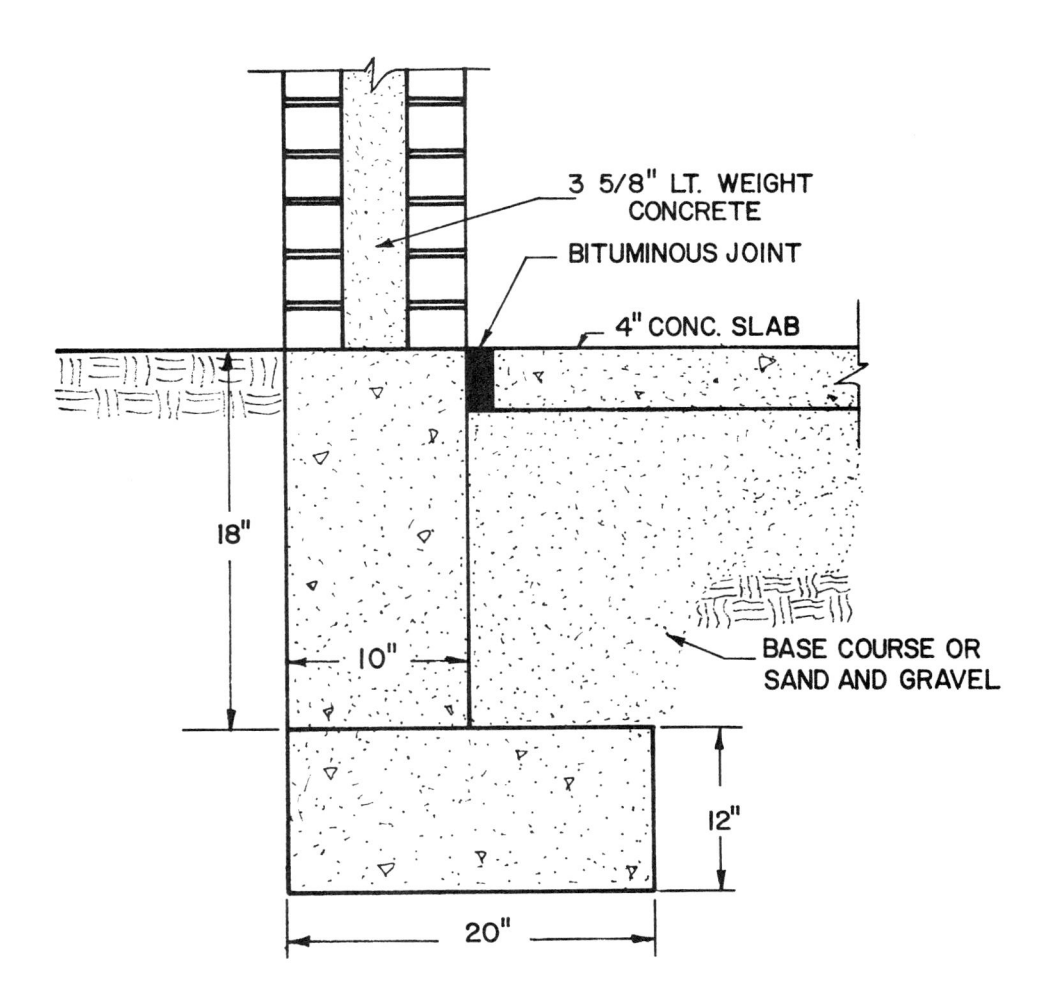

MASONRY WALL FOUNDATION DETAIL

**Figure 4–16** Application projects 16, 17, and 18.

**Project 19:** Figure 4–17 is a construction detail for a poured concrete foundation. Reconstruct Figure 4–17 on your CAD system as shown.

**Project 20:** Using Figure 4–17 as a guide, construct a similar foundation detail, but with the following differences:

1. Change the foundation wall to 10″ and the footing 20″.
2. Drop the brick siding.

**Project 21:** Using Figure 4–17 as a guide, construct a foundation detail that is the mirror image of Figure 4–17.

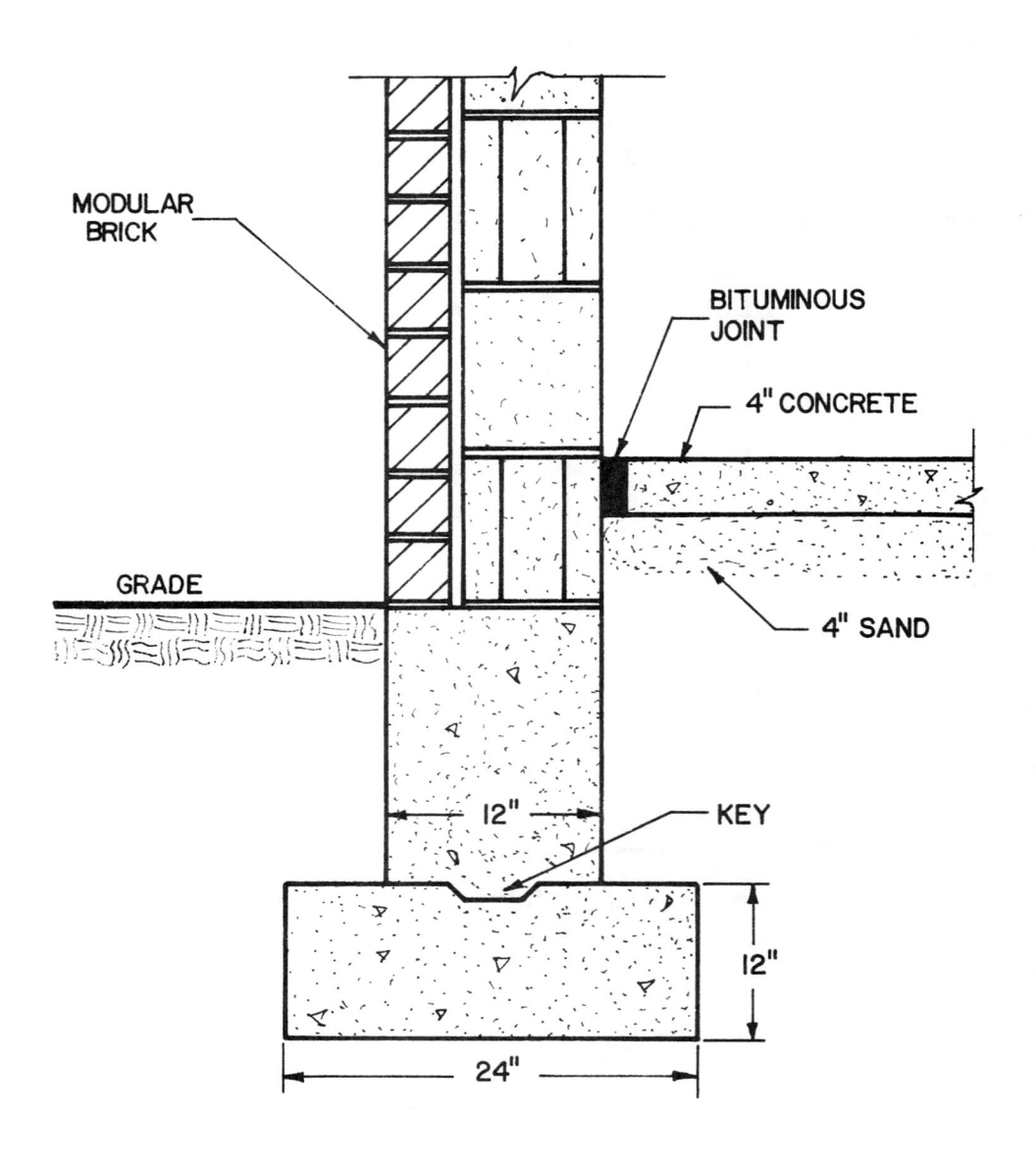

POURED CONCRETE FOUNDATION DETAIL
**Figure 4–17** Application projects 19, 20, and 21.

**Project 22:** Figure 4–18 is a construction detail for an outside wall of a residential dwelling. Reconstruct the wall detail on your CAD system as shown.

**Project 23:** Using Figure 4–18 as a guide, construct a similar wall detail, but with the following differences:

1. Drop the brick siding and add wood siding. Adjust all notes accordingly.
2. Change the roof pitch to 3–12 and adjust the detail accordingly.

**Project 24:** Using Figure 4–18 as a guide, construct a wall detail that is the mirror image of Figure 4–18.

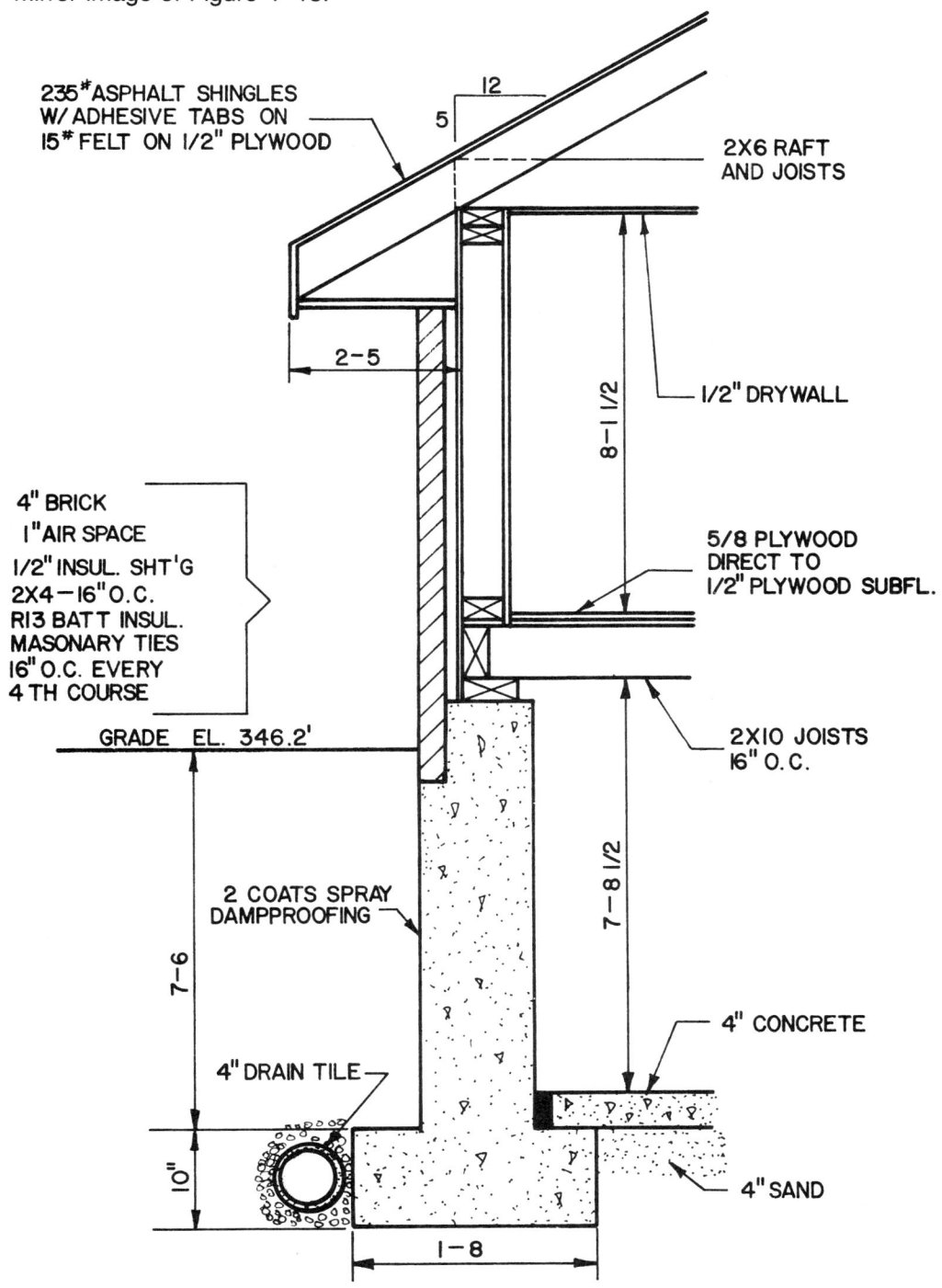

**Figure 4–18** Application projects 22, 23, and 24.

**Project 25:** Figure 4–19 is an architect's sketch of a construction detail. Reconstruct the sketch on your CAD system as a completed drawing.

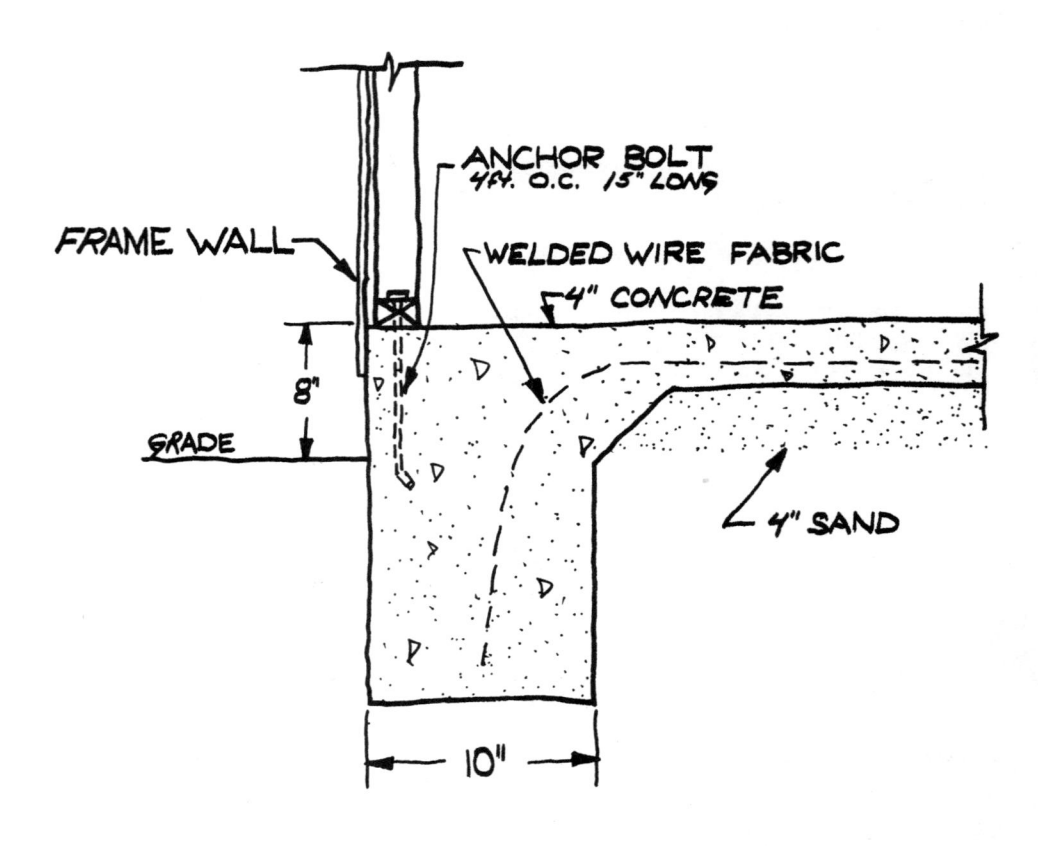

**Figure 4–19** Application project 25.

**Project 26:** Figure 4–20 is a construction detail of a ladder pad for a commercial building. Reconstruct the detail on your CAD system as shown.

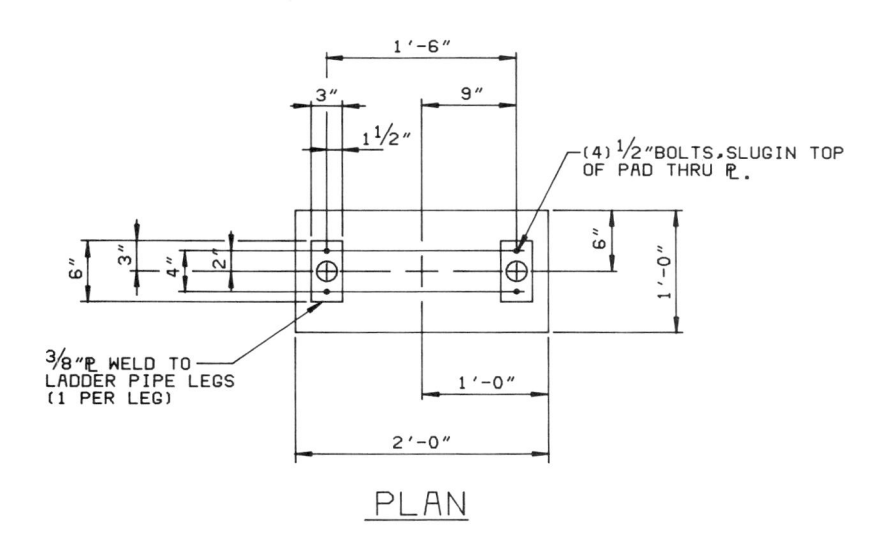

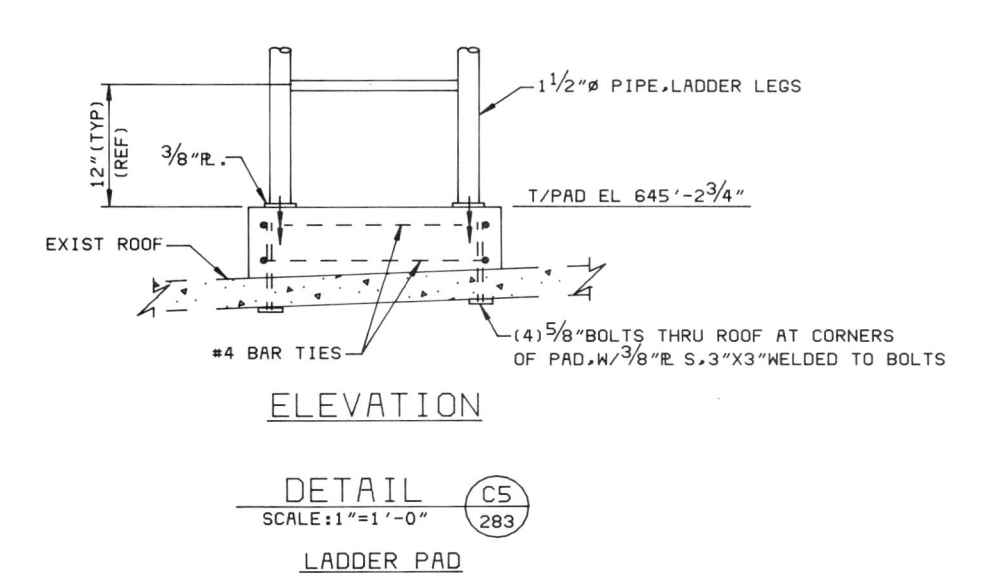

**Figure 4–20** Application project 26.

# chapter 5
# Elevations

## DEFINITION, PURPOSE, AND CONTENTS

Elevations are required in a complete set of architectural plans. While most components in a set of architectural plans are plan views in section, elevations are orthographic views. Although interior elevations are sometimes drawn to clarify interior relationships, the elevations required in a set of architectural plans are exterior elevations. Usually, when the term is used, it refers to exterior elevations.

An elevation is an orthographic view of a given side of a building. Normally, four elevations are drawn: one for the front, one for the back, and one for each side. Occasionally the design and configuration of a building might require that more than four elevations be drawn or, in some cases, less. However, four elevations is the norm.

Elevations are used in several ways: 1) to show lay and tradespeople what the finished building should look like, 2) to provide height information that cannot be shown on plan views, and 3) to show the types of materials used on the exterior of the building.

Information typically included on elevations is:

- grade line
- finished floor line
- ceiling line
- overall profile showing all corners
- windows
- doors
- roof lines
- chimneys
- special material symbols
- appropriate height dimensions

Figure 5–1 is the north elevation of an eight-story commercial building with a penthouse on the top floor. This elevation was produced on a modern CAD system. Notice the finished floor lines separating the various floors and the circular symbol used at one end of each line. Figure 5–2 is the south elevation of the same building. Look closely and see the differences between the north and south elevations. Figure 5–3 on page 66 contains the front and rear elevations for a two-story residential dwelling. From the material symbols, you can see that the first floor has brick veneer siding and the second floor has horizontal wood siding. Figure 5–4 on page 66 is the front elevation for a

**64** | CAD Applications: Architectural

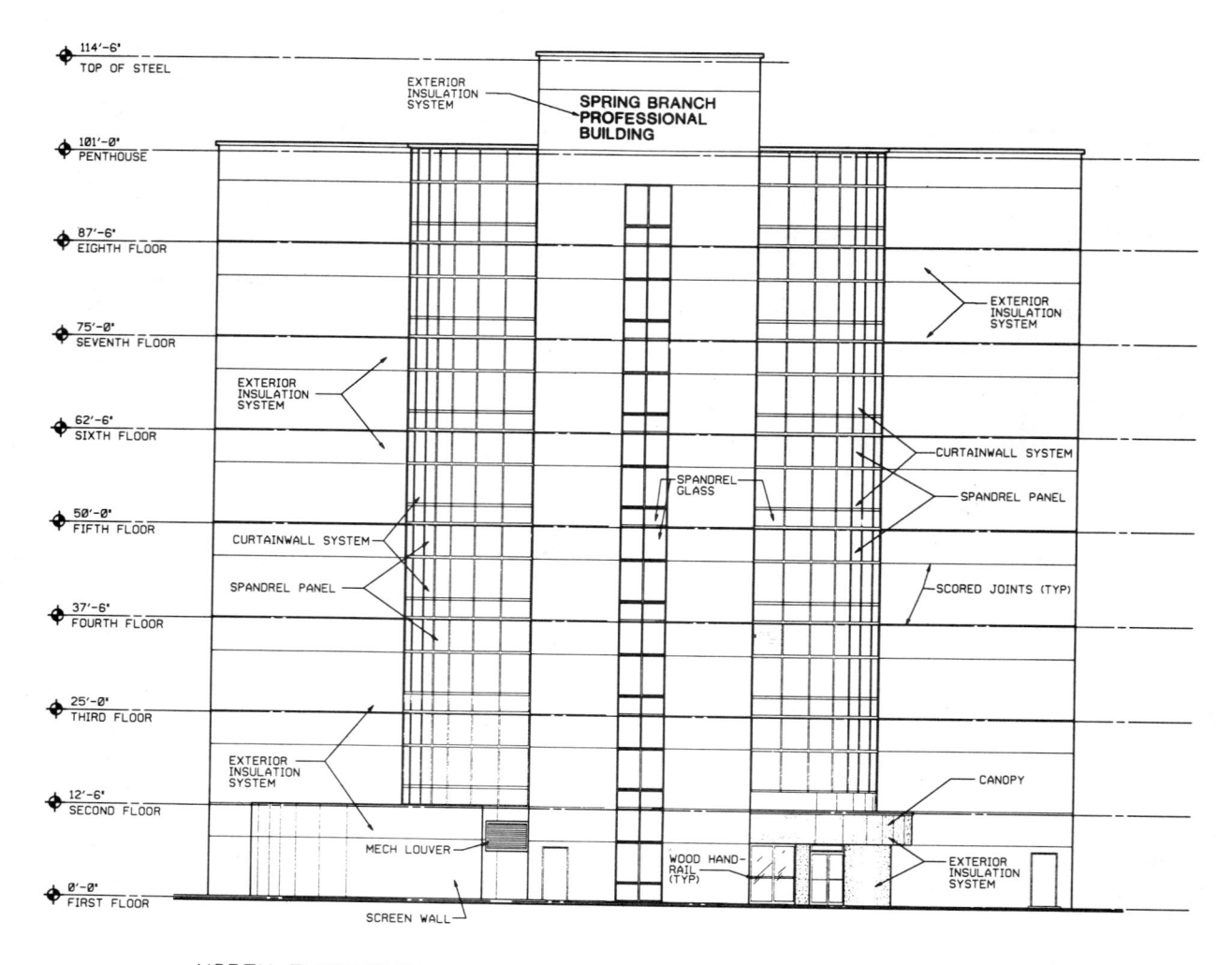

**Figure 5–1** Commercial elevation. *(Courtesy of Intergraph Corporation.)*

**Figure 5–2** Commercial elevation. *(Courtesy of Intergraph Corporation.)*

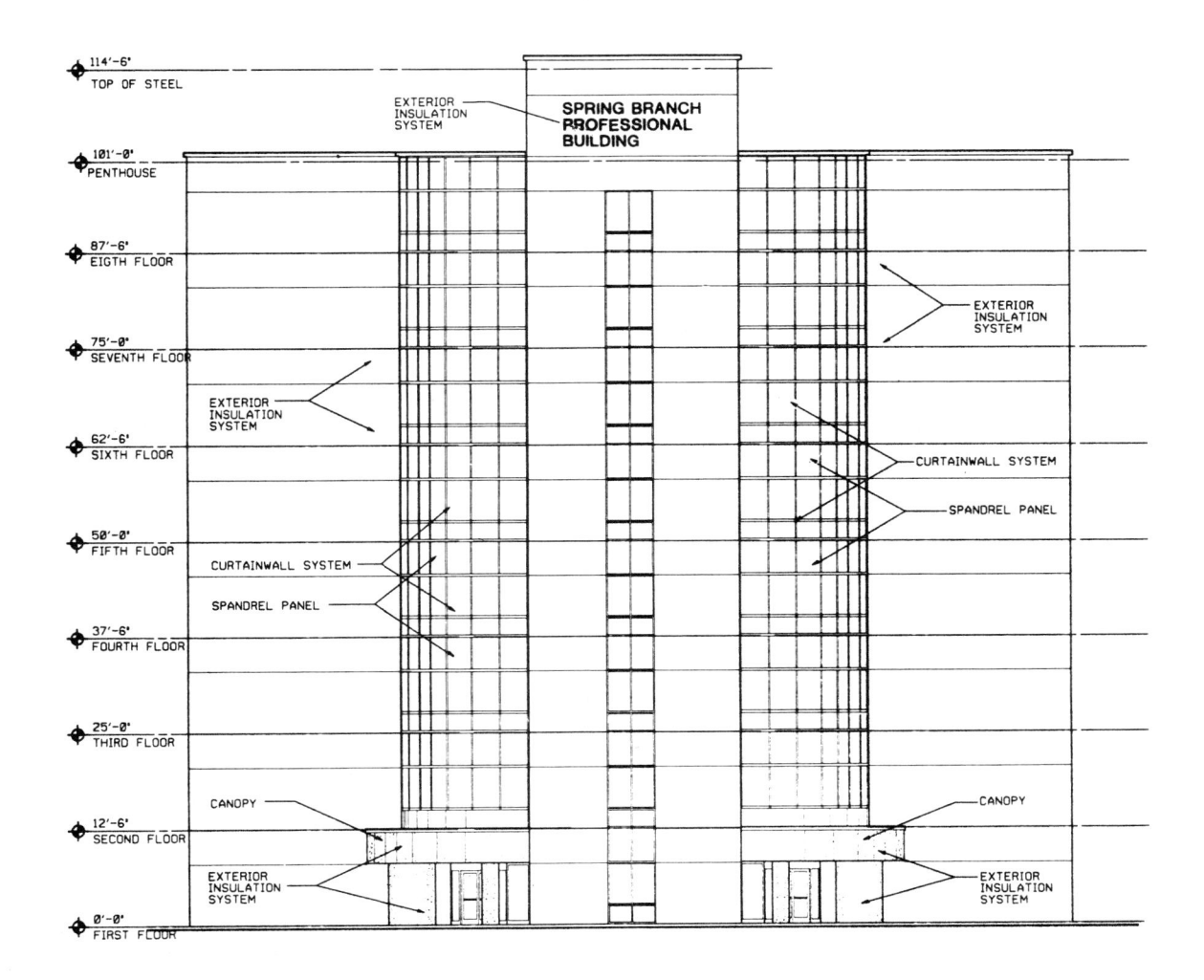

**Figure 5–3** Residential elevation. *(Courtesy of Bausch & Lomb/Houston Instrument.)*

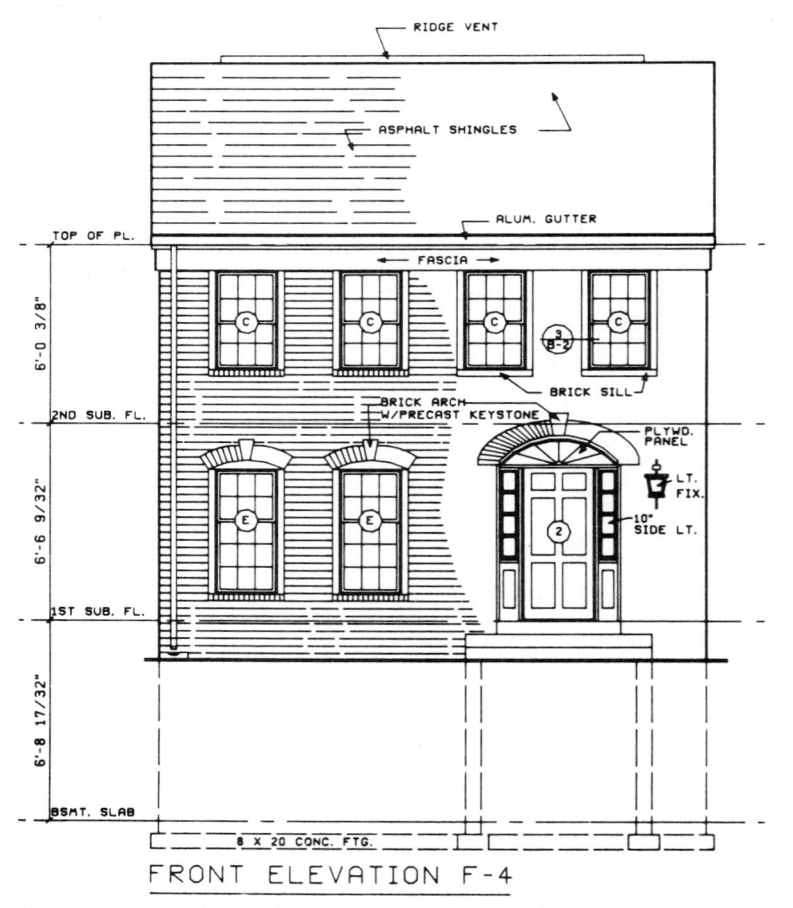

**Figure 5–4** Residential elevation. *(Courtesy of Sigma Design.)*

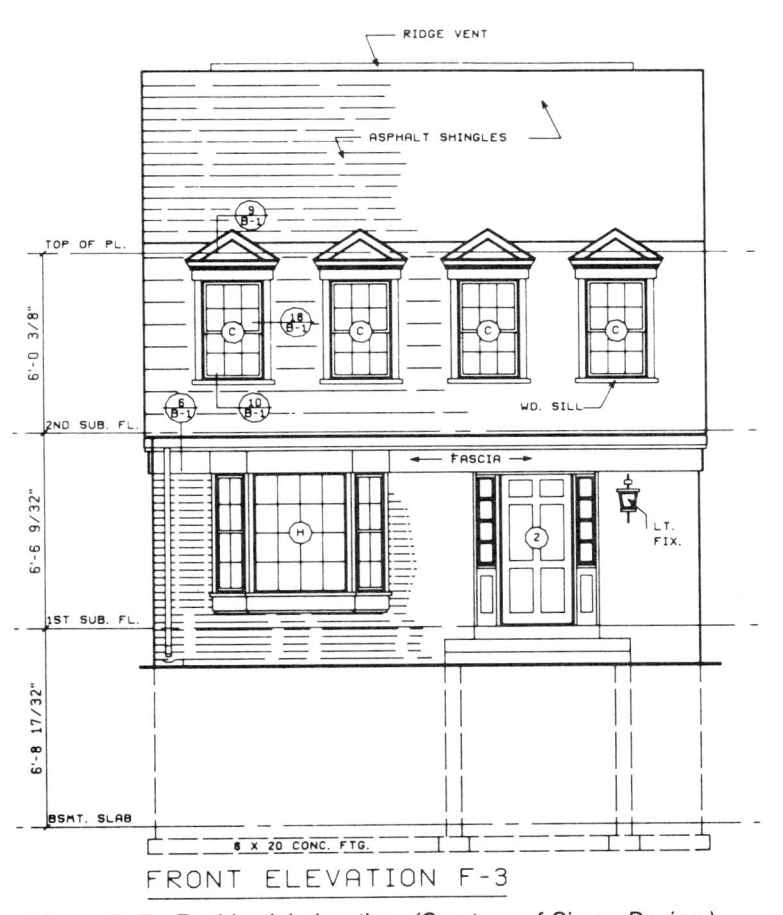

**Figure 5–5** Residential elevation. *(Courtesy of Sigma Design.)*

residential dwelling that has a basement and two stories. Notice the finely detailed windows and front door. This type of detail was accomplished using the ZOOM-IN function. Figure 5–5 is the front elevation for another residential dwelling with a basement and two stories. From the symbols, you can see that the house has one size of horizontal siding on the first floor, another on the second, and asphalt shingles on the roof. All of these examples of elevations were produced on modern CAD systems.

Note that elevations are technical drawings. They are *not* renderings. They *do not* contain secondary elements such as trees, bushes, people, automobiles, and so forth. These things are included on illustrations and renderings that are sometimes used on a separate cover sheet, but not as part of the architectural plans.

## SPECIAL SYMBOLS NEEDED

There are several special graphic symbols used in producing elevations on a CAD system. Those most frequently used are shown in Figure 5–6. Examine the symbols library of your CAD system to determine which of these symbols it contains. If the symbols library does not contain a particular symbol, you have two options:

1. Create the symbol and add it to the symbols library. This can only be done on those CAD systems that are programmed to accept user-defined symbols.
2. Construct the symbols on the drawing as they are needed, using the appropriate geometric characters and commands. For example, the "concrete block," "brick," and "siding" symbols can be made using the SOLID LINES command.

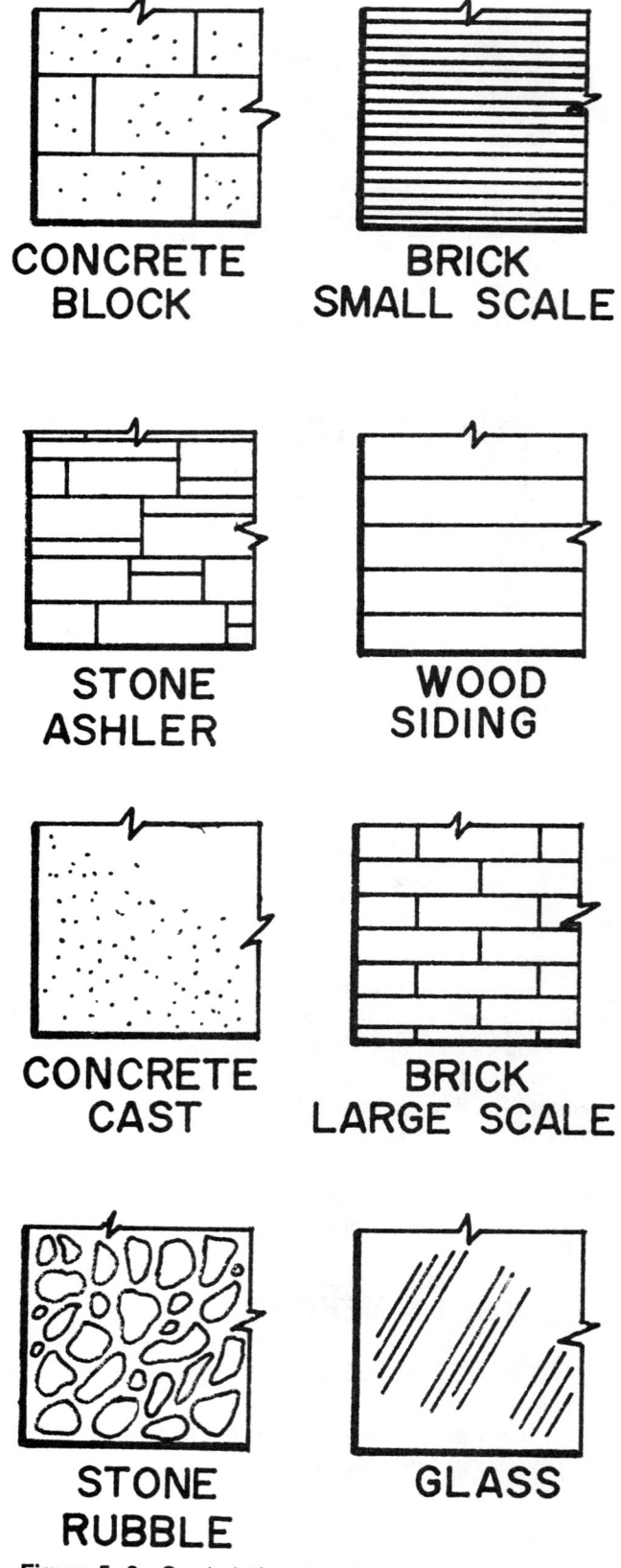

**Figure 5-6** Symbols for elevations.

Chapter 5 Elevations | 69

## CAD COMMANDS AND FUNCTIONS USED

There are several different commands and manipulation functions used in producing elevations on a CAD system. Most CAD systems have these commands and functions. However, they are often given different names on different systems (see Chapter 1).

The generic names for the commands and functions used to produce an elevation on a CAD system are listed in the Commands and Functions chart. Before attempting the application projects for Chapter 5, match these generic commands and functions with their corresponding commands and functions on your CAD system.

---

**COMMANDS AND FUNCTIONS**

**Graphic Creation Commands**

- ✓ Point
- ✓ Solid Line
- ✓ Hidden Line
- ✓ Construction Line
- ✓ Dashed Line
- ✓ Center Line
- ✓ Rectangle
- ✓ Circle
- ✓ Arc
- ✓ Irregular Curve
- ✓ Ellipse
- ___ Polygon
- ___ Grid
- ___ XYPT
- ___ Polar
- ___ Line Weight
- ___ Fillet
- ___ Chamfer

- ___ Leaders
- ___ Rect
- ___ Hatch

**Manipulation Commands**

- ✓ Move
- ✓ Copy
- ✓ Rotate
- ✓ Scale
- ✓ Zoom
- ✓ Pan
- ✓ Mirror

**Size Specification Commands**

- ✓ Auto. Dimension
- ___ Dimension
- ___ Tolerance
- ___ Calc. Area

**Output Commands**

- ✓ Plot
- ___ Print (Screen Dump)

**Text Creation Commands**

- ✓ Text

**Modification Commands**

- ✓ Edit
- ✓ Delete
- ✓ Redraw
- ___ Clip
- ✓ Erase

**Facilitation Commands**

- ✓ Save
- ✓ File
- ✓ Symbol Library
- ___ Layer
- ___ Quit
- ___ Default

---

## PROCEDURES FOR PREPARING THE ELEVATION

What follows is an illustrated, step-by-step description of how an elevation is produced on a CAD system. The example used is a front elevation for a residential dwelling. The same procedures would be used for commercial elevations and for rear and side elevations.

■ *Step 1*

Log-on to the system and create a drawing designation called ELVABC. Substitute your initials for the ABC. Decide what size medium you will plot the completed elevation on.

### ■ Step 2

Using the CONSTRUCTION LINES function if it is available and SOLID LINES if it is not, lay out the finished grade line. Use your foundation details to determine how far above the grade line the finished floor line should be and then lay out the finished floor line. Measuring up vertically and perpendicular to the finished floor line, lay out the ceiling line. Using these lines as the parameters, lay out the basic profile of the building, Figure 5–7. You will notice in this figure that two lines were used to indicate the grade. This is sometimes done for emphasis, but it is not required.

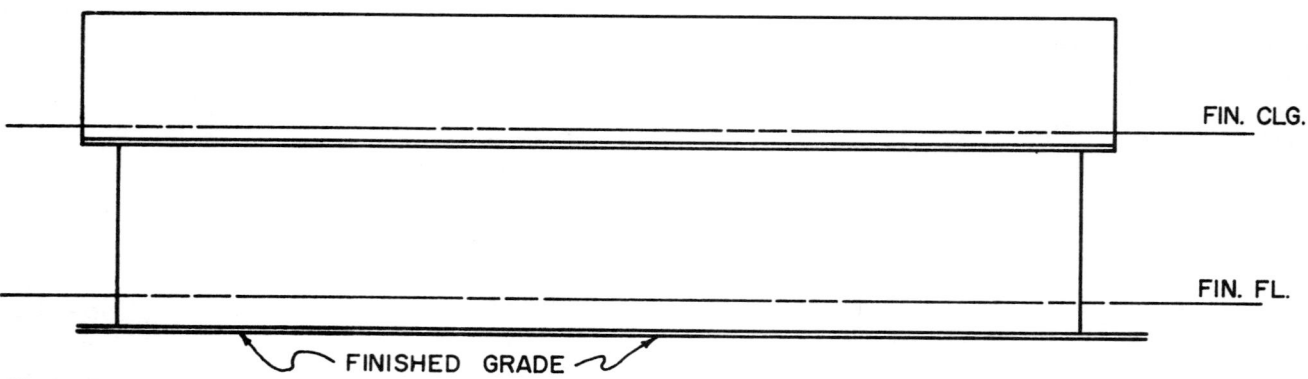

**Figure 5–7** Illustration for Step 2.

### ■ Step 3

Add permanent features such as windows, doors, and the chimney. Begin with the basic outline using the RECTANGLE function. Use the ZOOM-IN function to add detail to windows and doors. If the symbols library does not contain the symbol for glass, create the symbol using the SOLID LINE command. Use the ZOOM-IN command before applying the symbols to the windows, Figure 5–8. At this point, if you have been using the CONSTRUCTION LINES command, convert all lines to solid lines.

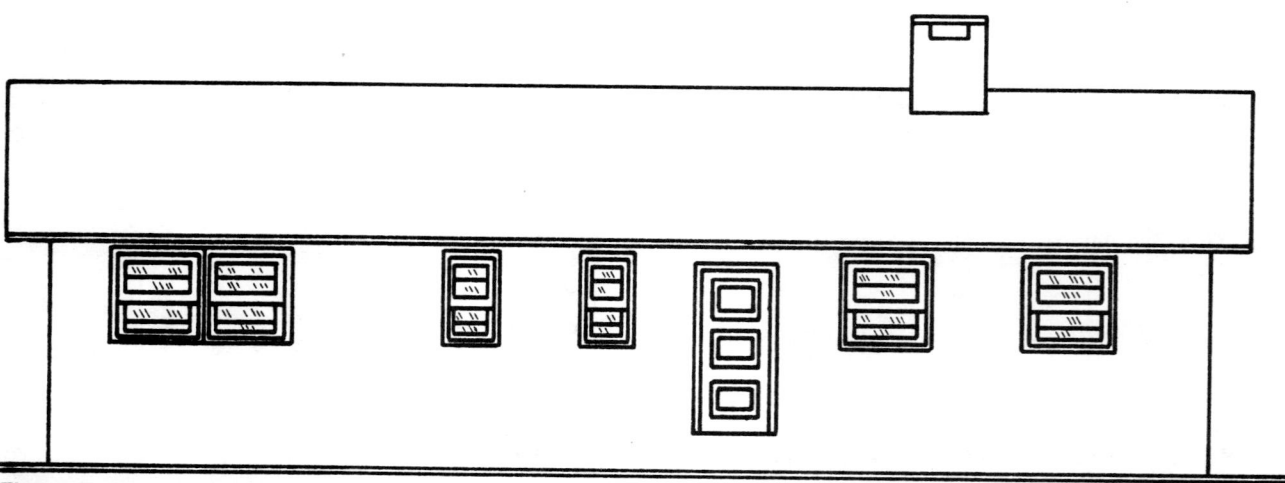

**Figure 5–8** Illustration for Step 3.

### ■ Step 4

Complete the elevation by adding the required symbols, dimensions, and text. Add the required symbols first, creating them if they are not contained in the symbols library. All of the symbols in Figure 5–9 were created without the benefit of the symbols library, using the SOLID LINES function. Switch to the DIMENSION mode and add the finished floor-to-ceiling and overhang dimensions. Switch to the TEXT mode and add all notation and called-out dimensional information, Figure 5–9.

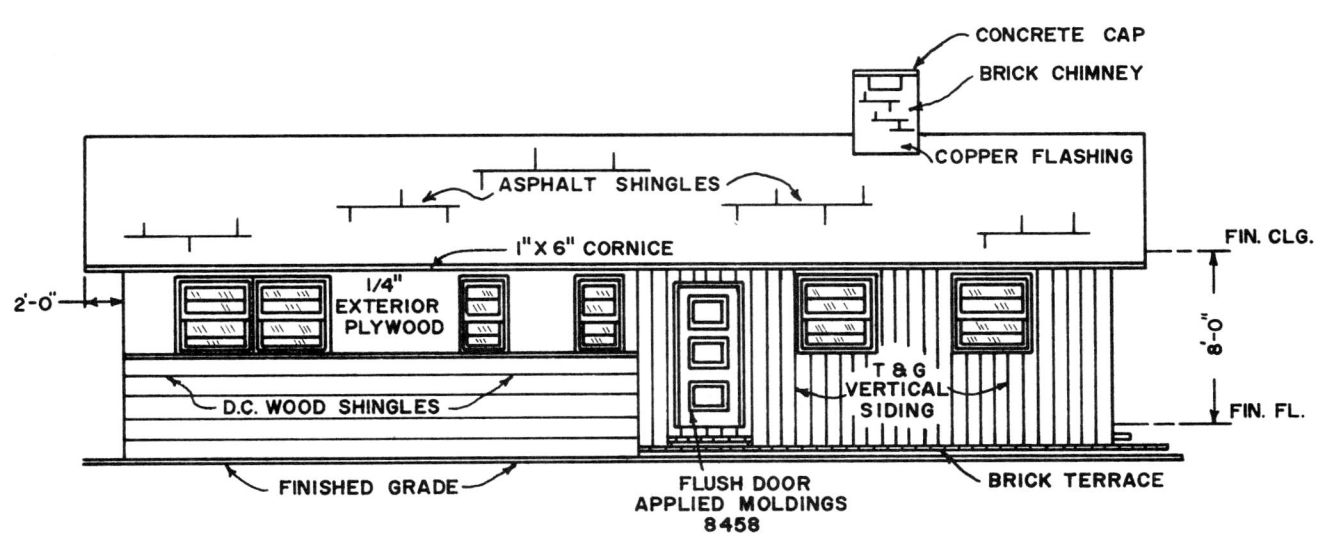

**Figure 5-9** Illustration for Step 4.

# REVIEW QUESTIONS

The following questions are provided as a review of Chapter 5 and should be completed before attempting the application projects for the chapter. Write your answers in the spaces provided.

1. Define "elevation."

2. List two ways in which elevations are used:

3. Sketch the symbols for the following:
   Concrete block—

   Small scale brick—

   Large scale brick—

   Wood siding—

5. List six items that might be included on a typical elevation:

6. What is your CAD system's command for the generic command CIRCLE?

7. What is your CAD system's command for the generic command IRREGULAR CURVE?

8. Explain the steps you would use to create the "large scale brick" symbol on a drawing if it is not contained in the symbols library of your CAD system.

# APPLICATION PROJECTS

The following application projects are provided to help you become proficient in producing elevations on a CAD system. To ensure that you use input, modification, and manipulation functions, you will be required to reconstruct elevations as shown and make modifications to them. To ensure that you use facilitation and output functions, SAVE each completed elevation and PLOT it on the size and type of medium specified by your instructor.

**Project 1:** Figure 5–10 is the outline of an elevation for a residential dwelling. The house is 42′-0″ long. Reconstruct the outline as shown or digitize it and display it in any size you choose on the graphics terminal by using the SCALE function. Then, make the following additions:

1. Add brick siding.
2. Add asphalt shingles.

**Project 2:** Call up the elevation developed in Project 1 (reconstruct it if you did not SAVE it permanently). Then, make the following additions:

1. Add front steps of poured concrete.
2. Add a chimney to the right side of the house.
3. Add a front doorknob and a light to the right and above the front door. Use the ZOOM-IN function to get accurate details.

**Project 3:** Call up the elevation developed in Project 2 (reconstruct it if you did not SAVE it permanently). Then, make the following changes:

1. Change the brick siding to vertical wood siding.
2. Change the asphalt shingles to cedar shank shingles.

**Project 4:** Call up the elevation in Project 3 (reconstruct it if you did not SAVE it permanently). Then, make the following changes:

1. Change the vertical siding to horizontal wood siding.
2. Change the chimney to the left side of the house.
3. Add a single-car carport to the right side of the house.

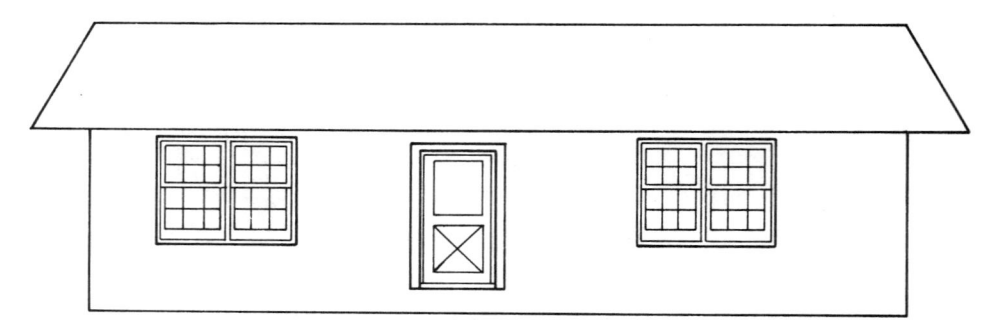

**Figure 5–10** Application projects 1, 2, 3, and 4.

**Project 5:** Figure 5-11 is the outline of an elevation for a residential dwelling. The house is 46'-0" long. Reconstruct the outline as shown or digitize it and display it in any size you choose on the graphics terminal by using the scale function. Then make the following additions:

1. Add brick siding.
2. Add asphalt shingles.

**Project 6:** Call up the elevation developed in Project 5 (reconstruct it if you did not SAVE it permanently). Then, make the following additions:

1. Add a poured concrete slab under the front door as a step-up.
2. Center the front door between the sets of windows.
3. Change the set of windows on the left to a 6'-0" square picture window.

**Project 7:** Call up the elevation developed in Project 6 (reconstruct it if you did not SAVE it permanently). Then make the following changes:

1. Change the brick siding to vertical wood siding.
2. Change the asphalt shingles to cedar shank shingles.

**Project 8:** Call up the elevation developed in Project 7 (reconstruct it if you did not SAVE it permanently). Then make the following changes:

1. Change the vertical wood siding to horizontal wood siding.
2. Add a two-car garage to the right side of the house.

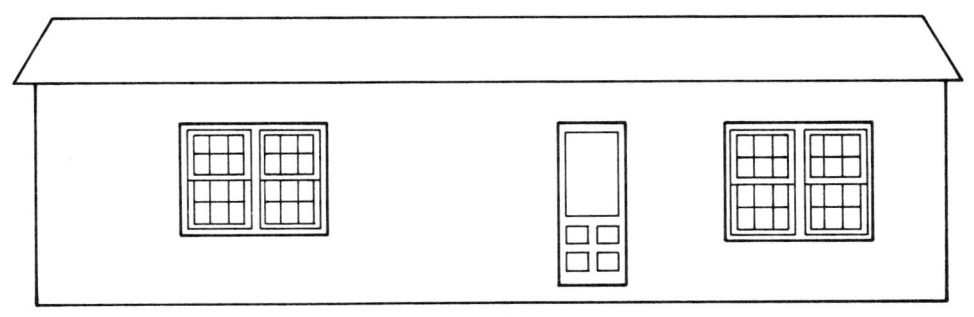

**Figure 5-11** Application projects 5, 6, 7, and 8.

**Project 9:** Figure 5–12 is the outline of the elevation for a residential dwelling. The house is 40'-0" long. Reconstruct the outline as shown or digitize it and display it any size you choose on the graphics terminal by using the SCALE function. Then make the following additions:

1. Add brick siding.
2. Add asphalt shingles.

**Project 10:** Call up the elevation developed in Project 9 (reconstruct it if you did not SAVE it permanently). Then make the following additions:

1. Add poured concrete front steps.
2. Add a chimney to the left side of the house.
3. Add a front doorknob and a light above the door. Use the ZOOM-IN command to achieve accurate detail.

**Project 11:** Call up the elevation you developed in Project 10 (reconstruct it if you did not SAVE it permanently). Then make the following changes:

1. Change the brick siding to vertical wood siding.
2. Change the asphalt shingles to cedar shank shingles.

**Project 12:** Call up the elevation developed in Project 11 (reconstruct it if you did not SAVE it permanently). Then make the following changes:

1. Change the vertical siding to horizontal wood siding.
2. Add a two-car carport on the right side of the house.

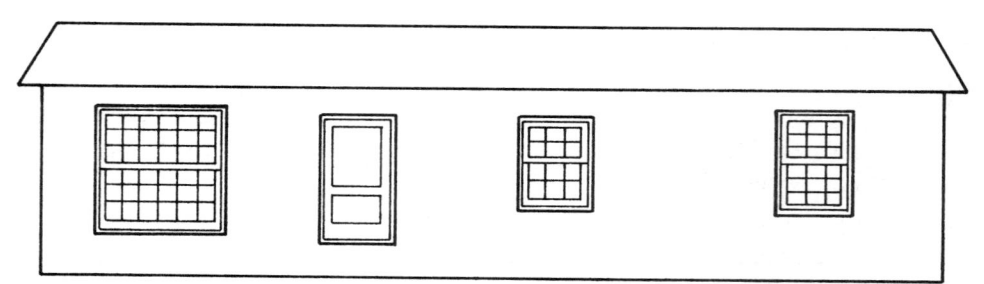

**Figure 5–12** Application projects 9, 10, 11, and 12.

**Project 13:** Figure 5–13 is the outline of an elevation for a residential dwelling. The house is 45'-0" long. Reconstruct the outline as shown or digitize it and display it in the size of your choice on the graphics terminal. Then make the following additions:

1. Add brick siding.
2. Add asphalt shingles.

**Project 14:** Call up the elevation developed in Project 13 (reconstruct it if you did not SAVE it permanently). Then make the following additions:

1. Add a poured concrete slab under the front door as a step-up.
2. Add a chimney to the right side of the house.
3. Add a front doorknob and a light above the front door. Use the ZOOM-IN function to achieve detail.

**Project 15:** Call up the elevation developed in Project 14 (reconstruct it if you did not SAVE it permanently). Then make the following changes:

1. Change the brick siding to vertical wood siding.
2. Change the asphalt shingles to cedar shank shingles.

**Project 16:** Call up the elevation developed in Project 15 (reconstruct it if you did not SAVE it permanently). Then make the following changes:

1. Change the vertical siding to horizontal wood siding.
2. Drop the chimney and add a two-car garage to the right side of the house.

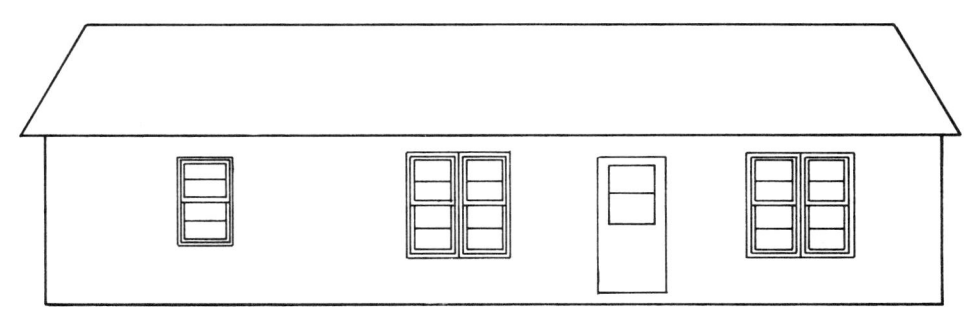

**Figure 5–13** Application projects 13, 14, 15, and 16.

**Project 17:** Figure 5–14 is the outline of an elevation for a residential dwelling. The house is 39'-6" long. Reconstruct the outline as shown or digitize it and display it in any size you choose on the graphics terminal by using the SCALE function. Then make the following additions:

1. Add stone siding.
2. Add asphalt shingles.

**Project 18:** Call up the elevation developed in Project 16 (reconstruct it if you did not SAVE it permanently). Then make the following additions:

1. Add a poured concrete slab under the front door as a step-up.
2. Add a front doorknob and a light over the front door. Use the ZOOM-IN function to achieve detail.
3. Add a chimney to the left side of the house.

**Project 19:** Call up the elevation developed in Project 17 (reconstruct it if you did not SAVE it permanently). Then make the following changes:

1. Change the top half of the stone siding to vertical wood siding.
2. Change the asphalt shingles to cedar shank shingles.

**Project 20:** Call up the elevation developed in Project 19 (reconstruct it if you did not SAVE it permanently). Then make the following changes:

1. Move the chimney to the rear of the house in the center.
2. Add a two-car garage to the left side of the house.

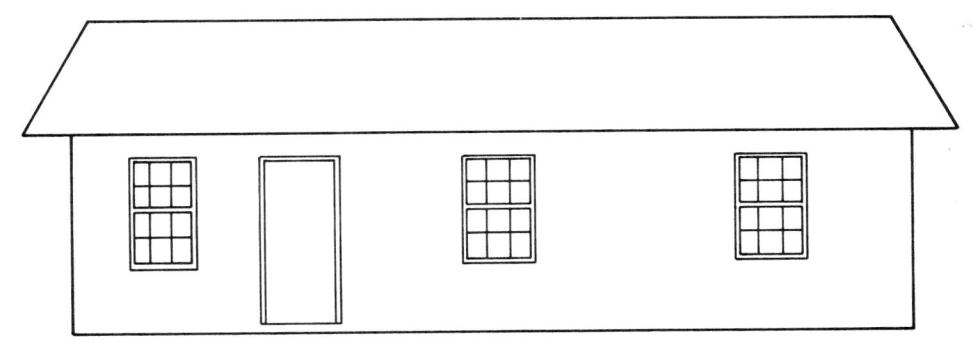

**Figure 5–14** Application projects 17, 18, 19, and 20.

**Project 21:** Figure 5–15 is a partial elevation for a commercial office building. Reconstruct the elevation as shown by digitizing the outline and using the ZOOM-IN function to achieve accurate detail. Assume the elevation is symmetrical and add the missing half.

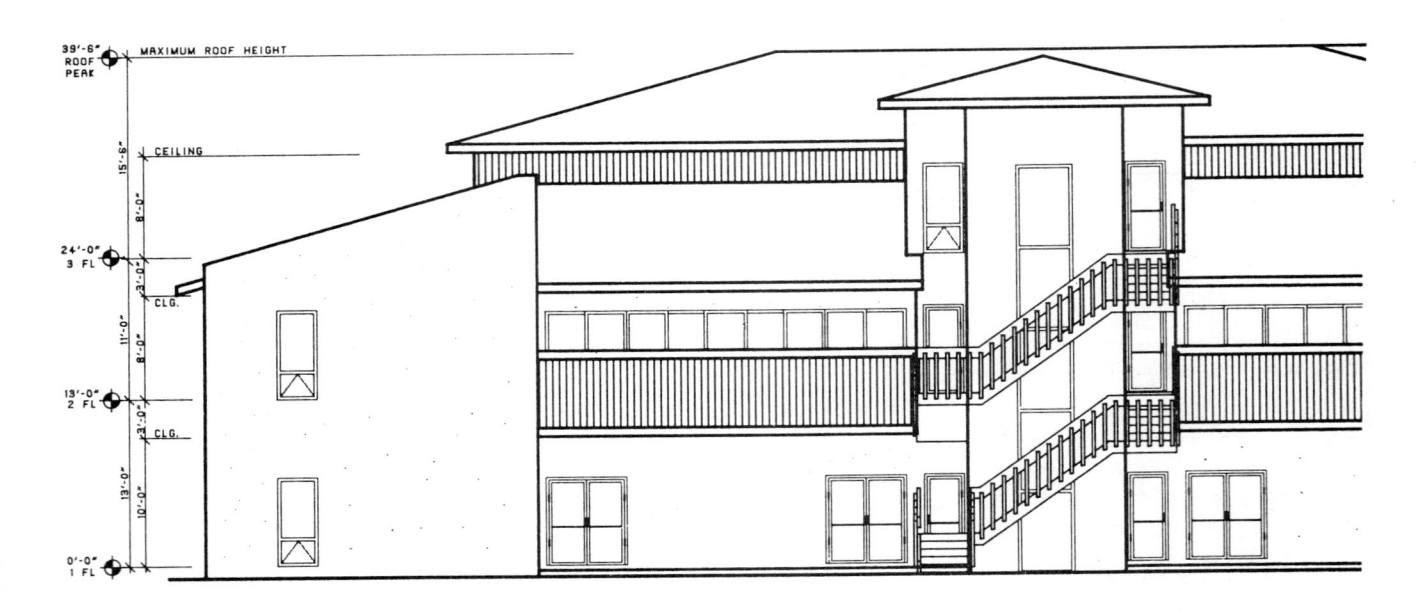

**Figure 5–15** Application project 21. *(Courtesy of Arrigoni Technology, Inc.)*

# chapter 6
# Foundation Plans

## DEFINITION, PURPOSE, AND CONTENTS

A foundation plan is required in a complete set of architectural plans. A foundation plan is a plan view in section showing all of the components of a building's foundation.

The foundation plan is used for guiding tradespeople in excavating for footings; pouring footings; building foundation walls; pouring the floor slab (in the case of on-grade foundations); and placing piers, beams, and floor joists (in the case of off-grade foundations). Figure 6–1 is an example of a foundation plan for a large commercial building that was produced on a modern CAD system.

Foundation plans for off-grade floor systems differ somewhat from those for slab on-grade floor systems. Figure 6–2 is a table that can be used as a guide in determining the basic components that should be contained in a foundation plan whether it is for an off-grade or an on-grade floor system.

## SPECIAL SYMBOLS NEEDED

There are a number of special graphic symbols used in producing foundation plans on a CAD system. Those most frequently used are shown in Figure 6–3. Examine the symbols library of your CAD system to determine which of the symbols in Figure 6–3 it contains. If the symbols library does not contain a particular symbol, you have two options:

1. Create the symbol and add it to the symbols library. This can be done only on those CAD systems that are programmed to accept user-defined symbols.
2. Construct the symbols on the drawing as they are needed, using the appropriate geometric characters and commands. For example, the "common brick" and "face brick" symbols can be made using the SOLID LINE command.

## CAD COMMANDS AND FUNCTIONS USED

There are several different commands and functions used in constructing a foundation plan on a CAD system. These commands and functions are the same whether the foundation plan is for a residential or commercial building. Most CAD systems have these

**78** | CAD Applications: Architectural

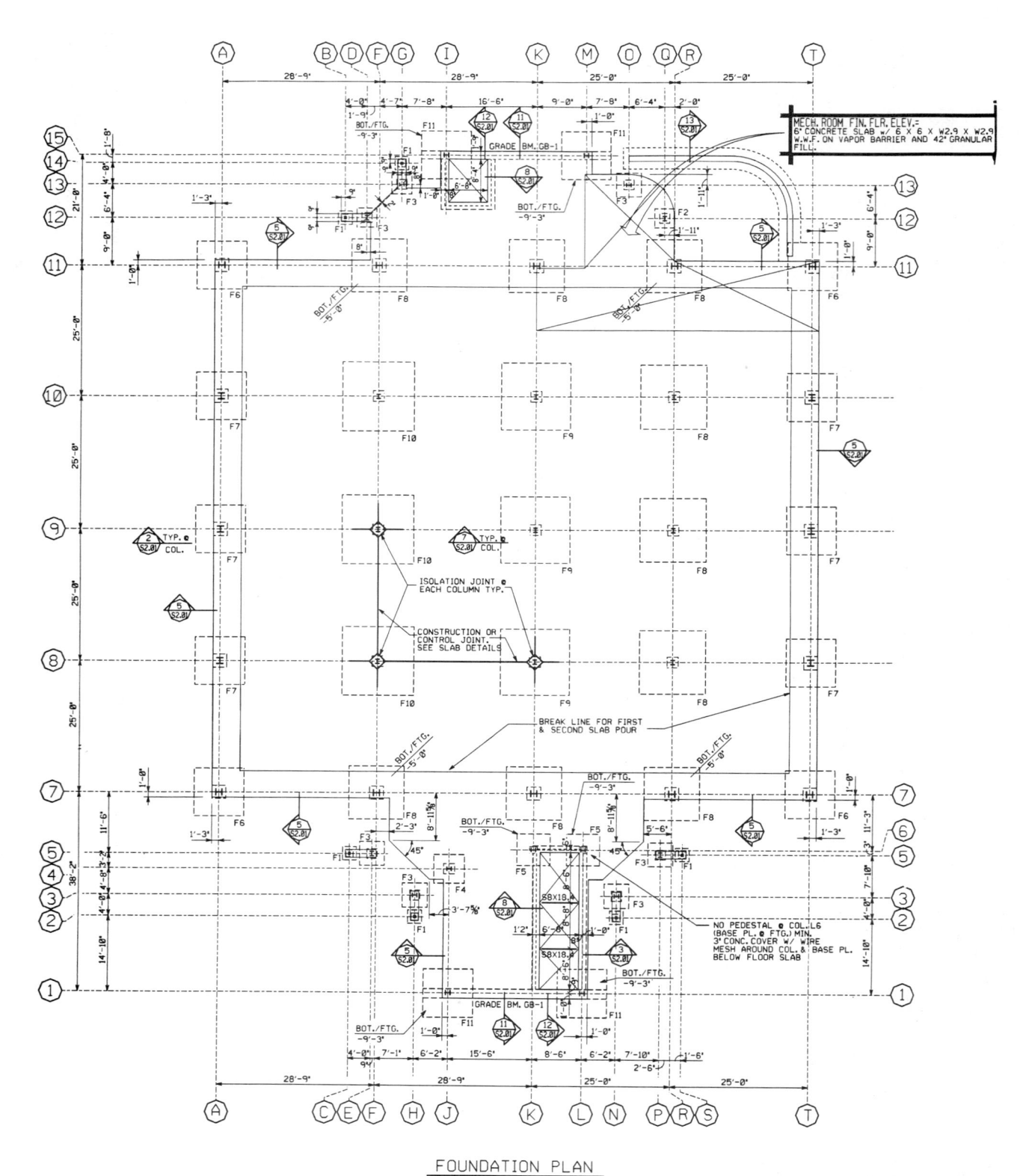

**Figure 6–1** Foundation plan for a large commercial building. *(Courtesy of Intergraph Corporation.)*

| CONTENT ITEM | OFF GRADE | ON GRADE |
|---|---|---|
| FOOTINGS | X | X |
| FOUNDATION WALLS | X | X |
| PIERS, POST, OR COLUMNS | X | |
| OPENINGS IN FOUNDATION WALLS | X | X |
| BEAMS | X | |
| PILASTERS | X | |
| FLOOR JOISTS | X | |
| DIMENSIONS | X | X |
| NOTES | X | X |
| SCALE | X | X |
| FLOOR SLAB | | X |
| SECTIONING ARROWS | X | X |

**Figure 6–2** Contents chart.

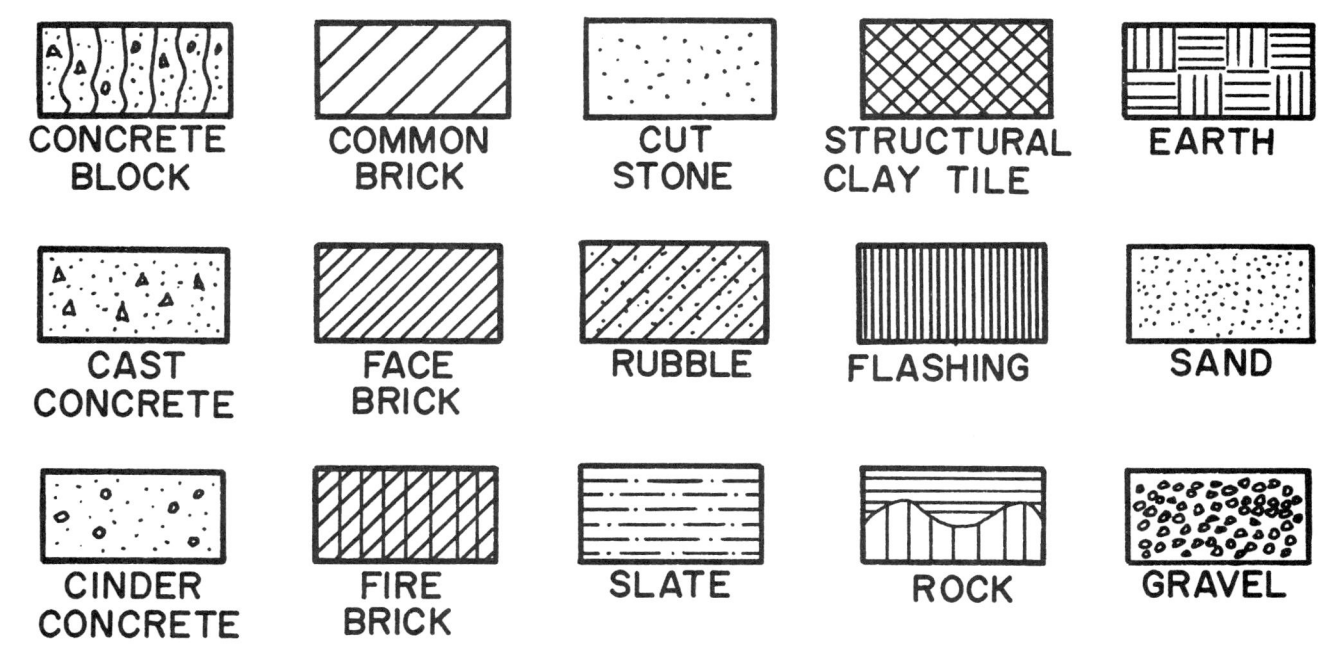

**Figure 6–3** Foundation plan symbols.

commands and functions. However, they are frequently given different names on different systems (see Chapter 1).

The generic names for the commands and functions used to produce a foundation plan on a CAD system are listed in the Commands and Functions chart. Before attempting the application projects for this chapter, match these generic commands and functions with their corresponding commands and functions on your CAD system.

## COMMANDS AND FUNCTIONS

**Graphic Creation Commands**

- √ Point
- √ Solid Line
- √ Hidden Line
- √ Construction Line
- √ Dashed Line
- √ Center Line
- √ Rectangle
- √ Circle
- √ Arc
- ___ Irregular Curve
- ___ Ellipse
- ___ Polygon
- ___ Grid
- ___ XYPT
- ___ Polar
- ___ Line Weight
- ___ Fillet
- ___ Chamfer
- ___ Leaders
- ___ Rect
- ___ Hatch

**Manipulation Commands**

- √ Move
- ___ Copy
- ___ Rotate
- √ Scale
- √ Zoom
- √ Pan
- ___ Mirror

**Size Specification Commands**

- √ Auto. Dimension
- ___ Dimension
- ___ Tolerance
- ___ Calc. Area

**Output Commands**

- √ Plot
- ___ Print (Screen Dump)

**Text Creation Commands**

- √ Text

**Modification Commands**

- √ Edit
- √ Delete
- √ Redraw
- ___ Clip
- √ Erase

**Facilitation Commands**

- √ Save
- √ File
- √ Symbol Library
- ___ Layer
- ___ Quit
- ___ Default

## PROCEDURES FOR PREPARING THE PLAN

What follows is an illustrated, step-by-step description of how a simple foundation plan (off-grade or on-grade) is produced on a CAD system. The example used to illustrate these procedures is an off-grade system for a residential dwelling. The procedures are basically the same for off-grade, on-grade, residential, and commercial foundation systems.

■ *Step 1*

Log-on to the system and create a drawing designation called FDNABC. Substitute your initials for the ABC. Determine the size you will produce by deciding on the size of paper that the foundation plan will be plotted on.

■ *Step 2*

Using the CONSTRUCTION LINES command, lay out the foundation walls with openings, piers, and pilasters. Once you are satisfied with the overall layout, convert the construction lines to solid lines, Figure 6–4. If your CAD system does not have a CONSTRUCTION LINES capability, lay out this step using the SOLID LINES command.

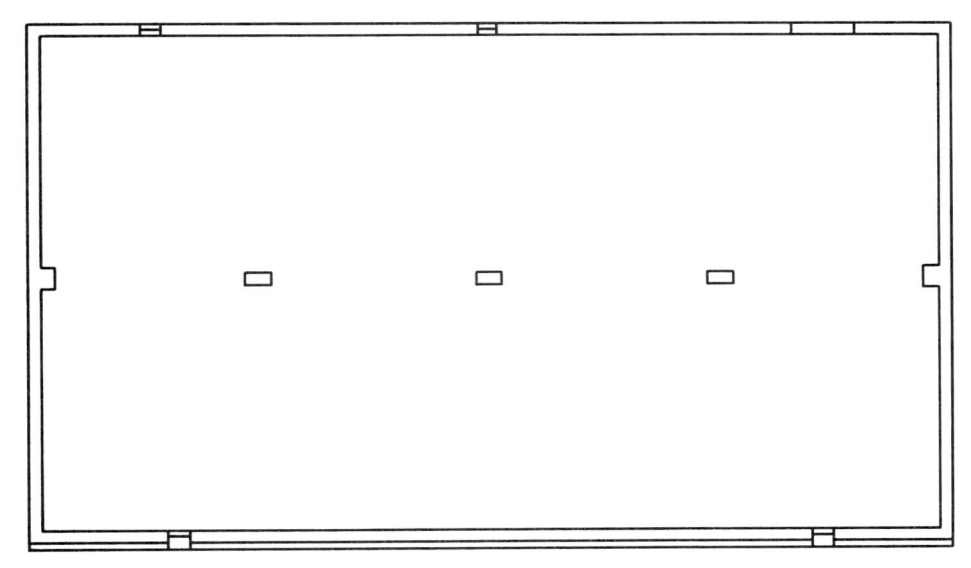

**Figure 6–4** Illustration for Step 2.

■ *Step 3*

Add the footing using the HIDDEN LINES command. The broken line representing the beams that span from pier to pier can be made using the SOLID LINES command and breaking the lines as needed. Cut Section A–A using either the SOLID LINES command or a SECTION CUTTING PLANE command if one is available on your CAD system. Create the direction symbol for the joists using the SOLID LINES command. Change to the TEXT mode and add the "A–A" on the cutting plane line, the pier note, and the joist size and spacing notes, Figure 6–5.

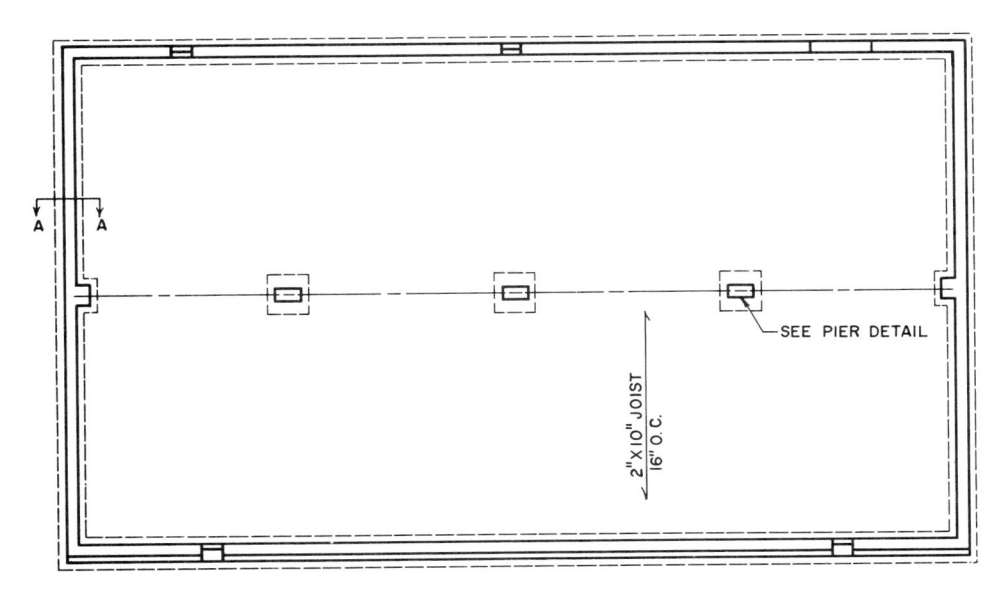

**Figure 6–5** Illustration for Step 3.

■ *Step 4*
Add the sectioning symbols for the foundation walls and the brick facing. Add all required dimensions using the DIMENSION command. Complete the drawing by adding any remaining text required, Figure 6-6.

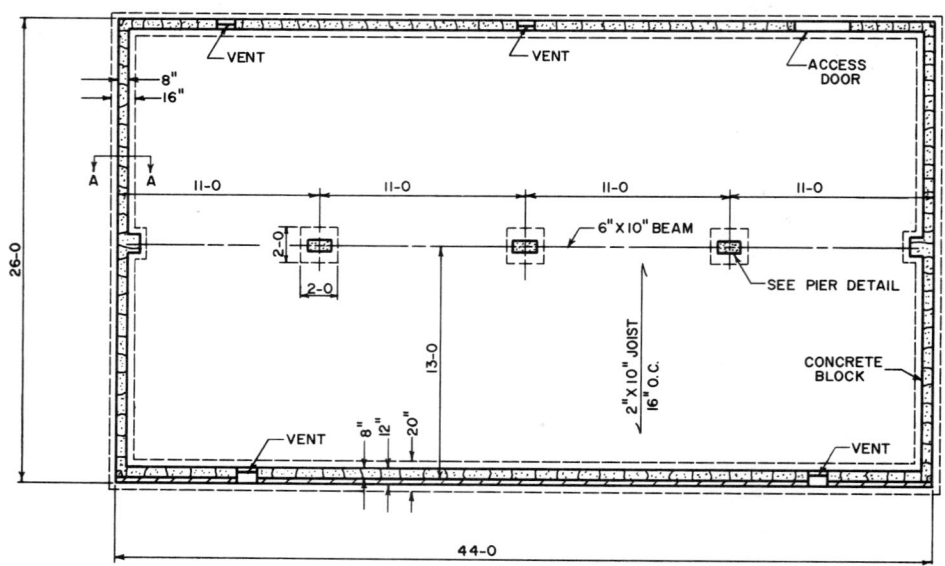

**Figure 6-6**  Illustration for Step 4.

## REVIEW QUESTIONS

The following questions are provided as a review of Chapter 6 and should be completed before attempting the application projects for the chapter. Write your answers in the spaces provided.

1. Define "foundation plan."

2. List four ways in which the foundation plan might be used.

3. Sketch the graphic symbols for the following:
   Common brick—

   Face brick—

   Earth—

   Sand—

   Rock—

Cast concrete—

Concrete block—

4. Indicate which of the following components would be found on an off-grade foundation plan and which would be found on an on-grade foundation plan (one item may be found on both).
   Beams—

   Footings—

   Floor joists—

   Floor slab—

   Sectioning cutting plane lines—

   Pilasters—

5. Explain the steps you would use on your CAD system to create the "cast concrete" symbol if it is not contained in the symbols library.

6. Explain the steps you would use on your CAD system to create the "rock" symbol if it is not contained in the symbols library.

7. Explain the steps you would use on your CAD system to create the "sand" symbol if it is not contained in the symbols library.

8. Several generic names for CAD commands are listed below. Give the name of the corresponding command on your CAD system.
   RECTANGLE—

   DIMENSION—

   TEXT—

   EDIT—

   DELETE—

# APPLICATION PROJECTS

The following application projects are provided to help you become proficient in producing foundation plans on a CAD system. To ensure that you use input, modification, and manipulation functions, you will be required to reconstruct projects as shown and make modifications to them. To ensure that you use facilitation and output functions, SAVE each completed foundation plan and PLOT it on the size and type of medium specified by your instructor.

**Project 1:** Figure 6–7 is a foundation plan for a large commercial building. The poured concrete footing is 24″ wide and 12″ thick. The foundation wall is of 12″ concrete block. Reconstruct the foundation plan as shown. Then make the following changes:

1. Increase the thickness of the floor slab by 1″.
2. Decrease the outside dimensions by 2′-0″ and adjust all other dimensions accordingly.

**Project 2:** Create a foundation plan for a large commercial building that is similar to Figure 6–7, but has the following differences:

1. A 4″ floor slab.
2. Is 30′-0″ × 60′-0″.

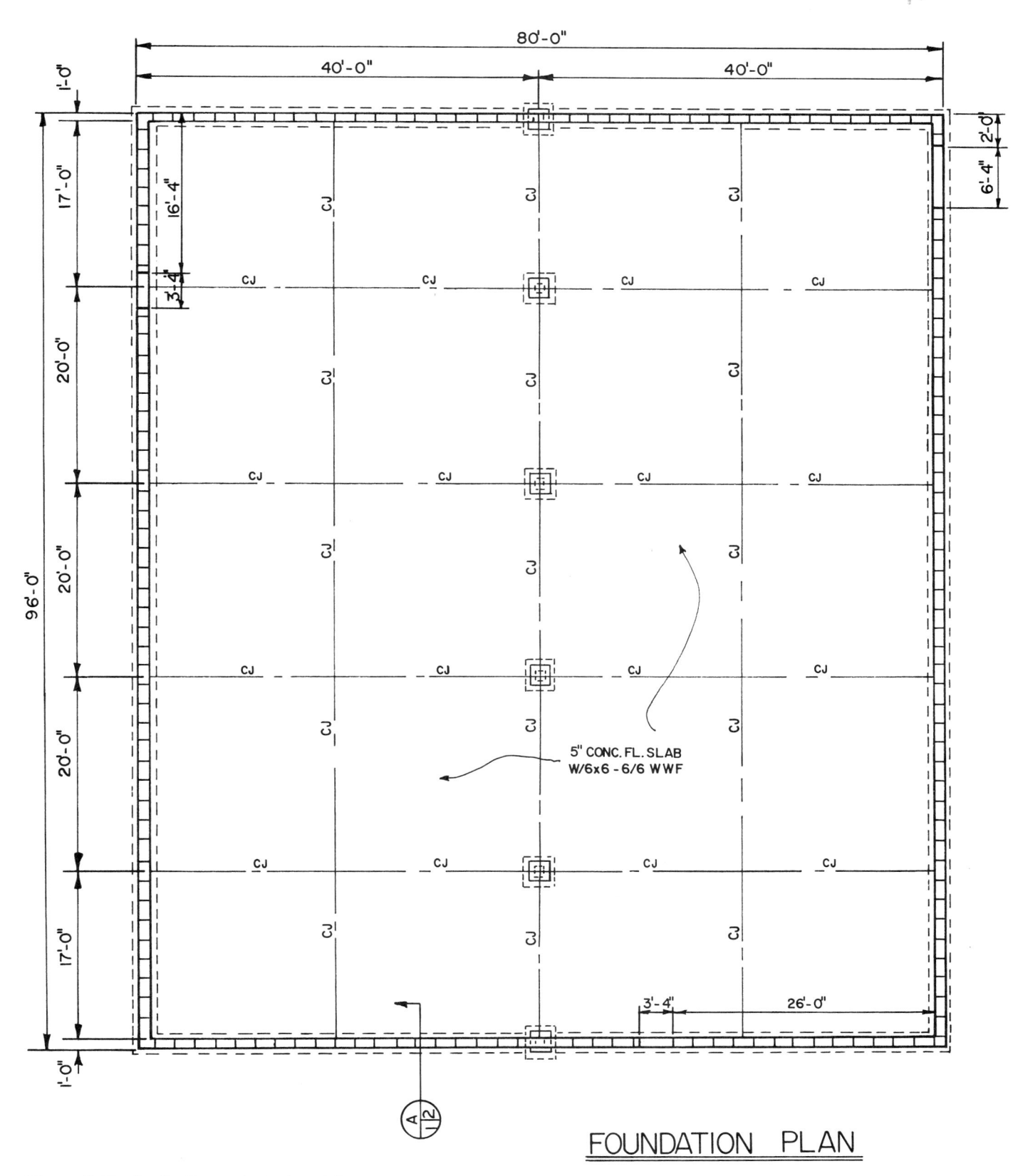

**Figure 6–7** Application projects 1 and 2.

**86** | CAD Applications: Architectural

**Project 3:** Figure 6–8 is a foundation plan for a residential dwelling with an off-grade floor system. Reconstruct the foundation plan on your CAD system as shown. Then make the following changes.

1. Add 4″ to the width of the footing.
2. Use 12″ concrete block for the foundation wall.

**Project 4:** Create a foundation plan for a residential dwelling that is similar to the one in Figure 6–8, but with the following differences:

1. Add 5′-0″ to the length and width of the house.
2. Recompute to determine (a) The number and spacing of piers, (b) The size of beams, and (c) The size and spacing of floor joists.

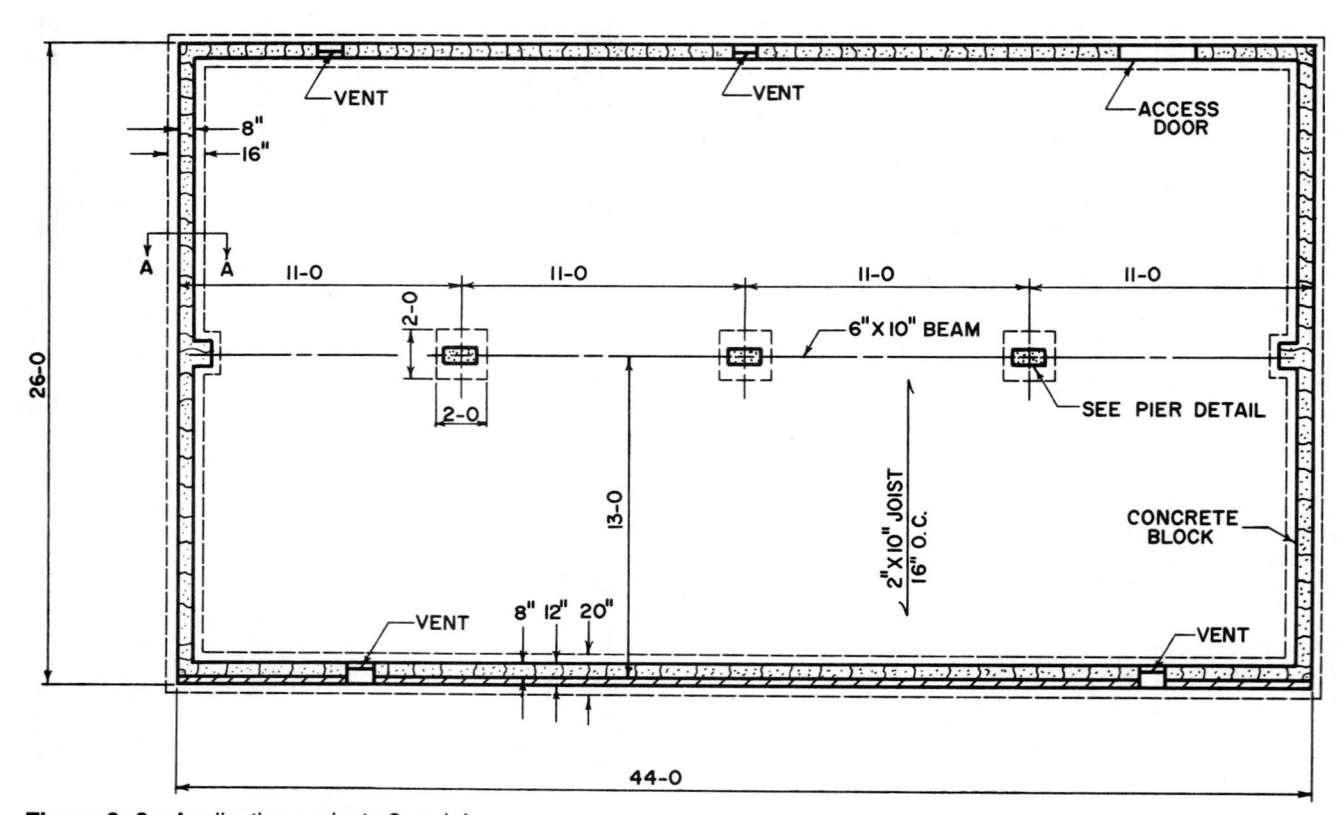

**Figure 6–8** Application projects 3 and 4.

**Project 5:** Figure 6–9 is the outside edge of the foundation wall for a residential dwelling. Construct a complete foundation plan for an off-grade floor system for the house.

**Project 6:** Construct a complete foundation plan for Figure 6–9 for a slab floor system.

**Figure 6-9** Application projects 5 and 6.

**Project 7:** Figure 6-10 is the outside edge of the foundation wall for a residential dwelling. Construct a complete foundation plan for an off-grade floor system for the house.

**Project 8:** Construct a complete foundation plan for Figure 6-10 for a slab floor system.

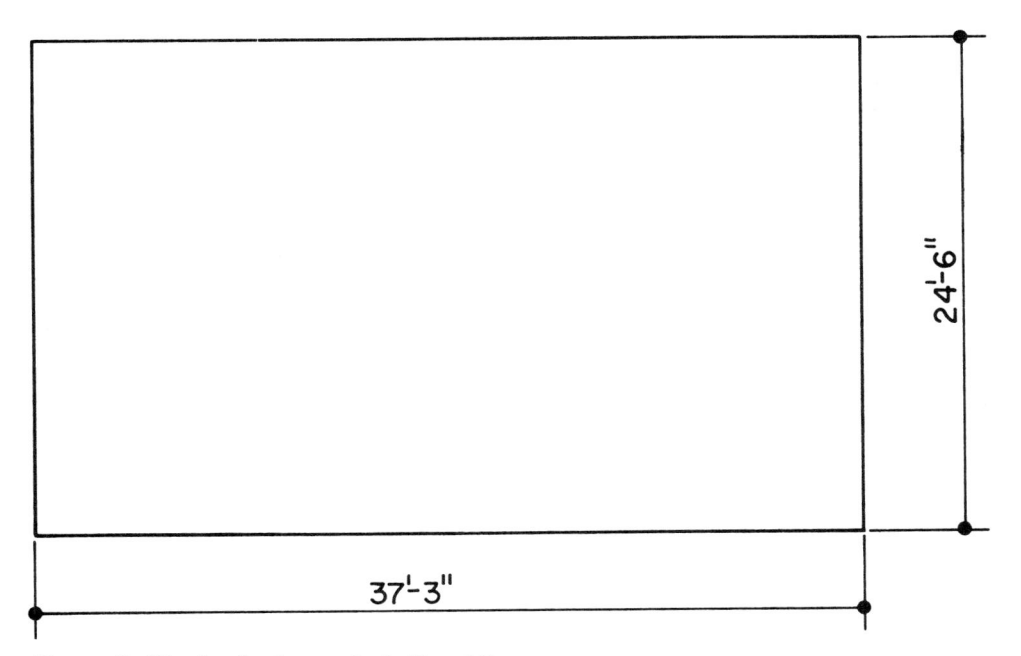

**Figure 6-10** Application projects 7 and 8.

**Project 9:** Figure 6–11 is the outside edge of the foundation wall for a residential dwelling. Construct a complete foundation plan for an off-grade floor system for the house.

**Project 10:** Construct a complete foundation plan for Figure 6–11 for a slab floor system.

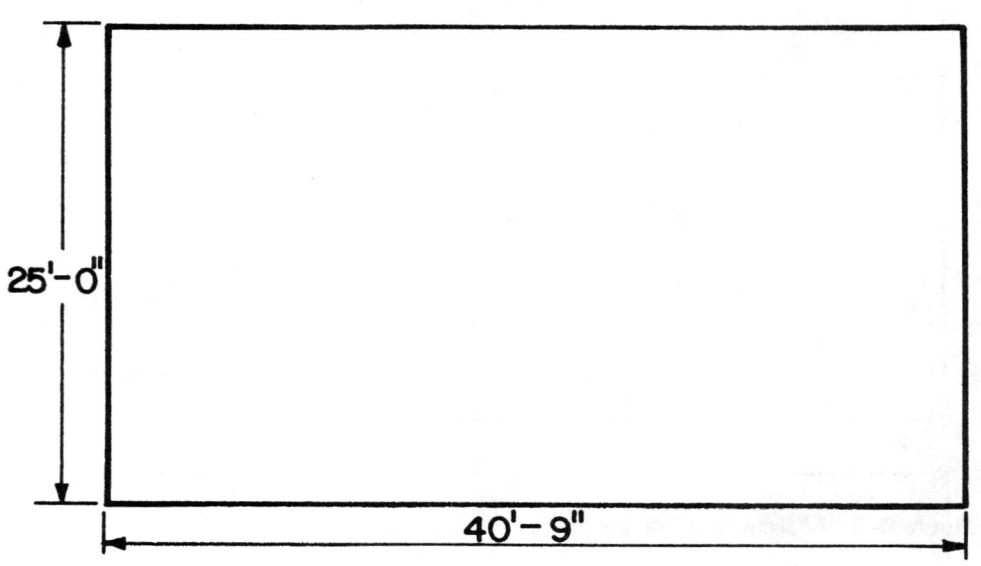

**Figure 6–11** Application projects 9 and 10.

**Project 11:** Figure 6–12 is the outside edge of the foundation wall for a residential dwelling. Construct a complete foundation plan for an off-grade floor system for the house.

**Project 12:** Construct a complete foundation plan for Figure 6–12 for a slab floor system.

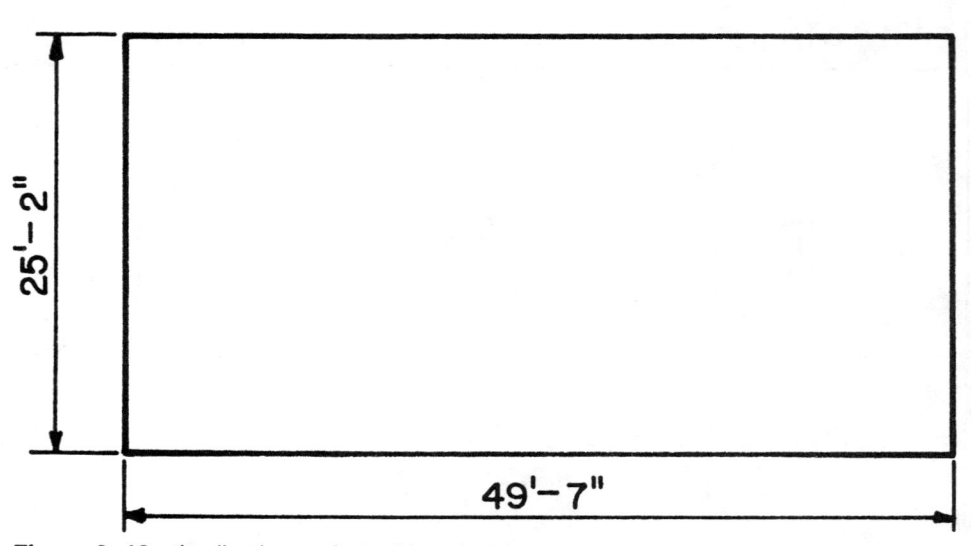

**Figure 6–12** Application projects 11 and 12.

**Project 13:** Figure 6–13 is the outside edge of the foundation wall for a residential dwelling. Construct a complete foundation plan for an off-grade floor system for the house.

**Project 14:** Construct a complete foundation plan for Figure 6–13 for a slab floor system.

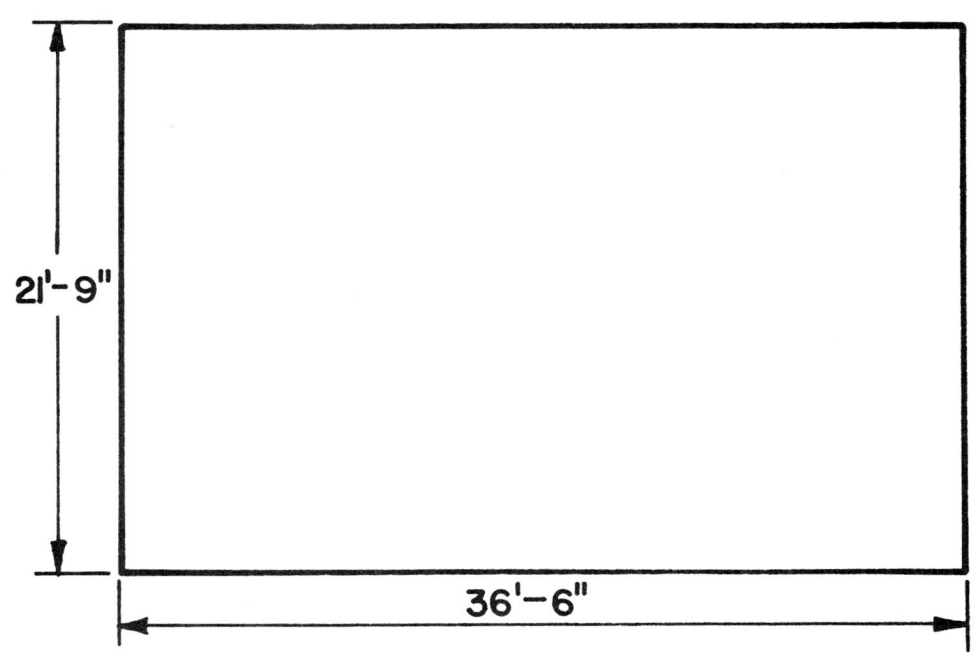

**Figure 6–13** Application projects 13 and 14.

**Project 15:** Figure 6–14 is the outside edge of the foundation wall for a residential dwelling. Construct a complete foundation plan for an off-grade floor system for the house.

**Project 16:** Construct a complete foundation plan for Figure 6–14 for a slab floor system.

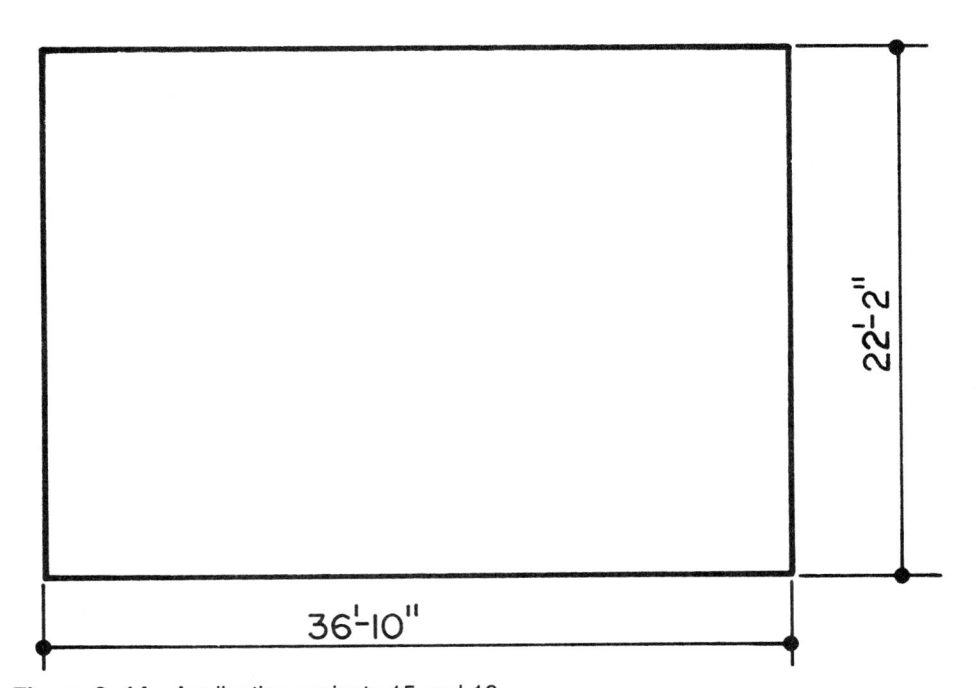

**Figure 6–14** Application projects 15 and 16.

**Project 17:** Figure 6–15 is the outside edge of the foundation wall for a residential dwelling. Construct a complete foundation plan for an off-grade floor system for the house.

**Project 18:** Construct a complete foundation plan for Figure 6–15 for a slab floor system.

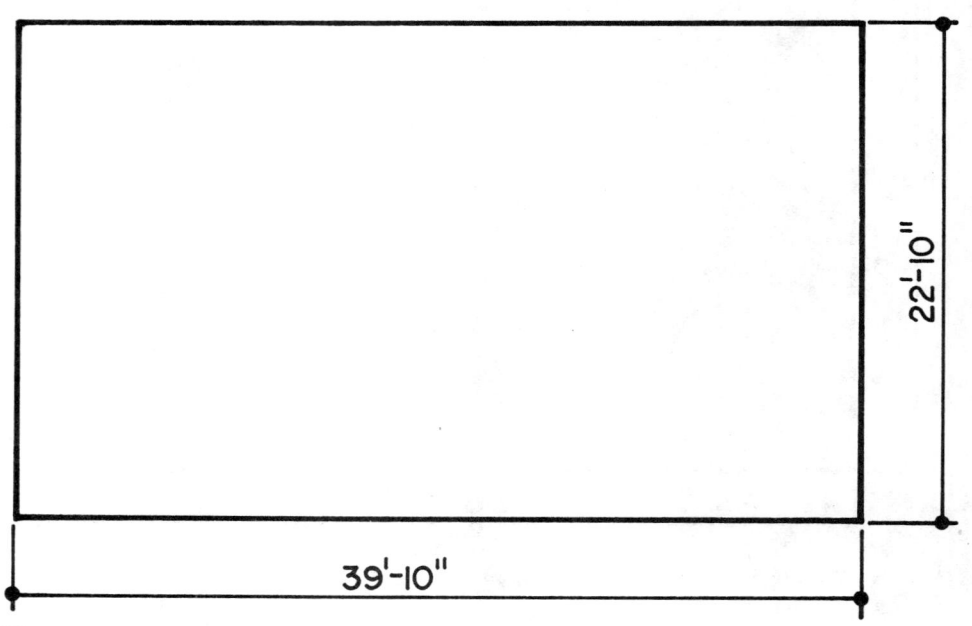

**Figure 6–15** Application projects 17 and 18.

**Project 19:** Figure 6–16 is the outside edge of the foundation wall for a residential dwelling. Construct a complete foundation plan for an off-grade floor system for the house.

**Project 20:** Construct a complete foundation plan for Figure 6–16 for a slab floor system.

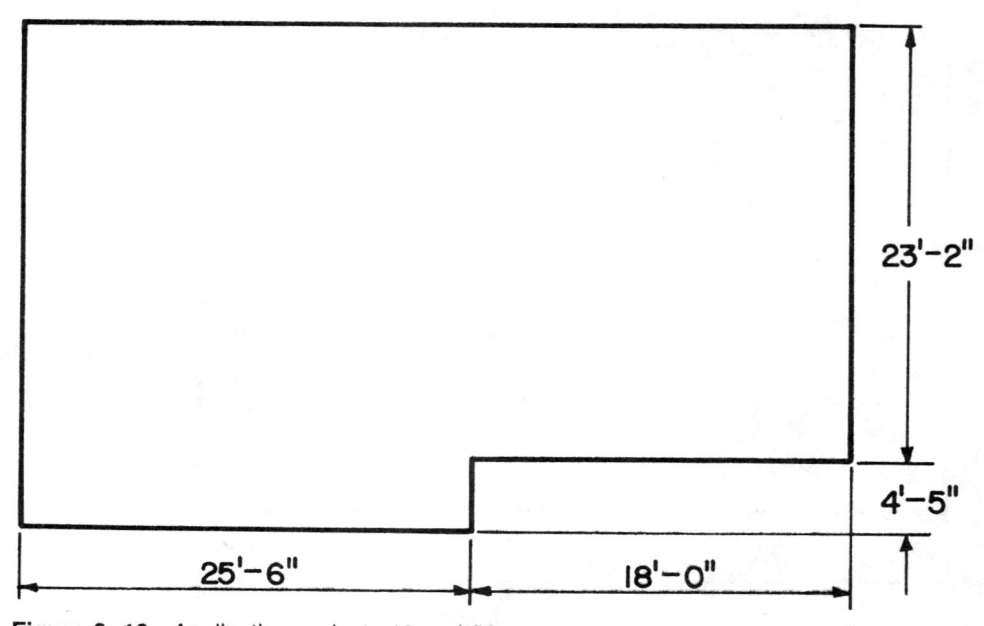

**Figure 6–16** Application projects 19 and 20.

**Project 21:** Figure 6-17 is the outside edge of the foundation wall for a residential dwelling. Construct a complete foundation plan for an off-grade floor system for the house.

**Project 22:** Construct a complete foundation plan for Figure 6-17 for a slab floor system.

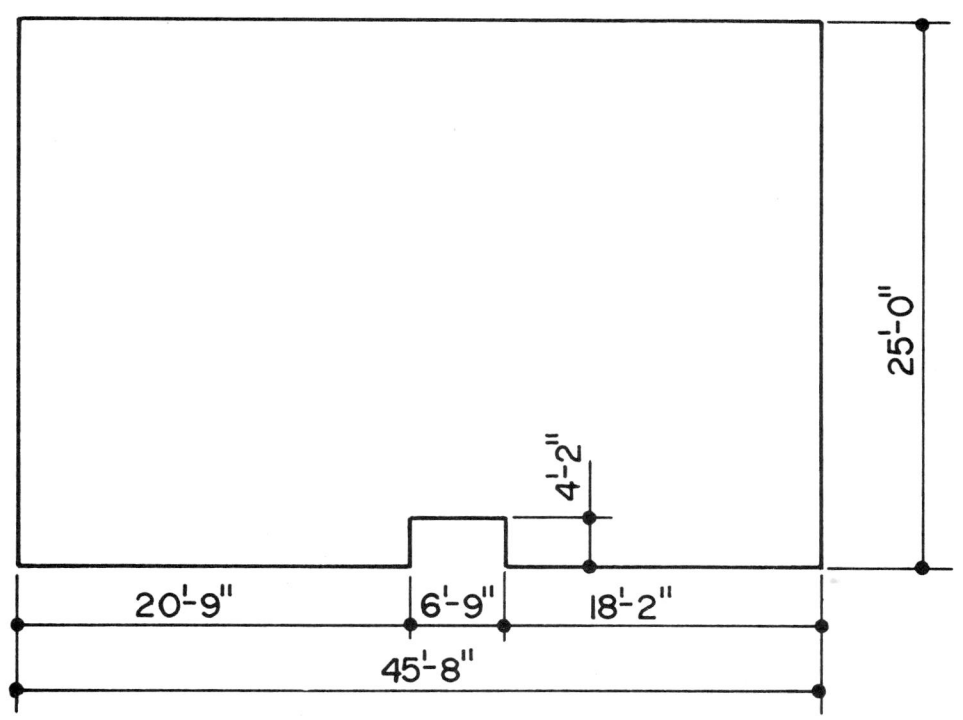

**Figure 6-17** Application projects 21 and 22.

**Project 23:** Figure 6-18 is a sketch of the foundation plan for a residential dwelling. The sketch contains a number of specifications for the foundation system. Convert the sketch to a completed foundation plan on your CAD system.

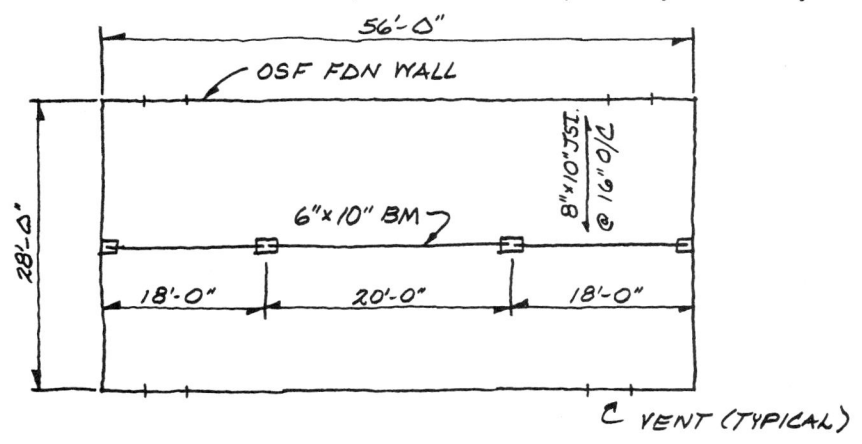

FOOTING SPECS: POURED CONCRETE 16" WIDE
FDN WALL SPECS: 8" BLOCK
PILASTER SPECS: 1- 8" BLOCK TURNED (BOTH WALLS)
PIERS SPECS: 8" BLOCK ON 24" SQ. CONC. FTG.
OPENINGS: 24" SQ. VENTS 4'-0" FROM CORNERS

**Figure 6-18** Application project 23.

# chapter 7
# Plumbing, Electrical, and HVAC Plans

## DEFINITION, PURPOSE, AND CONTENTS

The plumbing, electrical, and heating-ventilation-air conditioning (HVAC) plans are known as the "mechanical plans" in a set of architectural plans. The plumbing plan is a schematic diagram superimposed over a modified version of the floor plan that shows the water and waste removal systems for the building.

The electrical plan is a schematic diagram superimposed over a modified version of the floor plan that shows the electrical features of the building. The HVAC plan is a double-line drawing superimposed over a modified version of the floor plan that shows the heating, ventilation, and air conditioning system for the building.

The contents of the plumbing, electrical, and HVAC plans vary and must be treated separately.

### Contents of the Plumbing Plan

A typical plumbing plan should contain the following information: water lines, fixtures, drains, waste lines, vent stacks, pipe size notations, and any other miscellaneous notes required to describe the system. The plumbing plan may also include a plumbing fixture schedule. However, due to space limitations, the plumbing fixture schedule is sometimes placed on a special separate sheet.

### Contents of the Electrical Plan

A typical electrical plan should contain the following information: the meter and distribution panel, location of the service entrance, location of switches and notations indicating the types of switches, location and types of lighting fixtures, location of outlets and notations indicating the types of outlets, location of special features (e.g., thermostat, telephone outlets, intercom, television outlets, doorbells), and any notes required to describe the system. The electrical plan may also include a lighting fixture schedule and a table of circuit data. However, due to space limitations, these things are sometimes placed on a separate special sheet.

## Contents of the HVAC Plan

A typical HVAC plan should include the following information: size and location of all HVAC equipment, size and location of the distribution system, location of the return air duct, size and location of registers, location of the thermostat and any notes required to describe the system. The HVAC plan may also contain a summary of the heat loss–heat gain calculations. However, this information is usually contained on a special separate sheet.

Figures 7–1 through 7–5 on pages 94 through 98 are examples of mechanical plans produced on modern systems. Figure 7–1 is an electrical plan for a residential dwelling. Figure 7–2 is a plumbing plan for a commercial building. Figure 7–3 is an HVAC plan for a commercial building. Figure 7–4 is an electrical plan for a commercial building. Figure 7–5 is a set of riser diagrams that might accompany a plumbing plan.

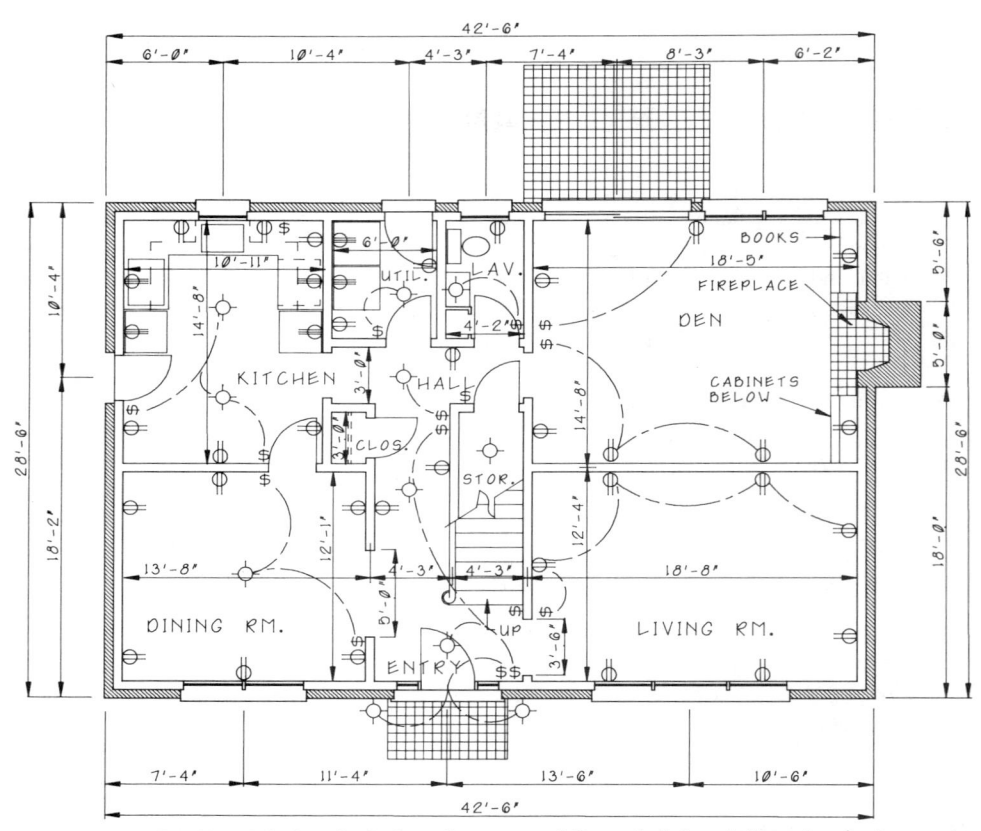

**Figure 7–1** Residential electrical plan. Courtesy of Bausch & Lomb/Houston Instrument.

## SPECIAL SYMBOLS NEEDED

There are numerous special symbols used in producing mechanical plans on a CAD system. The symbols used on plumbing, electrical, and HVAC plans are as different as the plans themselves. Figure 7–6 on page 99 contains symbols frequently used on plumbing plans. Figure 7–7 on page 99 contains symbols frequently used on electrical plans. Figure 7–8 on page 100 contains symbols frequently used on HVAC plans.

Chapter 7 Plumbing, Electrical, and HVAC Plans | 95

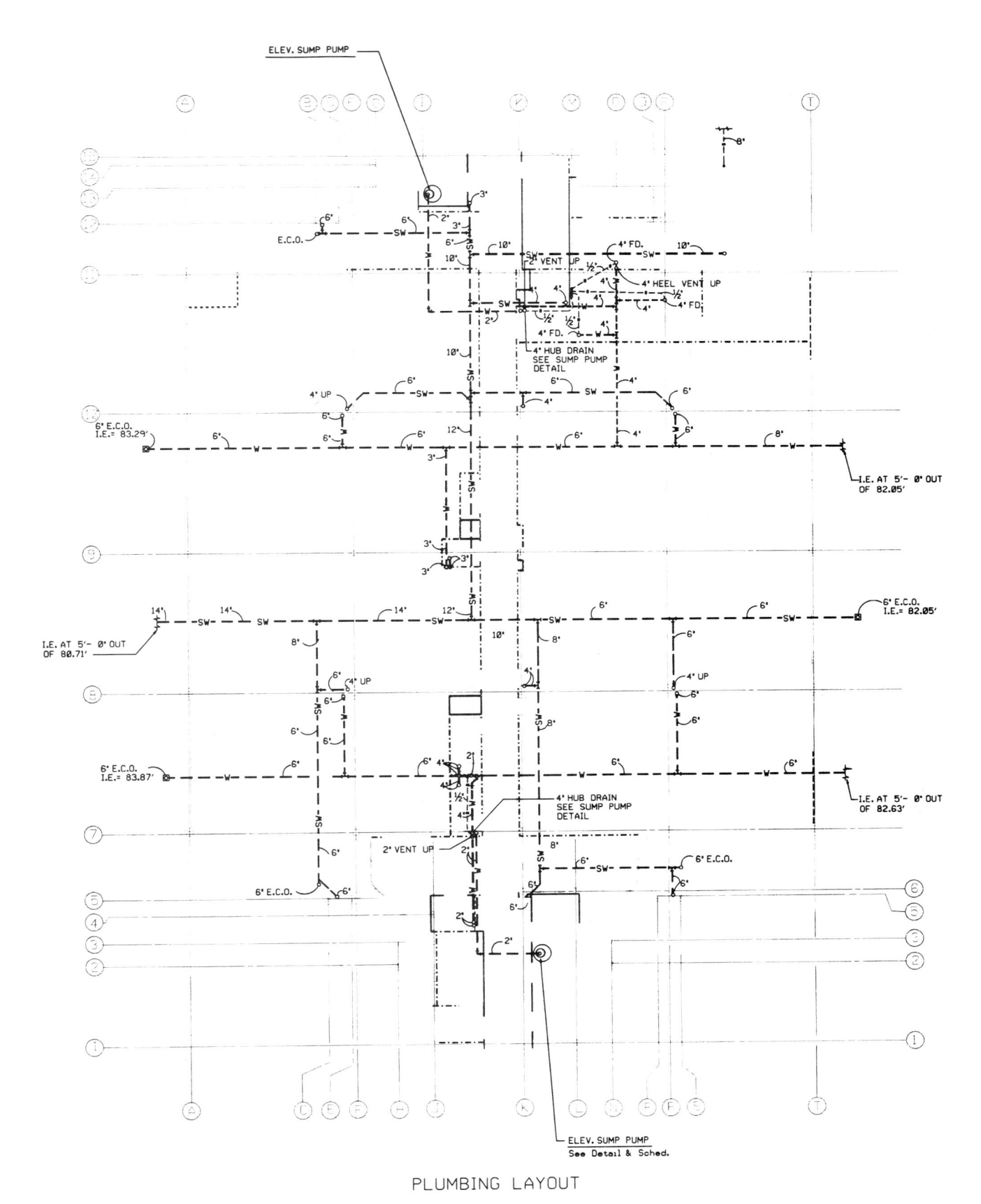

PLUMBING LAYOUT

**Figure 7–2** Commercial plumbing plan. *(Courtesy of Intergraph Corporation.)*

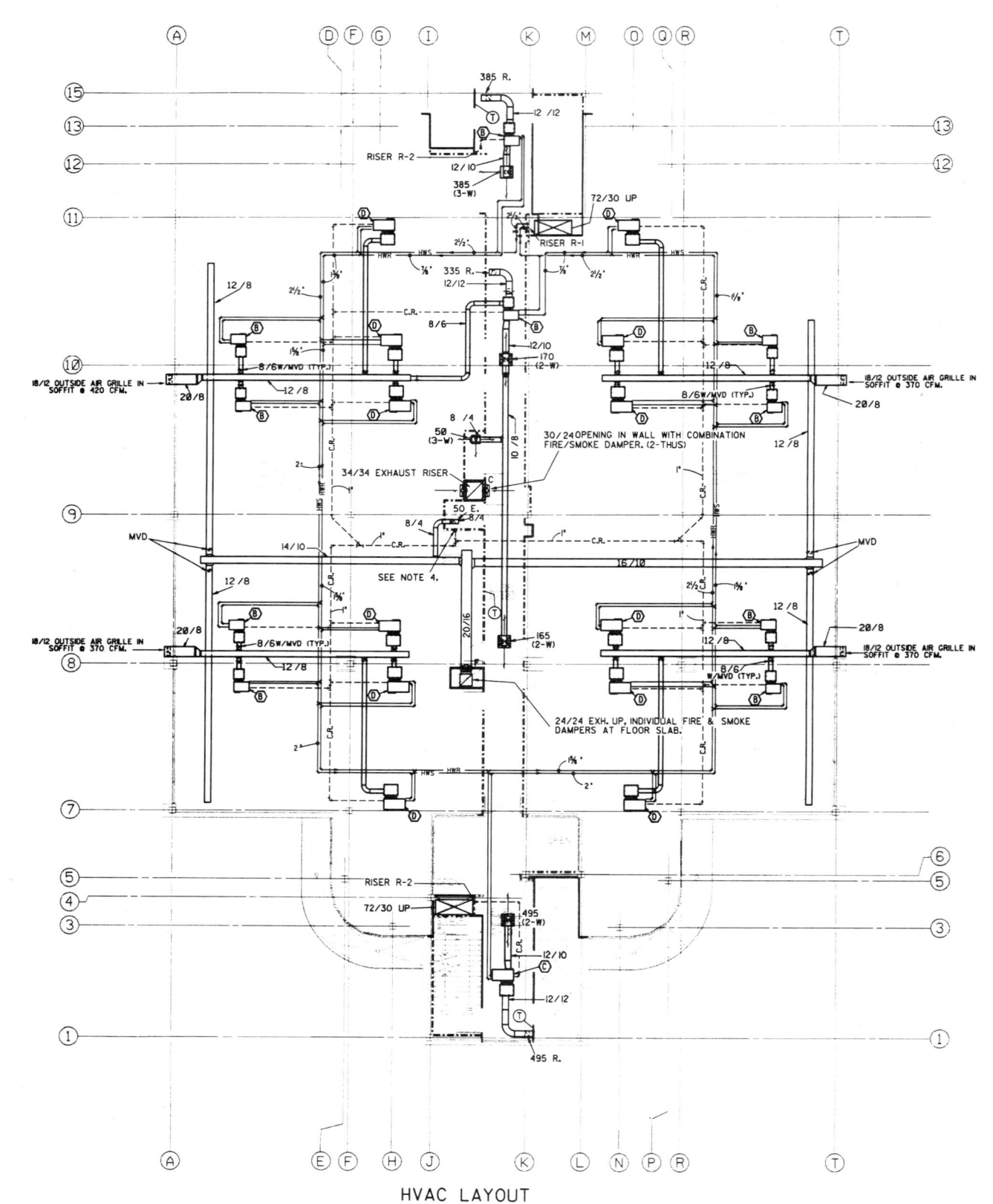

**Figure 7-3** Commercial HVAC plan. *(Courtesy of Intergraph Corporation.)*

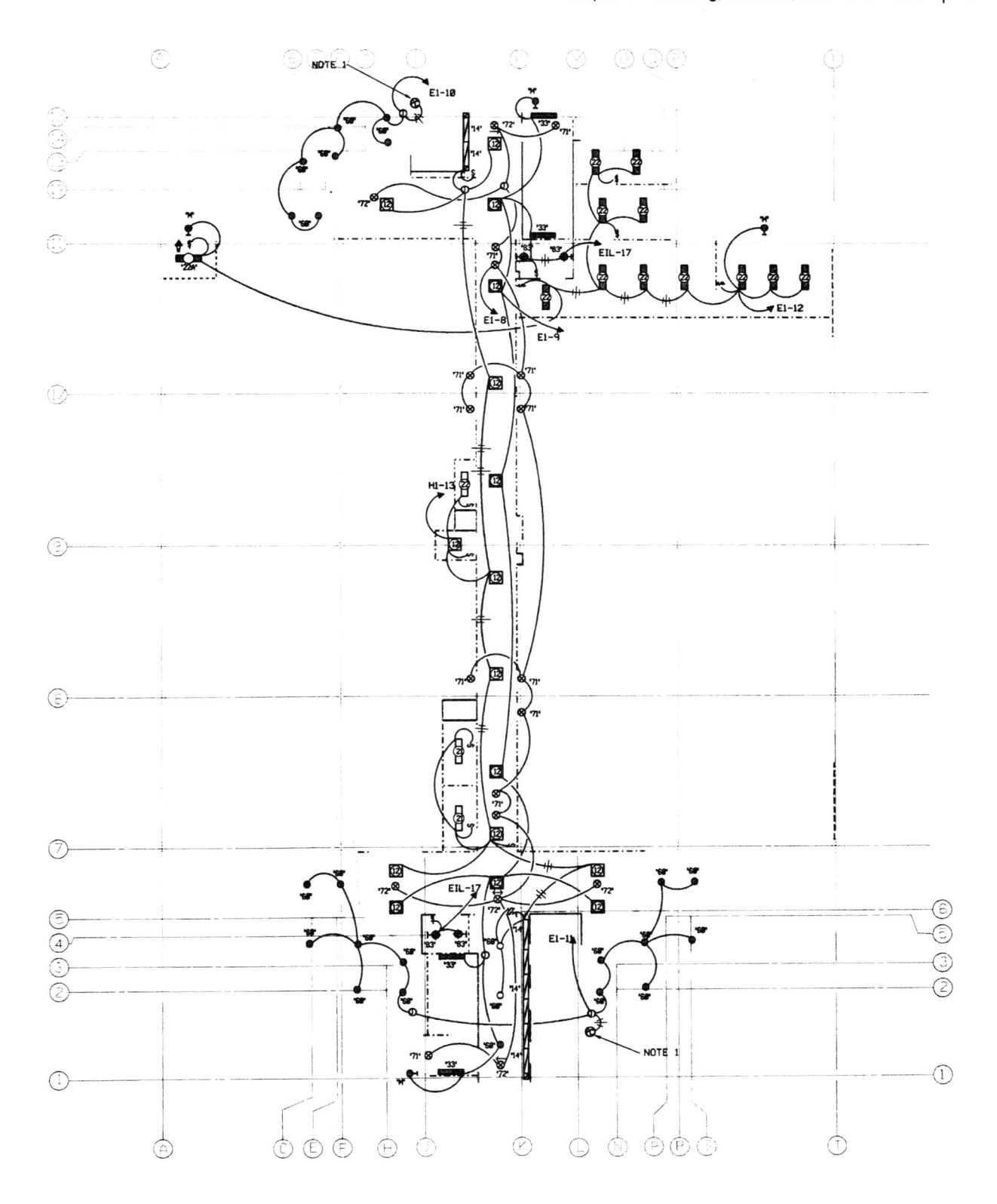

LIGHTING LAYOUT

**Figure 7–4** Commercial electrical plan. *(Courtesy of Intergraph Corporation.)*

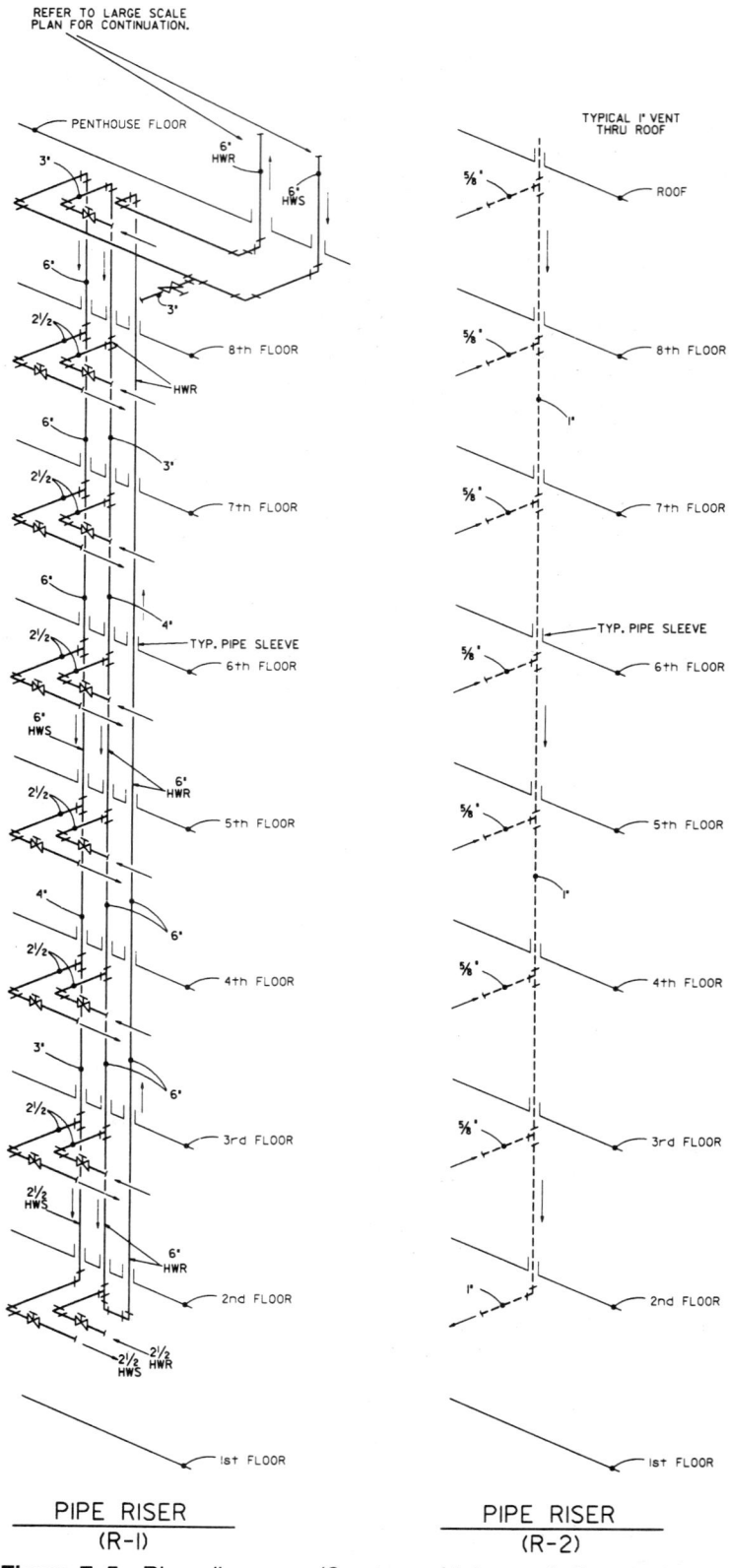

**Figure 7–5** Riser diagrams. *(Courtesy of Intergraph Corporation.)*

Examine the symbols library of your CAD system to determine which of these symbols it contains. If the symbols library does not contain a particular symbol, you have two options:

1. Create the symbol and add it to the symbols library. This can only be done on those CAD systems that are programmed to accept user-defined symbols.
2. Construct the symbols on the drawing as they are needed, using the appropriate geometric characters and commands. For example, the "register" symbol can be made using the SOLID LINES command.

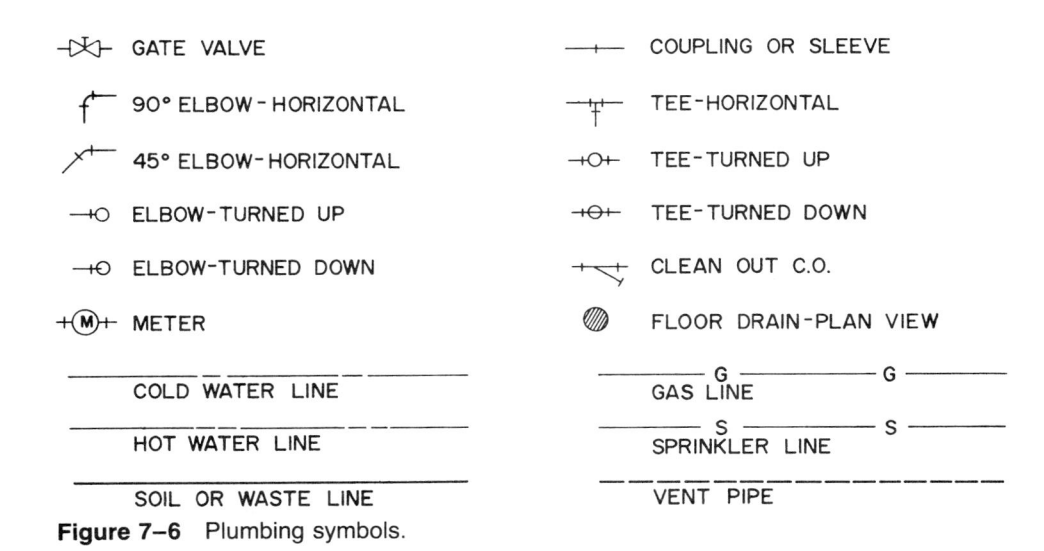

## PLUMBING SYMBOLS

| | | | |
|---|---|---|---|
| ⋈ | GATE VALVE | —— | COUPLING OR SLEEVE |
| | 90° ELBOW-HORIZONTAL | | TEE-HORIZONTAL |
| | 45° ELBOW-HORIZONTAL | | TEE-TURNED UP |
| | ELBOW-TURNED UP | | TEE-TURNED DOWN |
| | ELBOW-TURNED DOWN | | CLEAN OUT C.O. |
| | METER | | FLOOR DRAIN-PLAN VIEW |
| ———— | COLD WATER LINE | —G——G— | GAS LINE |
| ———————— | HOT WATER LINE | —S——S— | SPRINKLER LINE |
| ———————— | SOIL OR WASTE LINE | ———————— | VENT PIPE |

**Figure 7–6** Plumbing symbols.

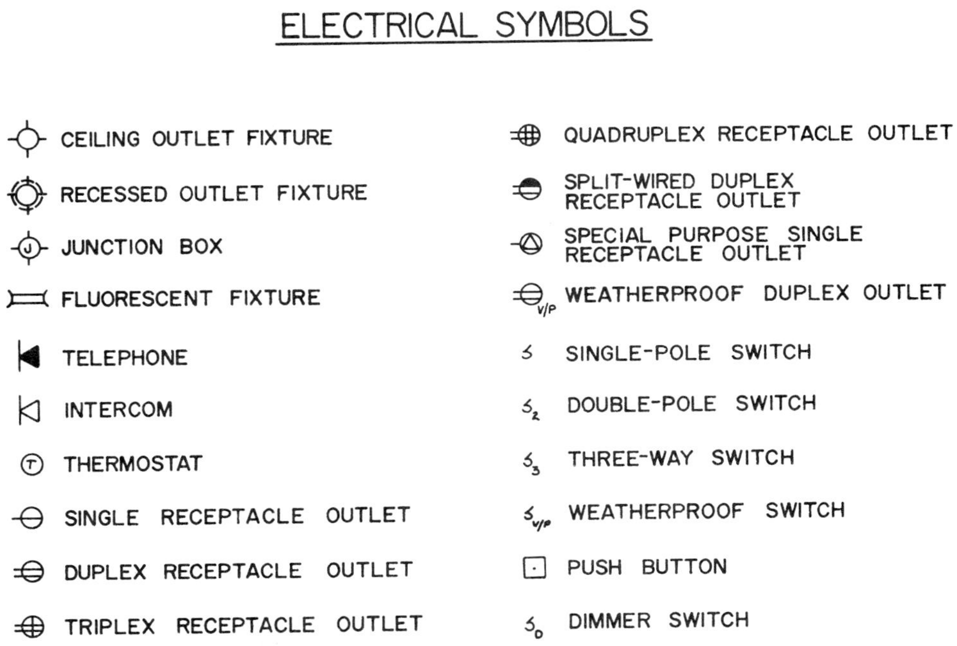

## ELECTRICAL SYMBOLS

| | | | |
|---|---|---|---|
| | CEILING OUTLET FIXTURE | | QUADRUPLEX RECEPTACLE OUTLET |
| | RECESSED OUTLET FIXTURE | | SPLIT-WIRED DUPLEX RECEPTACLE OUTLET |
| | JUNCTION BOX | | SPECIAL PURPOSE SINGLE RECEPTACLE OUTLET |
| | FLUORESCENT FIXTURE | | WEATHERPROOF DUPLEX OUTLET |
| | TELEPHONE | $S$ | SINGLE-POLE SWITCH |
| | INTERCOM | $S_2$ | DOUBLE-POLE SWITCH |
| | THERMOSTAT | $S_3$ | THREE-WAY SWITCH |
| | SINGLE RECEPTACLE OUTLET | $S_{WP}$ | WEATHERPROOF SWITCH |
| | DUPLEX RECEPTACLE OUTLET | | PUSH BUTTON |
| | TRIPLEX RECEPTACLE OUTLET | $S_D$ | DIMMER SWITCH |

**Figure 7–7** Electrical symbols.

# HVAC SYMBOLS

| | | | |
|---|---|---|---|
| | WARM AIR SUPPLY | ———————— | HOT WATER HEATING RETURN |
| | COLD AIR RETURN | ———————— | HOT WATER HEATING SUPPLY |
| | SECOND FLOOR SUPPLY | ⓣ | THERMOSTAT |
| | SECOND FLOOR RETURN | ⊠ | REGISTER |
| | DUCT SIZE AND AIR FLOW | ○ | CEILING DUCT OUTLET |

**Figure 7-8** HVAC symbols.

## CAD COMMANDS AND FUNCTIONS USED

There are several different commands and functions used in producing mechanical plans on a CAD system. Most CAD systems have these commands and functions. However, they are often given different names on different systems (see Chapter 2).

The generic commands and functions used to produce mechanical plans on a CAD system are listed in the Commands and Functions chart. Before attempting the application projects for this chapter, match the generic commands and functions listed with their corresponding commands and functions on your CAD system.

### COMMANDS AND FUNCTIONS

**Graphic Creation Commands**

- ✓ Point
- ✓ Solid Line
- ✓ Hidden Line
- ✓ Construction Line
- ✓ Dashed Line
- ✓ Center Line
- ✓ Rectangle
- ✓ Circle
- ✓ Arc
- ✓ Irregular Curve
- ___ Ellipse
- ___ Polygon
- ___ Grid
- ___ XYPT
- ___ Polar
- ___ Line Weight
- ___ Fillet
- ___ Chamfer
- ___ Leaders
- ___ Rect.
- ___ Hatch

**Manipulation Commands**

- ___ Move
- ___ Copy
- ___ Rotate
- ✓ Scale
- ✓ Zoom
- ✓ Pan
- ___ Mirror

**Size Specification Commands**

- ✓ Auto. Dimension
- ___ Dimension
- ___ Tolerance
- ___ Calc. Area

| Output Commands | Modification Commands | Facilitation Commands |
|---|---|---|
| √ Plot | √ Edit | √ Save |
| ___ Print (Screen Dump) | √ Delete | √ File |
|  | √ Redraw | √ Symbol Library |
| **Text Creation Commands** | ___ Clip | ___ Layer |
| √ Text | √ Erase | ___ Quit |
|  |  | ___ Default |

*Working with mechanical plans is one of the most opportune times for making best use of the Layering function. It is common practice in CAD to produce a modified floor plan once and SAVE it. Then you can use the same floor plan for producing the electrical, plumbing, and HVAC plans. Each time you need to produce a mechanical plan, you can call up the floor plan from storage rather than recreating it every time. In each case, the floor plan would be layer 1 and the mechanical plan layer 2. Another way to use this function to save time is to create the floor plan as layer 1. Then, superimpose each of the mechanical plans as layer 2, layer 3, and layer 4.

## PROCEDURES FOR PREPARING THE PLAN

Although the various mechanical plans use different symbols, the procedures used in preparing them are very similar. The procedures presented in this section may be used for plumbing, electrical, and HVAC plans. What follows is an illustrated, step-by-step description of how a mechanical plan is produced on a CAD system.

■ *Step 1*
Log-on to the system and create a drawing designation called MCHABC. Substitute your initials for the ABC. Decide what size medium the completed drawing will be plotted on.

■ *Step 2*
Create the modified floor plan using the CONSTRUCTION LINES function if it is available and SOLID LINES if it is not. Identify the floor plan as LAYER 1. Convert all construction lines to solid lines once you have completed the layout of the floor plan, Figure 7-9.

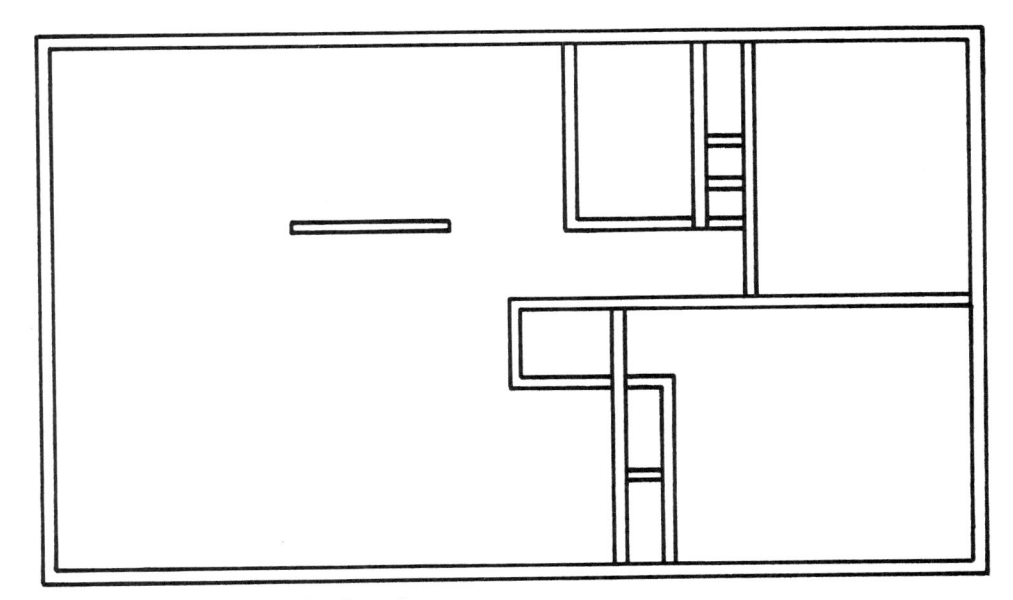

**Figure 7-9** Illustration for Step 2.

■ *Step 3*

Establish LAYER 2 superimposed on top of LAYER 1. Add switches, outlets, special outlets, and lighting fixtures. Switch to the HIDDEN LINE mode and use the IRREGULAR CURVE command to connect switches and fixtures together once you have added them. Add the meter and service entrance. Switch to the TEXT mode and add any notes needed to completely describe the system, Figure 7–10. SAVE the drawing and give the PLOT command.

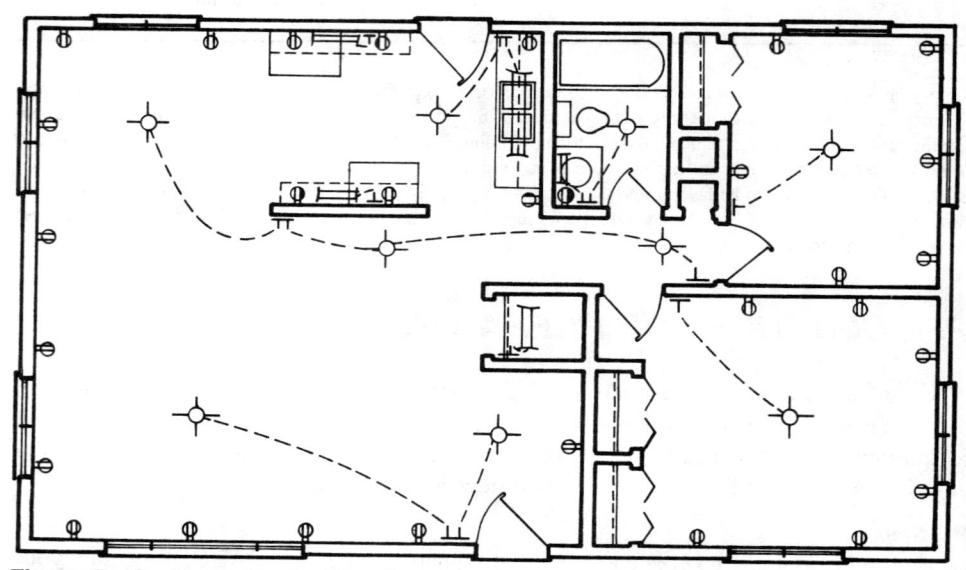

**Figure 7–10** Illustration for Step 3.

## REVIEW QUESTIONS

The following questions are provided as a review of Chapter 7 and should be completed before attempting the application projects for the chapter. Write your answers in the spaces provided.

1. Define the following terms:
   Plumbing plan—

   Electrical plan—

   HVAC plan—

   Mechanical plan—

2. Name four components that might be included on a plumbing plan.

3. Name four components that might be included on an electrical plan.

4. Name four components that might be included on an HVAC plan.

5. Sketch the symbols for the following:
   Ceiling outlet—

   Junction box—

   Thermostat—

   Duplex receptacle outlet—

   Weatherproof duplex outlet—

   Single-pole switch—

   90 degree elbow (horizontal)—

   Tee (horizontal)—

   Cold water line—

   Duct—

   Register—

6. Explain the steps used on your CAD system for setting up a series of layers.

# APPLICATION PROJECTS

The following application projects are provided to help you become proficient in producing mechanical plans on a CAD system. A floor plan is provided for each project. You are required to construct an electrical plan, a plumbing plan, and an HVAC plan for each floor plan. To save time, you may wish to SAVE the floor plan under a specific drawing designation and simply call it up and superimpose the mechanical plans on another layer. In reconstructing the given floor plans, you may use one of two options:

1. Reproduce the drawing through photocopying or place the page from the book on the digitizer and digitize it. Once you have input the drawing, you can use the SCALE function to display it in the desired size.
2. Use the room sizes provided for computing the needed dimensions and construct the drawing from scratch.

In either case, it is recommended that you construct each floor plan only once under one layer designation and construct the mechanical plan in question as another layer. You may even wish to construct all three mechanical plans for each floor plan as three superimposed layers. PLOT the finished plans on the size and type of medium specified by the instructor.

**Project 1:** Figure 7–11 is a floor plan for a residential dwelling. Reconstruct the floor plan on your CAD system as shown, but leave off the text. Superimpose an electrical plan over the floor plan.

**Project 2:** Superimpose a plumbing plan over the floor plan in Figure 7–11.

**Project 3:** Superimpose an HVAC plan over the floor plan in Figure 7–11.

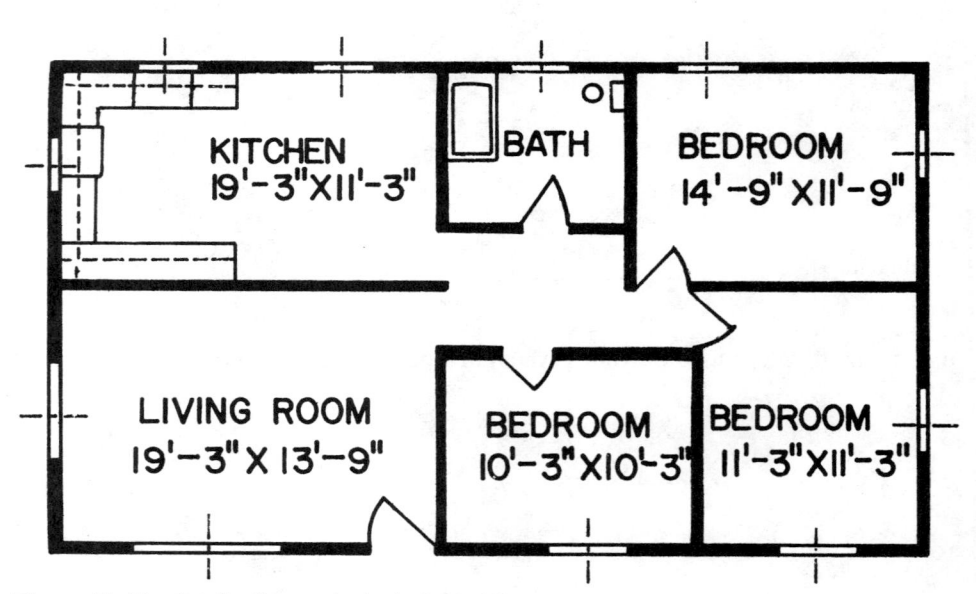

**Figure 7–11** Application projects 1, 2, and 3.

**Project 4:** Figure 7–12 is a floor plan for a residential dwelling. Reconstruct the floor plan on your CAD system as shown, but leave off the text. Superimpose an electrical plan over the floor plan.

**Project 5:** Superimpose a plumbing plan over the floor plan in Figure 7–12.

**Project 6:** Superimpose an HVAC plan over the floor plan in Figure 7–12.

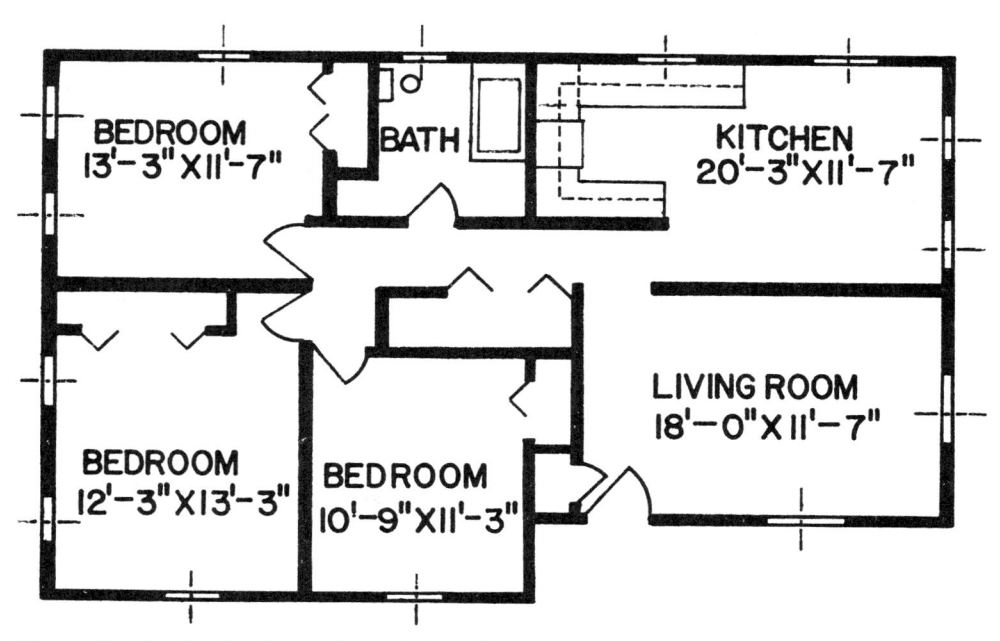

**Figure 7–12** Application projects 4, 5, and 6.

**Project 7:** Figure 7–13 is a floor plan for a residential dwelling. Reconstruct the floor plan on your CAD system as shown, but leave off the text. Superimpose an electrical plan over the floor plan.

**Project 8:** Superimpose a plumbing plan over the floor plan in Figure 7–13.

**Project 9:** Superimpose an HVAC plan over the floor plan in Figure 7–13.

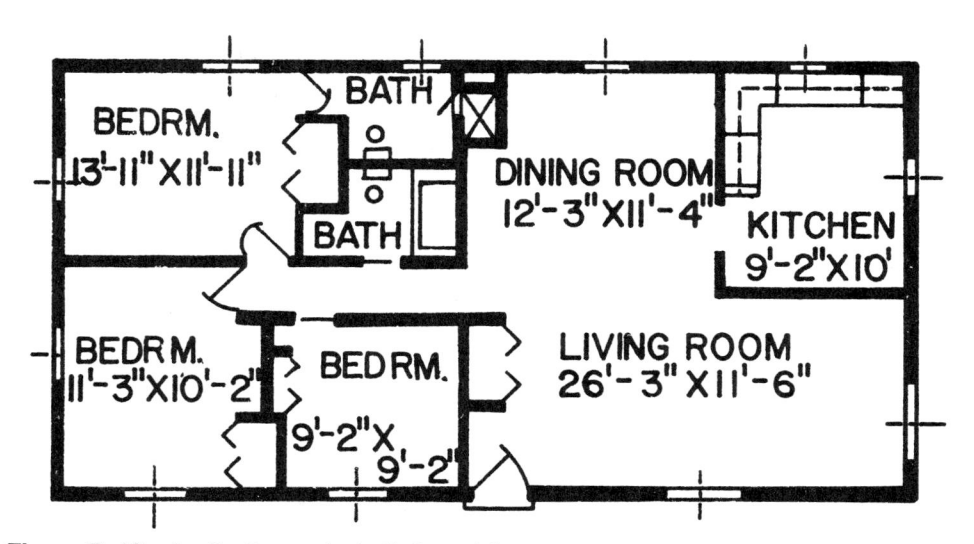

**Figure 7–13** Application projects 7, 8, and 9.

**Project 10:** Figure 7–14 is a floor plan for a residential dwelling. Reconstruct the floor plan on your CAD system as shown, but leave off the text. Superimpose an electrical plan over the floor plan.

**Project 11:** Superimpose a plumbing plan over the floor plan in Figure 7–14.

**Project 12:** Superimpose an HVAC plan over the floor plan in Figure 7–14.

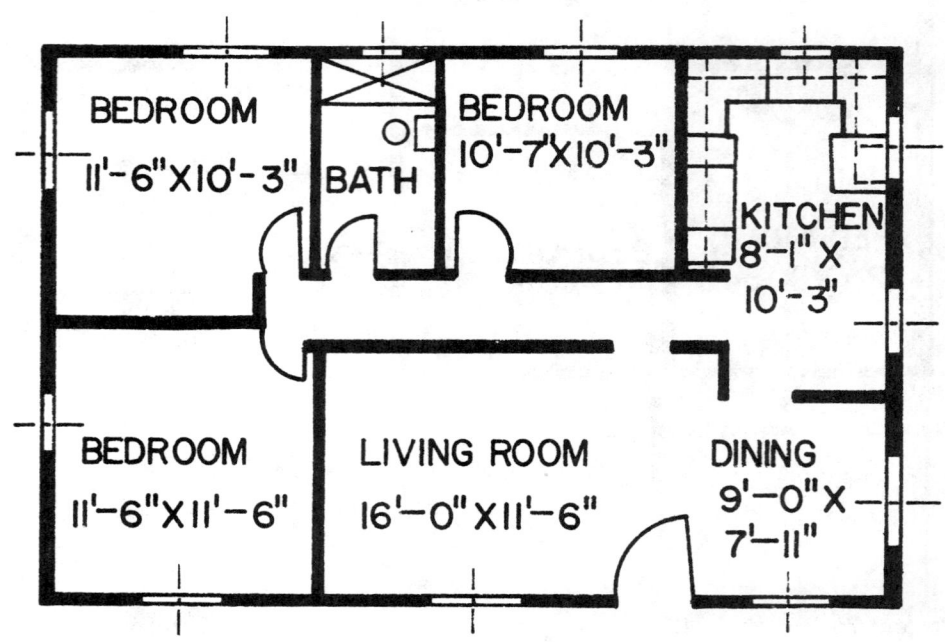

**Figure 7–14** Application projects 10, 11, and 12.

**Project 13:** Figure 7–15 is a floor plan for a residential dwelling. Reconstruct the floor plan on your CAD system as shown, but leave off the text. Superimpose an electrical plan over the floor plan.

**Project 14:** Superimpose a plumbing plan over the floor plan in Figure 7–15.

**Project 15:** Superimpose an HVAC plan over the floor plan in Figure 7–15.

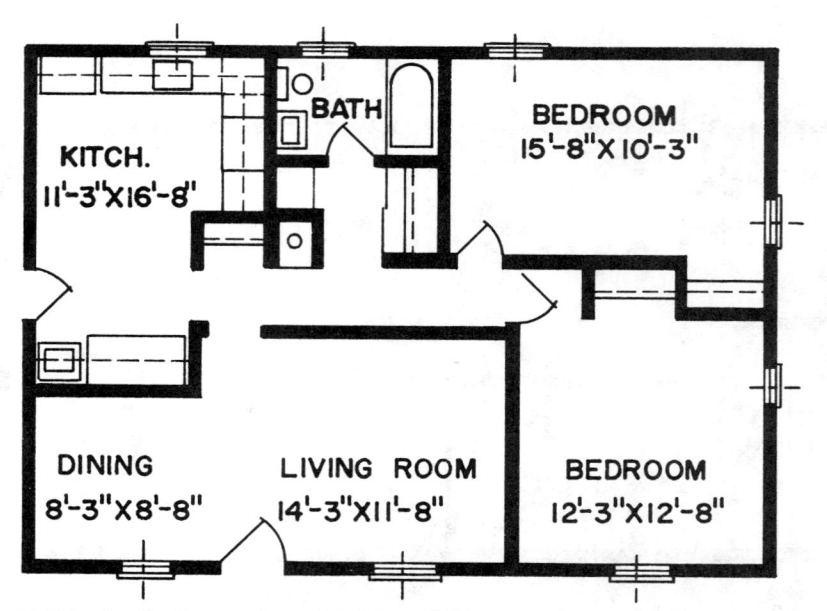

**Figure 7–15** Application projects 13, 14, and 15.

**Project 16:** Figure 7–16 is a floor plan for a residential dwelling. Reconstruct the floor plan on your CAD system as shown, but leave off the text. Superimpose an electrical plan over the floor plan.

**Project 17:** Superimpose a plumbing plan over the floor plan in Figure 7–16.

**Project 18:** Superimpose an HVAC plan over the floor plan in Figure 7–16.

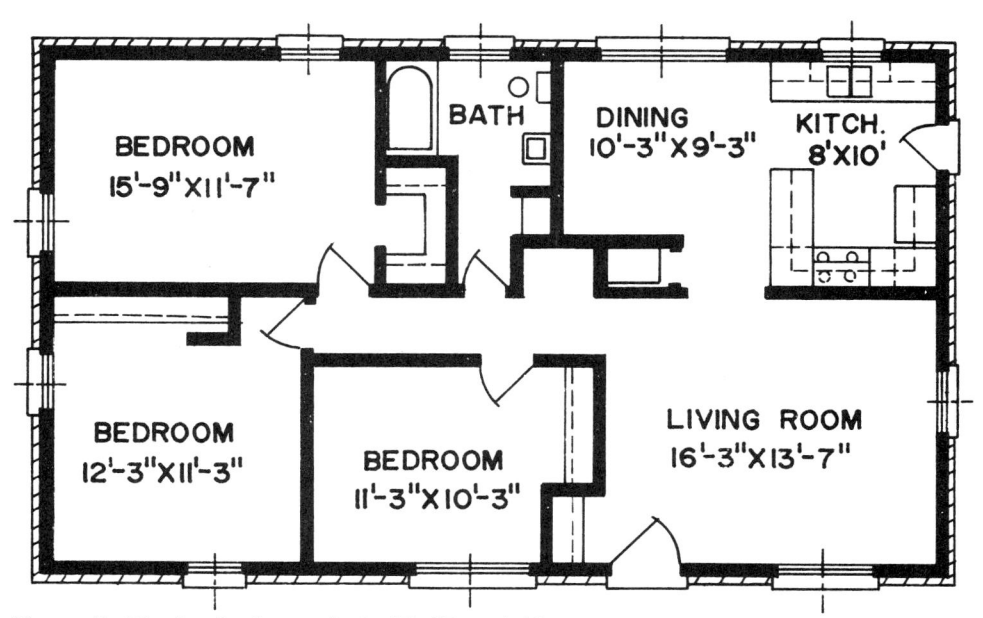

**Figure 7–16** Application projects 16, 17, and 18.

# 108 | CAD Applications: Architectural

**Project 19:** Figure 7–17 is a floor plan for a commercial building that was produced manually. Reconstruct the drawing on your CAD system, leaving off all dimensions and notes. SAVE the floor plan and give it a layer designation. Then, call it up and superimpose an electrical plan over it.

**Project 20:** Superimpose a plumbing plan over the floor plan in Figure 7–17.

**Project 21:** Superimpose an HVAC plan over the floor plan in Figure 7–17.

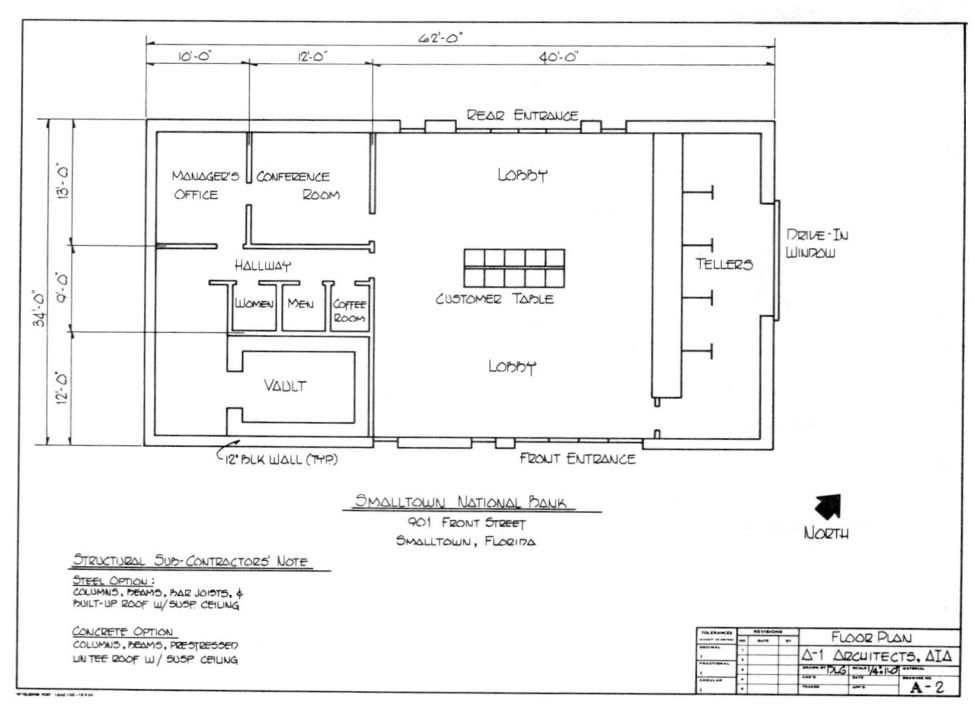

**Figure 7–17** Application projects 19, 20, and 21.

# chapter 8
# Plot Plans

## DEFINITION, PURPOSE, AND CONTENTS

A plot plan is required in both residential and commercial architectural plans. A plot plan is a plan view of a piece of property or construction site showing various items of information about the property and the building that will occupy it. A plot plan is *not* the same thing as a site plan. A site plan is used to show the property and vegetation on it prior to clearing, cut and fill, and any other alterations that will be made to the property. A plot plan is a view of the property after clearing, cut and fill, and other alterations have been made, and the foundation has been constructed. This chapter deals with plot plans, but the procedures for producing plot plans and site plans on a CAD system are similar.

The plot plan is used for staking out the footings and foundation; locating and installing utilities; communicating the elevation data on the property; and verifying compliance with planning, zoning, and setback restrictions. Figure 8–1 is an example of a partial plot plan for a commercial building that was produced on a modern CAD system.

Although the specific contents of a plot plan will vary depending on the details of the individual project, typical contents can be listed. Of course, not all elements listed appear on all plot plans. However, the elements listed below can be considered as being typical:

- property lines and descriptions
- an outline of the building
- out-to-out dimensions of the building
- location dimensions from property lines
- corner elevations
- contour lines (optional)
- streets and driveways
- sidewalks and walkways
- easements
- utilities
- fences and retaining walls
- lot and block or address information
- scale designation
- north arrow
- site location

**110** | CAD Applications: Architectural

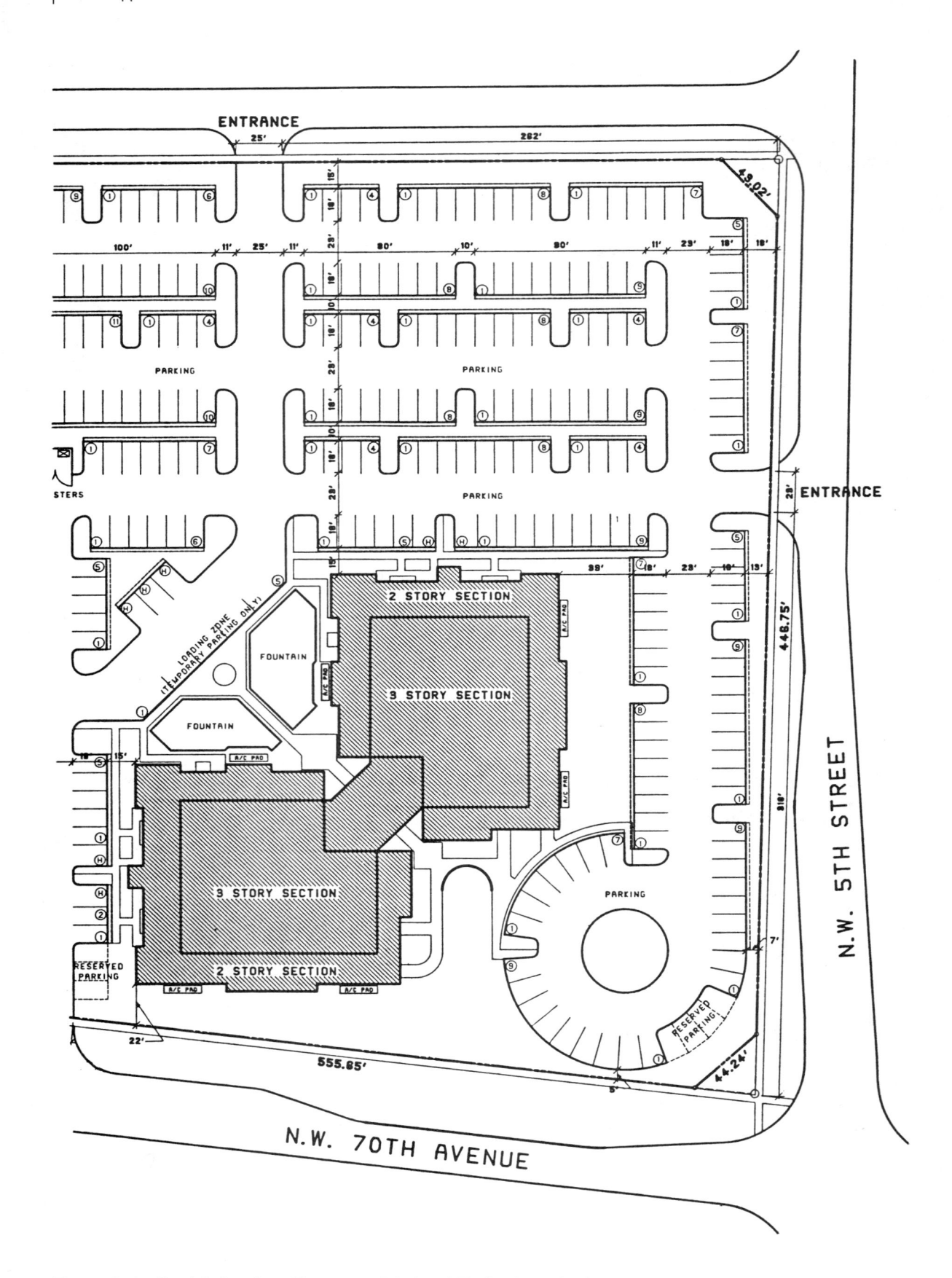

**Figure 8–1** Partial plot plan. *(Courtesy of Arrigoni Technology, Inc.)*

## SPECIAL SYMBOLS NEEDED

There are a number of special graphic symbols used in constructing a plot plan on a CAD system. Those most frequently used are shown in Figure 8–2. Examine the symbols library of your CAD system to determine which of these symbols it contains. If the symbols library does not contain a particular symbol, you have two options:

1. Create the symbol and add it to the symbols library. This can be done only on those CAD systems that are programmed to accept user-defined symbols.
2. Construct any symbols on the drawing as they are needed, using the appropriate geometric characters and commands. For example, the "fence" symbol can be made using the SOLID LINE command. The "sanitary sewer" symbol can be made using the SOLID LINE command to create a series of long, equally spaced dashes.

FENCE

GAS LINE

PAVED ROAD

SANITARY SEWER

UNPAVED ROAD

PROPERTY LINE

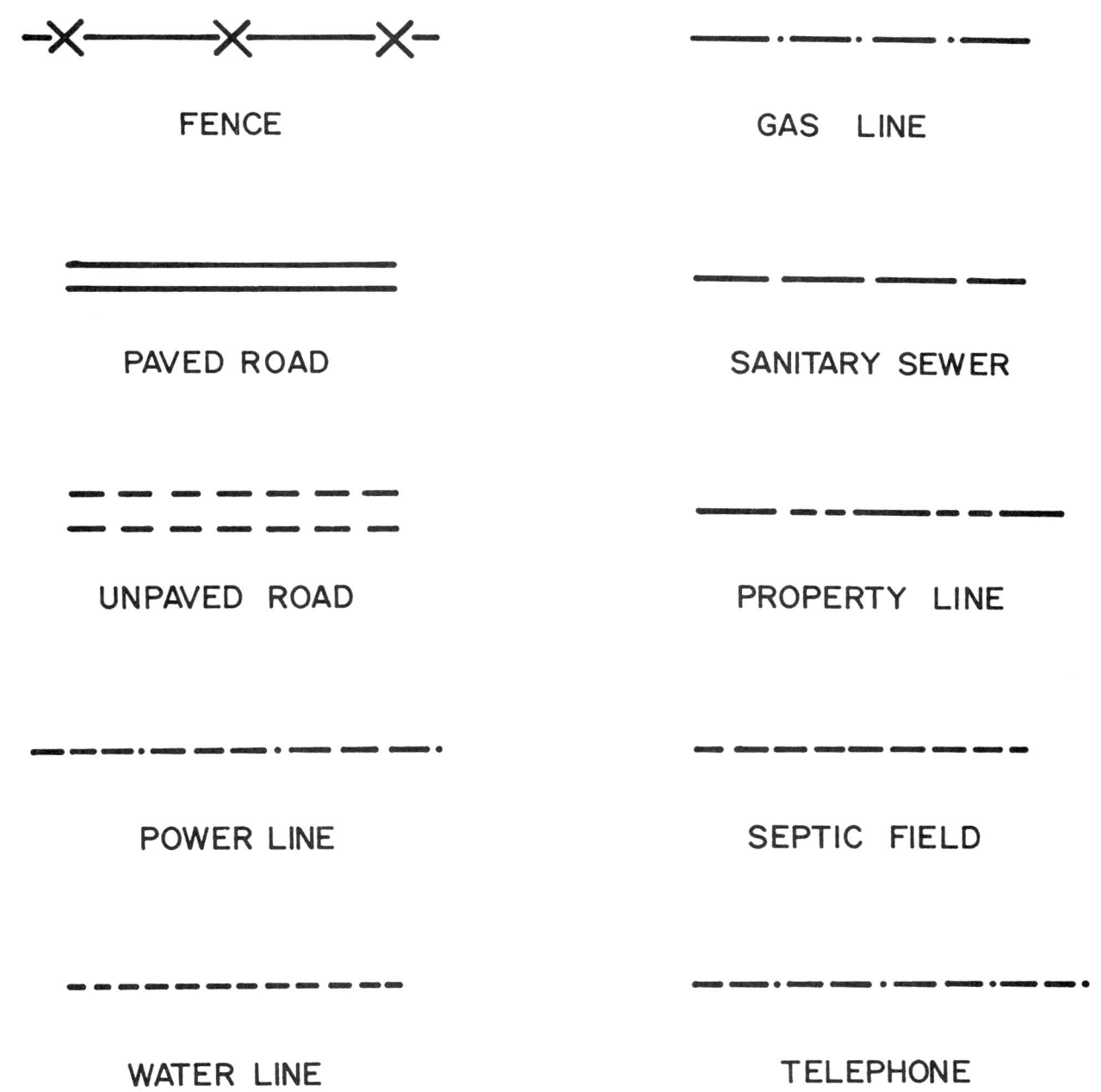

POWER LINE

SEPTIC FIELD

WATER LINE

TELEPHONE

**Figure 8–2** Graphic symbols for producing plot plans.

## CAD COMMANDS AND FUNCTIONS USED

There are a number of different commands and functions used in constructing a plot plan on a CAD system. Most CAD systems have these commands and functions, but they are frequently given different names on different systems (see Chapter 1).

The generic commands and functions used to produce a plot plan on a CAD system are listed in the Commands and Functions chart. Before attempting the application projects for this chapter, match these generic commands with their corresponding commands and functions on your CAD system.

### COMMANDS AND FUNCTIONS

**Graphic Creation Commands**

- ✓ Point
- ✓ Solid Line
- ✓ Hidden Line
- ✓ Construction Line
- ✓ Dashed Line
- ✓ Center Line
- ✓ Rectangle
- ✓ Circle
- ✓ Arc
- ✓ Irregular Curve
- ___ Ellipse
- ___ Polygon
- ___ Grid
- ___ XYPT
- ___ Polar
- ___ Line Weight
- ___ Fillet
- ___ Chamfer
- ___ Leaders
- ___ Rect.
- ___ Hatch

**Manipulation Commands**

- ✓ Move
- ✓ Copy
- ✓ Rotate
- ✓ Scale
- ✓ Zoom
- ✓ Pan
- ___ Mirror

**Size Specification Commands**

- ✓ Auto. Dimension
- ___ Dimension
- ___ Tolerance
- ___ Calc. Area

**Output Commands**

- ✓ Plot
- ___ Print (Screen Dump)

**Text Creation Commands**

- ✓ Text

**Modification Commands**

- ✓ Edit
- ✓ Delete
- ✓ Redraw
- ___ Clip
- ✓ Erase

**Facilitation Commands**

- ✓ Save
- ✓ File
- ✓ Symbol Library
- ✓ Layer*
- ___ Quit
- ___ Default

## PROCEDURES FOR PREPARING THE PLAN

What follows is an illustrated, step-by-step explanation of how to prepare a sample plot plan on a CAD system. The example used is a plot plan for a residential dwelling. However, the same basic procedures would be used for light commercial or commercial plot plans.

■ *Step 1*

Log-on to the system and create a drawing designation called "PLTABC." Substitute your initials for the ABC. This will allow you to identify your plot plan from among those of your classmates. After plotting, you might wish to "dump" your drawing on to your own diskette for storage. This will create your own file diskette and keep the system's main memory from overloading. Select the size of medium that you will plot on. This will dictate the scale of the drawing you will create.

■ *Step 2*

Select one property corner as a starting point (say the upper left-hand corner) and lay out the property lines using the CONSTRUCTION LINE command. If your system does not have this type of command, use the SOLID LINE command. Use the CIRCLE command to indicate corner markers. You will find it helpful to ZOOM-IN on the corners when placing the circles, Figure 8-3.

**Figure 8-3** Illustration for Step 2.

■ *Step 3*

If you began with the CONSTRUCTION LINES command in Step 1, convert the property lines to solid lines with long dashes evenly spaced. This can be done using just the SOLID LINES command and then breaking the lines. Or it can be done by using the SOLID LINES command to enter the lines and the ERASE command to take out portions, thereby creating dashes. Your system may have an automatic conversion command for converting construction lines to solid lines. Check this possibility first. Change to the TEXT mode and enter the bearing and distances for the property lines and the lot and block or address information. While still in the TEXT mode, label the corner elevations and the gas, water, and sewer lines, and the north arrow. Switch from the TEXT mode and draw the gas, water, sewer lines, and north arrow. If your CAD system's symbols library does not contain these symbols, they can be created using the SOLID LINES and POINT commands, Figure 8-4.

**114** | CAD Applications: Architectural

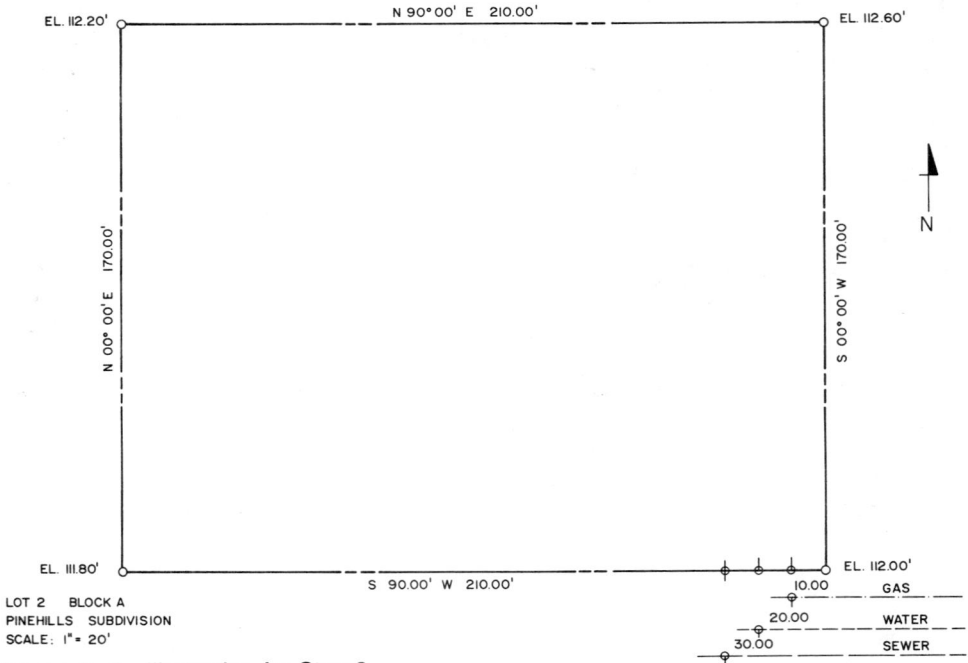

**Figure 8–4** Illustration for Step 3.

■ *Step 4*

Position the outline of the house on the lot using the CONSTRUCTION LINES command if your CAD system has it. Use the SOLID LINES command if not. Lay out the driveway. Convert all construction lines to solid lines. Add the out-to-out dimensions of the house and the width dimension for the driveway. Complete the plot plan by adding the dimension that locates the house on the lot, Figure 8–5. Notice in Figures 8–4 and 8–5 that the line terminators on the dimension lines for this plot plan are small circles. This is acceptable practice only in architectural, structural, and civil applications. Most CAD systems have

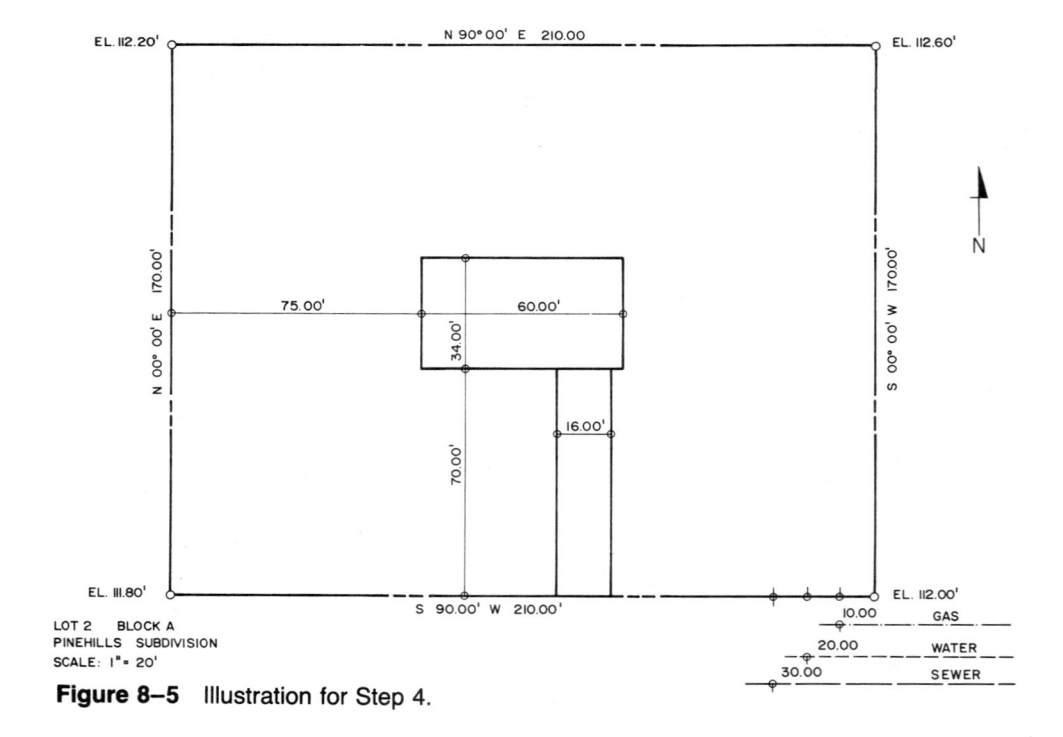

**Figure 8–5** Illustration for Step 4.

the capacity to create several different line termination options including circles, arrowheads (open), arrowheads (closed), and short slashes. This is particularly true in the case of systems designed for use in architectural applications.

## REVIEW QUESTIONS

The following questions are provided as a review of Chapter 3 and should be completed before attempting the application projects for the chapter. Write your answers in the spaces provided or on a separate sheet as directed by your teacher.

1. Define "plot plan."

2. Explain how a plot plan differs from a site plan.

3. List four ways in which a plot plan might be used:

4. List five of the typical elements that might be included on a plot plan:

5. Sketch the symbols for the following:
   Fence—

   Unpaved road—

   Property line—

   Gas line—

   Water line—

6. Explain the steps you would use in creating the "fence" symbol on a drawing if it is not available in the symbols library.

7. Several generic CAD commands are listed below. Give the name of the corresponding command for your CAD system.
   POINT—

   SOLID LINE—

   CONSTRUCTION LINE—

   CIRCLE—

   IRREGULAR CURVE—

   ZOOM-IN—

PAN—

ERASE—

DIMENSION—

TEXT—

8. Make a block diagram that explains the "log-on" sequence for your CAD system.

# APPLICATION PROJECTS

The following application projects are provided to help you become proficient in producing plot plans on a CAD system. Complete each problem as required and save it on your own file diskette under its figure number and your initials (e.g., 8–8DLG).

**Project 1:** Figure 8–6 contains the outline of an irregularly shaped piece of property. Redraw the plot plan using proper symbols. Add a north arrow and fictitious address information.

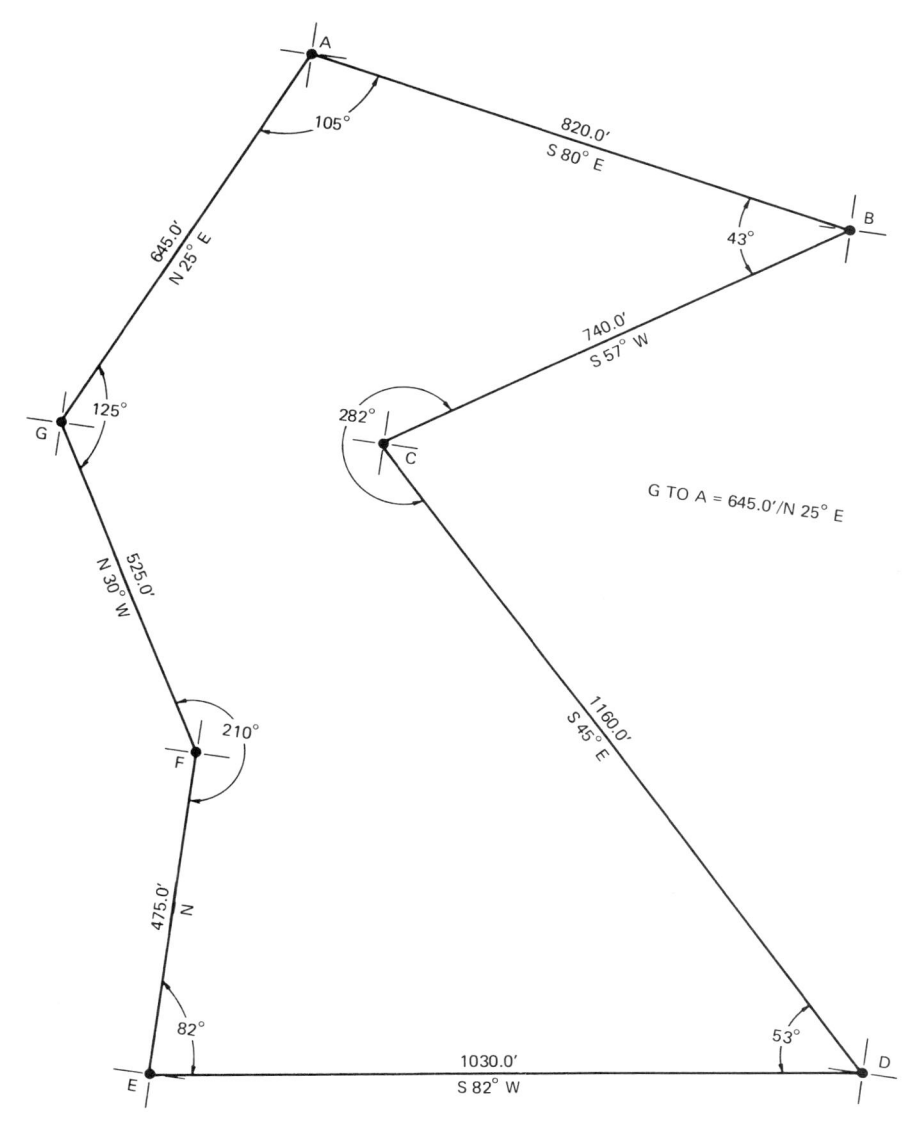

**Figure 8–6** Application project 1.

**Project 2:** Figure 8–7 contains the outline of an irregularly shaped piece of property. Redraw the plot plan using proper symbols. Add fictitious address information and label each corner with an elevation that would be realistic in your area of the country.

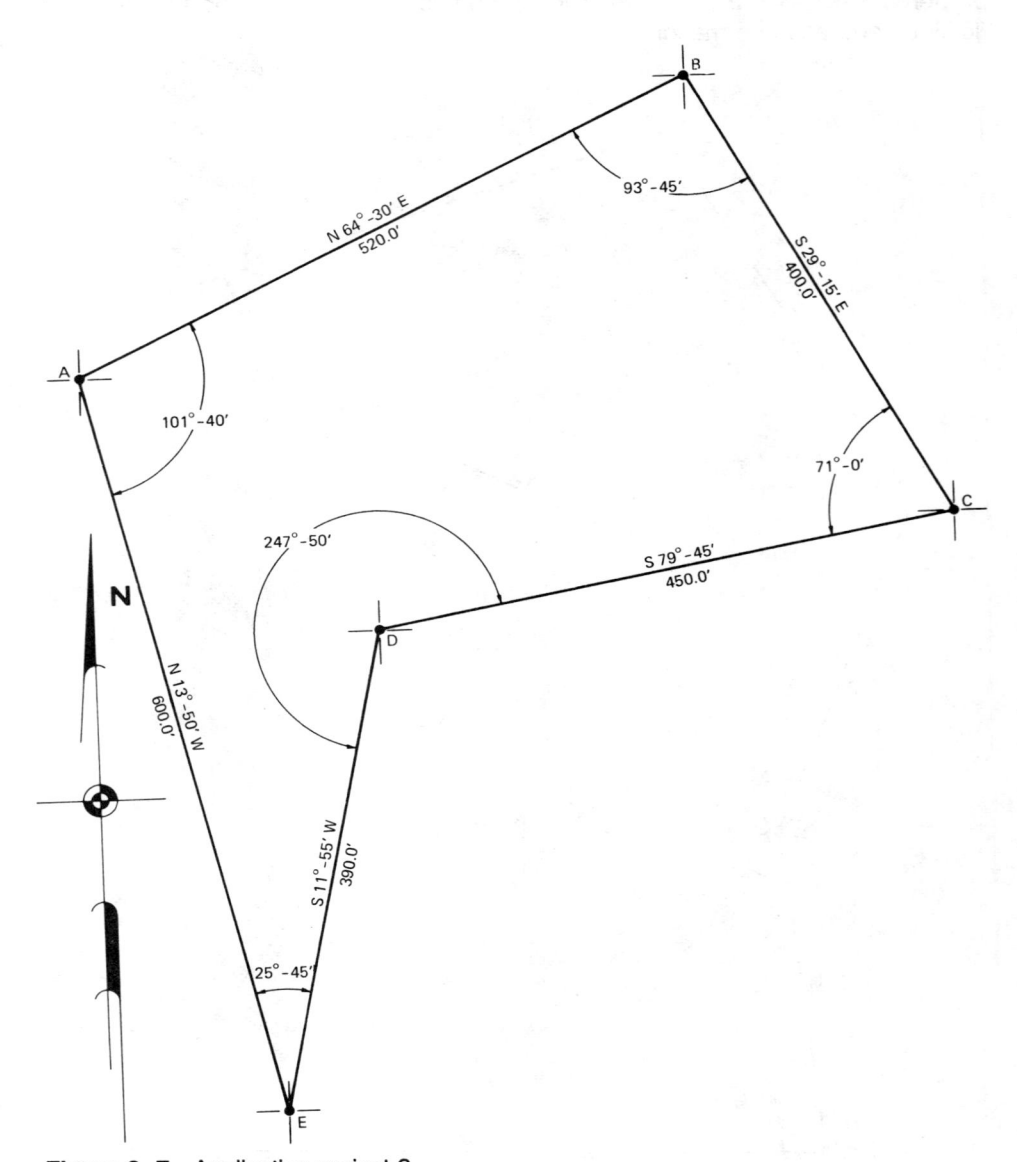

**Figure 8–7** Application project 2.

**Project 3:** Figure 8-8 contains the outline of an irregularly shaped piece of property. Redraw the plot plan using the proper symbols. Add a north arrow, fictitious address information, and a label to each corner with an elevation that would be realistic in your area of the country.

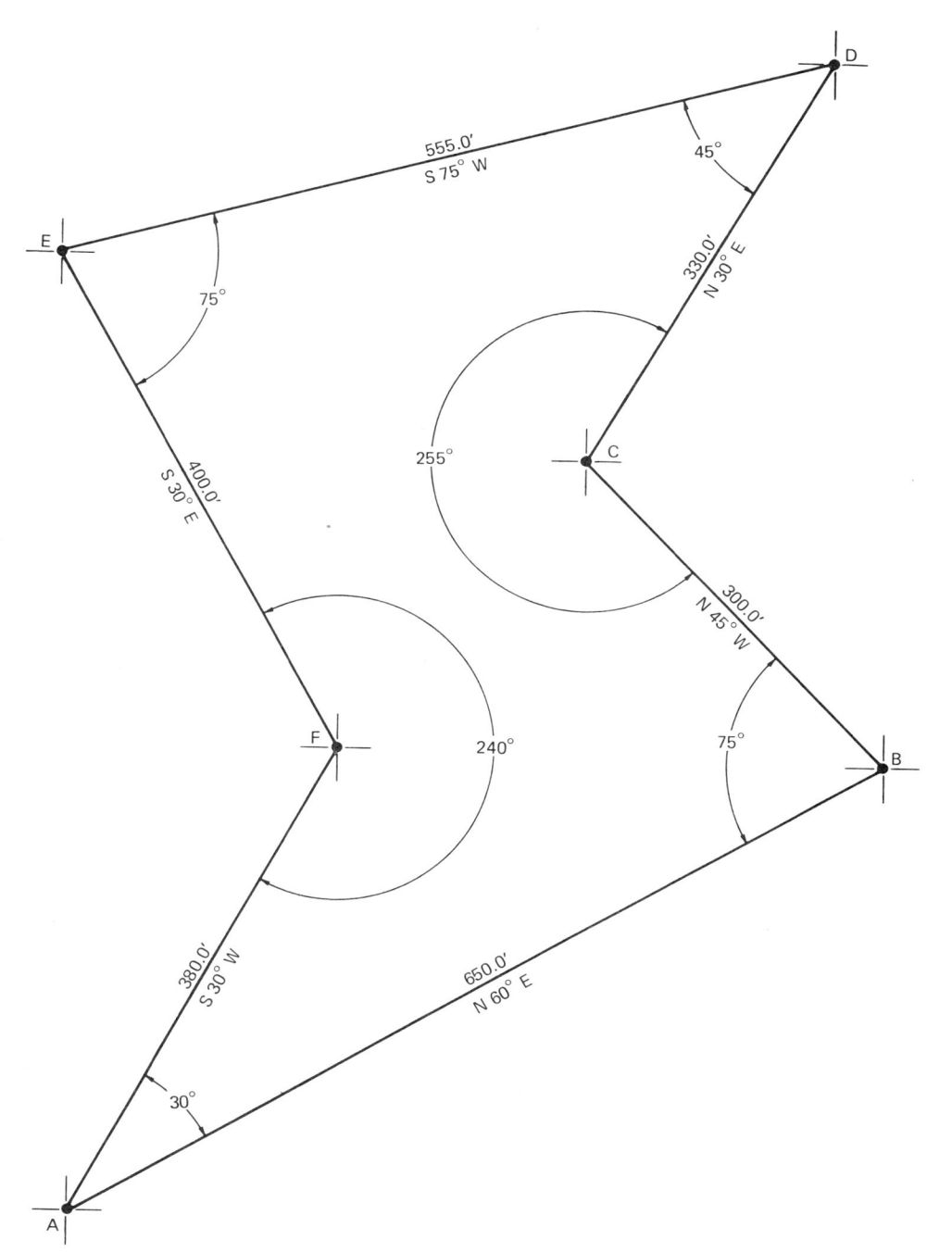

**Figure 8-8** Application project 3.

**Project 4:** Figure 8–9 contains a partially completed plot plan for a vacant lot and a description of the property lines. Redraw the plot plan and complete it by adding all required bearings to the plan. Add fictitious address information and label each corner with an elevation that would be realistic in your area of the country.

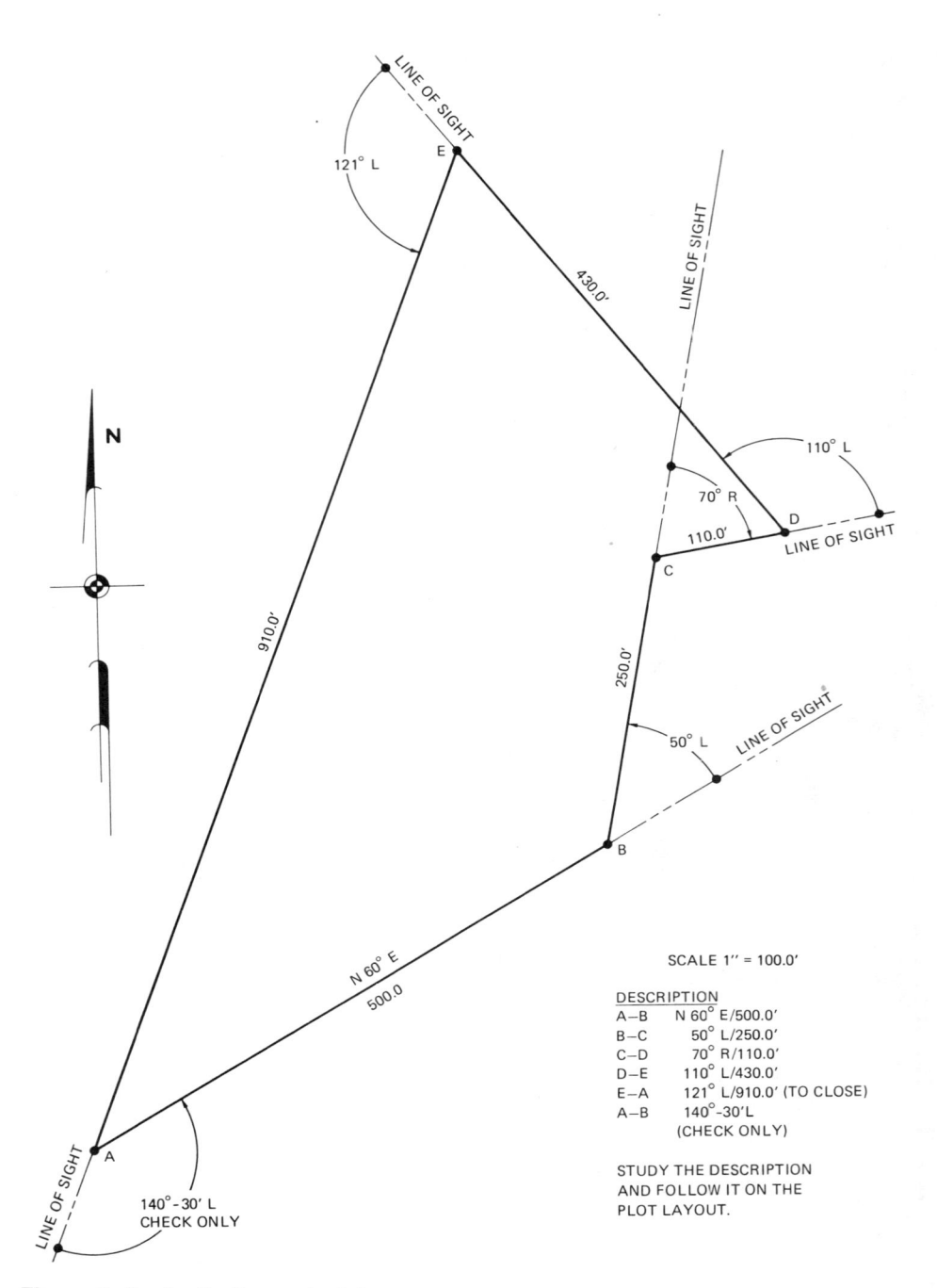

SCALE 1" = 100.0'

DESCRIPTION
A–B    N 60° E/500.0'
B–C    50° L/250.0'
C–D    70° R/110.0'
D–E    110° L/430.0'
E–A    121° L/910.0' (TO CLOSE)
A–B    140°-30'L
       (CHECK ONLY)

STUDY THE DESCRIPTION AND FOLLOW IT ON THE PLOT LAYOUT.

**Figure 8–9** Application project 4.

**Project 5:** Figure 8–10 contains a plot plan complete with all information except the outline of the house and utilities and corner elevations. Redraw the plot plan as shown. Add the outline of a house that is 60.00' long and 40.00' wide. The length of the house should run parallel to New Boston Road. The house should be centered in the lot. Add a note on the drawing that says: ALL UTILITIES AVAILABLE AT STREET.

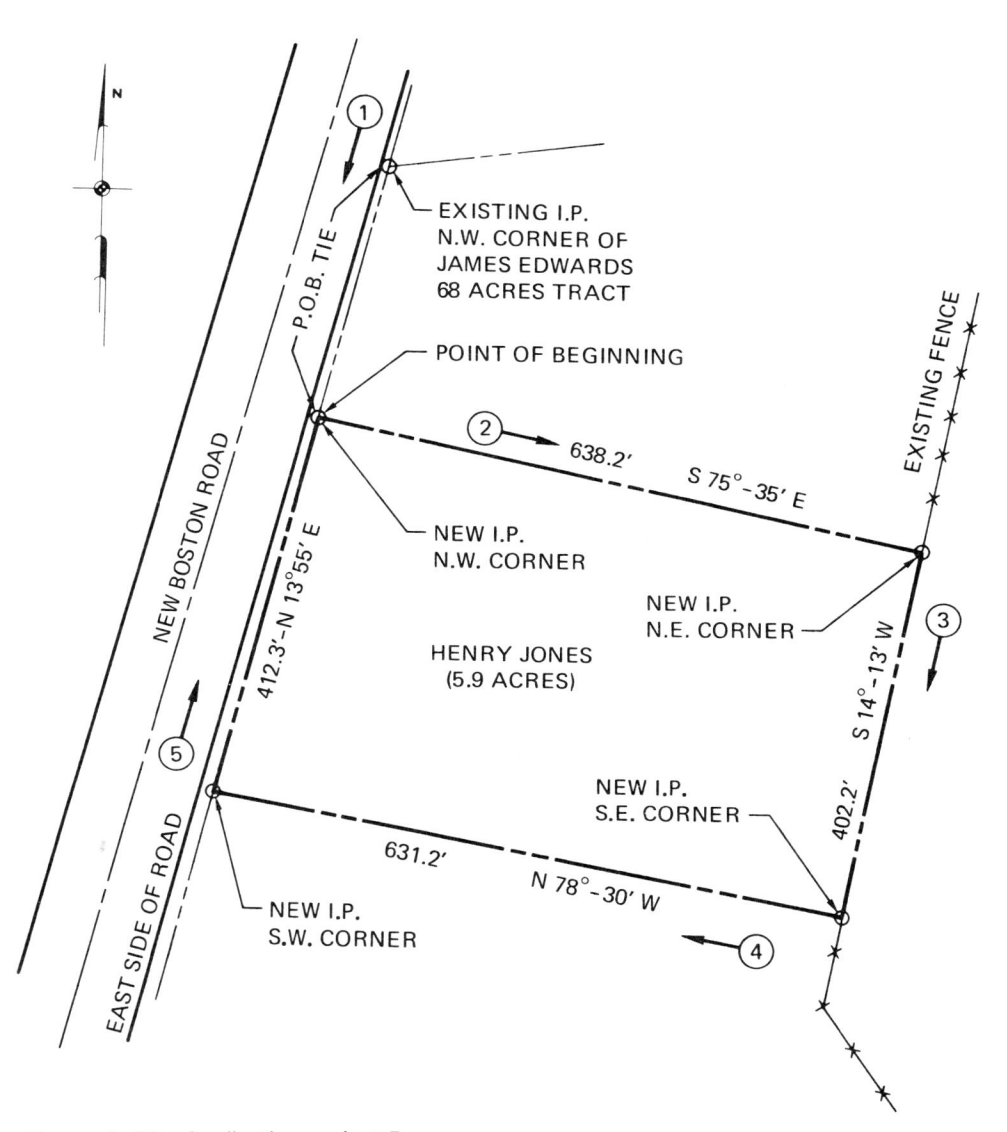

**Figure 8–10** Application project 5.

**Project 6:** Figure 8–11 contains a partial plot plan for a house. Redraw the plot plan as shown and complete it by adding bearings, corner elevations, and a house with utilities. The corner elevations should be realistic in your area of the country. The house should be 56.00' long and 38.00' wide. You may locate it on the lot. Add a gas, sewer, and water line at 10.00' intervals from the south property boundary and parallel to it.

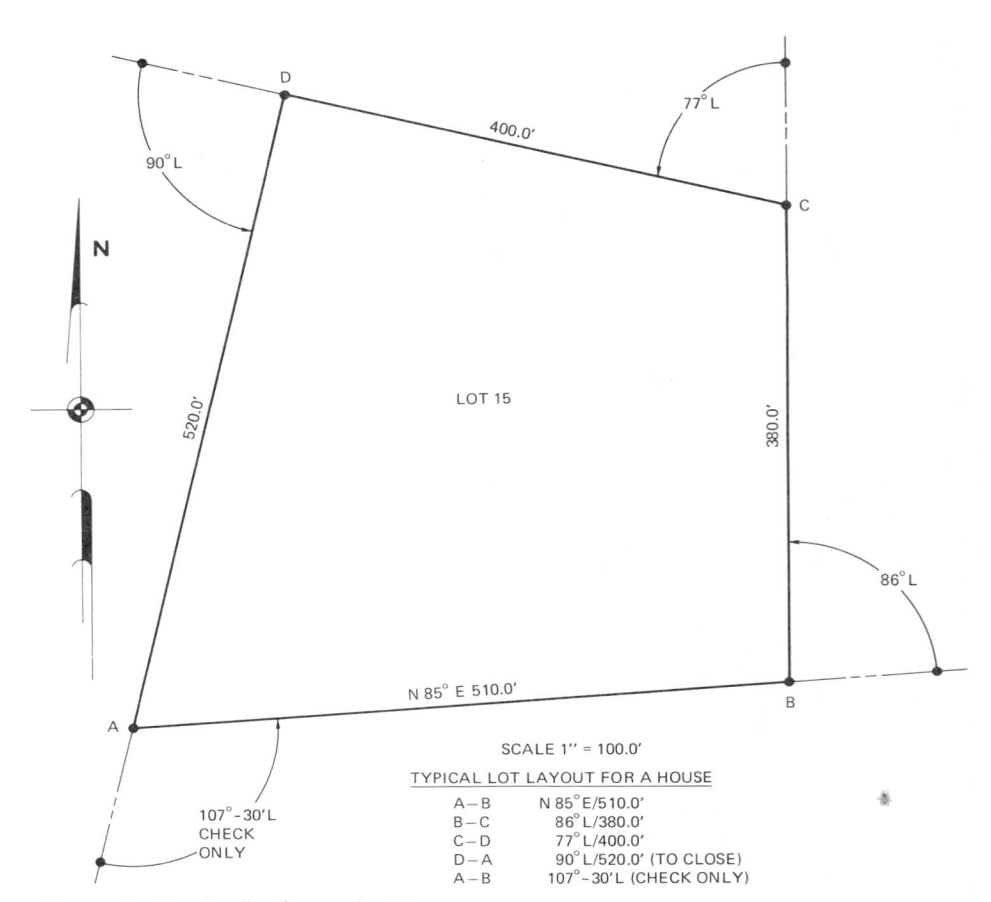

**Figure 8–11** Application project 6.

**Project 7:** Figure 8–12 is an engineer's sketch of a partial plot plan for Walton Acres. Redraw the partial plot plan as shown, taking notice of any notes the engineer might have left for you. Center a house on each lot that is 48.00' long and 36.00' wide with the length of the house running parallel to the west property boundary. Utilities should be located at five foot intervals under the street on the west side of the lots. Add realistic corner elevations for each lot and use proper symbols.

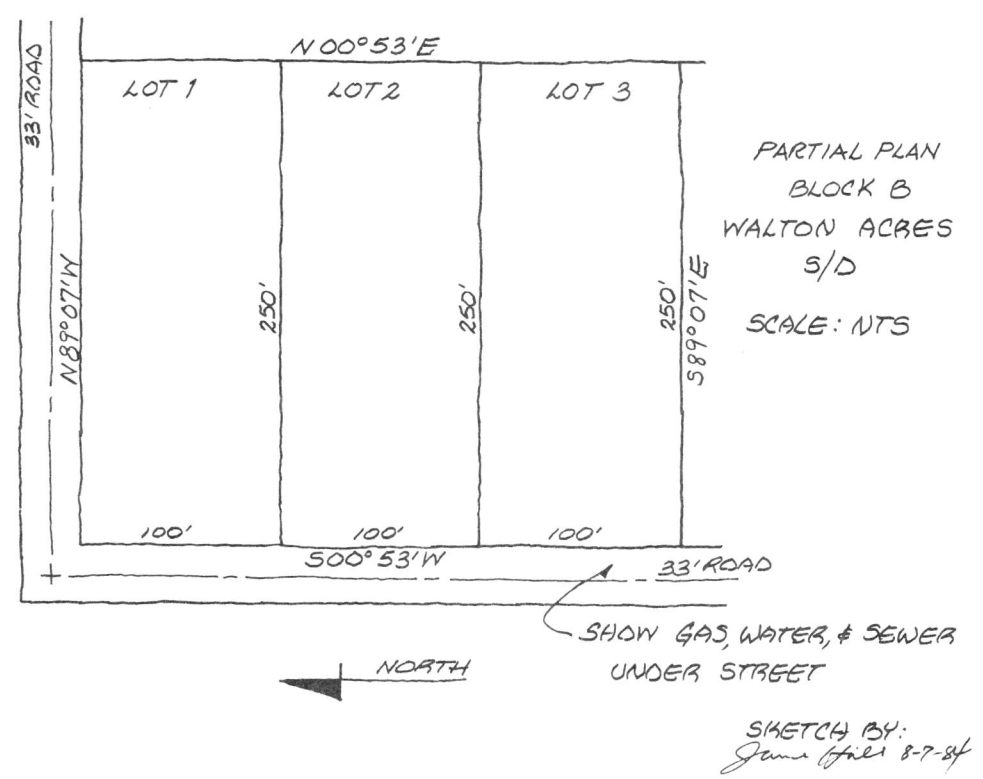

**Figure 8–12** Application project 7.

**Project 8:** Figure 8–13 is an engineer's sketch of a plot plan for a residential dwelling. Redraw the plot plan using proper symbols.

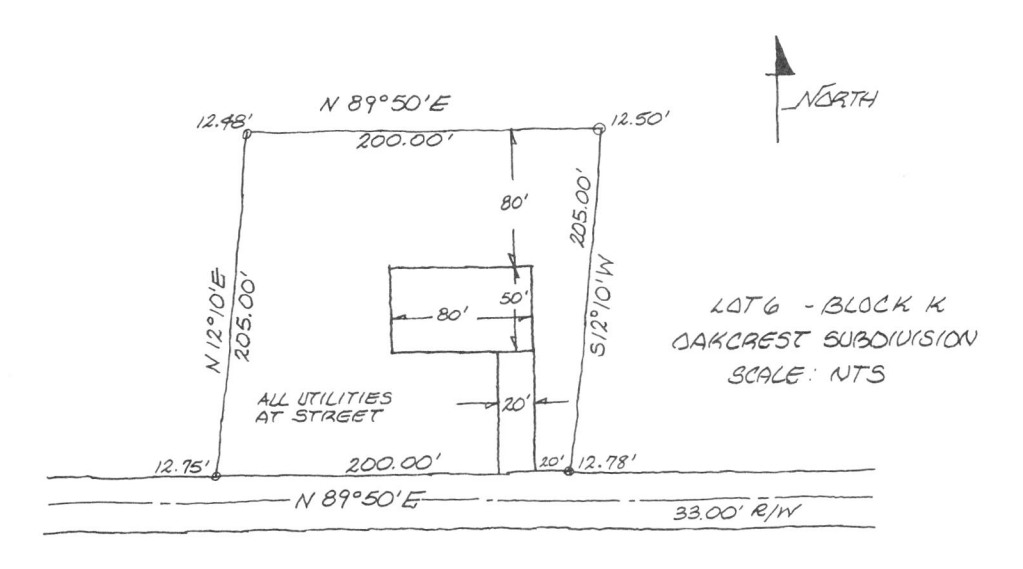

**Figure 8–13** Application project 8.

# chapter 9
# Structural Engineering Drawings

## DEFINITION, PURPOSE, AND CONTENTS

A complete set of architectural plans for a commercial or industrial building contains structural drawings prepared under the supervision of a structural engineer. Structural drawings are of two types: engineering drawings and shop drawings. This chapter deals with engineering drawings.

Structural engineering drawings are those required to define the structural or load-bearing components of the building. These components include such elements as footings, foundations, floor systems, wall systems, roof systems, columns, beams, and joists. In order to describe the design of these components, engineering drawings must include such things as framing plans, sections, and details. Figures 9–1 through 9–7 contain examples of engineering drawings produced on modern CAD systems.

Figure 9–1 contains two sectional views of the framing of a structural steel building that will have eight complete floors and a penthouse. Notice the notes that refer tradespeople to details. Figure 9–2 is a sectional view in elevation showing the rest of the framing configuration for the building in Figure 9–1. Figure 9–3 on page 128 is the roof framing plan for the same building. Notice the continuity in lettering and linework and the overall readability of the drawing. Figures 9–4 on page 129 and 9–5 on page 130 are column and wall framing plans for the building. Figures 9–6 and 9–7 on page 131 are sectional views in elevation showing two different views of the mechanical room for a large commercial building.

The purpose of a structural engineering drawing is to communicate the design of the structural or load-bearing'' skeleton of a building. Framing plans such as roof, floor, column, and beam plans serve the same purpose in the structural drawings that floor plans serve in architectural drawings. The contents of framing plans vary according to the type of framing plan. The contents of sections and details also vary just as they do in architectural plans. This makes it impossible to list the contents of a structural engineering drawing. However, there is a rule of thumb that drafters should follow in producing structural engineering drawings on a CAD system: INCLUDE ANY AND ALL INFORMATION THAT YOU WOULD NEED AS A TRADESPERSON TRYING TO CONSTRUCT THE BUILDING FROM THE DRAWING, BUT ONLY THAT INFORMATION.

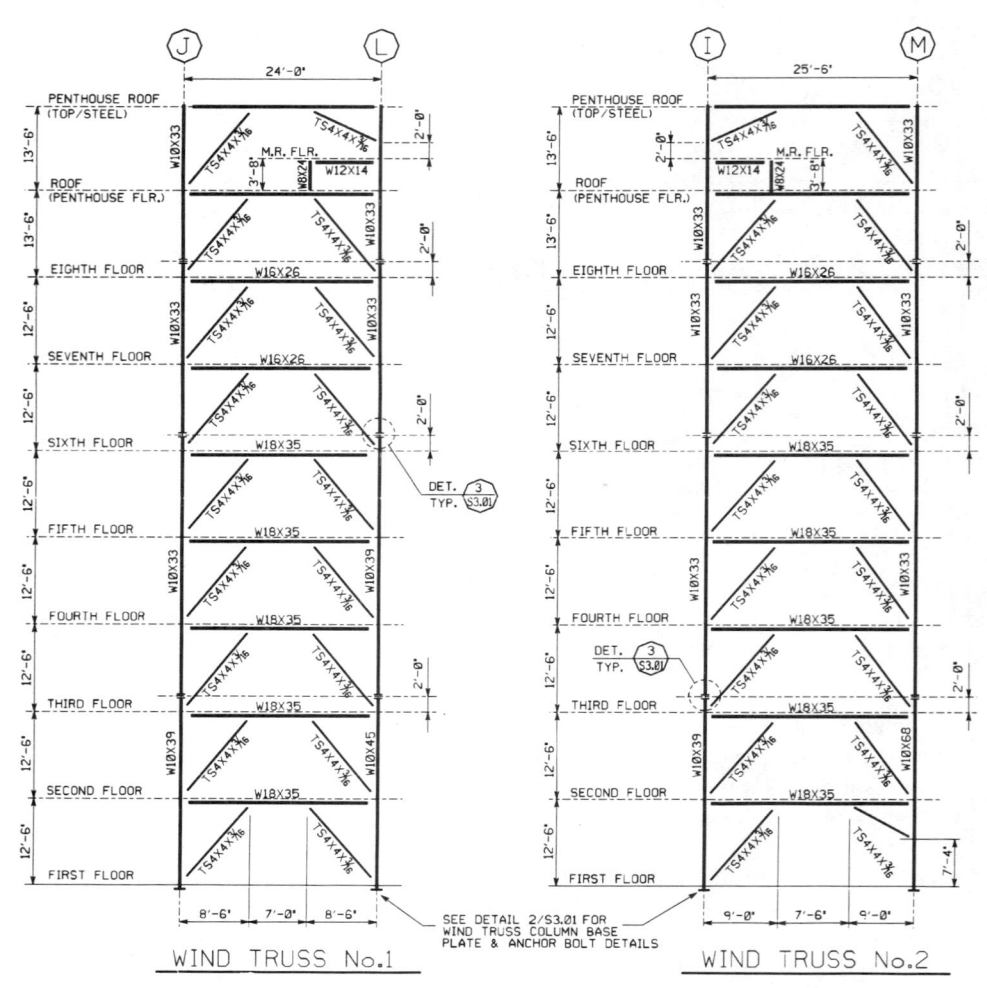

**Figure 9–1** Sectional engineering drawing. *(Courtesy of Intergraph Corporation.)*

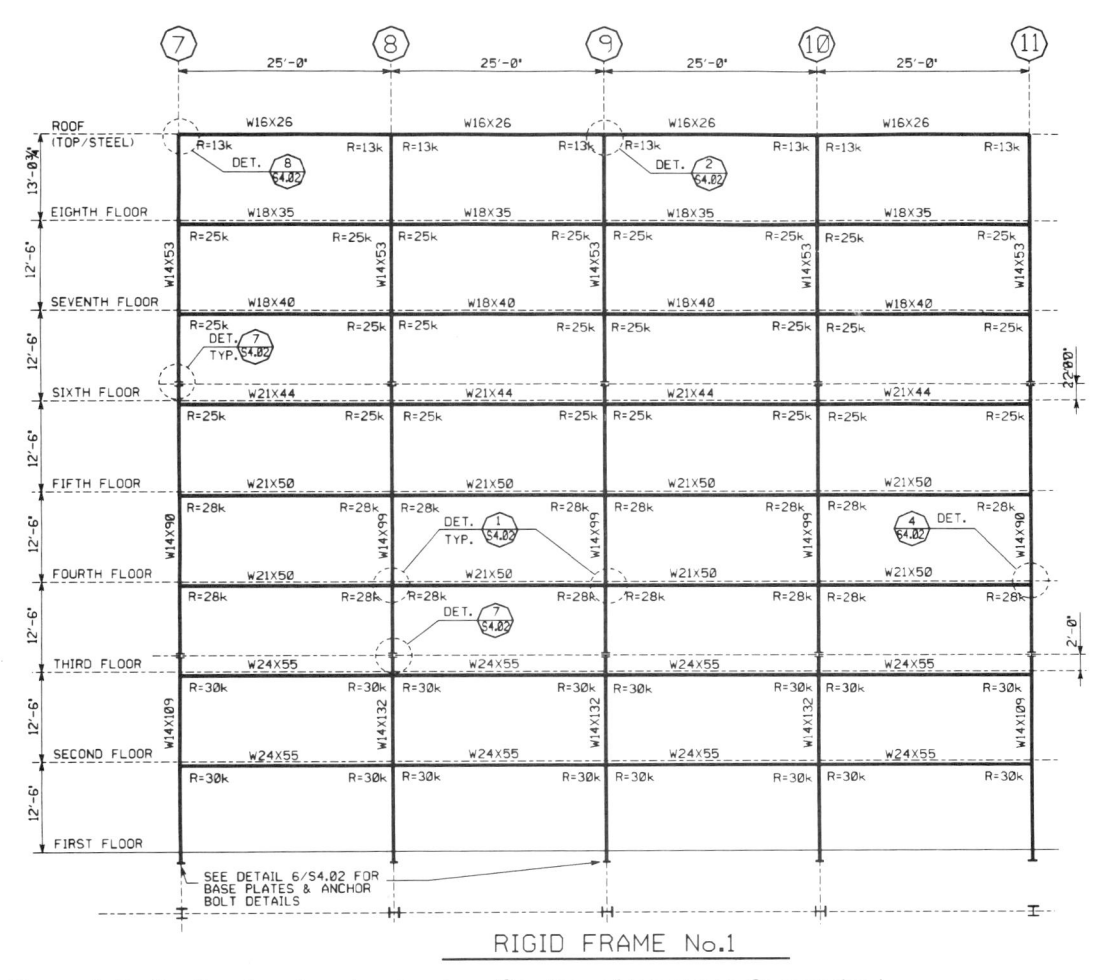

**Figure 9–2** Sectional engineering drawing. *(Courtesy of Intergraph Corporation.)*

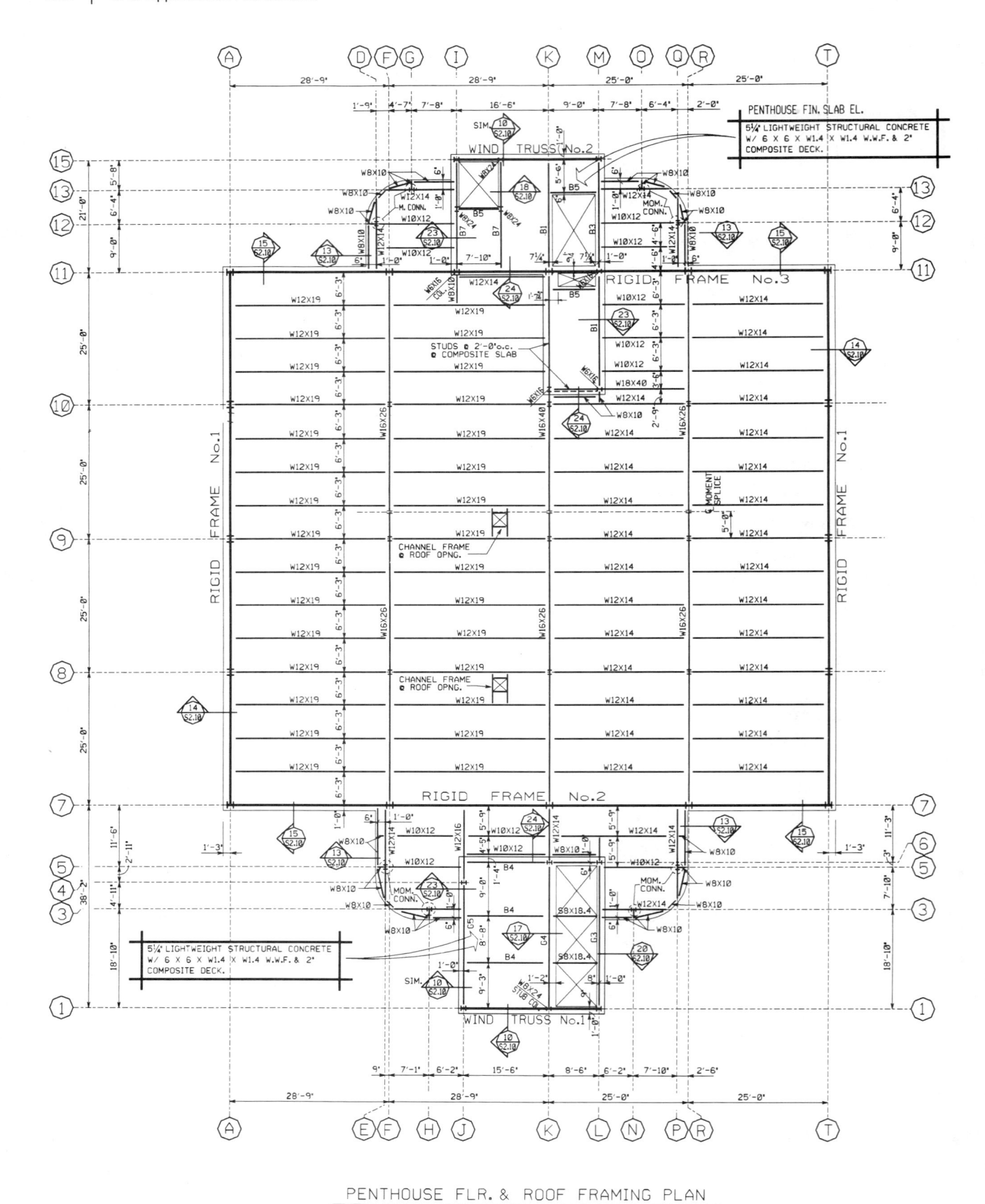

**Figure 9–3** Roof framing plan. *(Courtesy of Intergraph Corporation.)*

Chapter 9 Structural Engineering Drawings | **129**

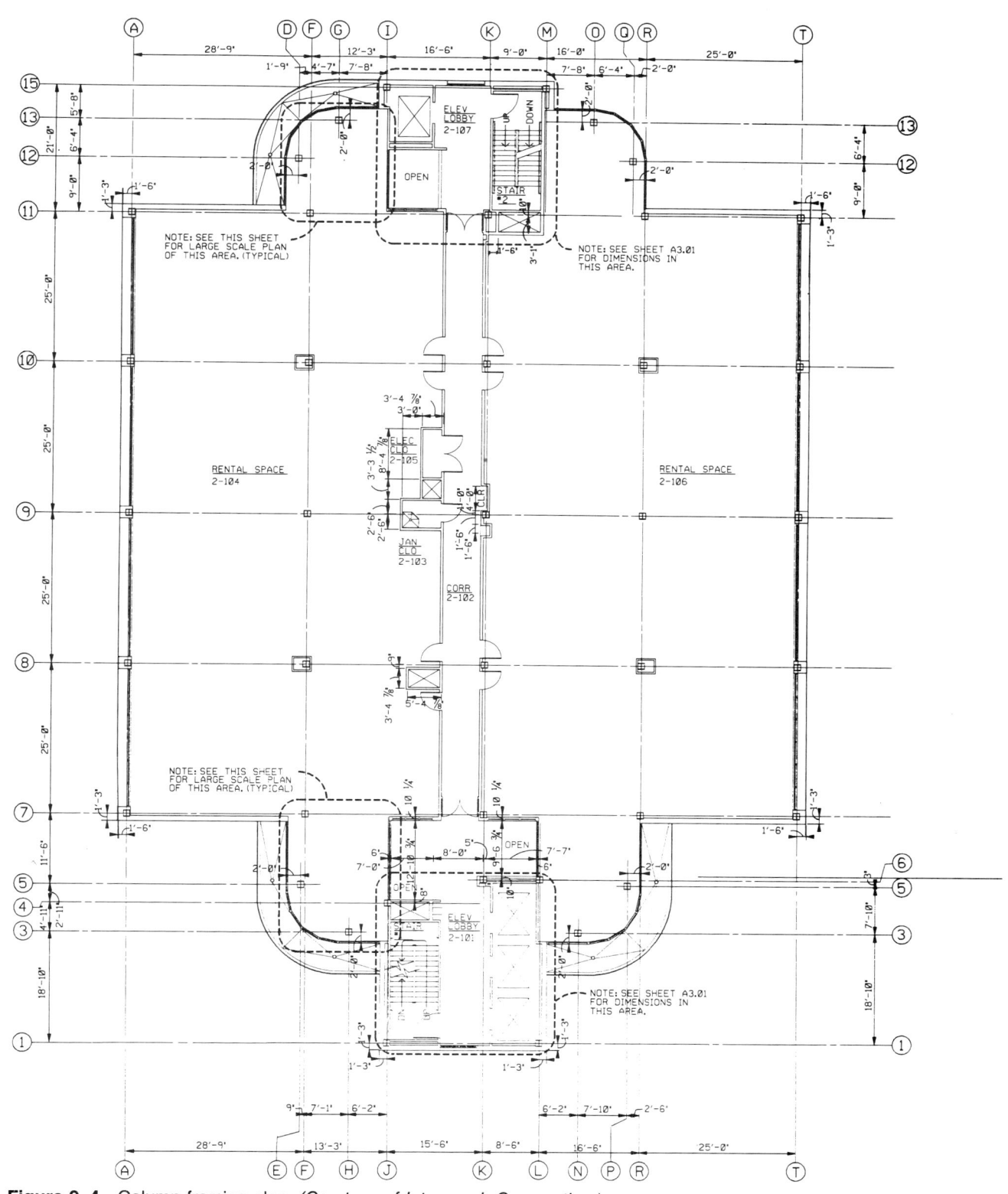

**Figure 9–4** Column framing plan. *(Courtesy of Intergraph Corporation.)*

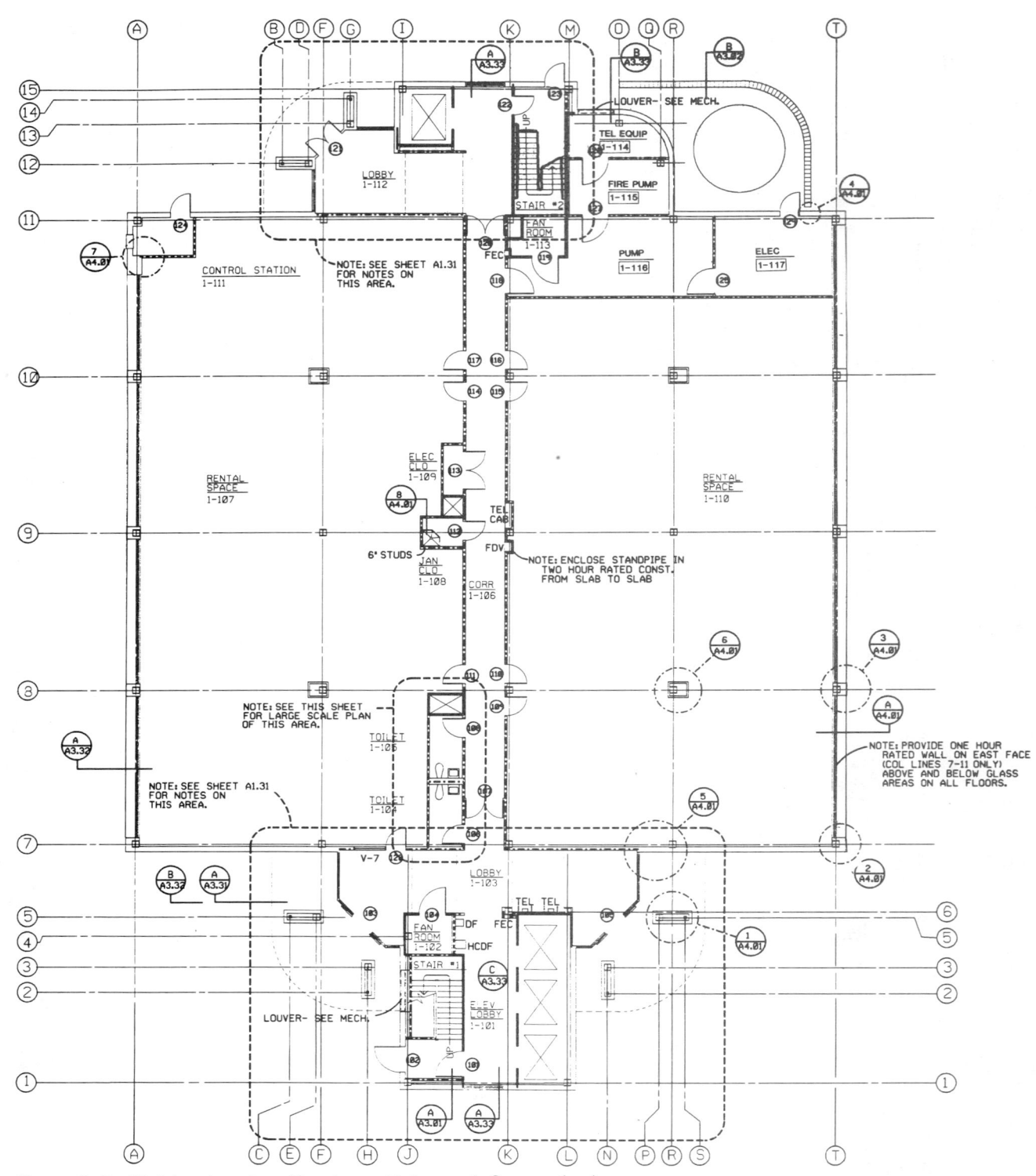

**Figure 9–5** Wall framing plan. *(Courtesy of Intergraph Corporation.)*

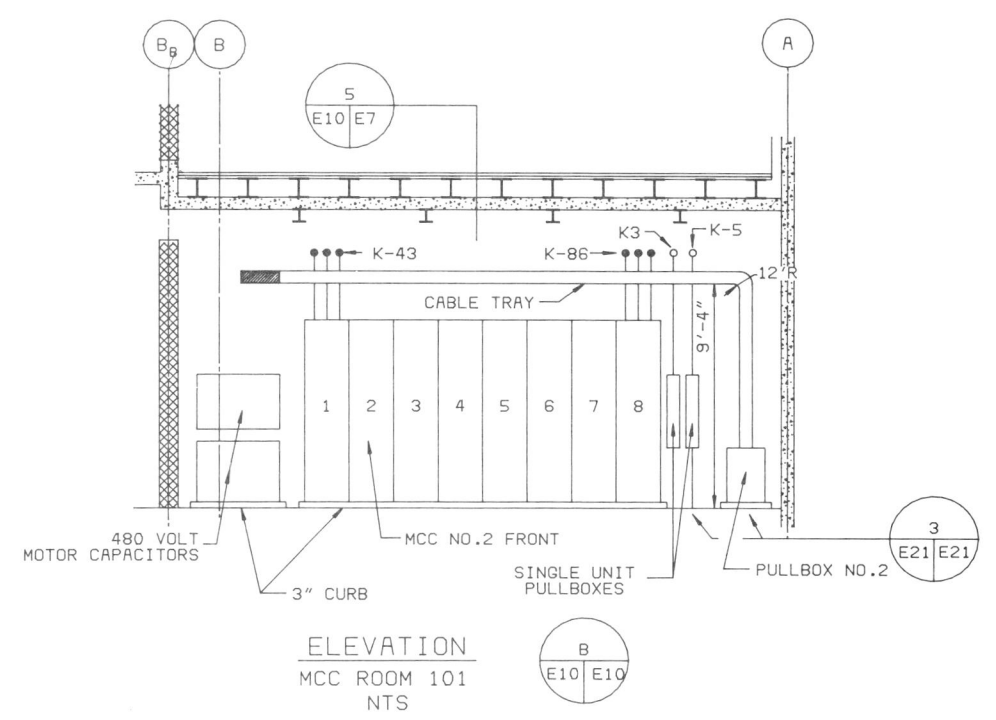

**Figure 9–6** Sectional elevation. *(Courtesy of Rust Engineering Company.)*

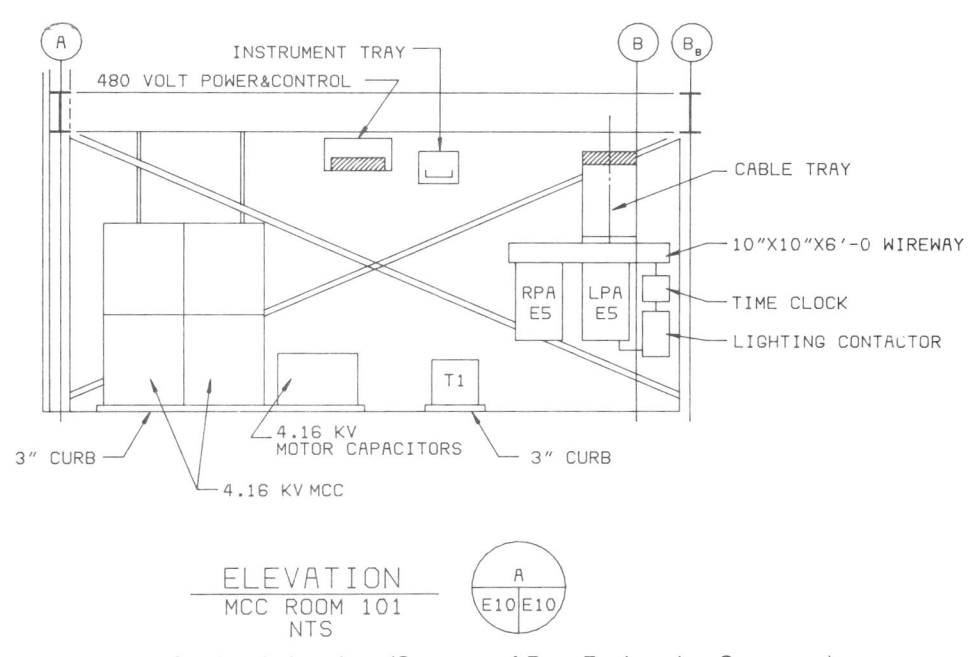

**Figure 9–7** Sectional elevation. *(Courtesy of Rust Engineering Company.)*

## SPECIAL SYMBOLS NEEDED

The symbols used in preparing structural engineering drawings on a CAD system vary as much as the drawings themselves. There are shape symbols and sectioning symbols. There are symbols for steel construction, symbols for concrete construction, and symbols for laminated wood and heavy timber construction. Figure 9–8 contains the shape and sectioning symbols used most frequently in preparing structural steel engineering drawings. Figure 9–9 contains the shape and sectioning symbols used most frequently in preparing precast and prestressed concrete engineering drawings. Of course, the sectioning symbols are also used in preparing poured-in-place concrete engineering drawings. Figure 9–10 combines the shape and sectioning symbols used most frequently in preparing laminated wood and heavy timber engineering drawings.

Examine the symbols library of your CAD system to determine which of these symbols it contains. If the symbols library does not contain a particular symbol, you have two options:

STRUCTURAL STEEL SHAPE SYMBOLS

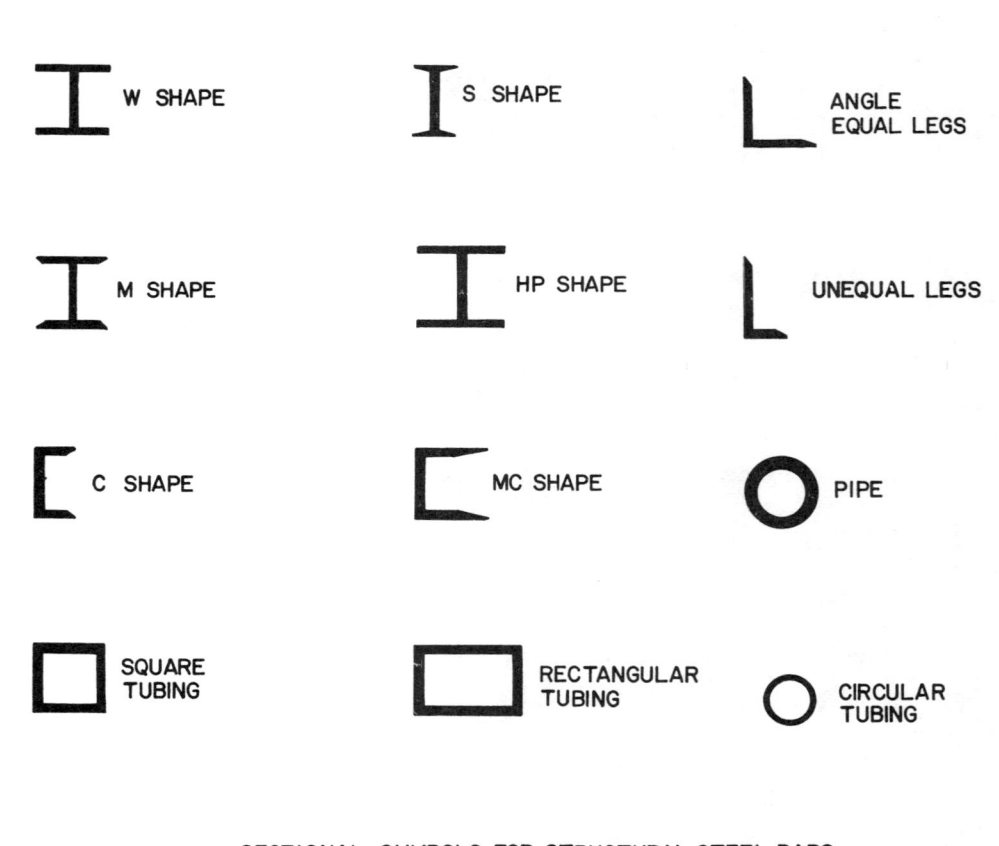

| W SHAPE | S SHAPE | ANGLE EQUAL LEGS |
| M SHAPE | HP SHAPE | UNEQUAL LEGS |
| C SHAPE | MC SHAPE | PIPE |
| SQUARE TUBING | RECTANGULAR TUBING | CIRCULAR TUBING |

SECTIONAL SYMBOLS FOR STRUCTURAL STEEL BARS

ROUND BAR   SQUARE BAR   RECTANGULAR BAR   HEXAGONAL BAR

**Figure 9–8** Structural steel symbols.

1. Create the symbol and add it to the symbols library. This can only be done on those CAD systems that are programmed to accept user-defined symbols.
2. Construct the symbols on the drawing as they are needed, using the appropriate geometric characters and commands. For example, the ''steel'' sectioning symbol can be made using the SOLID LINES command. The ''cast concrete'' symbol can be made using the POINT command.

PRECAST CONCRETE SHAPE SYMBOLS

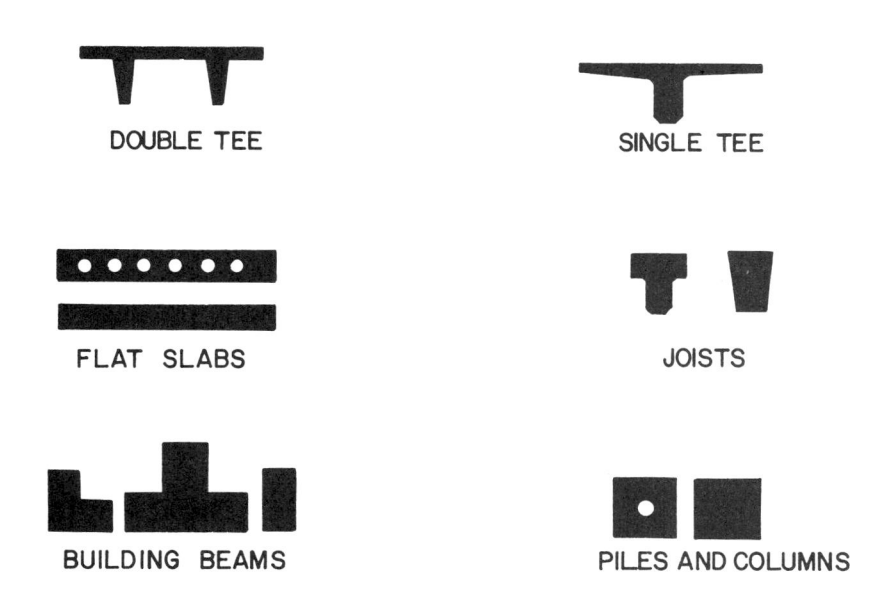

DOUBLE TEE

SINGLE TEE

FLAT SLABS

JOISTS

BUILDING BEAMS

PILES AND COLUMNS

CONCRETE SECTIONING SYMBOLS

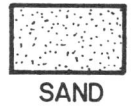

CONCRETE BLOCK  CAST CONCRETE  CINDER CONCRETE  EARTH  SAND

**Figure 9–9** Concrete symbols.

WOOD SHAPE AND SECTIONING SYMBOLS

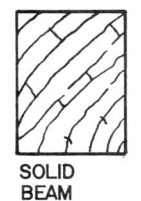

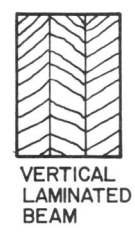

SOLID BEAM  HORIZONTAL LAMINATED BEAM  VERTICAL LAMINATED BEAM  STEEL REINFORCED BEAM  BOX BEAM

**Figure 9–10** Wood symbols.

## CAD COMMANDS AND FUNCTIONS USED

There are several different commands and functions used in producing structural engineering drawings on a CAD system. Most CAD systems have these commands and functions, but they are often given different names on different systems (see Chapter 2).

The generic names of the commands and functions used to produce structural engineering drawings on a CAD system are listed in the Commands and Functions chart. Before attempting the application projects in this chapter, match the generic commands and functions listed with their corresponding commands and functions on your CAD system.

### COMMANDS AND FUNCTIONS

**Graphic Creation Commands**

- √ Point
- √ Solid Line
- √ Hidden Line
- √ Construction Line
- √ Dashed Line
- √ Center Line
- √ Rectangle
- √ Circle
- √ Arc
- √ Irregular Curve
- √ Ellipse
- √ Polygon
- ___ Grid
- ___ XYPT
- ___ Polar
- ___ Line Weight
- ___ Fillet
- ___ Chamfer
- ___ Leaders
- ___ Rect.
- ___ Hatch

**Manipulation Commands**

- √ Move
- √ Copy
- √ Rotate
- √ Scale
- √ Zoom
- √ Pan
- ___ Mirror

**Size Specification Commands**

- √ Auto. Dimension
- ___ Dimension
- ___ Tolerance
- ___ Calc. Area

**Output Commands**

- √ Plot
- ___ Print (Screen Dump)

**Text Creation Commands**

- √ Text

**Modification Commands**

- √ Edit
- √ Delete
- √ Redraw
- ___ Clip
- √ Erase

**Facilitation Commands**

- √ Save
- √ File
- √ Symbol Library
- ___ Layer
- ___ Quit
- ___ Default

## PROCEDURES FOR PREPARING THE DRAWING

What follows is an illustrated, step-by-step description of how an engineering drawing is produced on a CAD system. These procedures can be applied to any of the many different types of structural engineering drawings.

■ *Step 1*

Log-on to the system and create a drawing designation called EGNABC. Substitute your initials for the ABC. Decide what size medium the completed drawing will be plotted on.

■ *Step 2*

Lay out the overall shape of the roof framing plan using the CONSTRUCTION LINES function if it is available and SOLID LINES if it is not. You can save time by beginning on the right side of the framing plan, creating one full-sized member using either CONSTRUCTION LINES or SOLID LINES, and using the COPY function to produce the other 10 full-sized members. Return to the CONSTRUCTION LINES or SOLID LINES command to create the member that is not a full width. You may wish to use the COPY command for creating the three blockouts in the roof also, Figure 9–11.

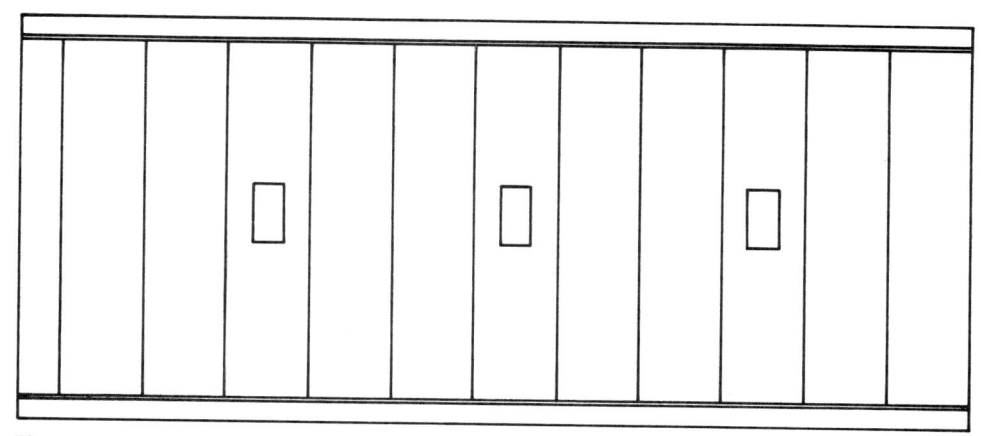

**Figure 9–11** Illustration for Step 2.

■ *Step 3*

Convert all construction lines to solid lines. Switch to the HIDDEN LINES mode and add the hidden lines for the beams under the roof members. Switch to the DASHED LINES mode and add the centerline of stem lines for each roof member, Figure 9–12.

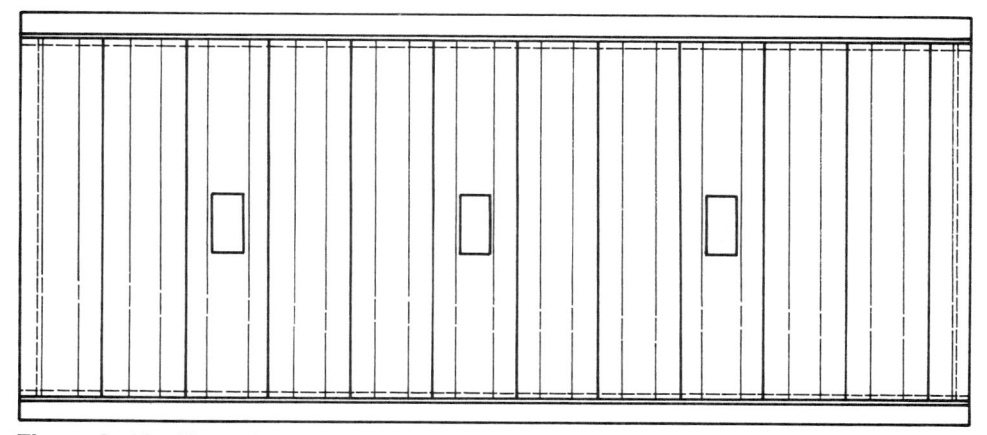

**Figure 9–12** Illustration for Step 3.

■ *Step 4*

Switch to the DIMENSION mode and add all required dimensions. Switch to the TEXT mode and add all required annotation. Add the sectioning symbols last. If your system has sectioning symbols in the symbols library, use them. If not, the symbols can be created using the CIRCLE, SOLID LINES, and ARC functions, Figure 9–13. SAVE the completed drawing and plot it.

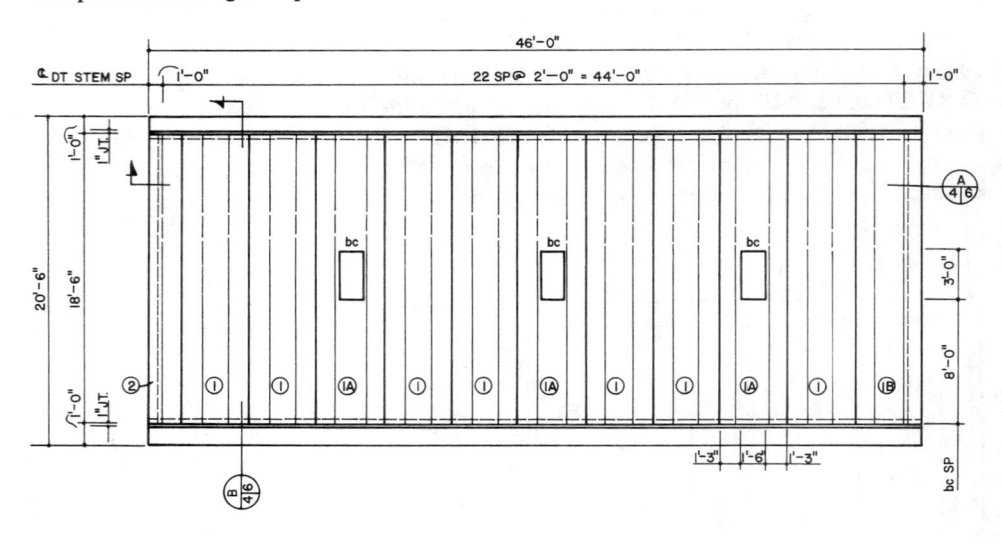

**Figure 9–13**   Illustration for Step 4.

## REVIEW QUESTIONS

The following questions are provided as a review of Chapter 9 and should be completed before attempting the application projects for the chapter. Write your answers in the spaces provided.

1. Define "structural engineering drawing."

2. Name four typical components of structural engineering drawings.

3. Name the three types of drawing normally required to describe the components listed in question 2.

4. What is meant by "load bearing"?

5. What is the rule of thumb to follow in deciding what should be contained on a structural engineering drawing?

6. Sketch the symbols for the following:
   Steel (in section)—

   Circular steel tubing (shape)—

Square steel tubing (shape)—

Concrete block (in section)—

Earth (in section)—

Solid beam (in section)—

Vertical laminated beam (in section)—

7. What is your CAD system's command for the generic command IRREGULAR CURVE?

8. Explain the steps you would use to create the "solid beam" symbol on a drawing if it is not contained in the symbols library of your CAD system.

9. Explain the steps you would use to create the "earth" symbol on a drawing if it is not contained in the symbols library of your CAD system.

10. Explain the steps you would use to create the "vertical laminated beam" symbol on a drawing if it is not contained in the symbols library of your CAD system.

# APPLICATION PROJECTS

The following application projects are provided to help you become proficient in producing structural engineering drawings on a CAD system. To ensure that you use input, modification, and manipulation functions, you will be required to reconstruct an engineering drawing as shown and make modifications to it. To ensure that you use facilitation and output functions, SAVE each completed drawing and PLOT it on the size and type of medium specified by your instructor.

**Project 1:** Figure 9–14 is an engineering drawing for a commercial building with a concrete foundation system. Reconstruct the engineering drawing as shown on your CAD system. Then, make the following changes:

1. Change the overall dimensions of the foundation from 80'-0" × 96'-0" to 86'-0" × 98'-0" and adjust all affected dimensions accordingly.
2. Change the concrete slab to 6" thick.
3. Add another 3'-4" door to the front wall, spaced in from the left side the same as the existing door opening.
4. Take out the 6'-4" door opening in the right-hand wall.

FOUNDATION PLAN

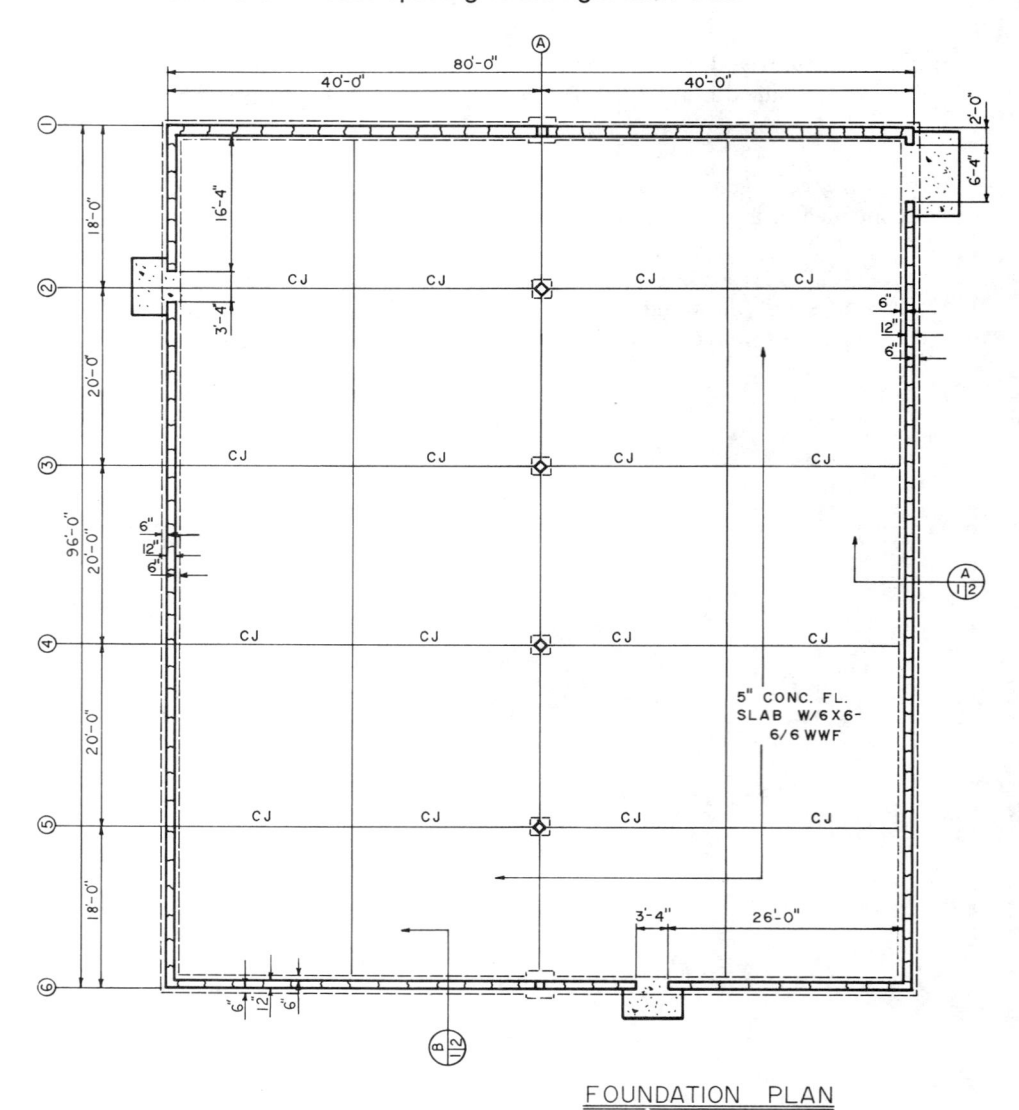

**Figure 9–14** Application projects 1 and 2.

**Project 2:** Using Figure 9–14 as a guide, create a foundation plan for a commercial building with a 4" concrete floor. The drawing should have the same configuration as Figure 9–14, but the overall dimensions are 70'-0" × 86'-0".

**Project 3:** Figure 9–15 is an engineering drawing of a roof-framing plan for a concrete roof that will be poured in place. Reconstruct the engineering drawing on your CAD system as shown. Then, make the following changes:

1. Change the overall dimensions from 61'-4" to 64'-0" and adjust all affected dimensions accordingly.
2. Change the longitudinal reinforcing from #6 bars at 6" on center to #4 bars at 6" on center.
3. Change the cross reinforcing from #5 bars at 6" on center to #4 bars at 6" on center.
4. Change Section B to Section A and Section C to Section B.

**Project 4:** Using Figure 9–15 as a guide, create a roof-framing plan for a building with the exact same configuration, but with the following outside dimensions: 56'-0" × 56'-0".

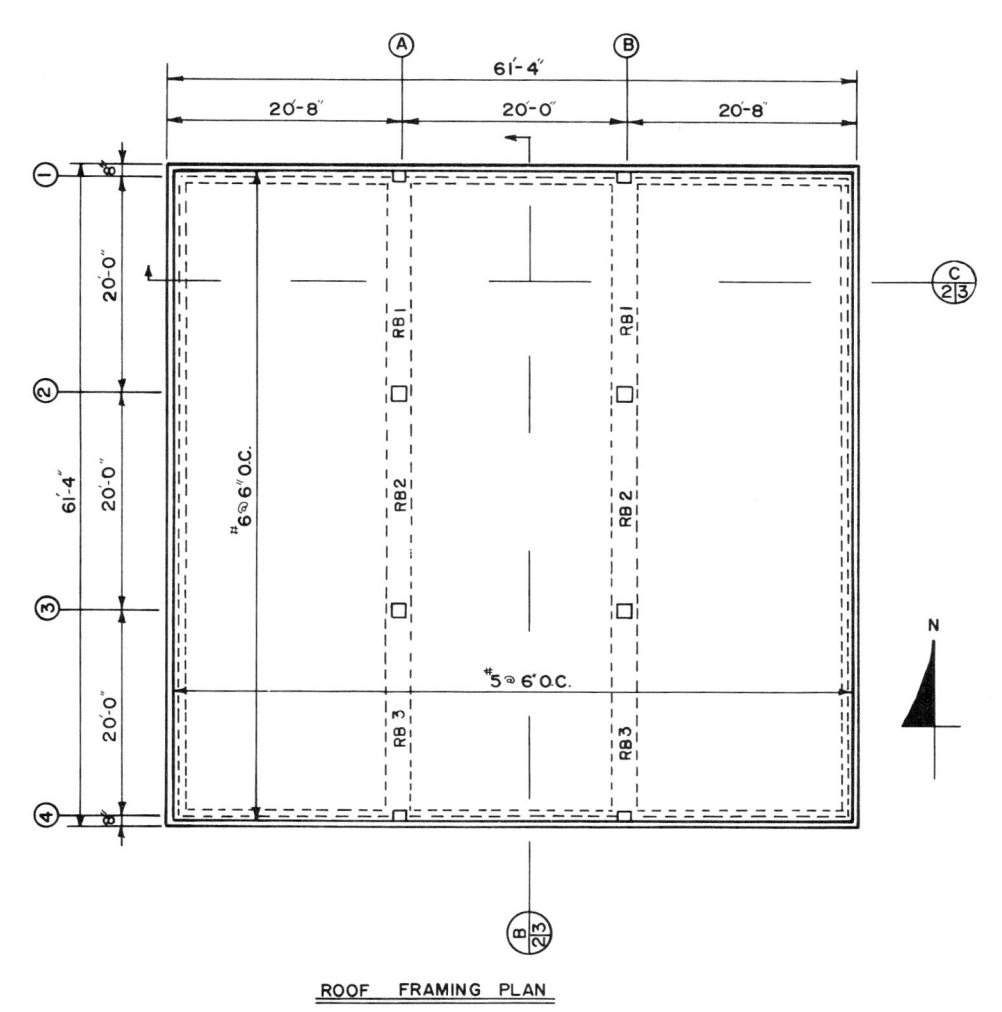

**Figure 9–15** Application projects 3 and 4.

**Project 5:** Figure 9–16 is a sectional engineering drawing for a commercial building with concrete columns, beams, wall panels, and a concrete roof. Reconstruct the engineering drawing as shown on your CAD system. Then, make the following changes:

1. Change the 61'-4" dimension to 64'-0" and adjust all affected dimensions accordingly.
2. Change the 4" facia panels to 6" facia panels.
3. Change all 12" square concrete columns to 14" square concrete columns.
4. Change the 12" concrete beam to a 10" concrete beam.

**Project 6:** Using Figure 9–16 as a guide, create a sectional engineering drawing for a commercial building with the same configuration and design, but with the following differences: 12" double tee wall panels instead of facia panels and a 6" thick concrete roof.

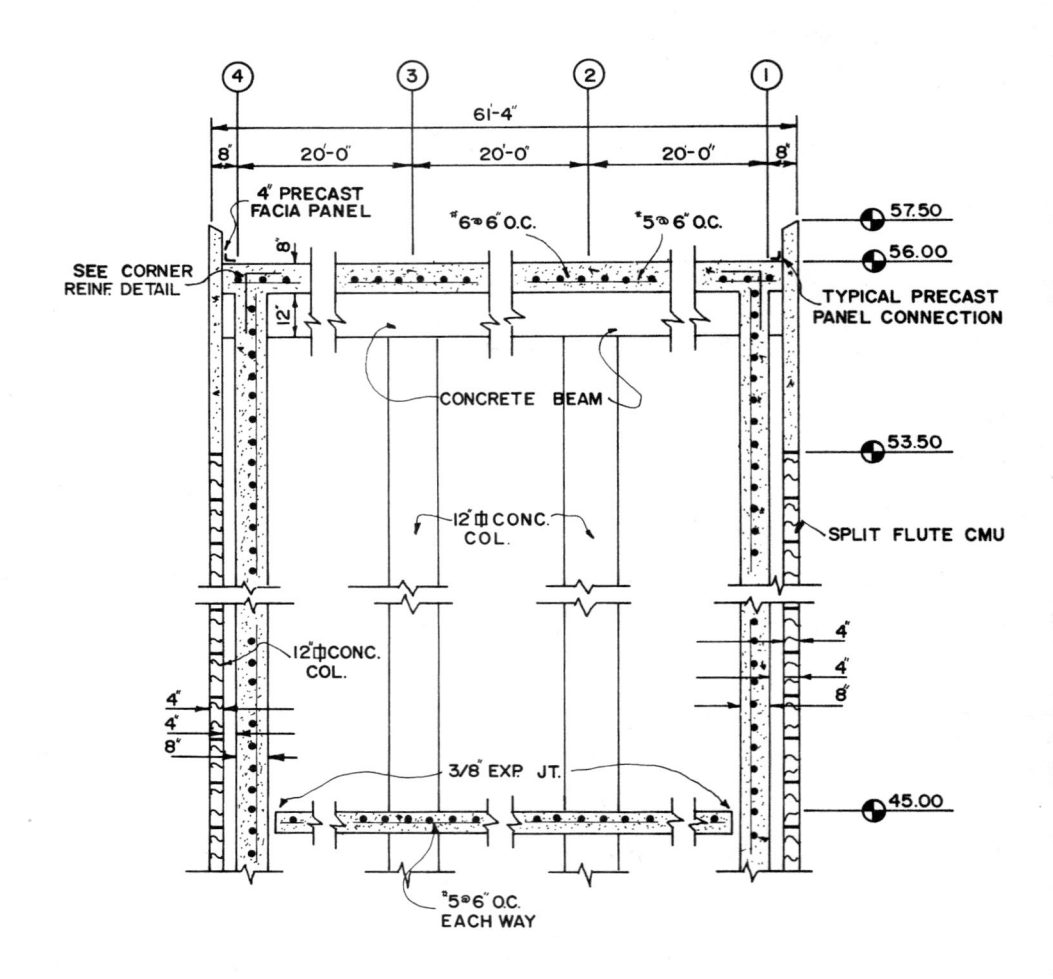

**Figure 9–16** Application projects 5 and 6.

**Project 7:** Figure 9–17 is a sectional engineering drawing for a commercial building with concrete facia panels, columns, beams, and a concrete roof. Reconstruct the engineering drawing on your CAD system as shown. Then, make the following changes:

1. Change the 61'-4" dimension to 56'-0" and adjust all affected dimensions accordingly.
2. Change the depth of the beams from 12" to 10".
3. Change the width of the beams from 20" to 18" and adjust the reinforcements accordingly.
4. Change the 12" square columns to 14" square columns.

**Project 8:** Using Figure 9–17 as a guide, create a sectional engineering drawing for a commercial building with the same configuration and design, but with the following differences: 12" double tee wall panels instead of facia panels and a 6" thick concrete roof.

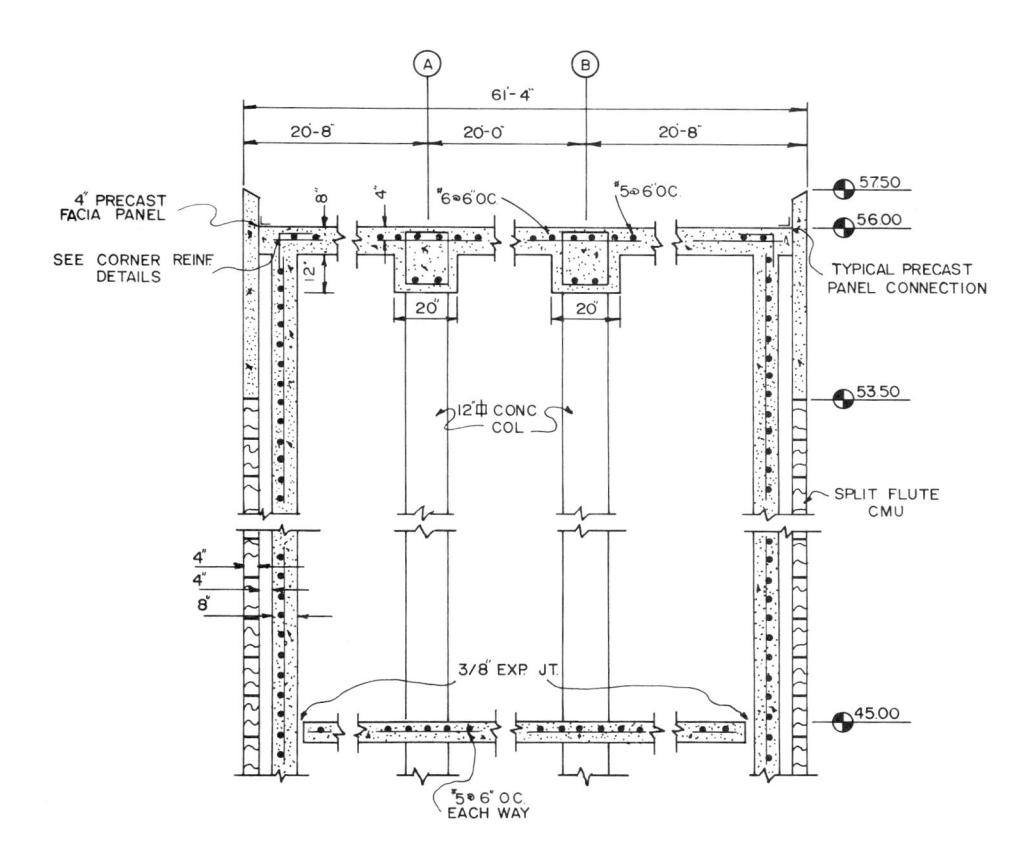

**Figure 9–17** Application projects 7 and 8.

**142** | CAD Applications: Architectural

**Project 9:** Figure 9–18 contains an engineering drawing of the layout of a power room for a commercial building with precast concrete walls. Reconstruct the engineering drawing as shown on your CAD system. A scale has been provided to assist you. Then, make the following changes:

1. Add 2'-0" to the outside dimensions and adjust the layout accordingly.
2. Take out the stairs and grating on the right side of the drawing.
3. Take out all electrical symbols and notations.

**Project 10:** Reconstruct the engineering drawing in Figure 9–18 exactly as shown, except that the new drawing should be a mirror image of Figure 9–18.

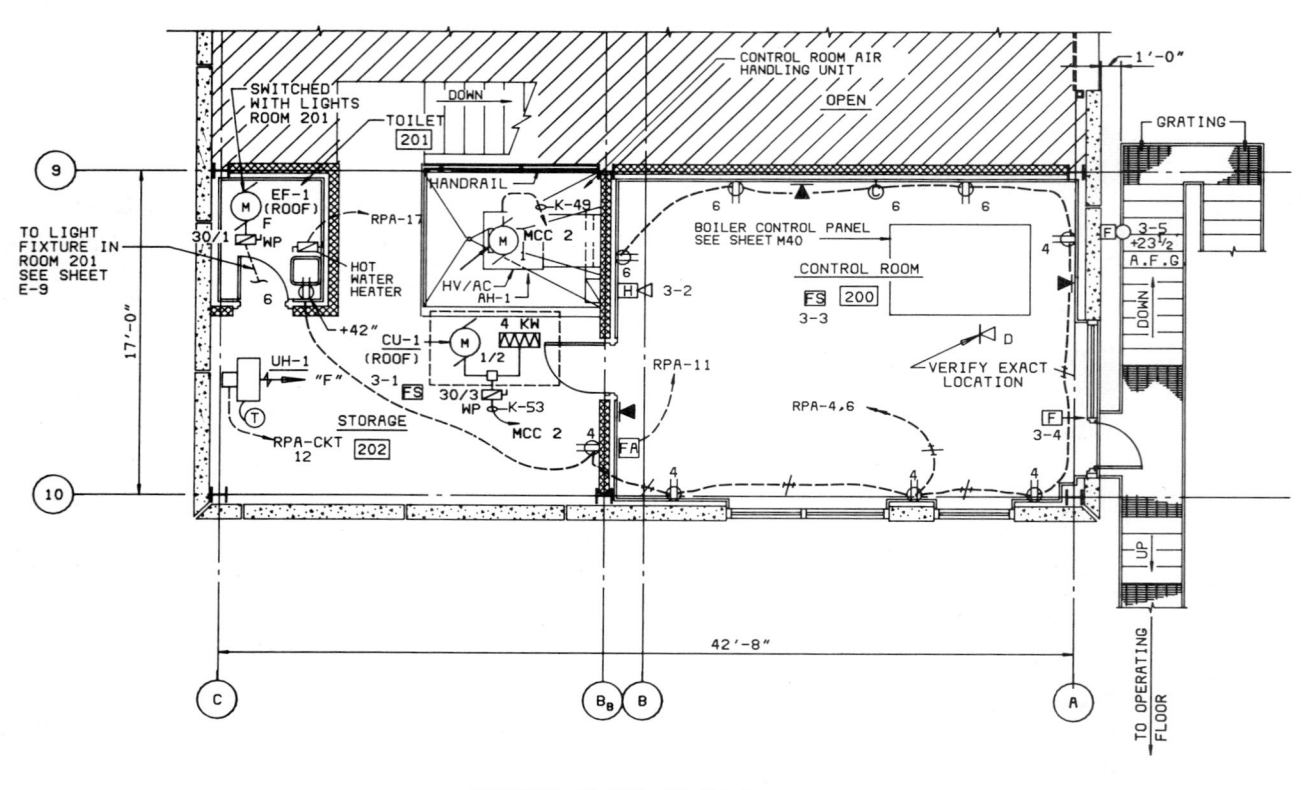

**Figure 9–18** Application projects 9 and 10.

**Project 11:** Figure 9–19 is an engineering drawing showing the foundation for a car wash. Reconstruct the engineering drawing on your CAD system as shown. Then, make the following changes:

1. Add 1'-6" to the outside dimensions and adjust accordingly.
2. Add 2" to the width of the foundation walls and adjust accordingly.
3. Add 2" to the length and width of the 2'-0" × 4'-6" hole in the floor and adjust accordingly.

**Project 12:** Reconstruct the engineering drawing in Figure 9–19 exactly as shown, except that the new drawing should be a mirror image of Figure 9–19.

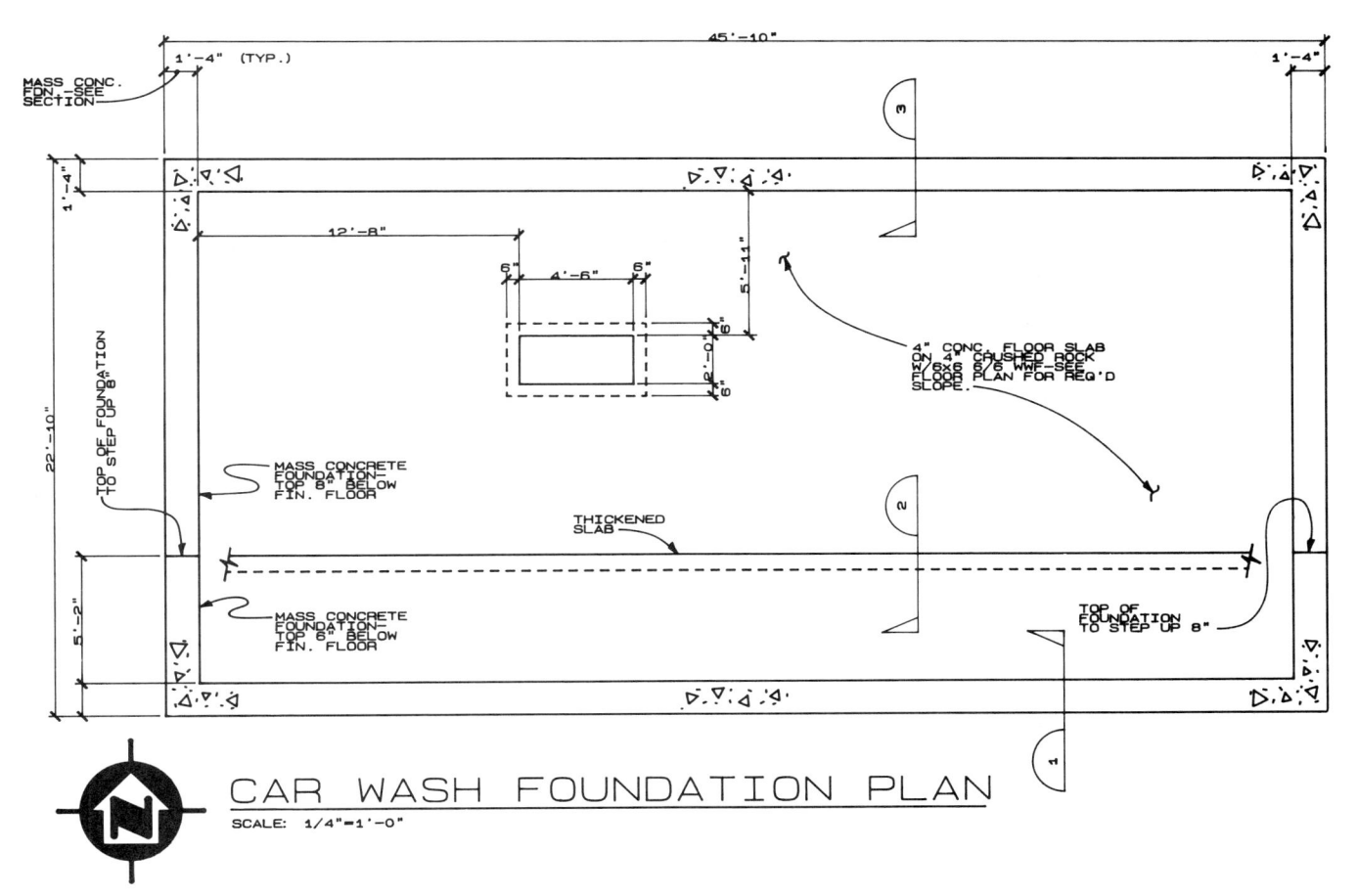

**Figure 9–19** Application projects 11 and 12. *(Courtesy of PSI Systems Corp.)*

**144** | CAD Applications: Architectural

**Project 13:** Figure 9–20 is an engineering drawing showing the foundation for a kiosk. Reconstruct the engineering drawing on your CAD system as shown. Then, make the following changes:

1. Add 1'-2" to all outside dimensions and adjust accordingly.
2. Change the width of the foundation wall to 1'-2" and adjust accordingly.
3. Take out both layers of rigid styrofoam insulation under the floor slab.

**Project 14:** Reconstruct the engineering drawing in Figure 9–20 exactly as shown, except that the new drawing should be a mirror image of Figure 9–20.

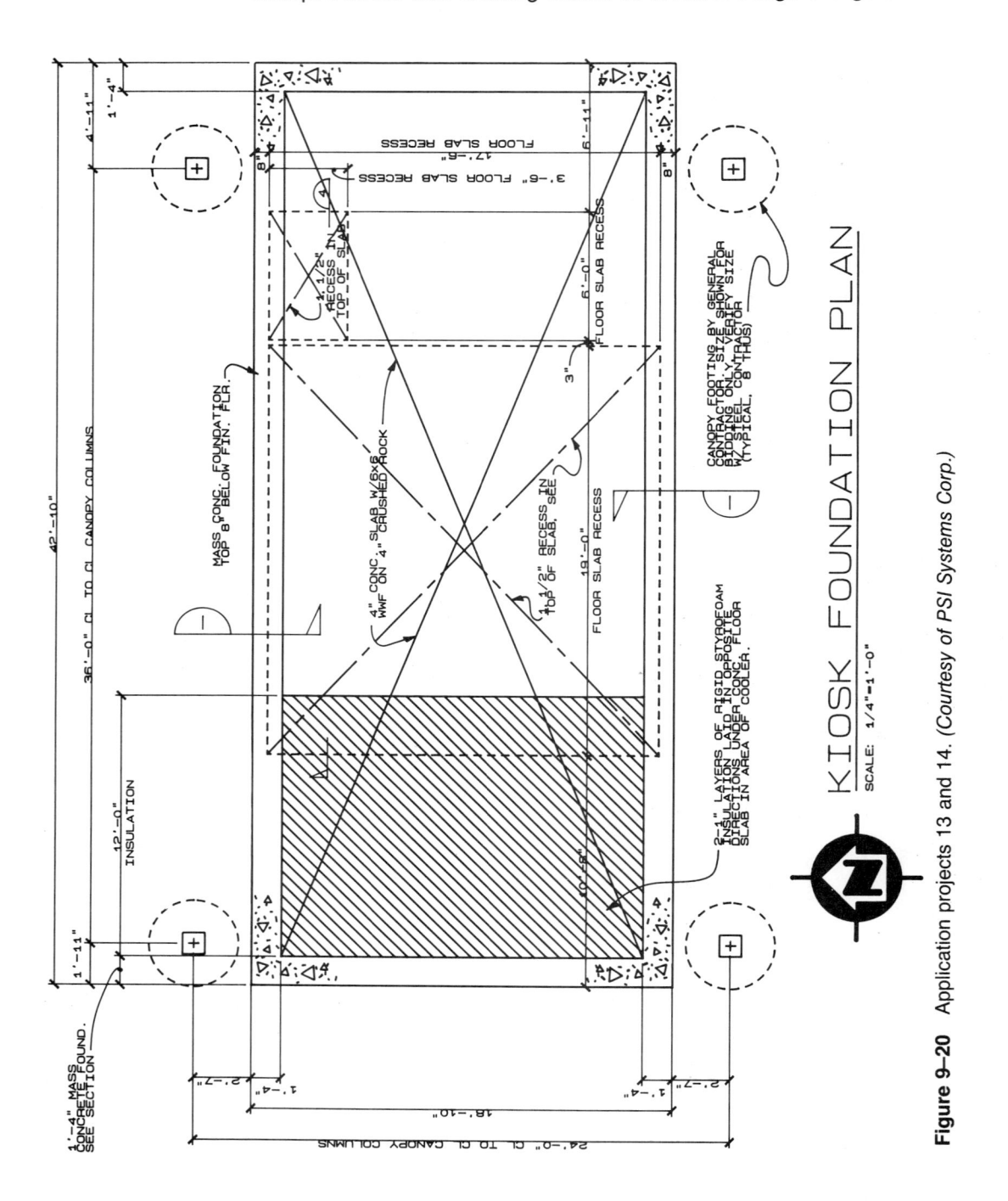

**Figure 9–20** Application projects 13 and 14. *(Courtesy of PSI Systems Corp.)*

**Project 15:** Figure 9–21 is an engineering drawing showing the floor layout of a car wash. Reconstruct the engineering drawing as shown on your CAD system. Then, make the following changes:

1. Add 1'-6" to the length and width of the car wash and adjust all affected dimensions accordingly.
2. Flip-flop the entrance and exit to the car wash and adjust accordingly.

**Project 16:** Reconstruct the engineering drawing in Figure 9–21 exactly as shown, except that the new drawing should be a mirror image of Figure 9–21.

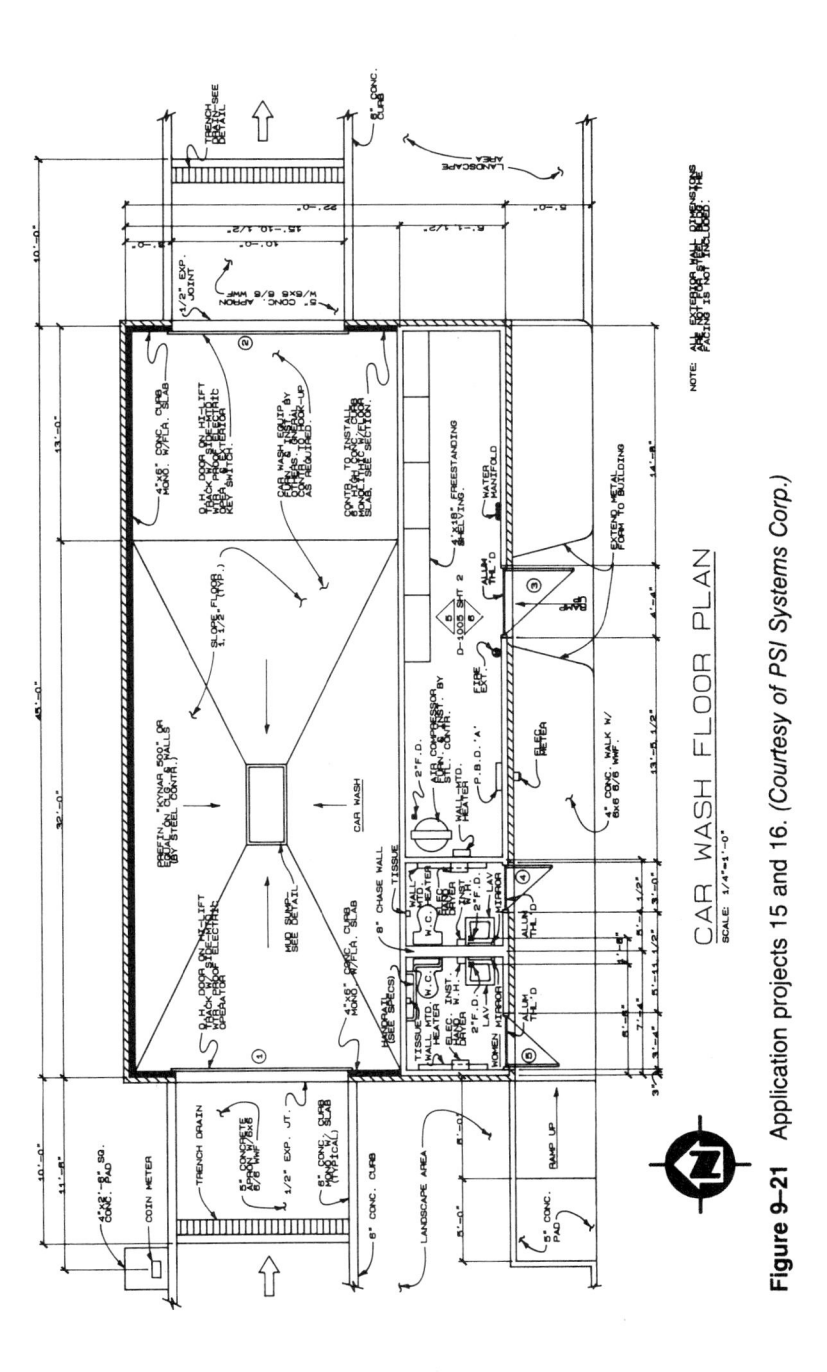

**Figure 9–21** Application projects 15 and 16. *(Courtesy of PSI Systems Corp.)*

**146** CAD Applications: Architectural

**Project 17:** Figure 9–22 contains an engineering drawing for an island kiosk. Reconstruct the engineering drawing as shown on your CAD system. Then make the following changes:

1. Add 1'-2" to the outside dimensions and adjust accordingly.
2. Flip-flop the cooler and cash register/storage areas.

**Project 18:** Reconstruct the engineering drawing in Figure 9–22 exactly as shown, except that the new drawing should be a mirror image of Figure 9–22.

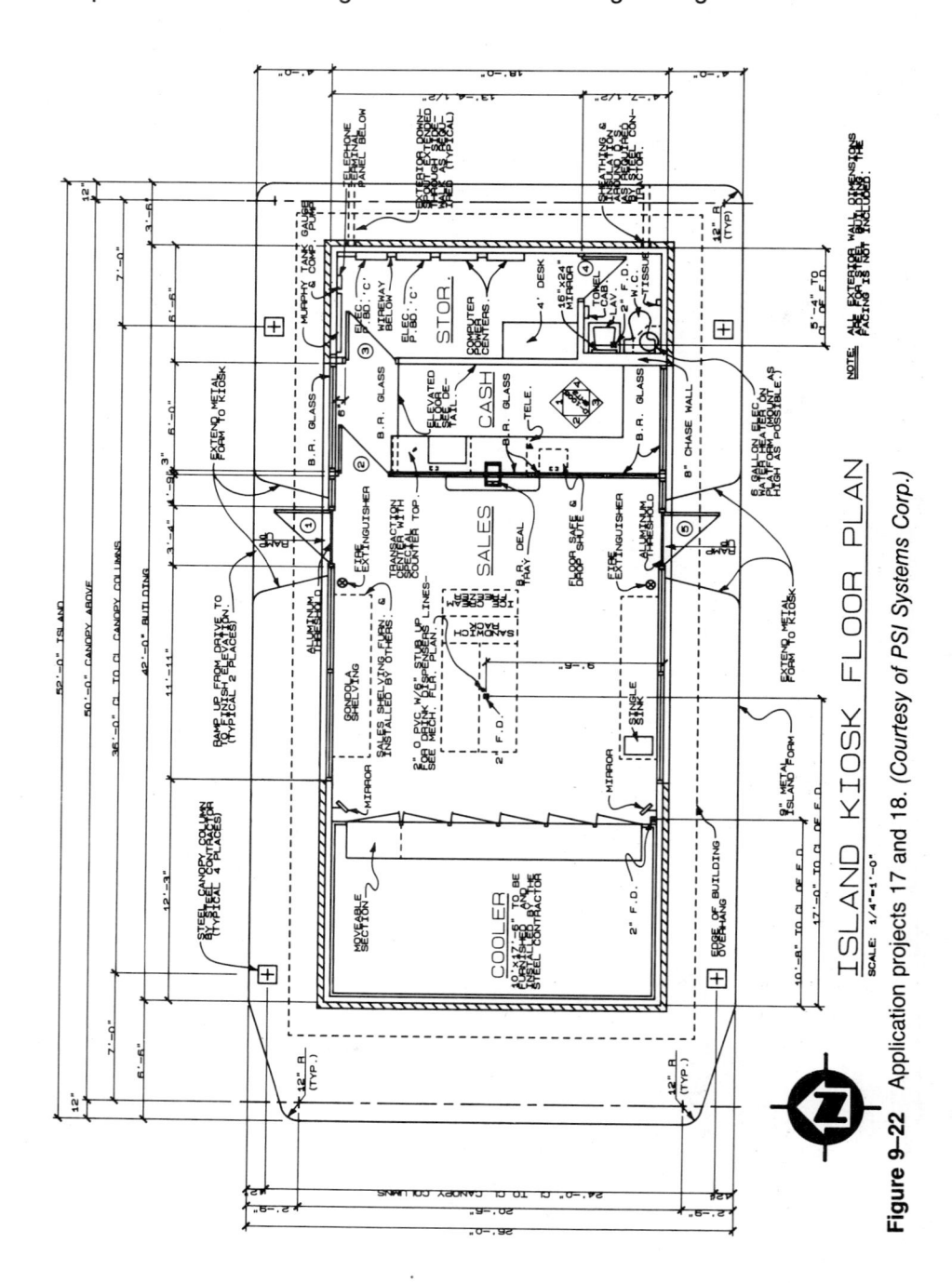

**Figure 9–22** Application projects 17 and 18. (*Courtesy of PSI Systems Corp.*)

**Project 19:** Figure 9–23 contains a sectional drawing for a commercial building with a concrete foundation wall and basement and a wooden floor and wall structure. Reconstruct the sectional drawing as shown on your CAD system. Use the following specifications for the basement area: 12″ poured concrete foundation wall, 16″ × 12″ poured concrete footing, 10′-0″ from the top of the basement floor to the bottom of the floor joists. Make the following additions:

1. Show two #4 bars 2″ off the bottom of the footing running continuously. Call them out using leader lines.
2. Show a #4 bar longitudinal reinforcement at 6″ on center throughout the foundation wall with #3 bar ties at 6″ on center. Call out the reinforcing bars and allow 1½″ of cover.

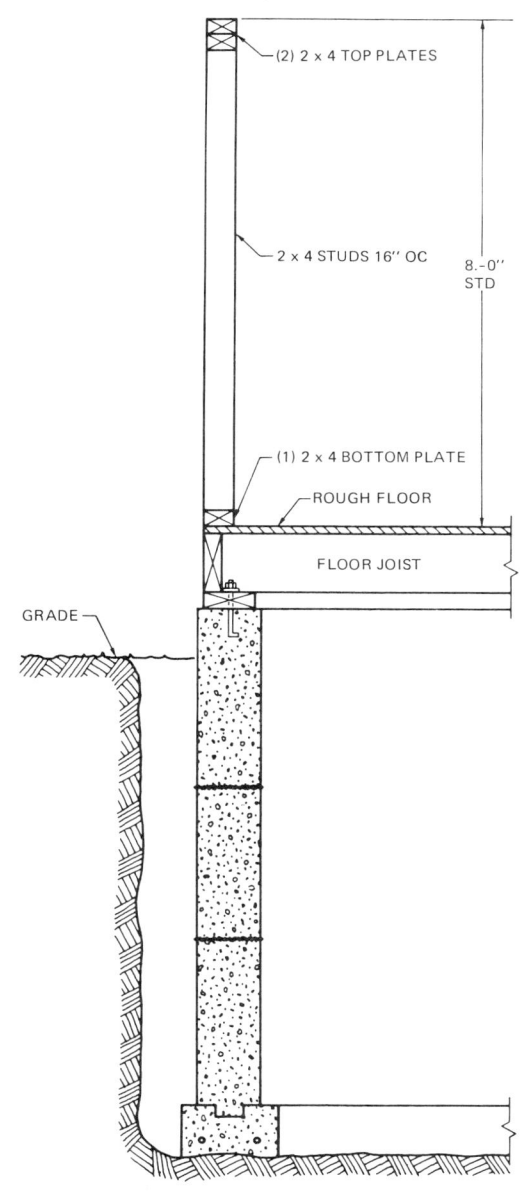

**Figure 9–23** Application project 19.

**Project 20:** Figure 9–24 contains a sectional drawing similar to the one in Figure 9–23. Repeat the instructions for Figure 9–23.

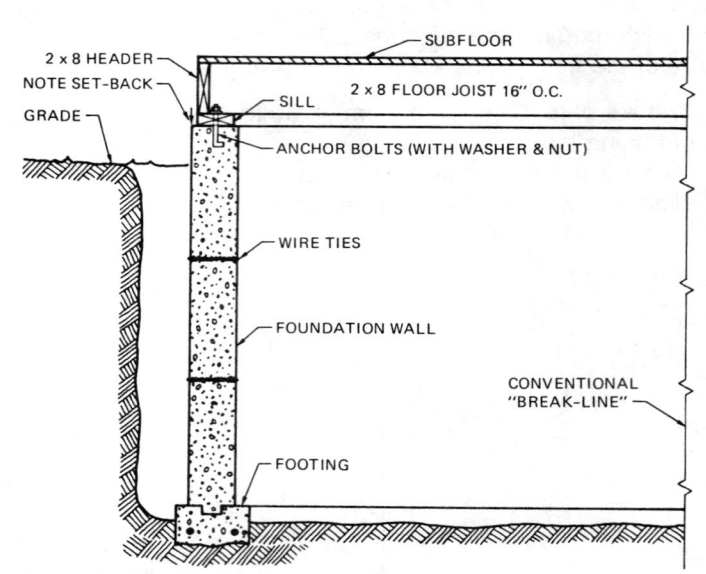

**Figure 9–24** Application project 20.

**Project 21:** Figure 9–25 contains a sectional drawing showing the formwork for a concrete foundation wall. Create a drawing of the foundation wall with the formwork stripped away, but with the reinforcing bars showing. Use the same design for the reinforcing that was used in Figure 9–23.

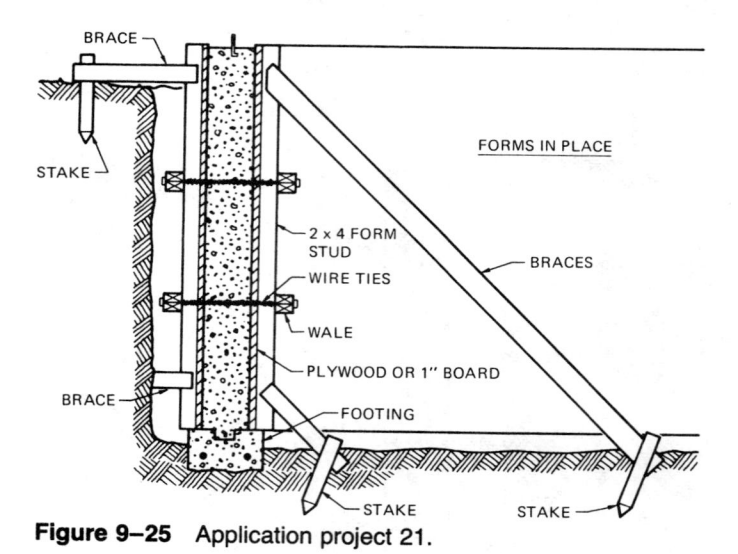

**Figure 9–25** Application project 21.

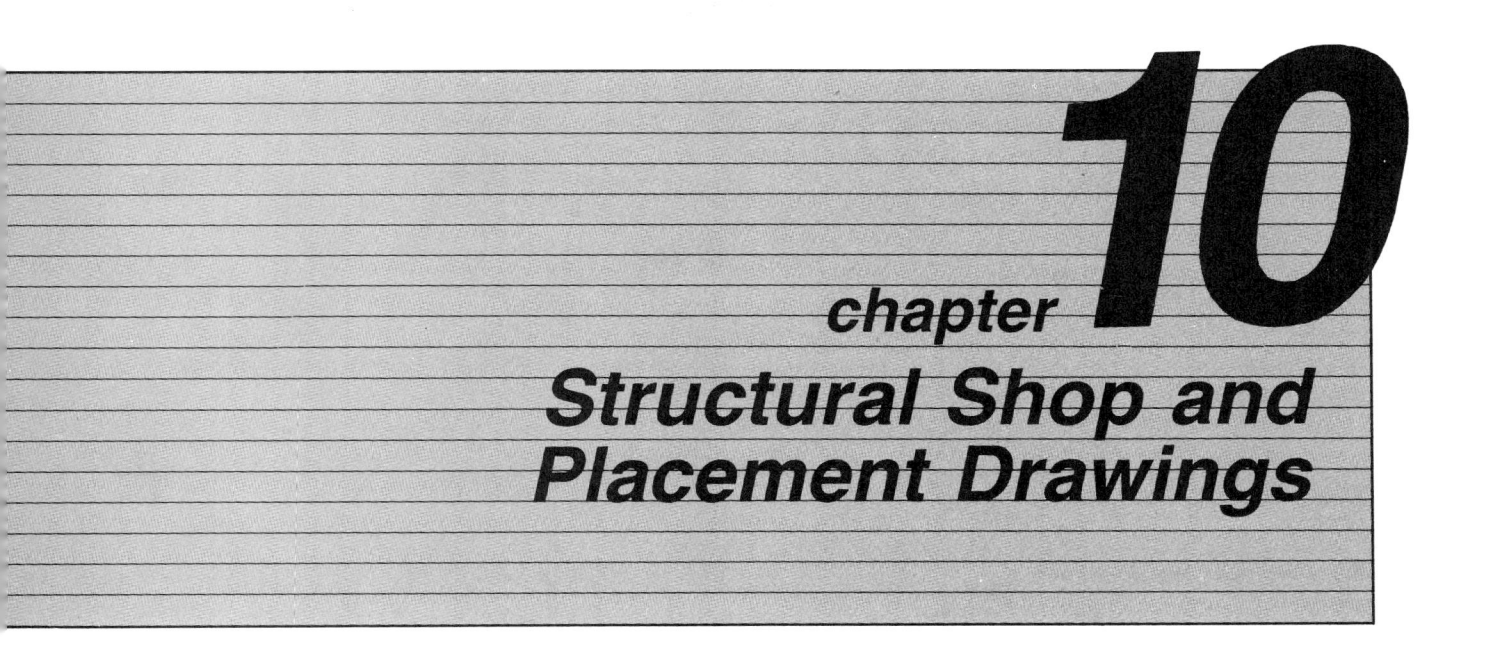

# chapter 10
# Structural Shop and Placement Drawings

## DEFINITION, PURPOSE, AND CONTENTS

Structural shop drawings are detail drawings of the structural products used in construction projects involving prefabricated products. These prefabricated products include beams, columns, joists, rafters, wall studs, wall members, floor members, and roof members. They might be made of steel, prestressed concrete, aluminum, precast concrete, laminated wood, or heavy timber.

Structural placing drawings are detail drawings used on-site for constructing structural members made of concrete that is poured in place. They are used in placing the steel reinforcing bars and in building the forms needed.

The purpose of structural shop drawings is to guide shop workers in performing all of the various tasks required to fabricate the various structural members of a prefabricated job. Drafters work from engineering drawings to produce shop drawings. A shop drawing will be made for every different structural member contained in the engineering drawings.

The purpose of placing drawings is the same. The major difference is that the work is done on-site rather than in a shop. Figures 10–1, 10–2, and 10–3 are examples of structural shop drawings produced on modern CAD systems. Figure 10–1 is a shop drawing of a structural steel column. Figure 10–2 contains two shop drawings of steel braces for a structural steel project. Figure 10–3 on page 152 is a shop drawing for a 12" prestressed concrete double tee roof or floor member.

As you can see from these figures, the information contained on shop drawings and on placing drawings is too varied to simply be listed. The contents vary according to the type of product and type of material it is made of, as well as the design specifications of the individual member. In preparing shop or placing drawings, drafters should apply a rule of thumb similar to the one used in producing engineering drawings: INCLUDE ANY AND ALL INFORMATION REQUIRED FOR THE PROPER FABRICATION OF THE PRODUCT, BUT ONLY THAT INFORMATION.

## SPECIAL SYMBOLS NEEDED

The special symbols used in producing shop and placing drawings are the same as those used in producing engineering drawings in Chapter 9. For convenience the symbols shown in Chapter 9 are repeated here as Figures 10–4 on page 152 and Figures 10–5 and 10–6 on page 153. Examine the symbols library of your CAD system to determine which

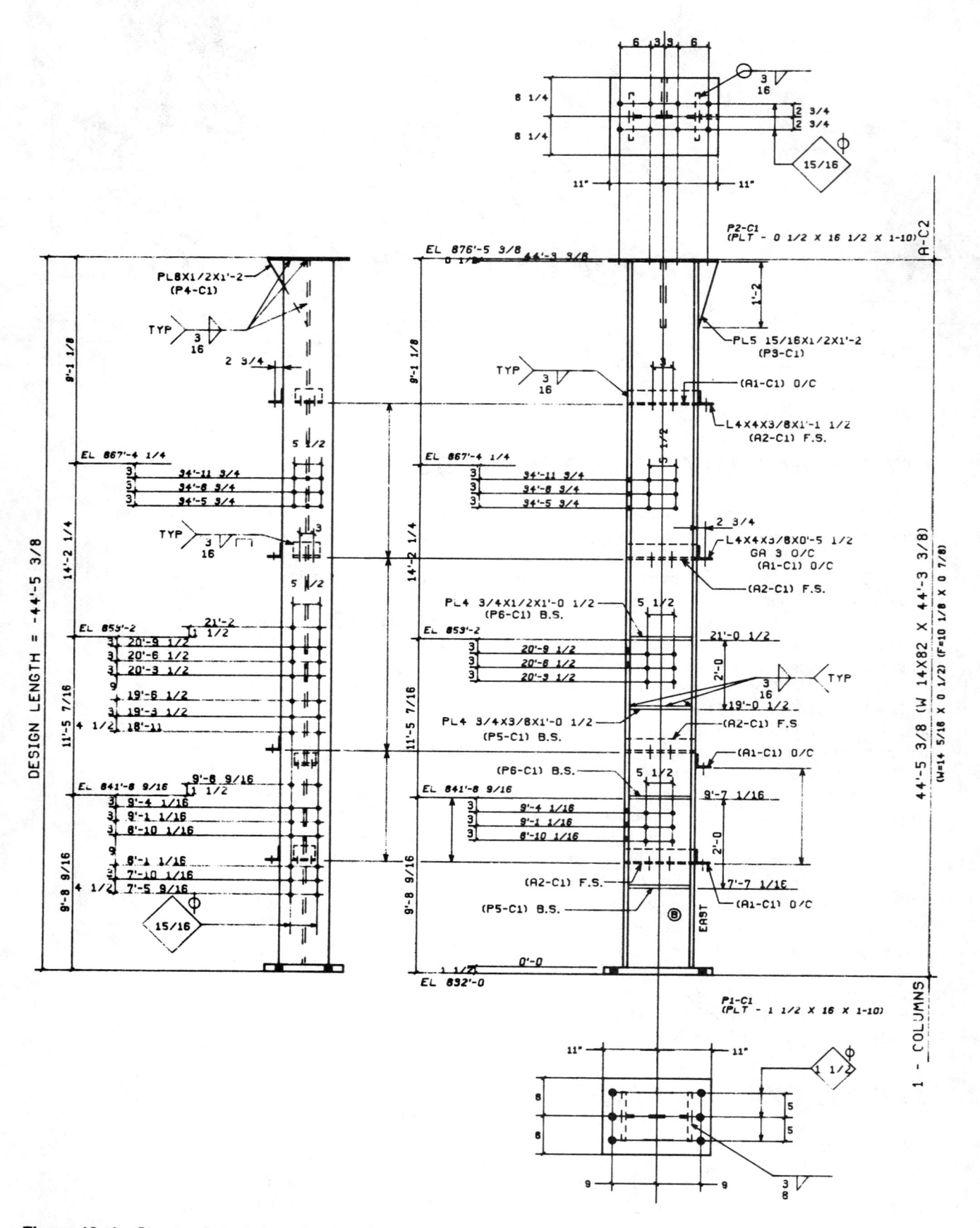

**Figure 10–1** Structural steel shop drawing. *(Courtesy of Sigma Design.)*

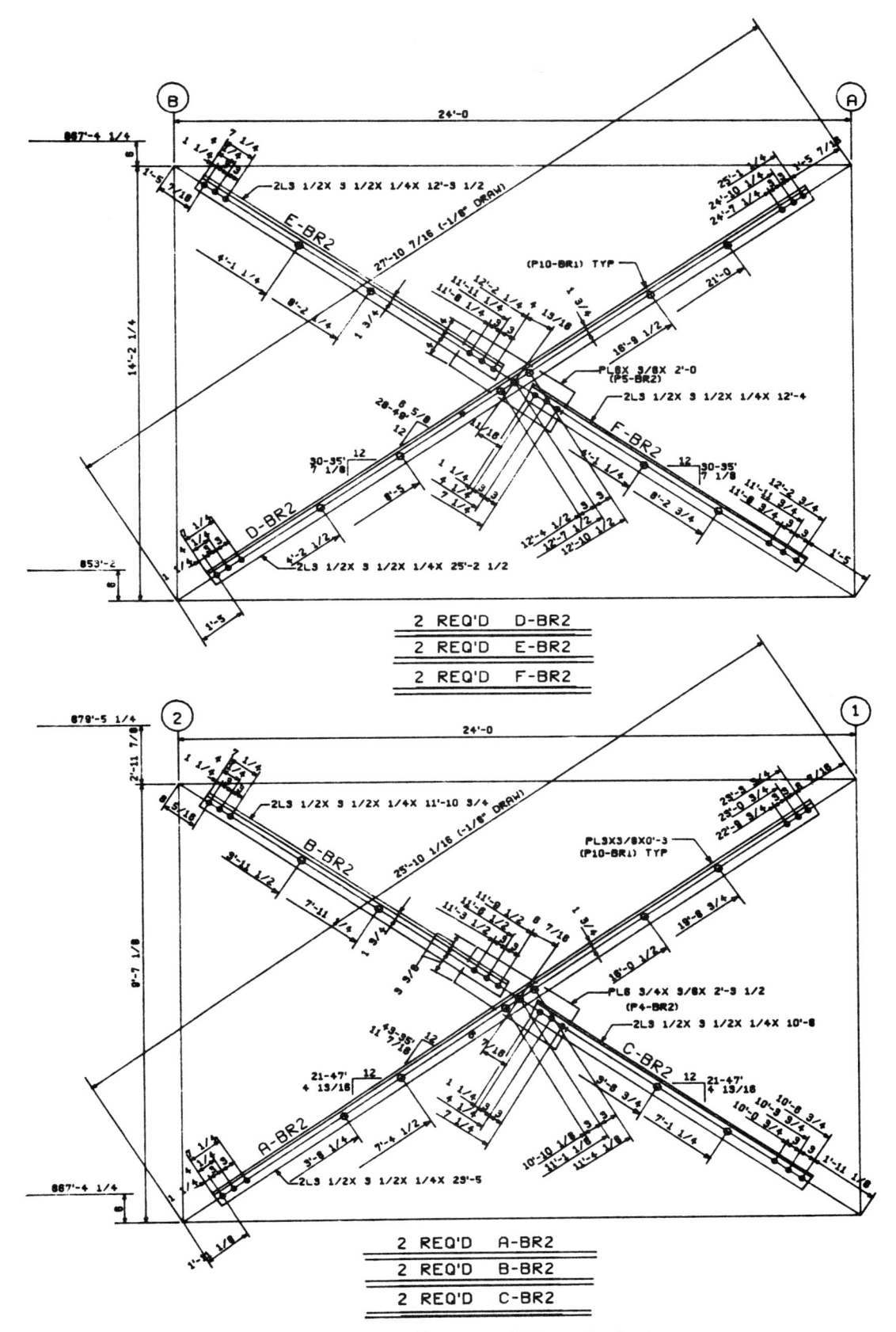

**Figure 10–2** Structural steel shop drawing. *(Courtesy of Sigma Design.)*

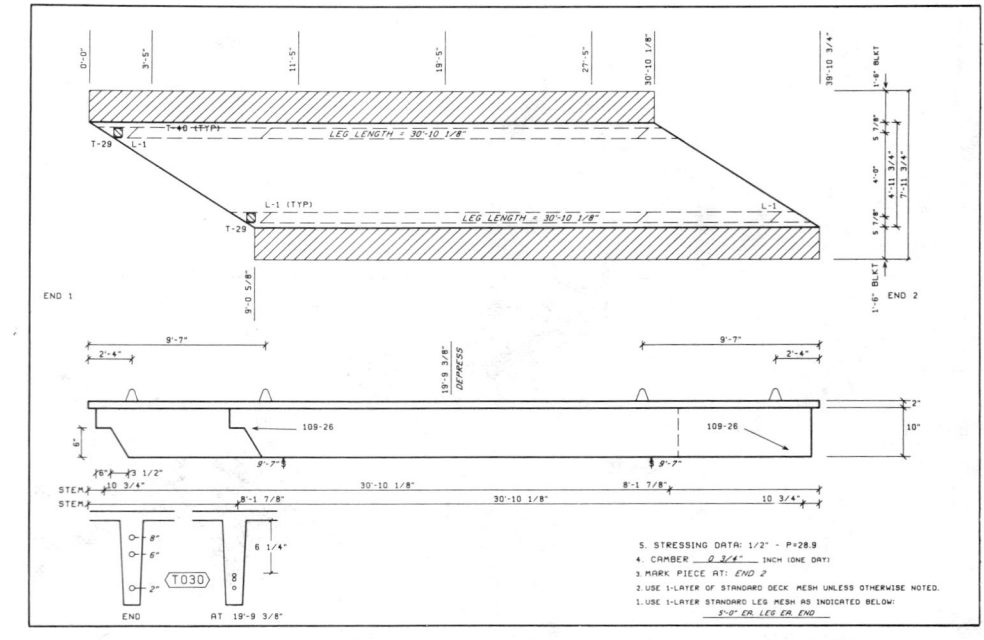

**Figure 10–3** Prestressed concrete shop drawing. *(Courtesy of Sigma Design.)*

## STRUCTURAL STEEL SHAPE SYMBOLS

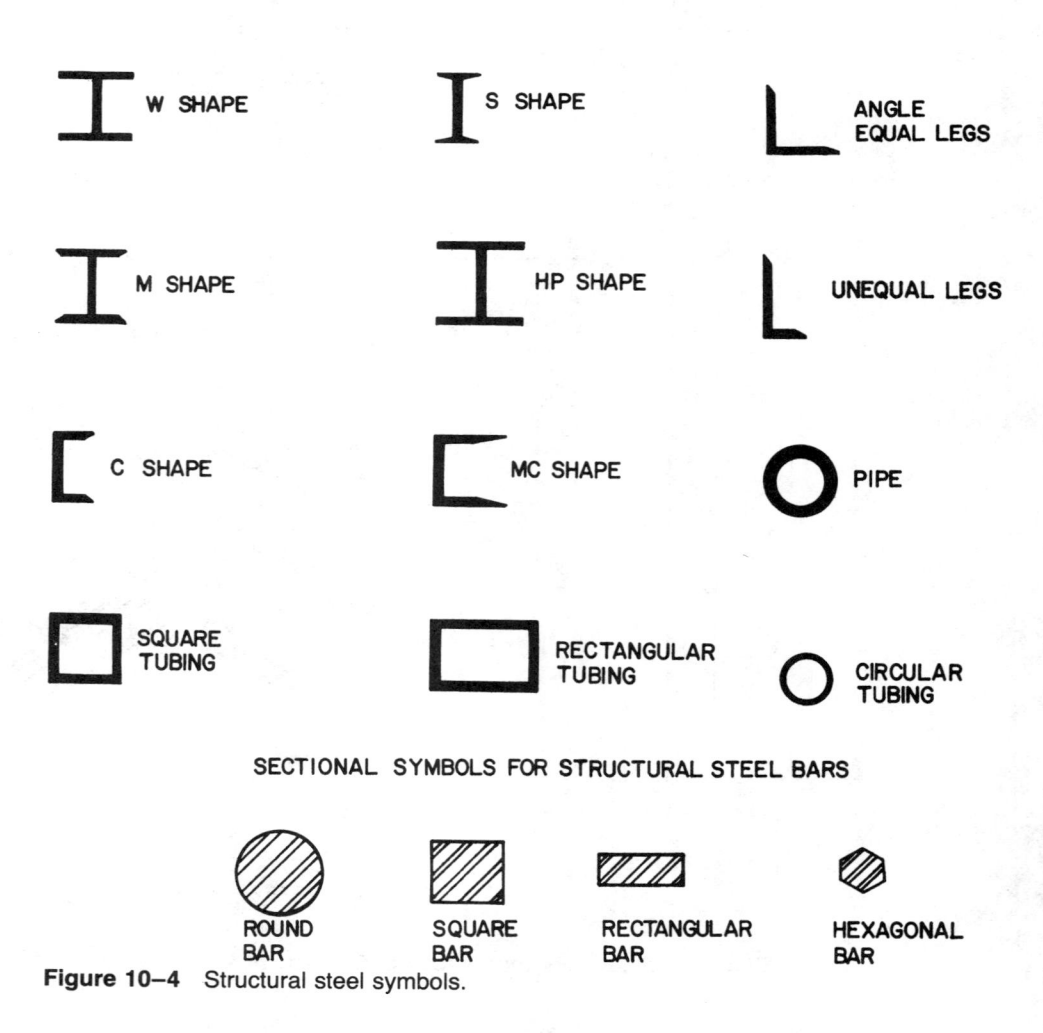

- W SHAPE
- S SHAPE
- ANGLE EQUAL LEGS
- M SHAPE
- HP SHAPE
- UNEQUAL LEGS
- C SHAPE
- MC SHAPE
- PIPE
- SQUARE TUBING
- RECTANGULAR TUBING
- CIRCULAR TUBING

## SECTIONAL SYMBOLS FOR STRUCTURAL STEEL BARS

- ROUND BAR
- SQUARE BAR
- RECTANGULAR BAR
- HEXAGONAL BAR

**Figure 10–4** Structural steel symbols.

## PRECAST CONCRETE SHAPE SYMBOLS

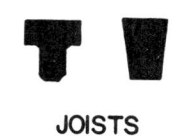

DOUBLE TEE

SINGLE TEE

FLAT SLABS

JOISTS

BUILDING BEAMS

PILES AND COLUMNS

## CONCRETE SECTIONING SYMBOLS

CONCRETE BLOCK

CAST CONCRETE

CINDER CONCRETE

EARTH

SAND

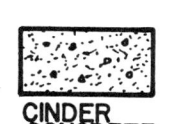

**Figure 10–5** Concrete symbols.

## WOOD SHAPE AND SECTIONING SYMBOLS

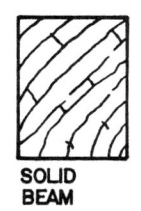

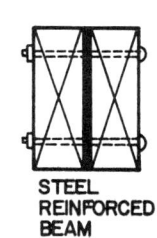

SOLID BEAM

HORIZONTAL LAMINATED BEAM

VERTICAL LAMINATED BEAM

STEEL REINFORCED BEAM

BOX BEAM

**Figure 10–6** Wood symbols.

of these symbols it contains. If the symbols library does not contain a particular symbol, you have two options:

1. Create the symbol and add it to the symbols library. This can be done only on those CAD systems that are programmed to accept user-defined symbols.
2. Construct the symbols on the drawing as they are needed, using the appropriate geometric characters and commands.

## CAD COMMANDS AND FUNCTIONS USED

There are several different commands and functions used in producing shop and placing drawings on a CAD system. Most CAD systems have these commands and functions. However, they are often given different names on different systems (see Chapter 2).

The generic names for the commands and functions used to produce shop and placing drawings on a CAD system are listed in the Commands and Functions chart. Before attempting the application projects for this chapter, match these generic commands and functions with their corresponding commands and functions on your CAD system.

### COMMANDS AND FUNCTIONS

**Graphic Creation Commands**

- √ Point
- √ Solid Line
- √ Hidden Line
- √ Construction Line
- √ Dashed Line
- √ Center Line
- √ Rectangle
- √ Circle
- √ Arc
- √ Irregular Curve
- √ Ellipse
- √ Polygon
- ___ Grid
- ___ XYPT
- ___ Polar
- ___ Line Weight
- ___ Fillet
- ___ Chamfer
- ___ Leaders
- ___ Rect.
- ___ Hatch

**Manipulation Commands**

- √ Move
- √ Copy
- √ Rotate
- √ Scale
- √ Zoom
- √ Pan
- ___ Mirror

**Size Specification Commands**

- √ Auto. Dimension
- ___ Dimension
- ___ Tolerance
- ___ Calc. Area

**Output Commands**

- √ Plot
- ___ Print (Screen Dump)

**Text Creation Commands**

- √ Text

**Modification Commands**

- √ Edit
- √ Delete
- √ Redraw
- ___ Clip
- √ Erase

**Facilitation Commands**

- √ Save
- √ File
- √ Symbol Library
- ___ Layer
- ___ Quit
- ___ Default

# PROCEDURES FOR PREPARING THE DRAWING

What follows is an illustrated, step-by-step generic description of how to produce a shop or placing drawing on a CAD system. These procedures can be applied to any of the many different types of shop drawings or placing drawings that might be produced on a CAD system.

■ *Step 1*

Log-on to the system and create a drawing designation SHPABC. Substitute your initials for the ABC. Decide what size medium you will use to plot the completed drawing on.

■ *Step 2*

Lay out the overall shape of the beam detail using the CONSTRUCTION LINES command if available. If not, use SOLID LINES, Figure 10–7.

■ *Step 3*

Convert all construction lines to solid lines. Using the CIRCLE command, create the circular end views of the longitudinal reinforcing bars in the end view. If your system does not have a FLOODING capability for filling in the circles, you can accomplish the same results by ZOOMING-IN on each circle and creating a series of successively smaller concentric circles. In this way, when the plotter plots the circles, the lines will run together and fill in the circles. Switch to the HIDDEN LINES mode and draw the bars that wrap around the longitudinal reinforcing. While still in the HIDDEN LINES mode, draw the vertical blockouts for anchor bolts in the elevation view of the beam. Switch to the SOLID LINES mode and draw the longitudinal reinforcing bars in the elevation view of the beam. Be sure that you break each line at least twice, Figure 10–8.

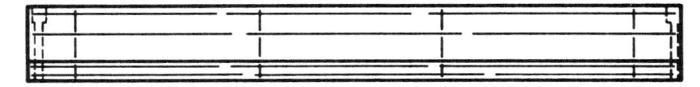

**Figure 10–8** Illustration for Step 3.

■ *Step 4*

Switch to the DIMENSIONING MODE and add all required dimensions. Switch to the TEXT MODE and add the remaining size callouts and other required annotation. SAVE the completed drawing and give the PLOT command, Figure 10–9.

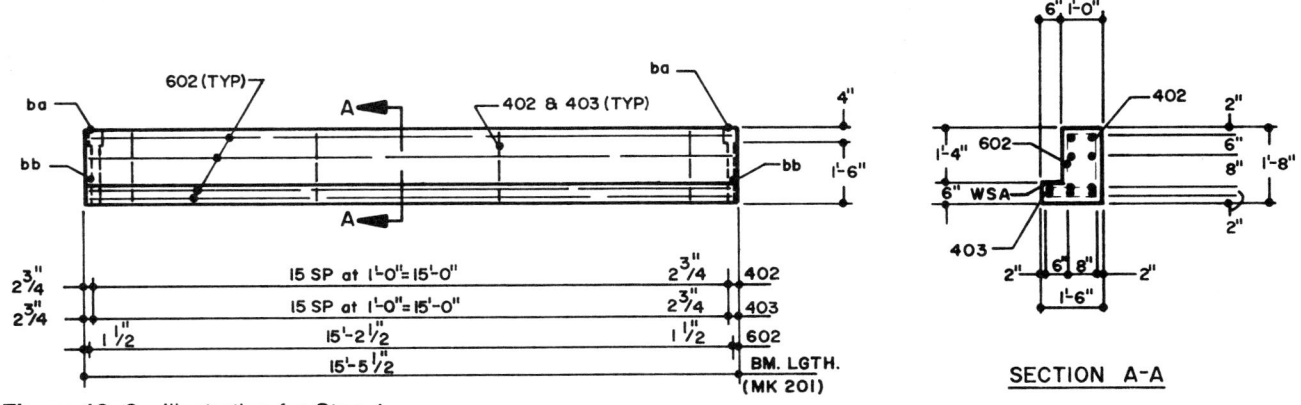

**Figure 10–9** Illustration for Step 4.

## REVIEW QUESTIONS

The following questions are provided as a review of Chapter 10 and should be completed before attempting the application projects for the chapter. Write your answers in the spaces provided.

1. Define "structural shop drawing."

2. Define "structural placing drawing."

3. What is the difference between a shop drawing and a placing drawing?

4. What is the rule of thumb to follow in preparing shop or placing drawings?

5. Sketch the symbols for the following:
    W shape (shape)—

    S shape (shape)—

    Double tee (shape)—

    Single tee (shape)—

6. What are your CAD system's commands for the following generic commands?
    CONSTRUCTION LINE—

    HIDDEN LINE—

    RECTANGLE—

    CIRCLE—

8. Explain the steps you would use to create the W shape symbol on a drawing if it is not contained in the symbols library of your CAD system.

9. Explain the steps you would use to create the "double tee" symbol on a drawing if it is not contained in the symbols library of your CAD system.

10. Explain the steps you would use to create the "single tee" symbol on a drawing if it is not contained in the symbols library of your CAD system.

# *APPLICATION PROJECTS*

The following application projects are provided to help you become proficient in producing structural shop drawings on a CAD system. The projects range from simple to complex, beginning with the easier projects and getting progressively more difficult. To ensure that you must use input, modification, manipulation, and functions, you will be required to reconstruct a given shop drawing and make several modifications to it. To ensure that you use facilitation and output functions, you should SAVE each completed drawing and PLOT it on the type and size of medium specified by your instructor.

**Project 1:** Figure 10–10 is a shop drawing of a W16 × 31 structural steel beam. Reconstruct the shop drawing as shown.

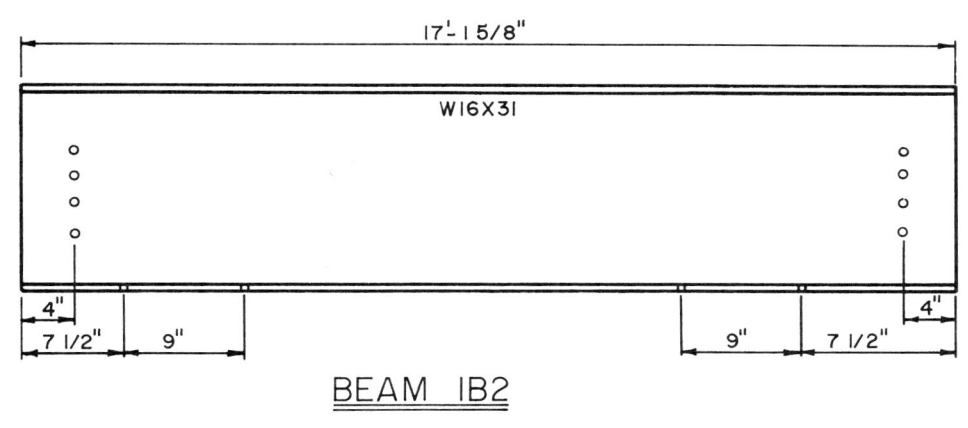

**Figure 10–10** Application project 1.

**Project 2:** Figure 10–11 is a shop drawing containing a fabrication detail for two structural steel beams with identical configurations, but different lengths. Notice that only one end of the beam configuration has been drawn. This means that the beam is symmetrical. Reconstruct the shop drawing on your CAD system as shown, but add the missing right-hand end of the beam configuration.

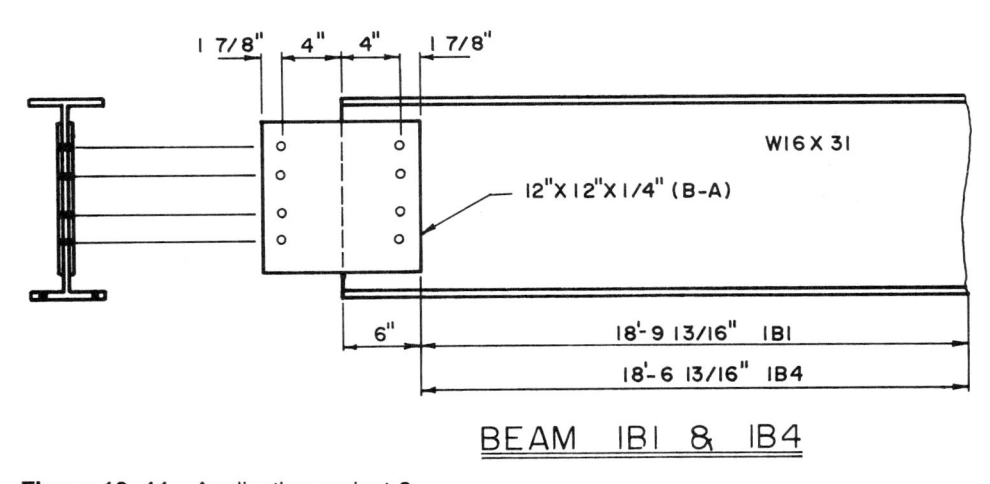

**Figure 10–11** Application project 2.

**Project 3:** Figure 10–12 is a shop drawing for two structural steel columns made of tubing and plates. The configurations for the two columns are identical. Only the lengths are different. Reconstruct the shop drawing as shown. Then make the following changes:

1. Reconstruct the shop drawing as shown, but change the length to 15'-11".
2. Construct a separate shop drawing for IC2. Change the length to 15'-10" and remove the plate from the left-hand end of the configuration as drawn. Move Section A–A to the right side of the drawing.

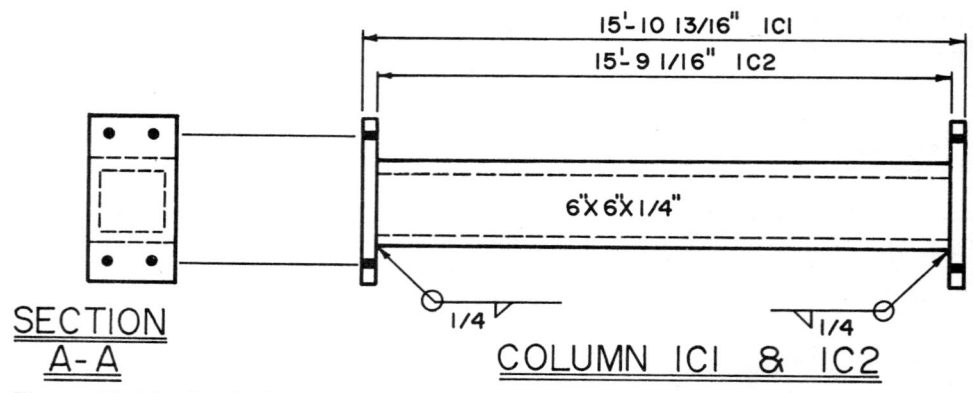

**Figure 10–12** Application project 3.

**Project 4:** Figure 10–13 is a shop drawing for a structural steel beam that will be erected using bolts. Bolts will also be used to attach the connection plates to the beam. Reconstruct the shop drawing on your CAD system as shown. Then make the following changes:

1. Attach the connection plates to the beam using a ½" fillet weld. The beams will still be erected using bolts.
2. Increase the length of the beam by 2".
3. Add a fifth hole to the connection plates and change the spacing to 1½" each.

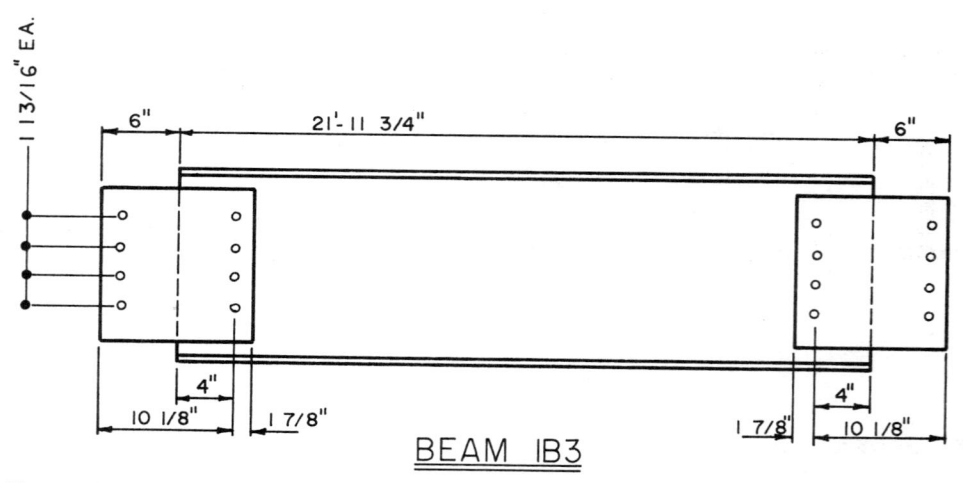

**Figure 10–13** Application project 4.

**Project 5:** Figure 10–14 is a shop drawing containing a group of fabrication details for eight structural steel beams. Assume you work for a company that has just converted to CAD. Your job is to take all of the drawings on file and input them so they can be stored on disks or tapes, and your first project is Figure 10–14.

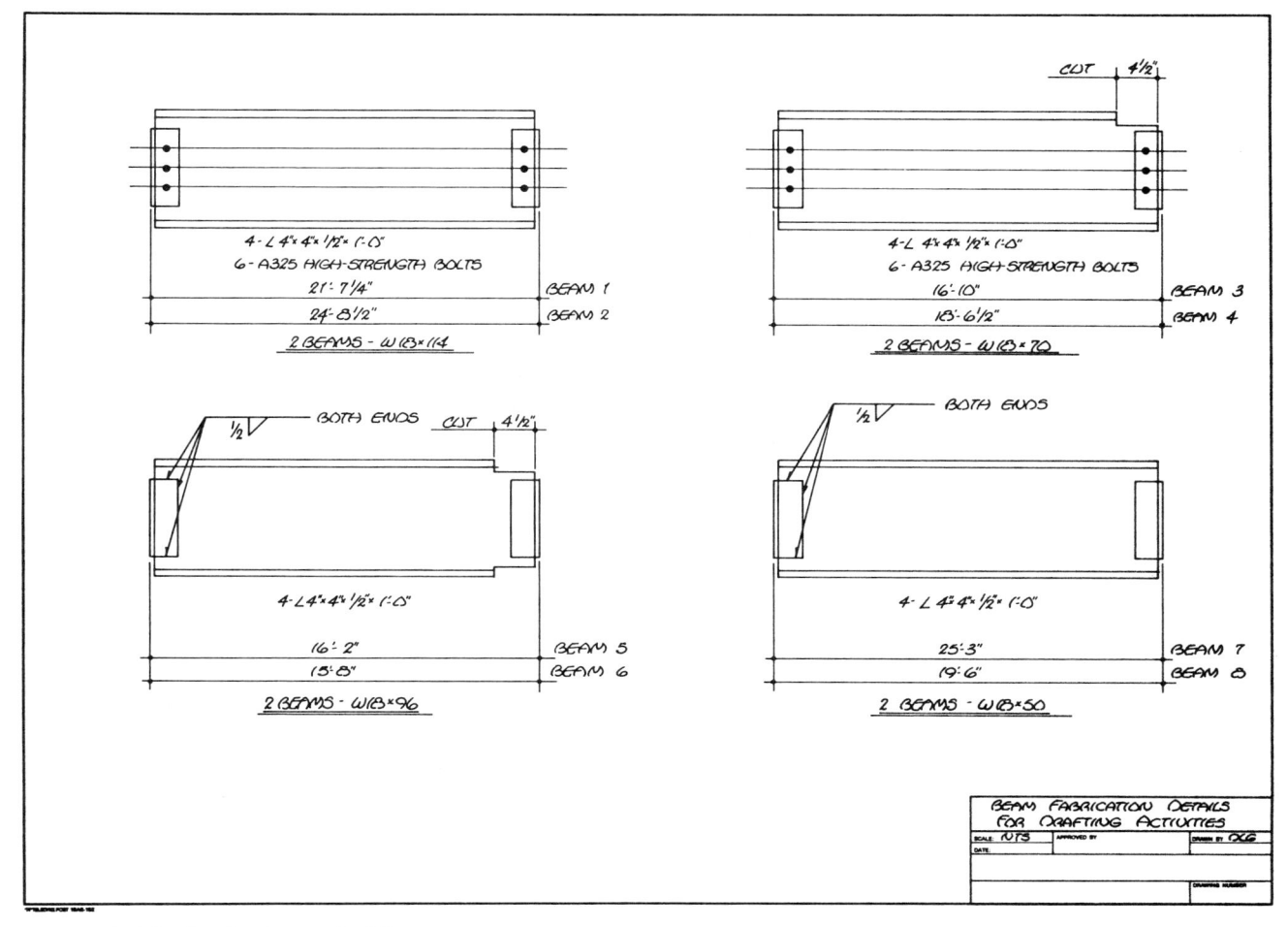

Figure 10–14 Application project 5.

**160** | CAD Applications: Architectural

**Project 6:** Figure 10–15 is a shop drawing containing fabrication details for three structural steel beams. Reconstruct the shop drawing as shown. Then make the following changes:

1. Add 5″ to all beam lengths.
2. All "cuts" should be 10″.
3. All welds should be ½″.

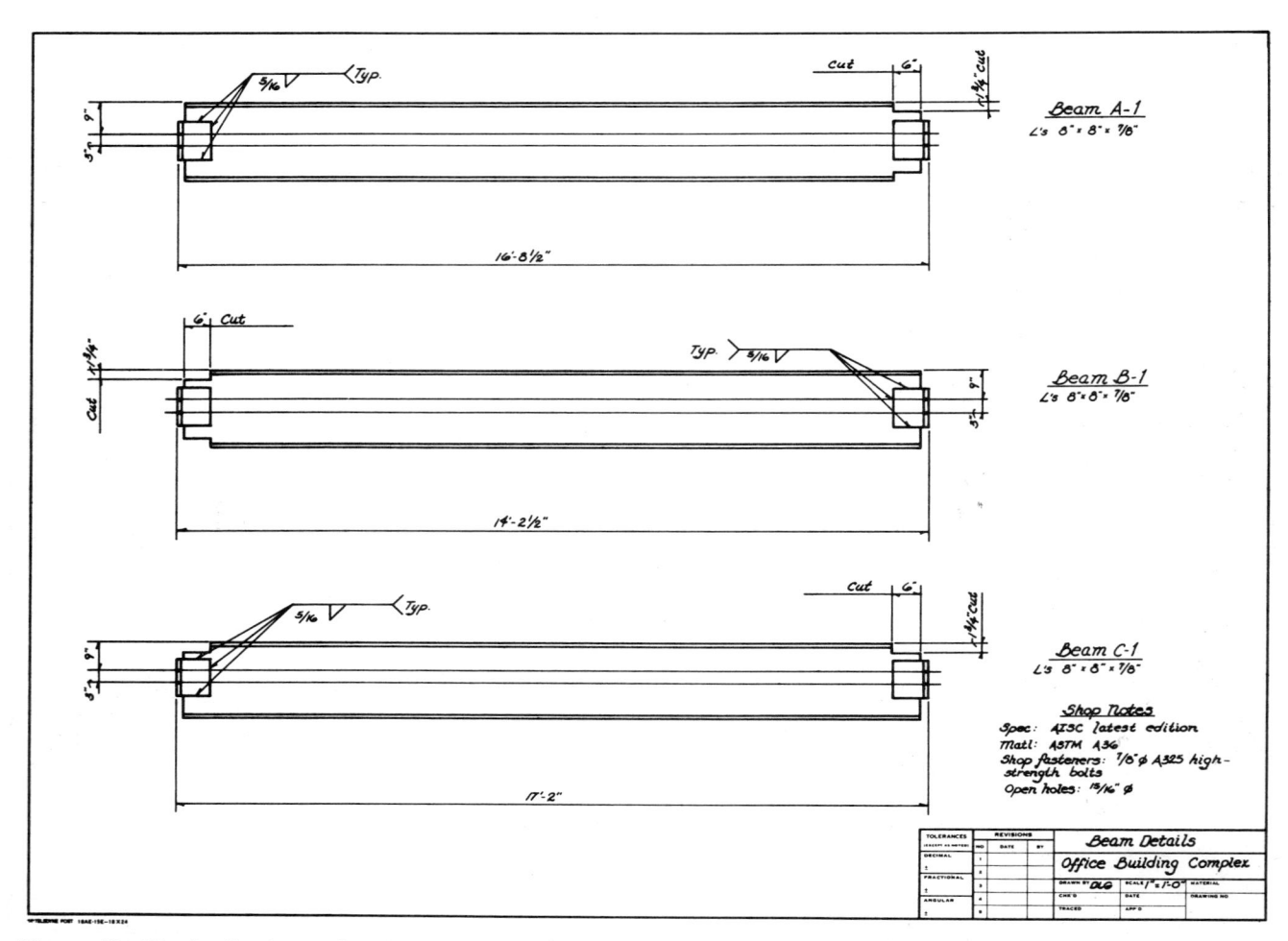

**Figure 10–15** Application project 6.

**Project 7:** Figure 10–16 is a shop drawing for a W14 × 53 structural steel column. Reconstruct the shop drawing on your CAD system as shown. Then make the following changes:

1. Change the baseplate from 2'-0" × 1'-3" to 2'-6" × 1'-6", but leave the bolt holes 3" in from each side.
2. Change the length of the column to 29'-9" and adjust all length dimensions accordingly.
3. Rewrite the shop notes as shown, but number each note.

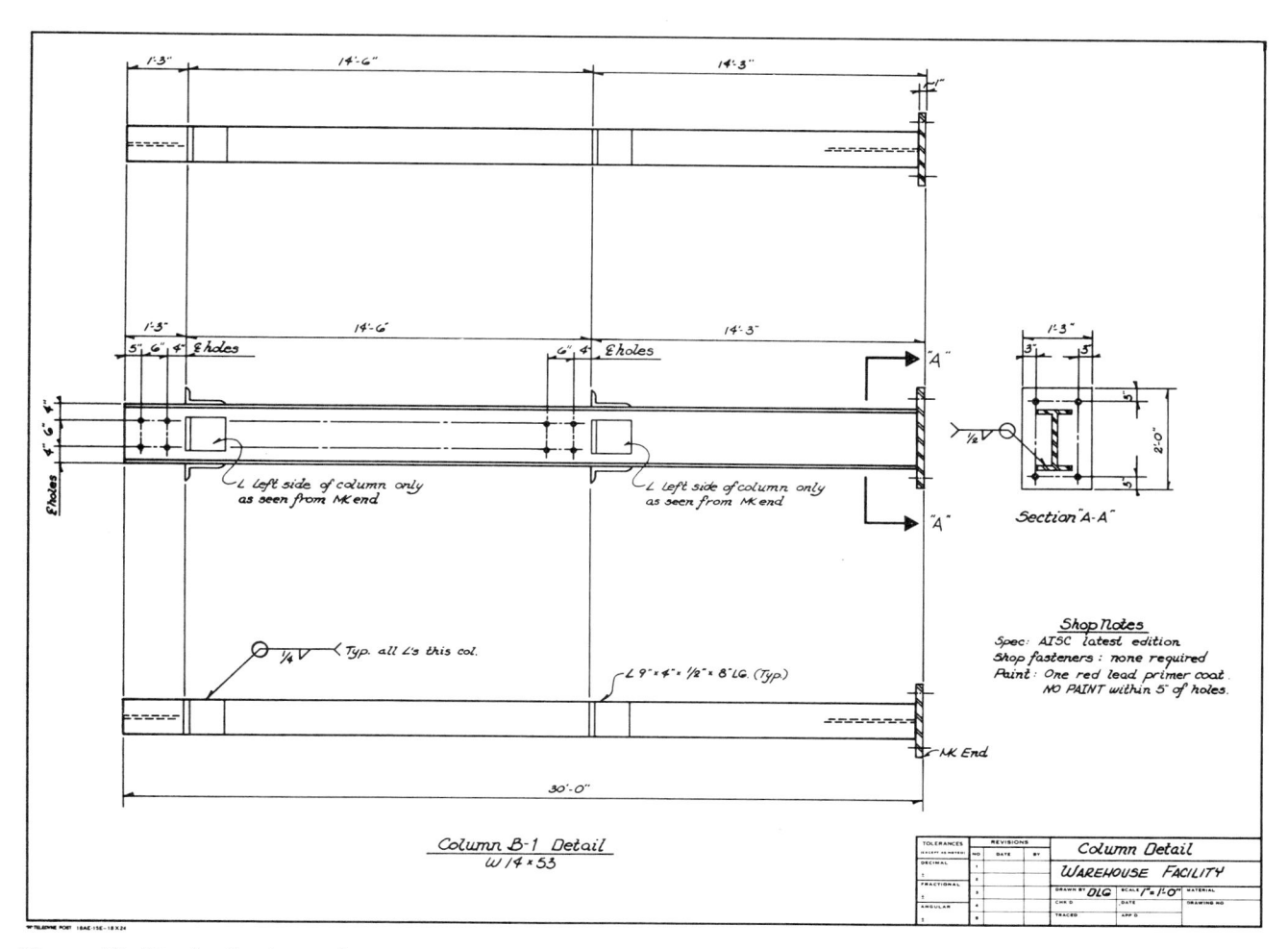

**Figure 10–16** Application project 7.

**Project 8:** Figure 10–17 is a placing drawing for a building with a poured concrete footing, 12" concrete block foundation wall (cores filled), and a 4" concrete floor system. Reconstruct the placing drawing on your CAD system as shown. Then make the following changes:

1. Change the footing dimensions from 3'-0" × 12" to 24" × 12".
2. Reinforce the footing as follows: (A) length reinforcing—five #5 bars, and (B) width reinforcing—#4 bars at 12".
3. Call out 6 × 6 10/10 welded wire mesh (WWM) for floor reinforcing.

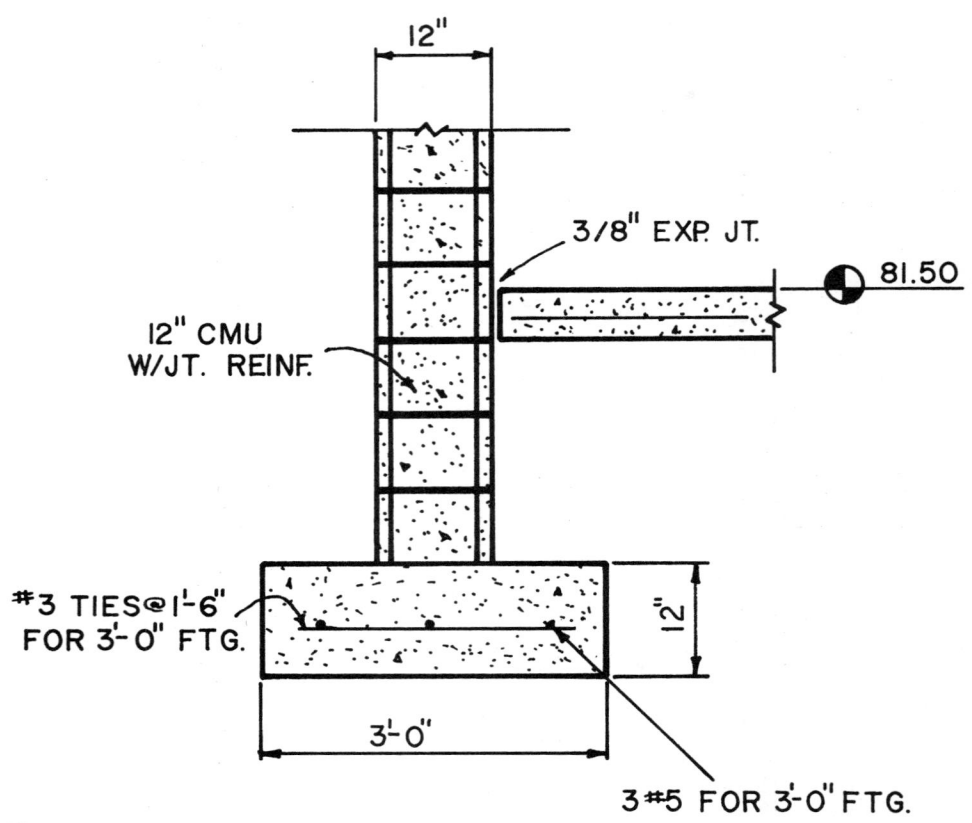

**Figure 10–17** Application project 8.

**Project 9:** Figure 10–18 is a placing drawing showing a typical corner reinforcing for a commercial building. Reconstruct the placing drawing on your CAD system as shown. Then make the following changes:

1. Change the corner dowels to #3 bars at 9" on center and 36" long.
2. Make the walls 6" thick.

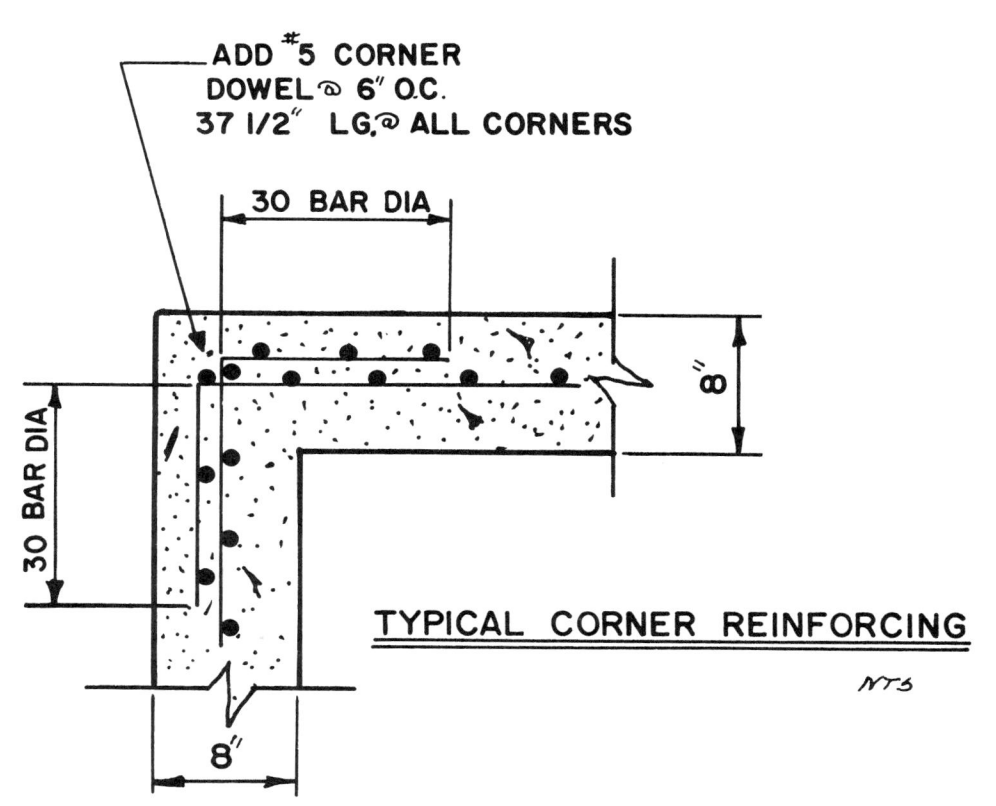

**Figure 10–18** Application project 9.

**Project 10:** Figure 10–19 is a placing drawing showing a typical column and beam reinforcing situation at a discontinuous column. Using Figure 10–19 as a guide, construct a similar placing drawing with the beam extending over the column to form a "T" configuration. Change the reinforcing as follows:

1. Allow 1¾" cover at the top and bottom of the beam.
2. Use #4 ties at 12" on center beginning 1¾" below the beam.

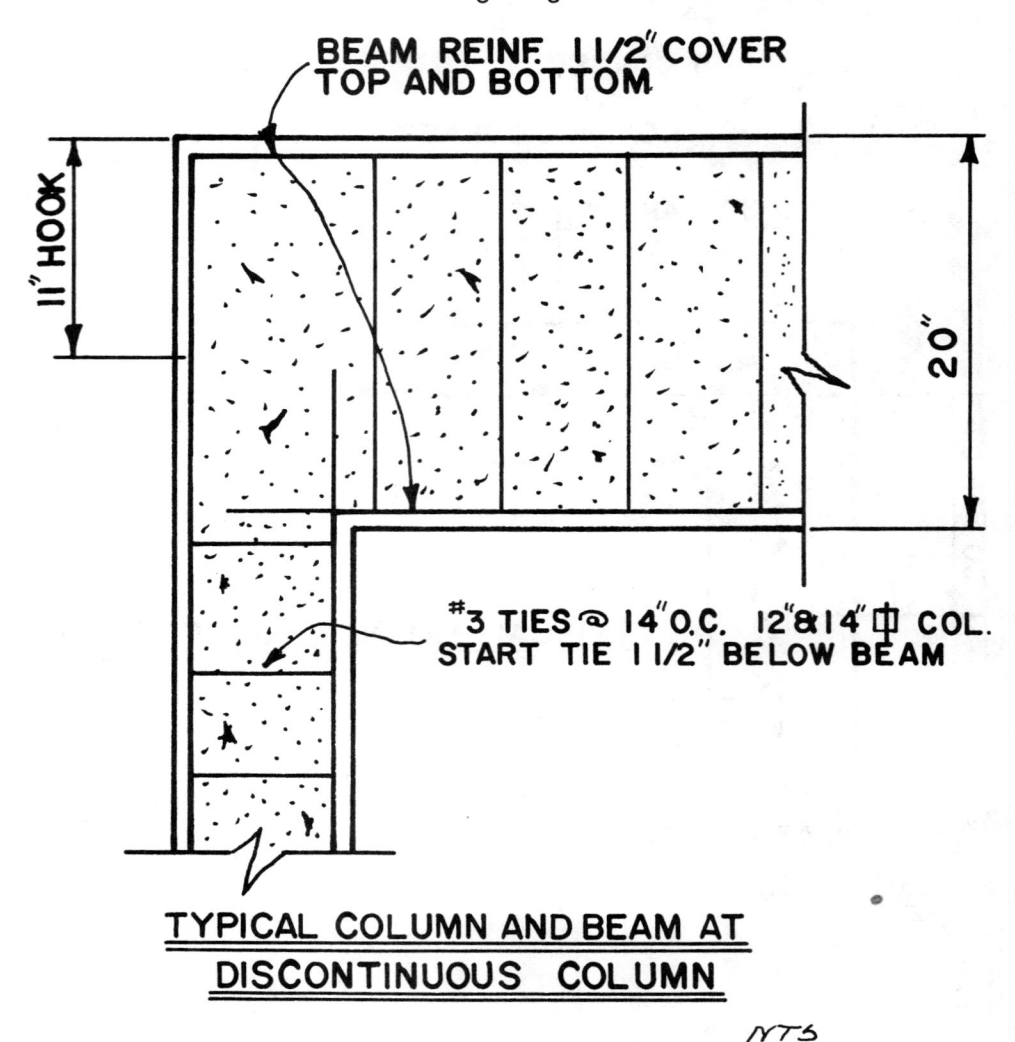

**Figure 10–19** Application project 10.

**Project 11:** Figure 10–20 is a placing drawing showing a typical reinforcing situation for a column and beam at a discontinuous column. Reconstruct the placing drawing on your CAD system as shown. Then make the following changes:

1. Allow 1¾" cover at the top and bottom of the beam.
2. Use #4 ties at 12" on center beginning 1¾" below the beam.

**Project 12:** Figure 10–21 is a foundation plan for a self-service gas station. Section A–A on the drawing serves the same purpose as a placing drawing. Reconstruct the entire drawing on your CAD system as shown. Then make the following changes to Section A–A:

1. Respace the #8 bars at 4".
2. Make the space between the anchor bolts 1'-6".
3. Project the anchor bolts 6" out of the concrete.

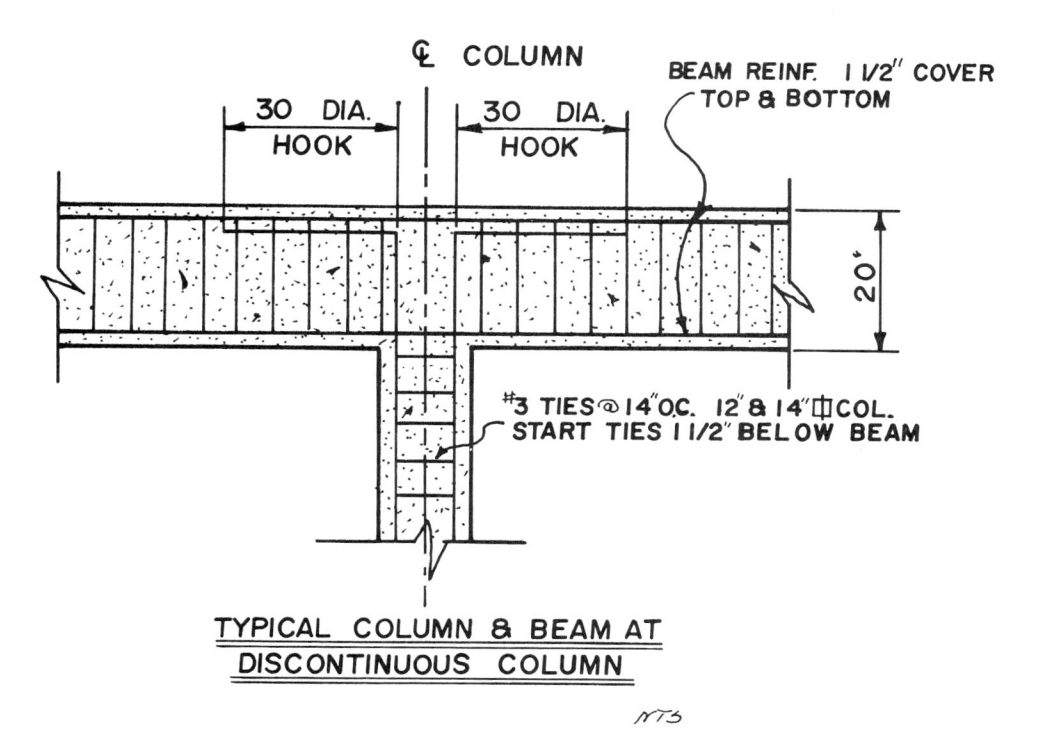

**Figure 10–20** Application project 11.

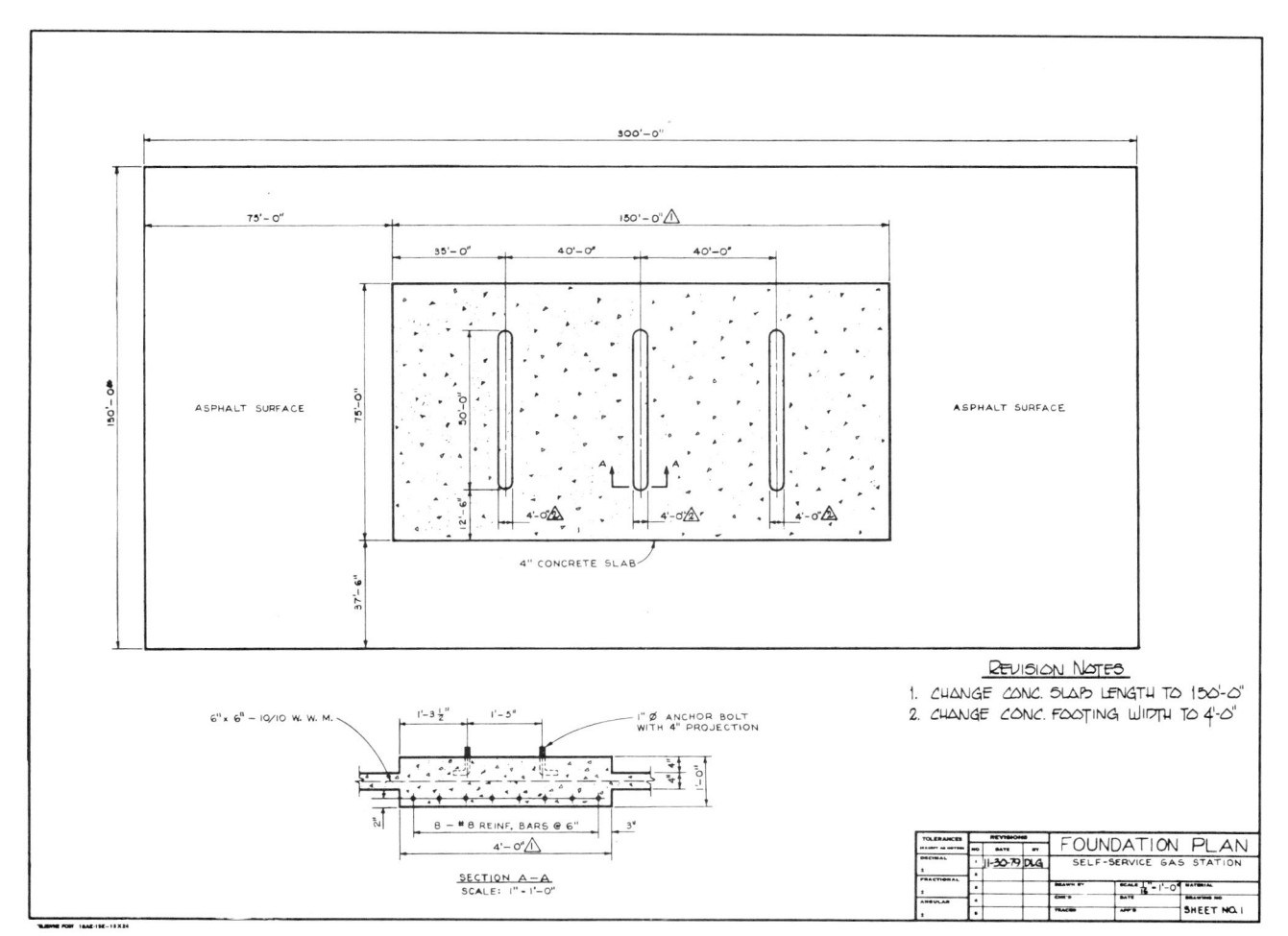

**Figure 10–21** Application project 12.

**166** | CAD Applications: Architectural

**Project 13:** Figure 10–22 is a shop drawing containing fabrication details for the miscellaneous metals and materials for a precast concrete project. Reconstruct the shop drawing on your CAD system as shown. Then make the following changes:

1. Change the dimensions of "bpa" from 2'-2" × 1'-8" to 2'-0" × 1'-6", but leave the holes 2½" in from the sides.
2. Increase the length of "tra" to 3'-6", but leave the thread length 6".
3. Change the dimensions of "wpa" from 9" × 7" to 10" × 8" and adjust all other dimensions accordingly.
4. Revise the LEGEND to reflect the changes made in 1 through 3 above.

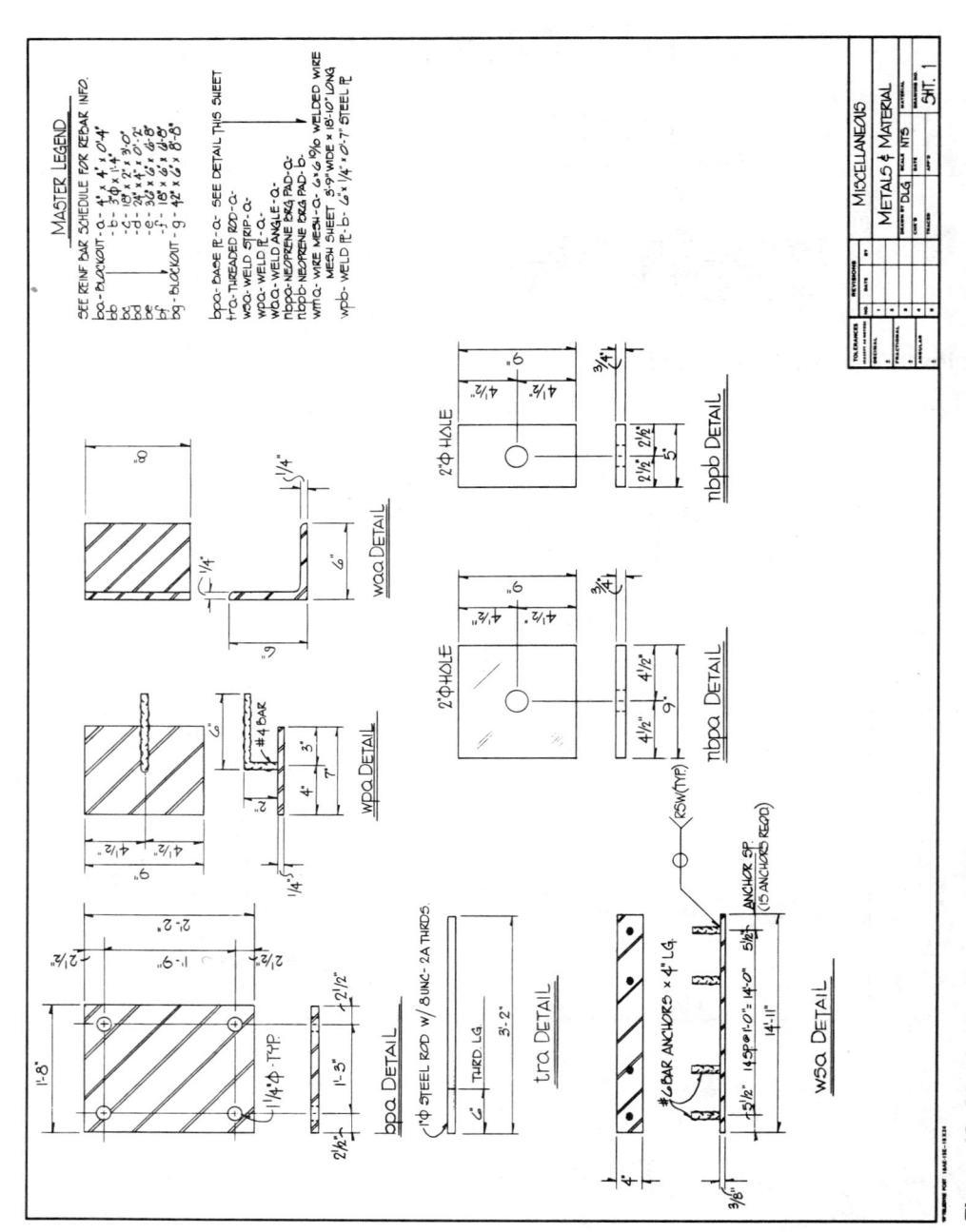

**Figure 10–22** Application project 13.

Chapter 10 Structural Shop and Placement Drawings | **167**

**Project 14:** Figure 10–23 is a shop drawing for a 14″ prestressed concrete roof member. Reconstruct the shop drawing on your CAD system as shown. Then make the following changes:

1. Change the member length to 18′-6″ and adjust all length dimensions accordingly.
2. Increase the size of "bc" from 3′-0″ × 1′-6″ to 3′-2″ × 1′-7″ and adjust all related dimensions accordingly.
3. Change the size of the strands in the sectional view from ½″ diameter to ⅜″ diameter.

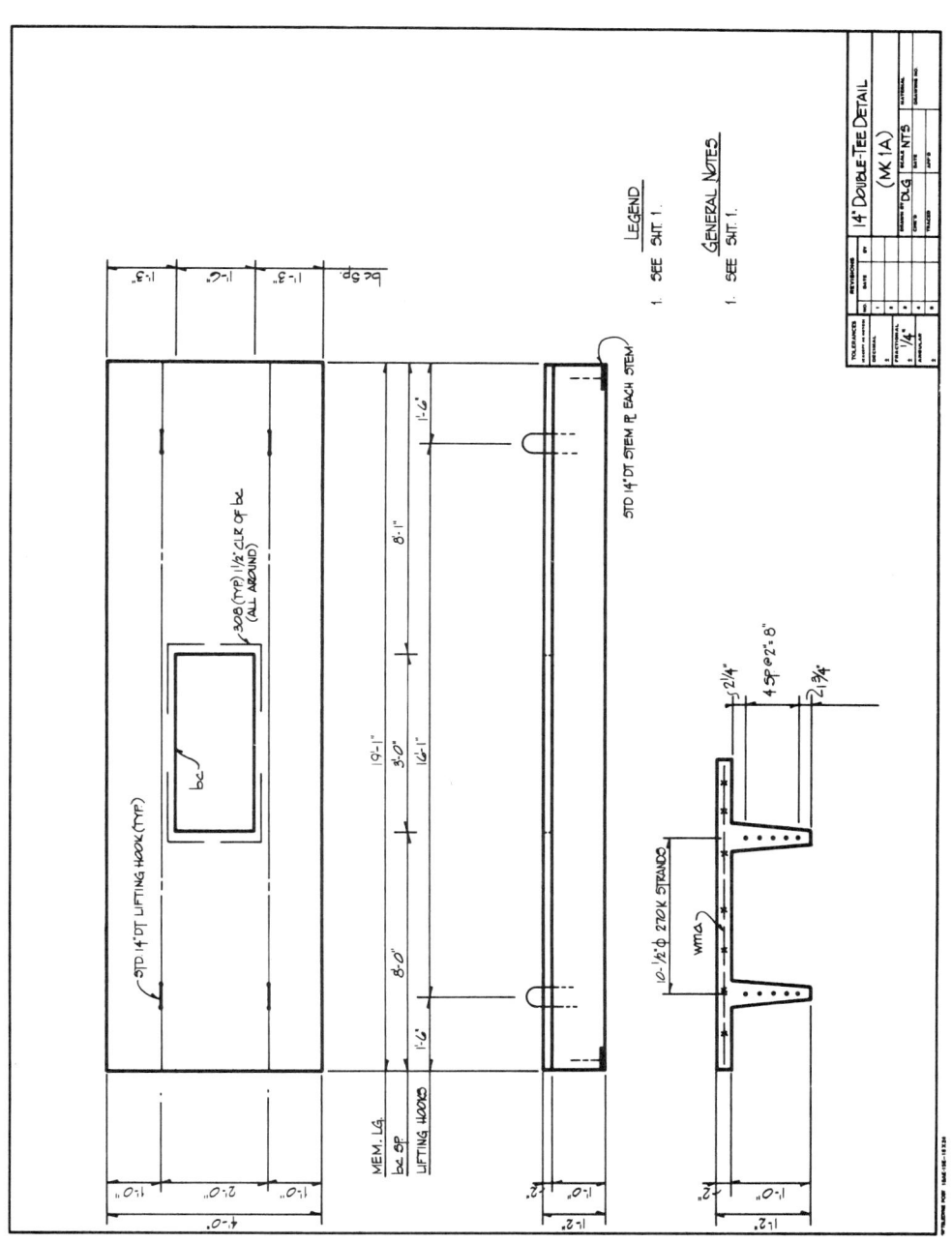

**Figure 10–23** Application project 14.

**Project 15:** Figure 10–24 is a shop drawing for a precast concrete beam. The overall width of the beam is 24″ and each ledge is 6″. Reconstruct the beam on your CAD system as shown. Then make the following changes:

1. Change the member length to 16′-6″ and adjust all length dimensions accordingly.
2. Take out all "ba's" and extend the "bb's" through the beam.
3. Change all #4 bars to #3 bars and correct the drawing accordingly.
4. Change the length of the #602 bars to 15′-2″ and adjust all related dimensions accordingly.

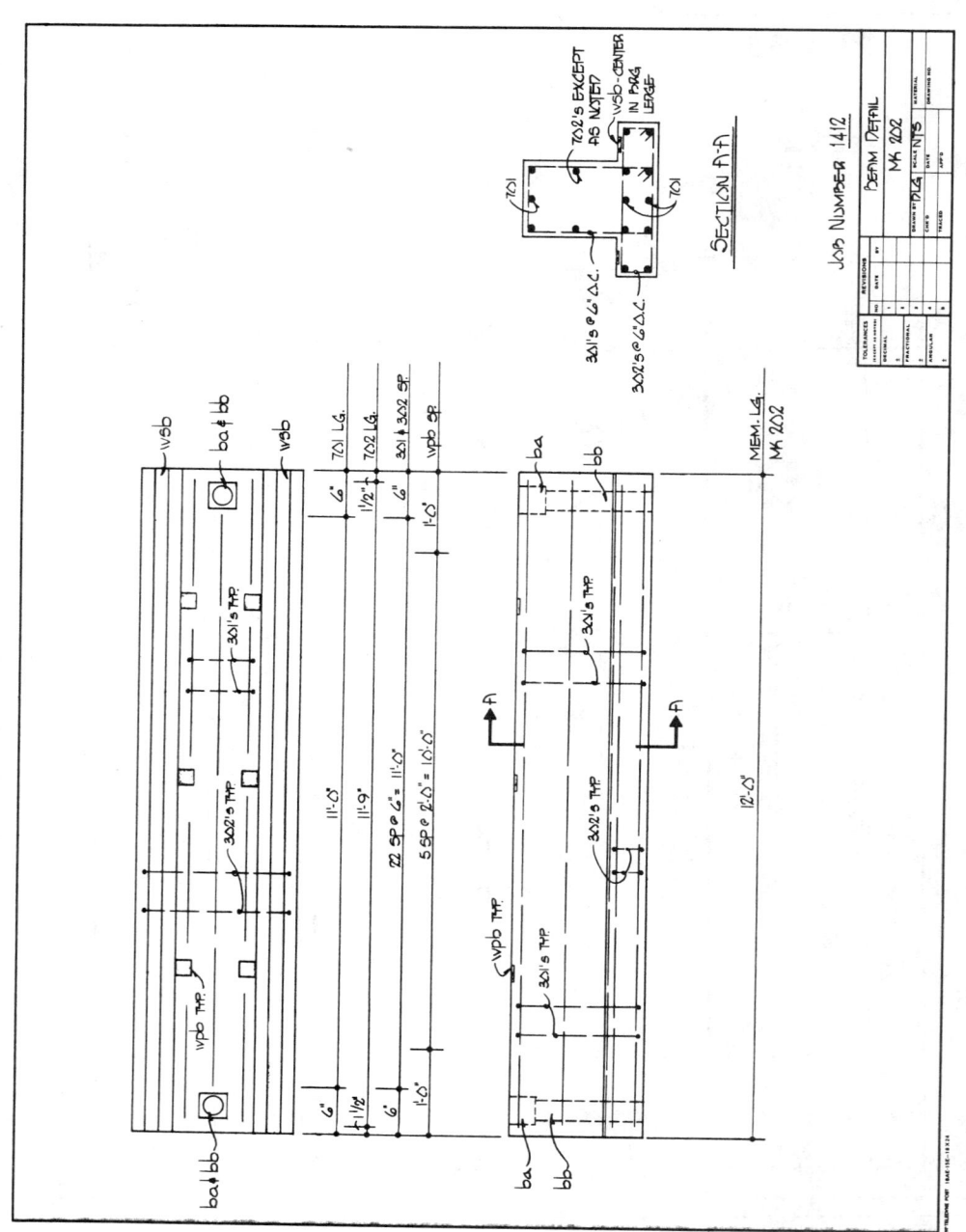

**Figure 10–24** Application project 15.

**Project 16:** Figure 10–25 is a shop drawing containing fabrication details for two precast concrete columns. Reconstruct the shop drawing on your CAD system as shown. Then make the following changes:

1. Change the member length to 10'-6½" and adjust all length dimensions accordingly.
2. Add 2" to the length and width of "bpa." The bolt holes should remain 2½" in from each side. Make all related changes.
3. Change the 401 bar spacing to 6" on center and adjust accordingly.
4. Extend the "tra's" out of the columns an additional 6" and make all related changes.

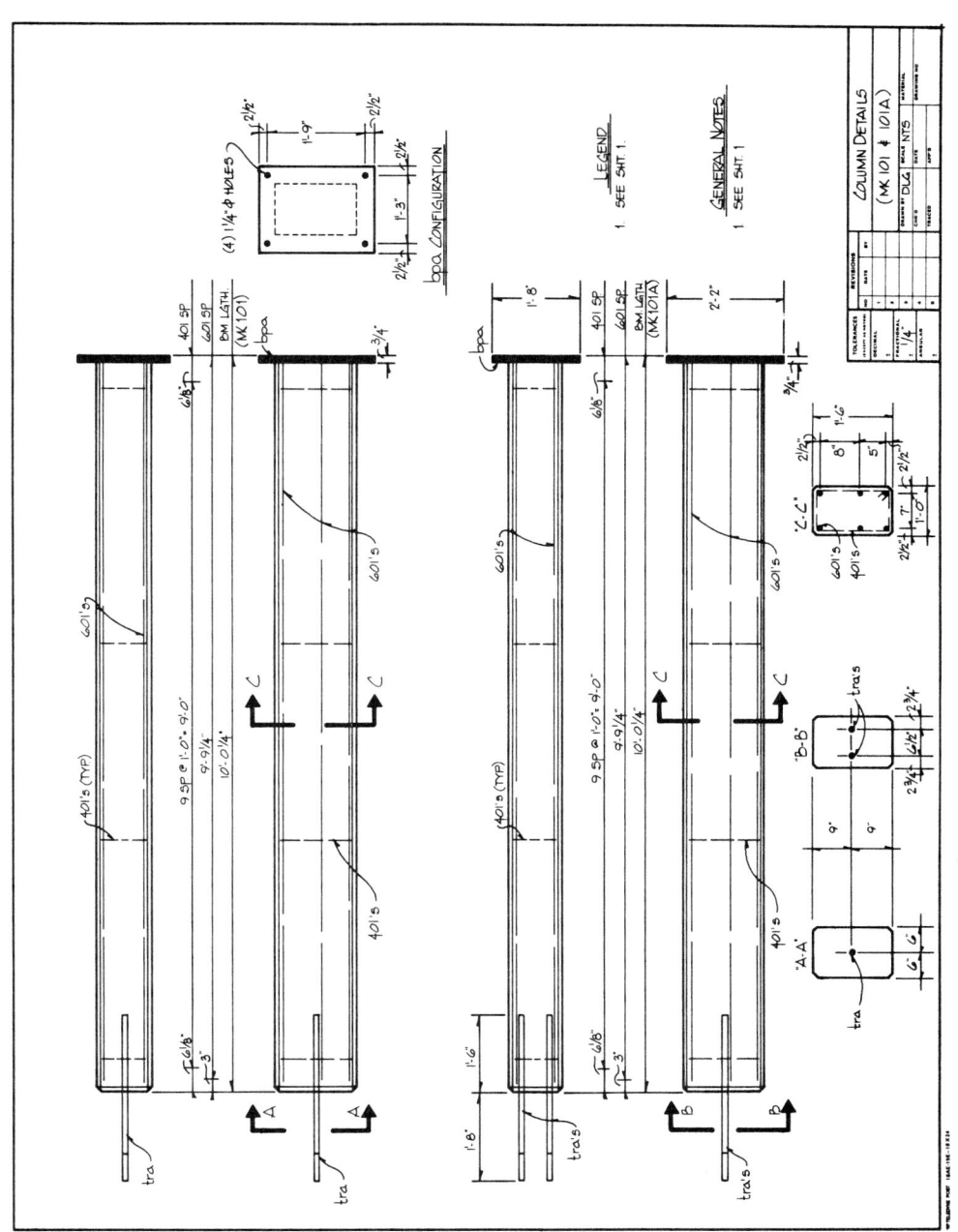

**Figure 10–25** Application project 16.

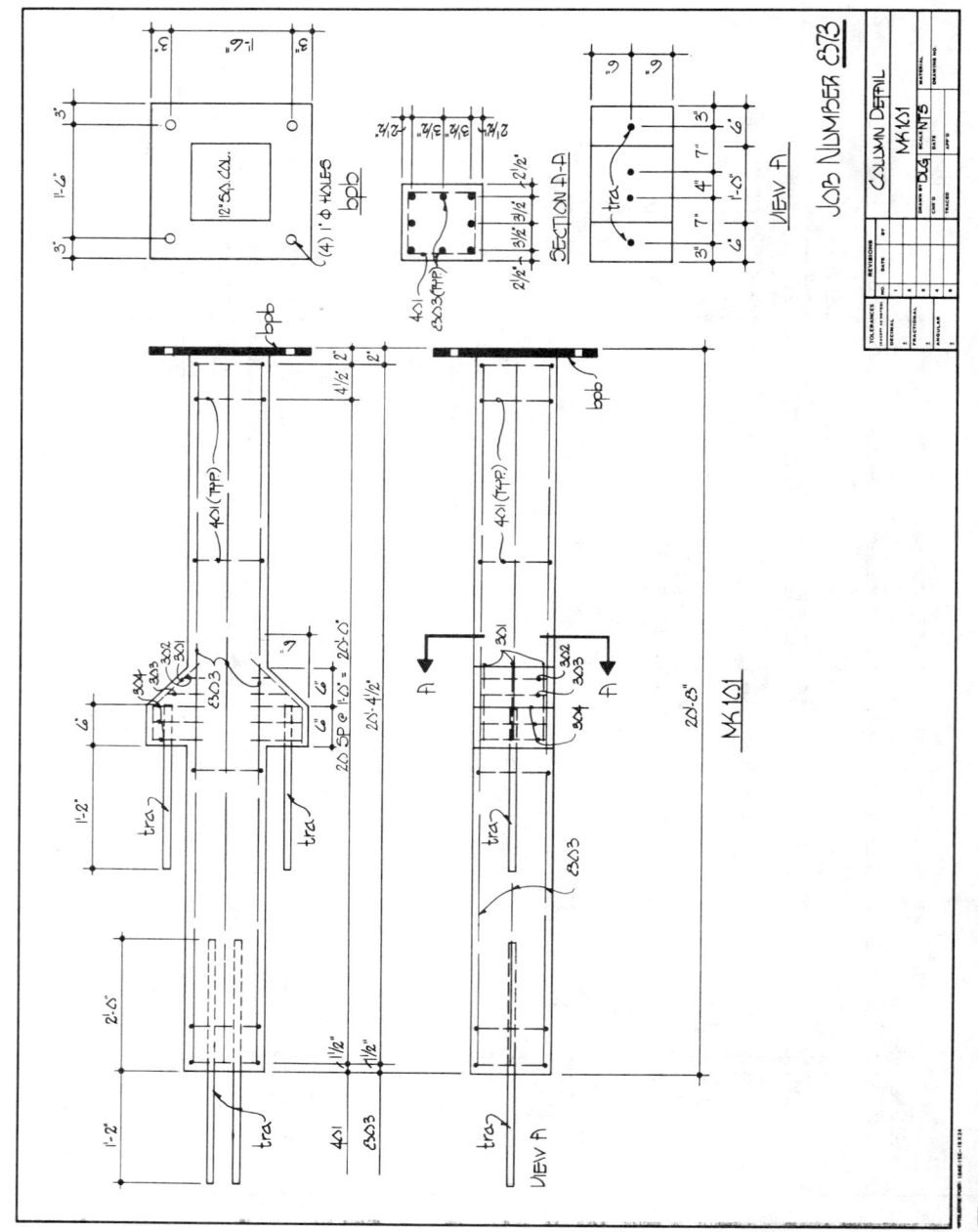

**170** | CAD Applications: Architectural

**Project 17:** Figure 10–26 is a shop drawing containing a fabrication detail for a precast concrete column. Reconstruct the column detail on your CAD system as shown. Then make the following changes:

1. Change the member length to 21'-0" and adjust all length dimensions accordingly.
2. Change all #3 bars to #4 bars.
3. Add 2" to the length and width of "bpb" and make all related changes. The holes should be changed to 3½" in from each side.
4. Change all #8 bars to #7 bars.

**Figure 10–26** Application project 17.

**Project 18:** Figure 10–27 is a shop drawing containing a fabrication detail for a precast concrete flat-slab wall panel. Reconstruct the wall panel detail on your CAD system as shown. Then make the following changes:

1. Change the member length to 15'-6" and adjust all length dimensions accordingly.
2. Take out blockout "bf" and make all related changes.
3. Add two more "wpa's." Center one additional "wpa" between each existing set and adjust the dimensions involved accordingly.
4. Change the thickness of the flat slab to 8" and adjust all related dimensions.

**Project 19:** Construct a complete shop drawing for a precast concrete flat-slab wall panel that is exactly like the detail in Figure 10–27, but with "bf" and "bh" removed to make the member a rectangle.

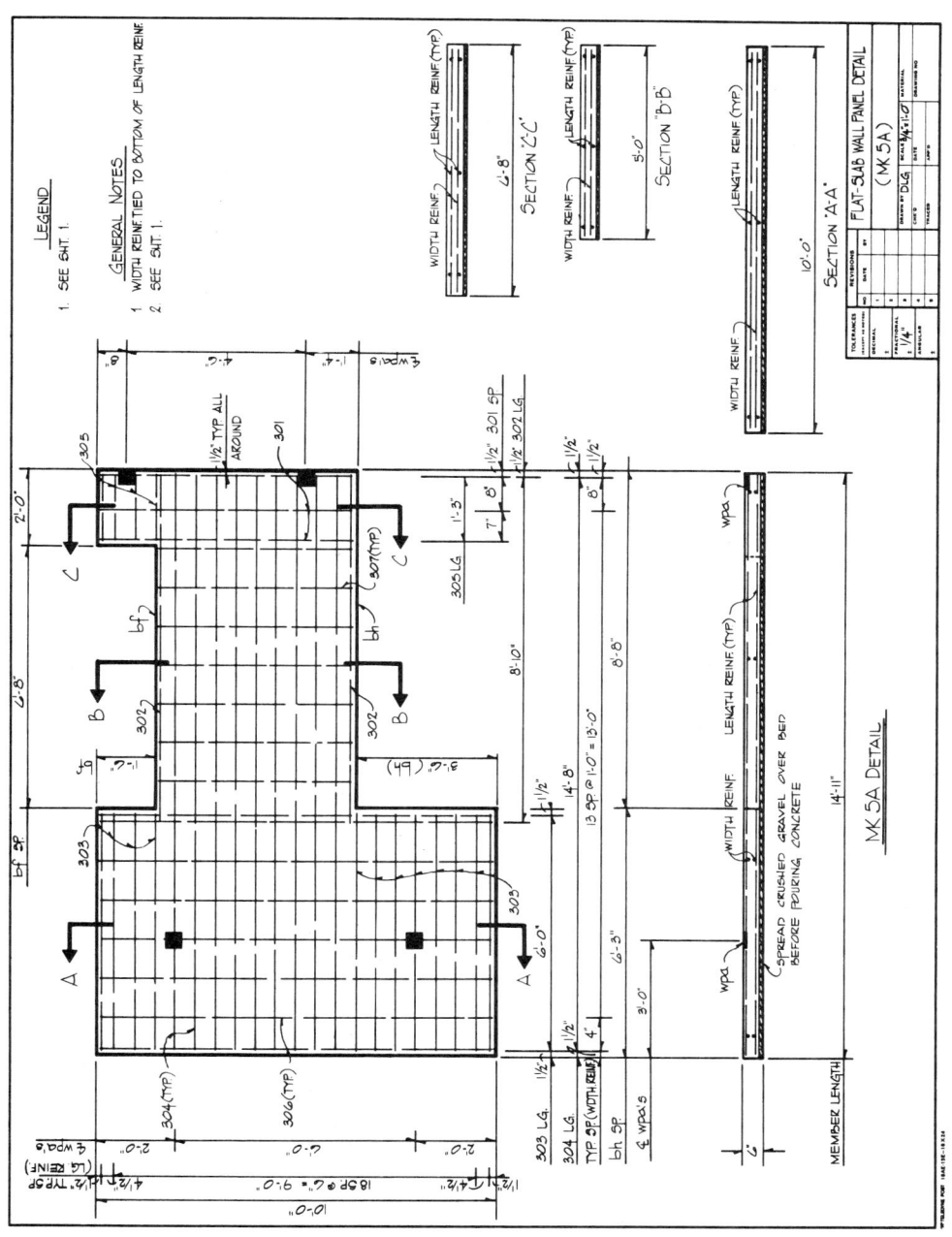

**Figure 10–27** Application projects 18 and 19.

# Appendix A
## Advanced Application Projects

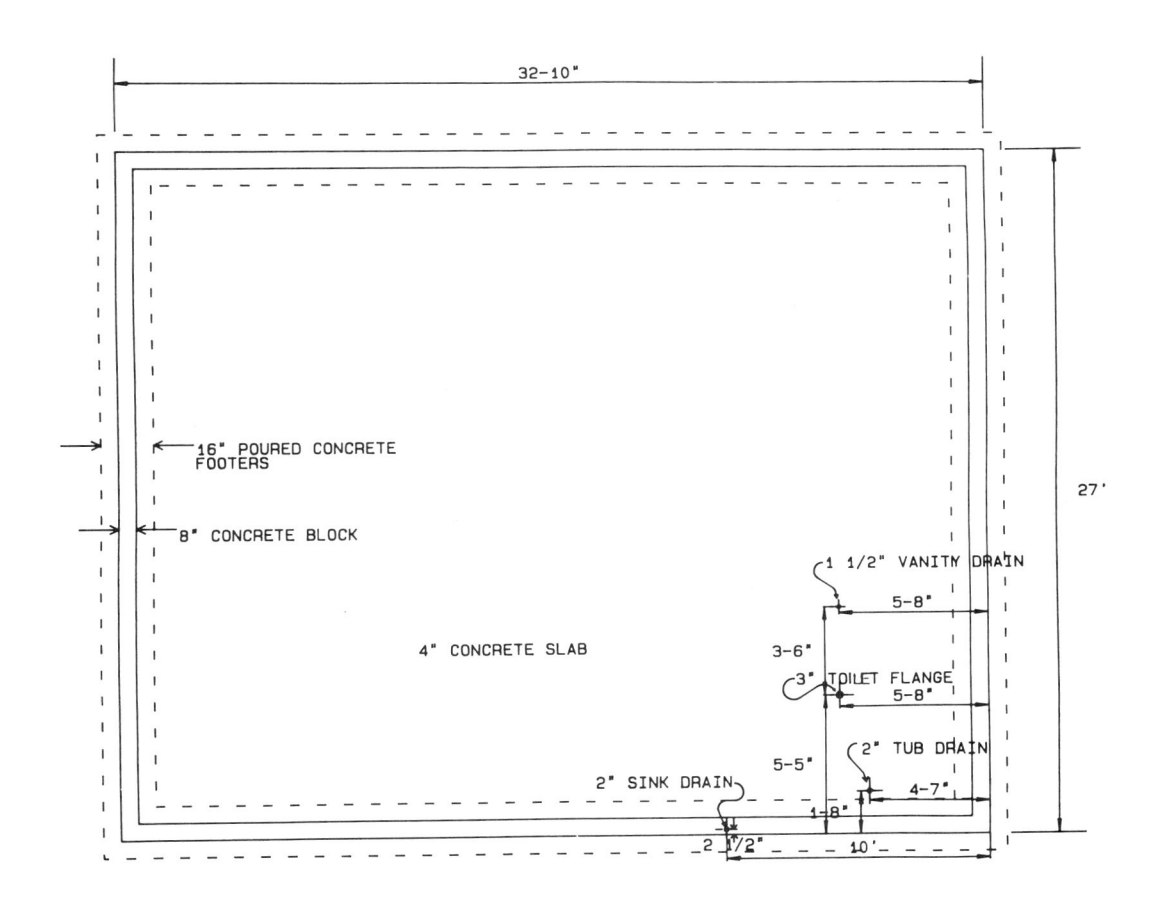

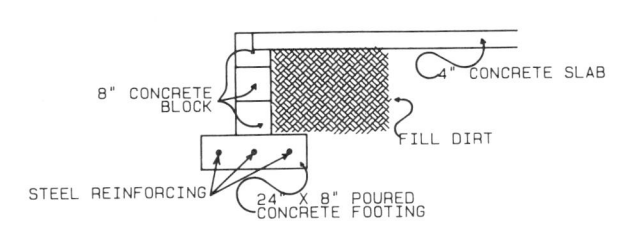

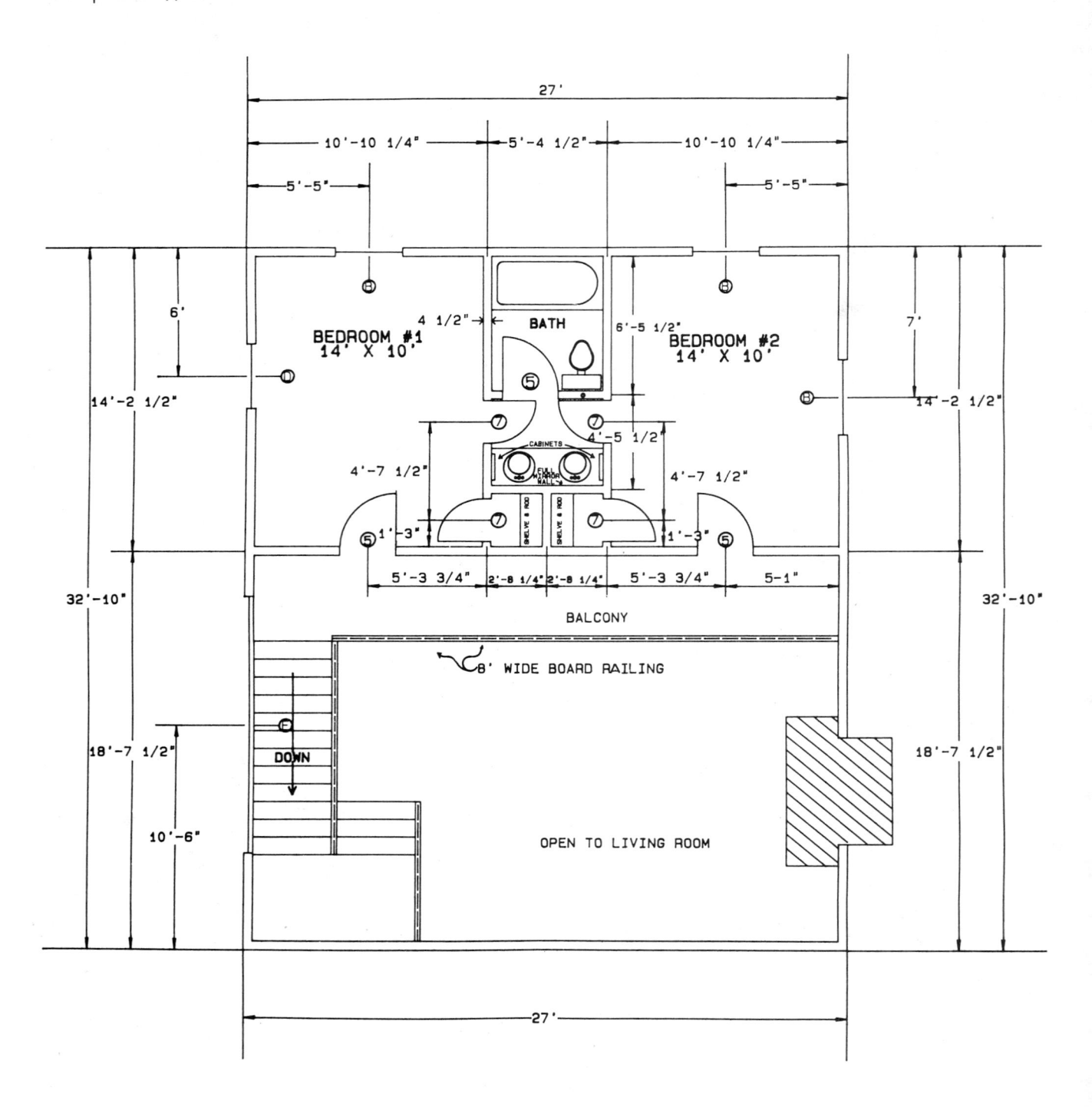

**174** | CAD Applications: Architectural

Appendix A Advanced Application Projects | 175

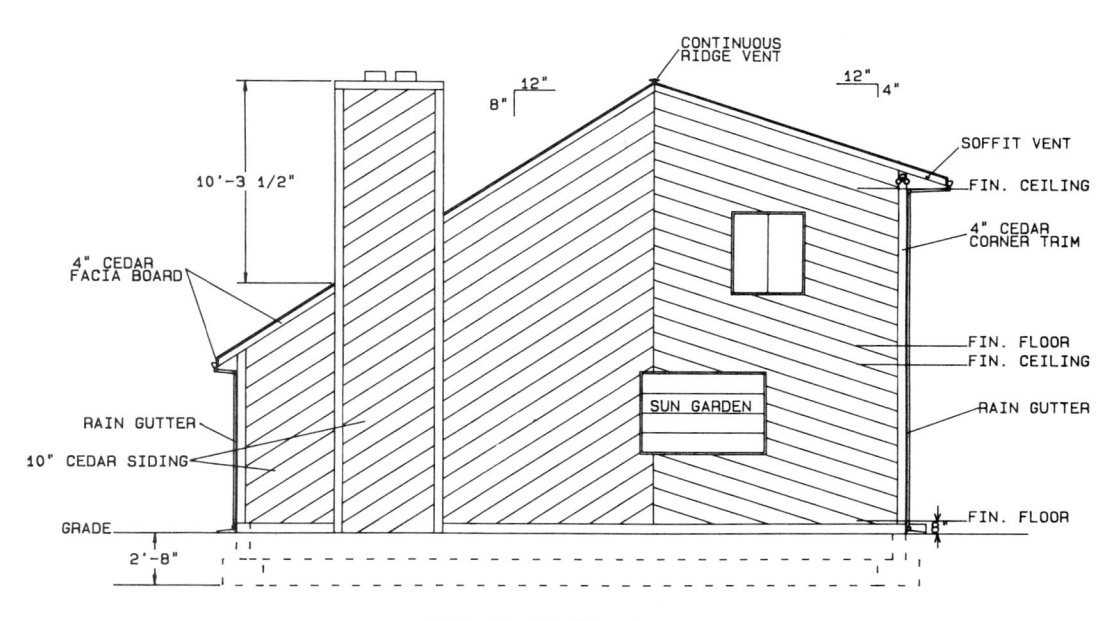

REAR ELEVATION

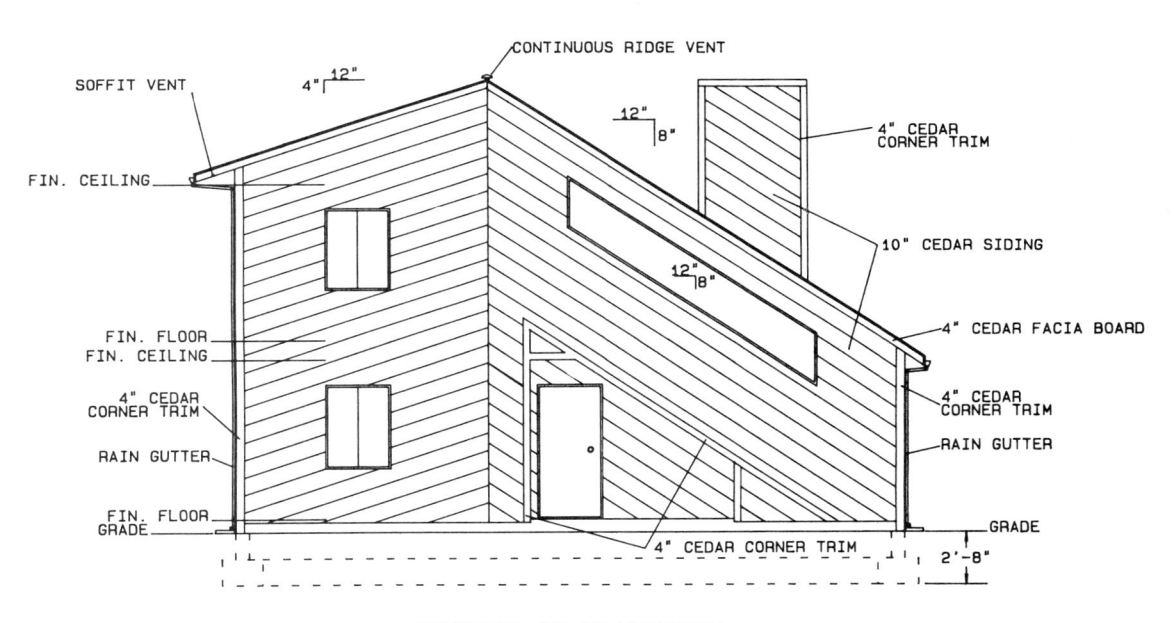

FRONT ELEVATION

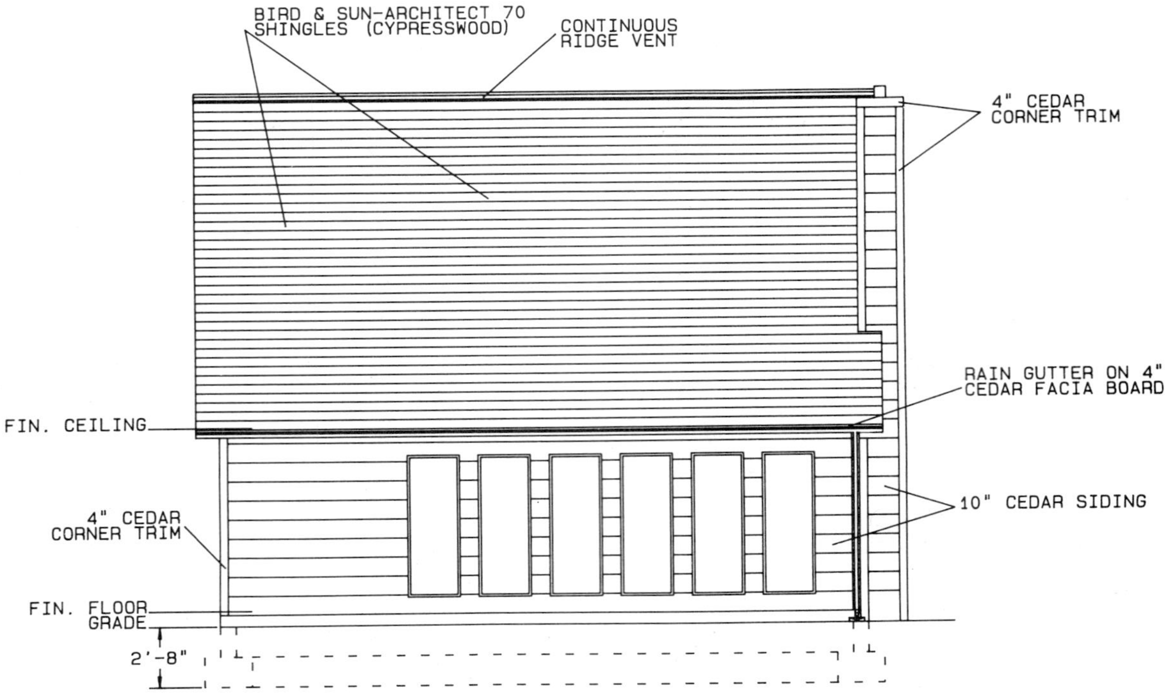


RIGHT SIDE ELEVATION

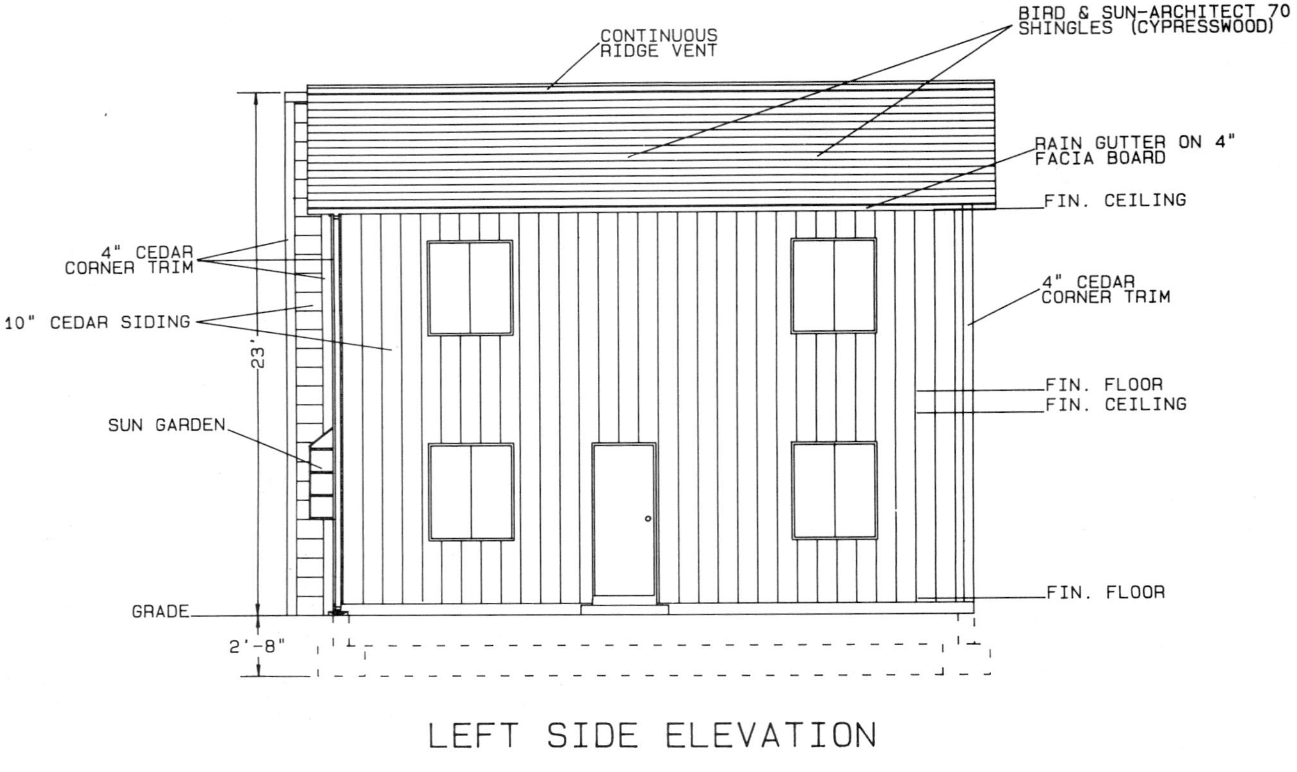


LEFT SIDE ELEVATION

| | | |
|---|---|---|
| NUMBER A-4 | DRAWN: PHILLIP OWENS<br>SCALE: 1/4"=1'<br>DATE: 02/16/84<br>C'RSE NO: ARC 2122<br>CH'D BY: MR. VANDERVEST | GULF COAST COMMUNITY COLLEGE<br>TITLE: LEFT & RIGHT SIDE ELEVATIONS<br>FOR:<br>ARCHITECTURAL DRAFTING DEPARTMENT<br>PANAMA CITY, FLORIDA |

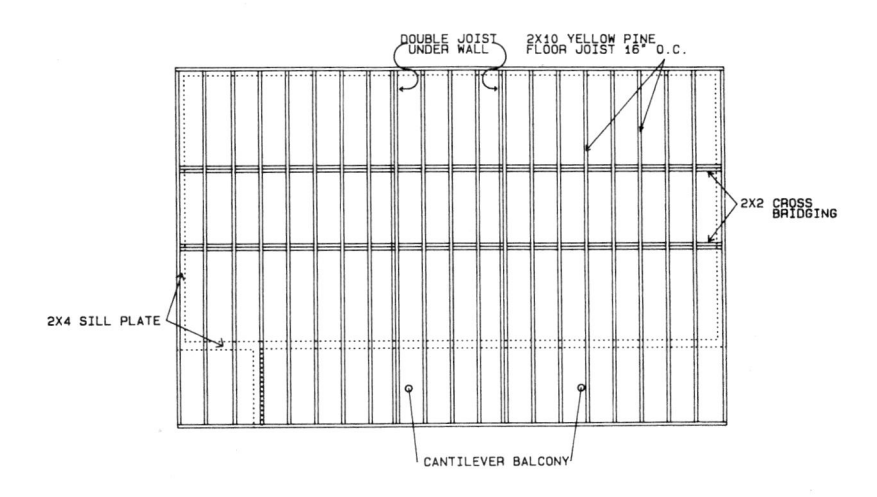

## FLOOR FRAMING PLAN (SECOND FLOOR)

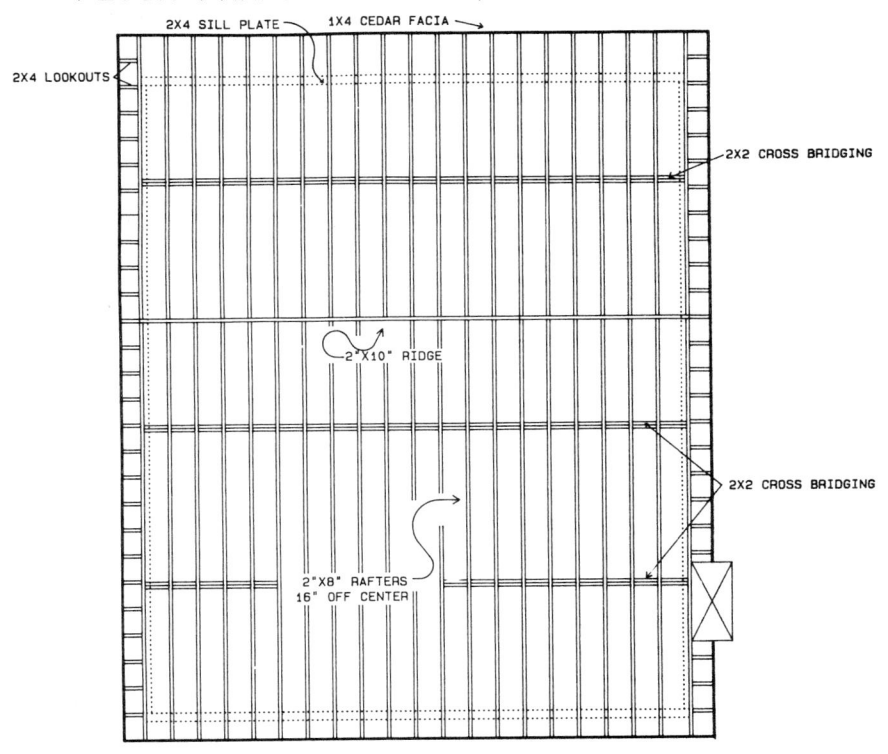

## ROOF FRAMING PLAN

178 | CAD Applications: Architectural

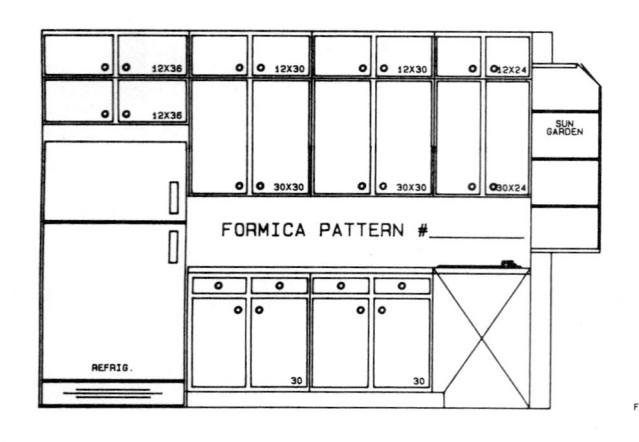

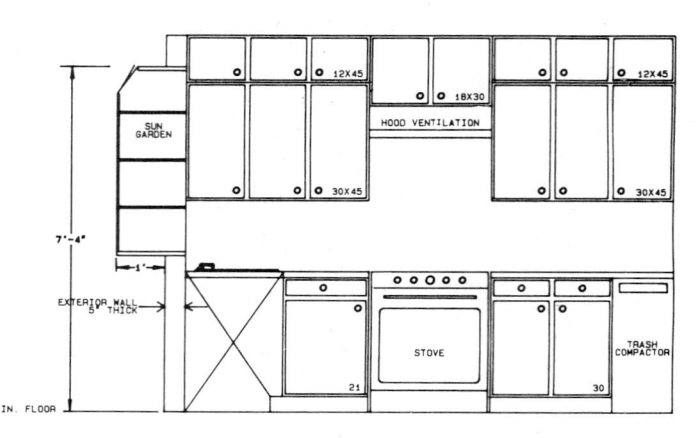

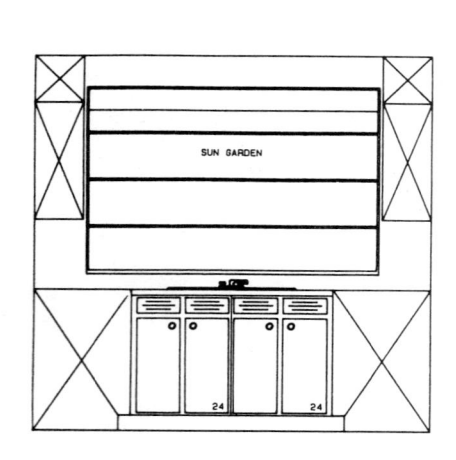

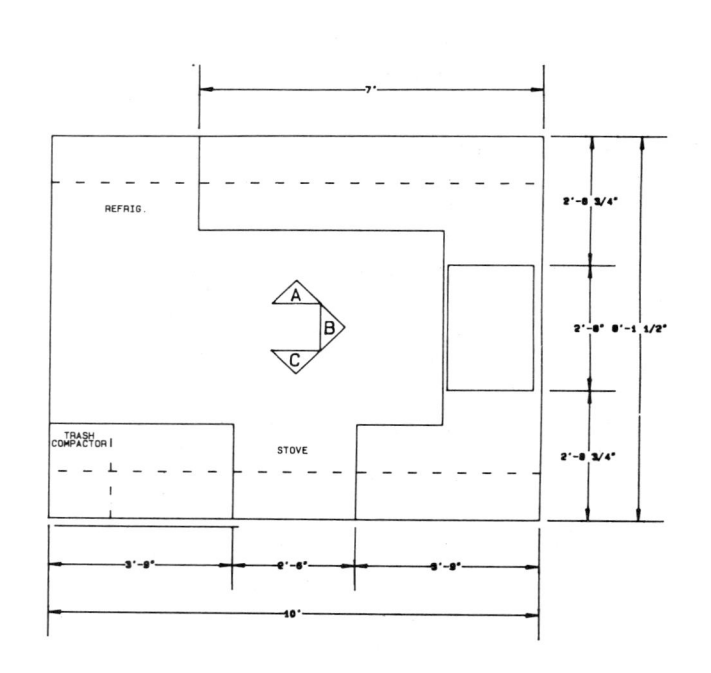

Appendix A Advanced Application Projects | 179

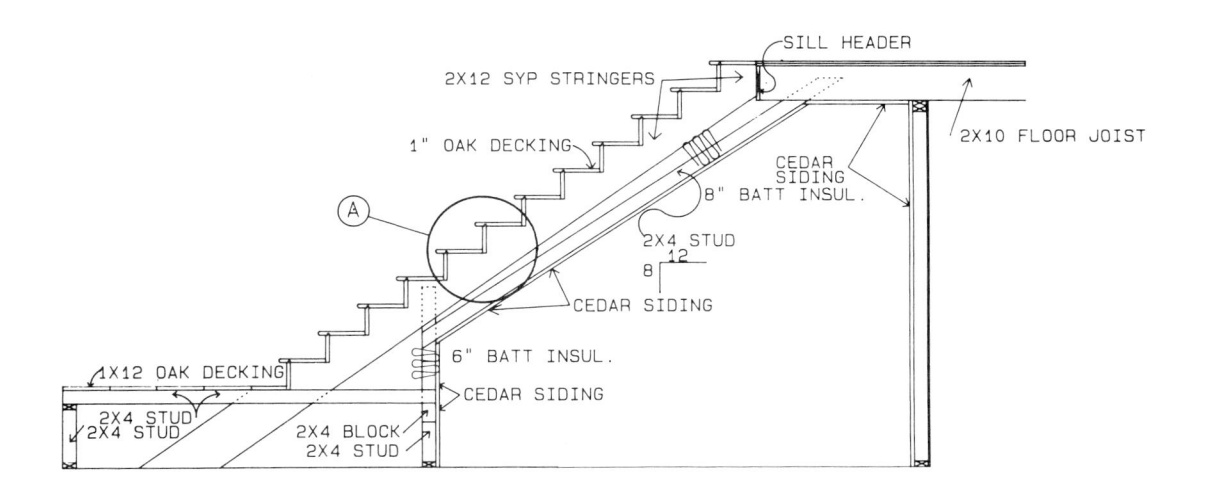

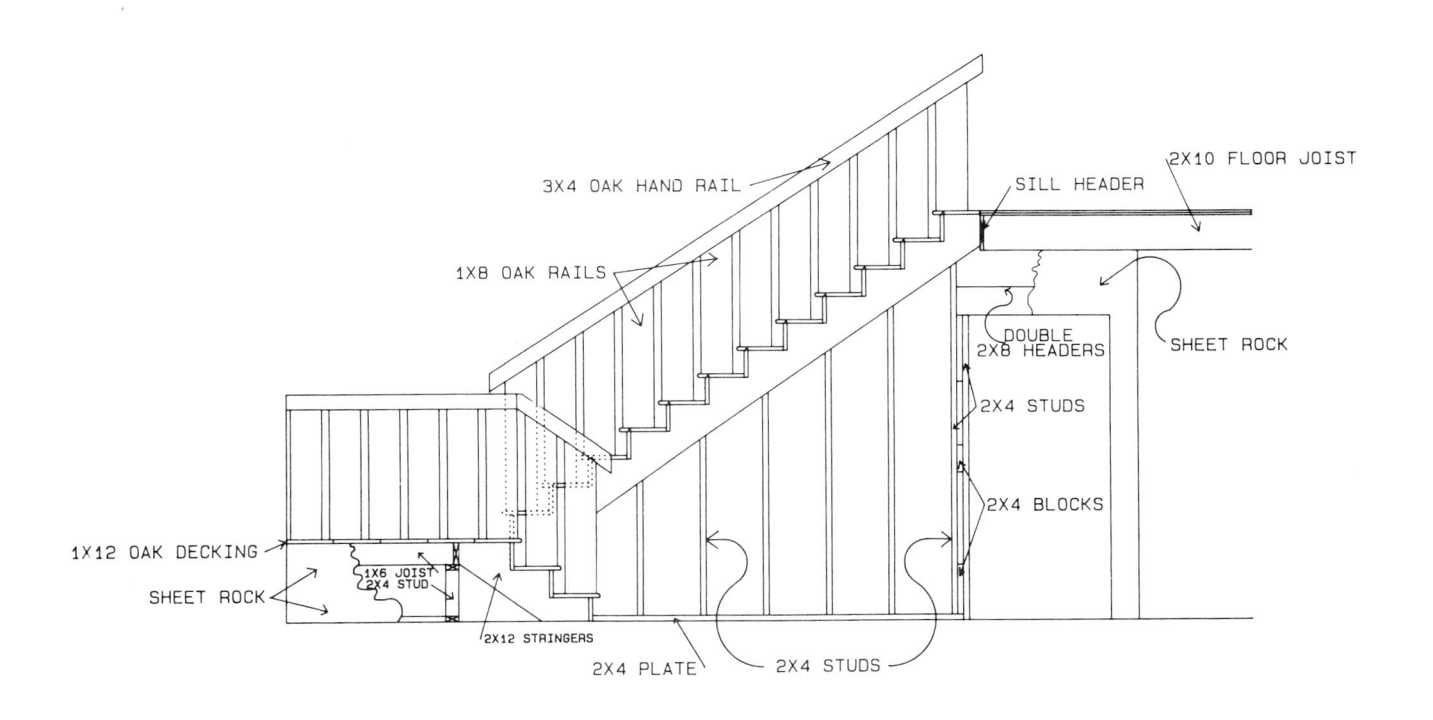

**180** | CAD Applications: Architectural

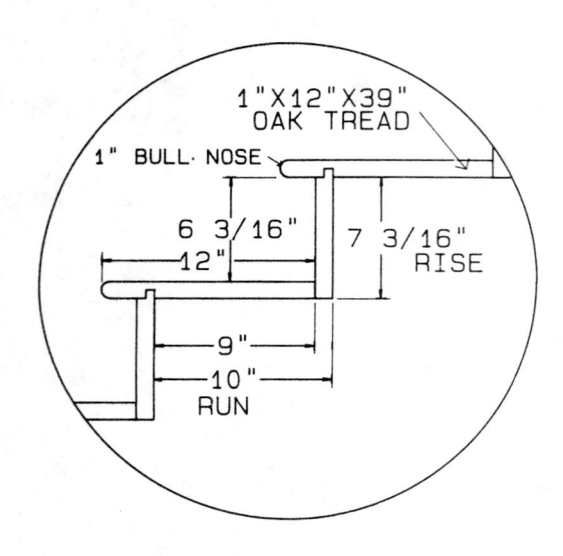

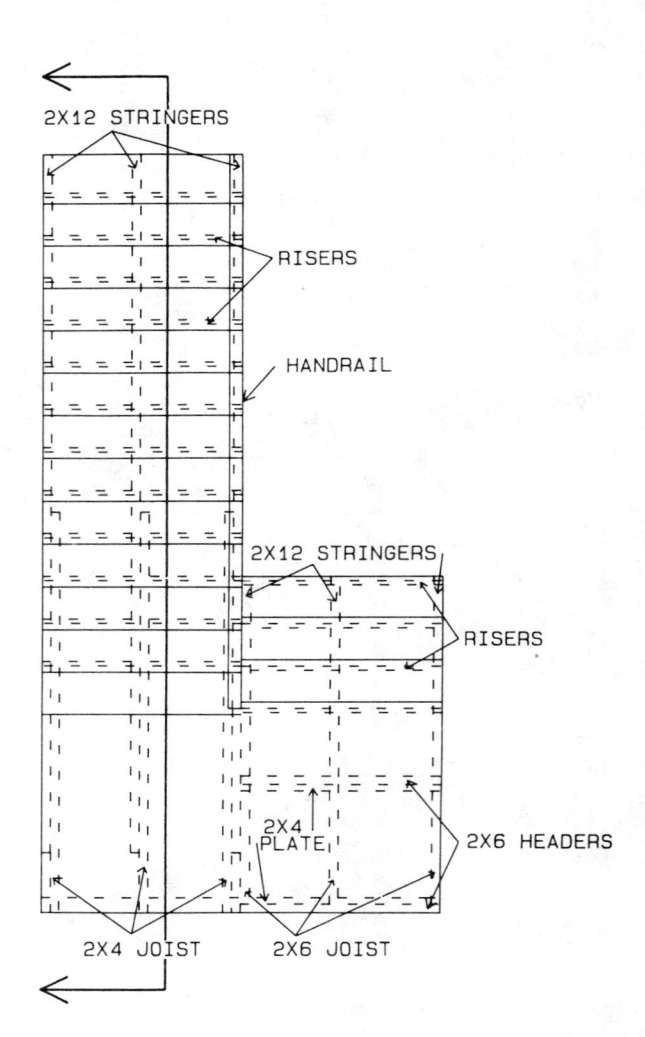

Appendix A  Advanced Application Projects | 181

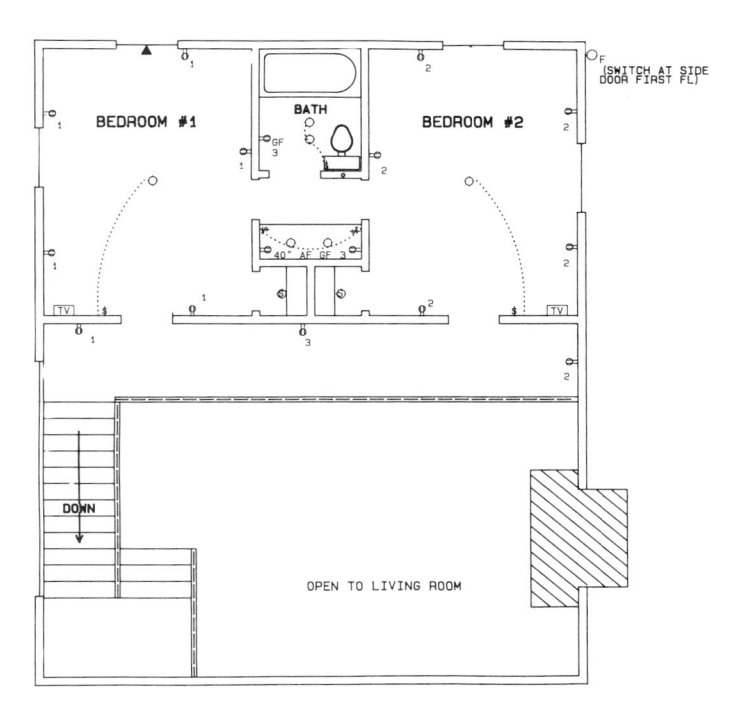

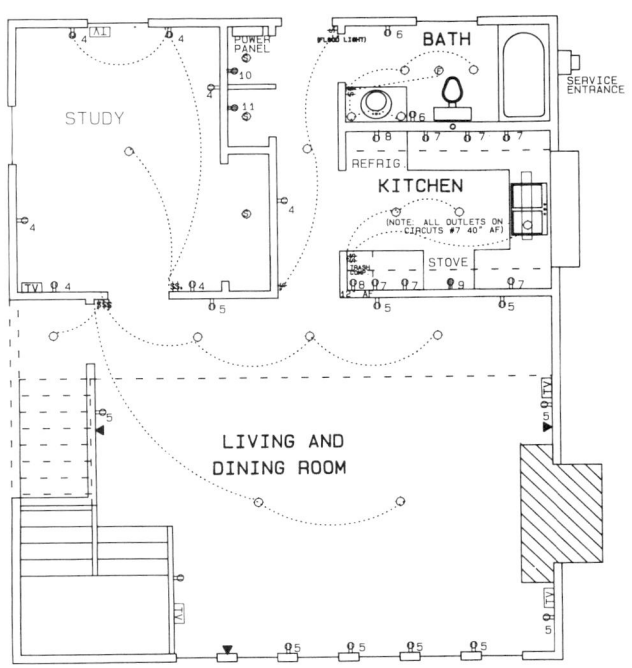

| CIRCUIT LEGEND |||||
|---|---|---|---|---|
| | ROOM | APPLIANCES | AMPS | VOLT |
| #1 | BEDROOM #1 | OUTLETS & LIGHTS | 20 | 110 |
| #2 | BEDROOM #2 | OUTLETS & LIGHTS | 20 | 110 |
| #3 | BATH #2 | OUTLETS & LIGHTS | 20 | 110 |
| #4 | STUDY | OUTLETS & LIGHTS | 20 | 110 |
| #5 | LIVING ROOM | OUTLETS & LIGHTS | 20 | 110 |
| #6 | BATH #1 | OUTLETS & LIGHTS | 20 | 110 |
| #7 | KITCHEN | OUTLETS & LIGHTS | 20 | 110 |
| #8 | KITCHEN | REFRIG. & TRASH COMP. | 20 | 110 |
| #9 | KITCHEN | STOVE | 50 | 220 |
| #10 | HALL CLS. | WATER HEATER | 50 | 220 |
| #11 | HALL CLS. | FURNACE | 50 | 220 |

| LEGEND ||
|---|---|
| TV | TELEVISION CABLE |
| | TELEPHONE |
| | DUPLEX CONVENIENCE OUTLET |
| GF | DUP OUTLET (GROUND FAULT) |
| | DUP OUTLET 1/2 W/SWITCH CONTROL |
| | 220 V OUTLET |
| $ | SINGLE POLE SWITCH |
| | SWITCH THREE WAY |
| | FLUORESCENT LIGHT |
| | CEILING LIGHT OUTLET |
| | PULL SWITCH |
| F | OUTSIDE FLOODLIGHT |
| | OUTSIDE WALL FIXTURE |

NUMBER A-9

DRAWN: PHILLIP OWENS
SCALE: 1/4" = 1'
DATE: 02/16/84
C'RSE NO: ARC 2122
CH'D BY: MR. VANDERVEST

TITLE: ELECTRICAL PLAN
FOR: FIRST & SECOND FLOOR

GULF COAST COMMUNITY COLLEGE
ARCHITECTURAL DRAFTING DEPARTMENT
PANAMA CITY, FLORIDA

## WINDOW SCHEDULE

| SYM | SIZE | TYPE | MANUFACTURER | CAT. NO | GLAZING | MATERIAL | REMARKS | QUAN |
|---|---|---|---|---|---|---|---|---|
| A | 2' X 6' | PICTURE | ANDERSON | 1N5 | TRIPLE | WOOD | DOUBLE GLAZED WITH TINTED STORM WINDOW | 6 |
| B | 3' X 4' | SLIDING | BETTER-BILT ALUMINUM | 3040 | DOUBLE | ALUMINUM | | 5 |
| C | 6' X 4' | BAY | SUN GARDEN | 6040 | DOUBLE | ALUMINUM | | 1 |
| D | 3.5'X4' | SLIDING | BETTER-BILT ALUMINUM | 3540 | DOUBLE | ALUMINUM | | 2 |
| E | 14.5'X2' | PICTURE | MARVIN GUARD | SPECIAL | DOUBLE | WOOD | PARALLELOGRAM WITH A 12/8 PITCH | 1 |

## DOOR SCHEDULE

| SYM | SIZE | THK | TYPE | MANUFACTURER | CAT. NO | MATERIAL | FINISH | JAMB | REMARKS | QUAN |
|---|---|---|---|---|---|---|---|---|---|---|
| 1 | 3'X6'8" | 7/4" | EXTERIOR | PEACH TREE | W500 | WOOD | STAIN | WOOD | | 1 |
| 2 | 2.5'X6'8" | 7/4" | EXTERIOR | PEACH TREE | A100 | WOOD | STAIN | WOOD | | 1 |
| 3 | 3'X6'8" | 7/4" | EXTERIOR | PEACH TREE | W100 | WOOD | STAIN | WOOD | | 1 |
| 4 | 2.5'X6'8" | 11 | BIFOLD | ACME | 1421 | WOOD | STAIN | WOOD | | 2 |
| 5 | 5'X6'8" | 11/8 | INTERIOR | MOHAWK (WOOD FLUSH) | BIRCH | WOOD | STAIN | WOOD | | 4 |
| 6 | 6'X6'8" | 11/8 | BIFOLD | ACME | 1423 | WOOD | STAIN | WOOD | | 4 |
| 7 | 4'X6'8" | 11/8 | INTERIOR | MOHAWK (WOOD FLUSH) | BIRCH | WOOD | STAIN | WOOD | | 1 |

## ROOM FINISH SCHEDULE

Remarks:
- A = 3 COATS ENAMEL
- B = SEAL & VARNISH
- C = STAIN, SEAL & VARNISH
- D = SPRAYED PLASTER

Floor options: CARPET OVER 5/8 PARTICAL BD. / VINYL FLOOR OVER PLYWOOD / VINYL FLOOR OVER CONCRETE / CONCRETE

Base options: CONCRETE / 5/8 PLYWOOD

Wall options (N, E, S, W): LATH & PLASTER / VERTICAL T&G 1X4 PINE / 1/4" PANELING & 1/4" PLYWOOD / UNFINISHED CEDAR / EXTERIOR TRIM

Ceiling: LATH & PLASTER / T&G 1X4 PINE

Trim: CROWN MOLDING – PINE / BASE MOLDING – PINE / CORNER TRIM – PINE

| NO. | NAME | Floor | Base | N | E | S | W | Ceiling | Wainscot Ht. | Cabinet Door Ht. | Trim |
|---|---|---|---|---|---|---|---|---|---|---|---|
| #1 | LIVING ROOM | Carpet | Concrete | A | A | A | A | D | OPEN | | A A A |
| #2 | KITCHEN | Vinyl/Plywood | 5/8 Plywood | X | X | X | X | D | 8' | | C C C |
| #3 | BATH 1ST FL | Vinyl/Plywood | 5/8 Plywood | X | X | X | X | D | 8' | | C C C |
| #4 | HALL | Carpet | 5/8 Plywood | | | | | D | 8' | | C C C |
| #5 | STUDY | Carpet | 5/8 Plywood | B | B | B | B | B | 8' | | B B B |
| #6 | STUDY CL. | Carpet | 5/8 Plywood | X | X | X | X | D | 8' | | |
| #7 | HALL CLS. | Carpet | 5/8 Plywood | A | A | A | A | D | 8' | | |
| #8 | 1ST BEDROOM | Carpet | 5/8 Plywood | A | A | A | A | D | 8' | | A A A |
| #9 | 1ST BR CLS. | Carpet | 5/8 Plywood | X | X | X | X | D | 8' | | |
| #10 | 2ND BEDROOM | Carpet | 5/8 Plywood | A | A | A | A | D | 8' | | A A A |
| #11 | 2ND BR CLS. | Carpet | 5/8 Plywood | X | X | X | X | D | 8' | | |
| #12 | WASH ROOM | Vinyl/Plywood | 5/8 Plywood | X | X | X | X | D | 8' | | |
| #13 | BATH | Vinyl/Plywood | 5/8 Plywood | A | A | A | A | D | 8' | | C C C |
| | EXTERIOR TRIM | | | B | B | B | B | | | | A A A |

---

NUMBER: A-10
DRAWN: PHILLIP OWENS
SCALE: 1/4"=1'
DATE: 02/16/84
C'RSE NO: ARC 2122
CH'D BY: MR. VANDERVEST

TITLE: WINDOW, DOOR & ROOM FINISH SCHEDULE

GULF COAST COMMUNITY COLLEGE
ARCHITECTURAL DRAFTING DEPARTMENT
PANAMA CITY, FLORIDA

# Appendix B
## Design Data

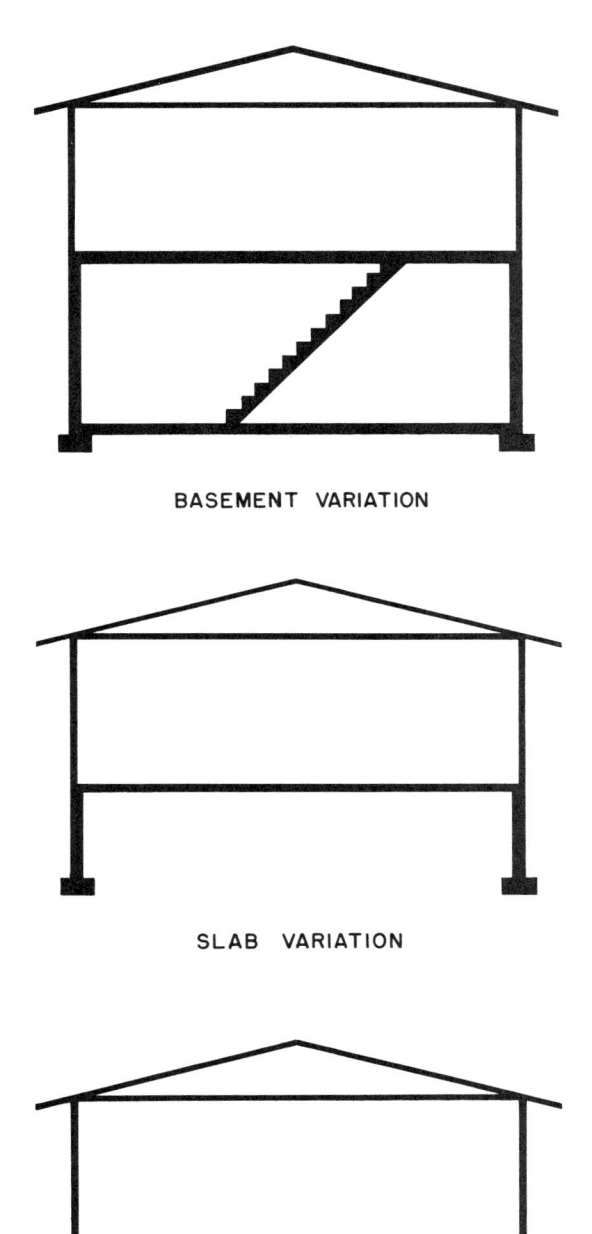

BASEMENT VARIATION

SLAB VARIATION

CRAWL SPACE VARIATION

**Figure B-1** One-story house variations.

BASEMENT VARIATION

SLAB VARIATION

CRAWL SPACE VARIATION

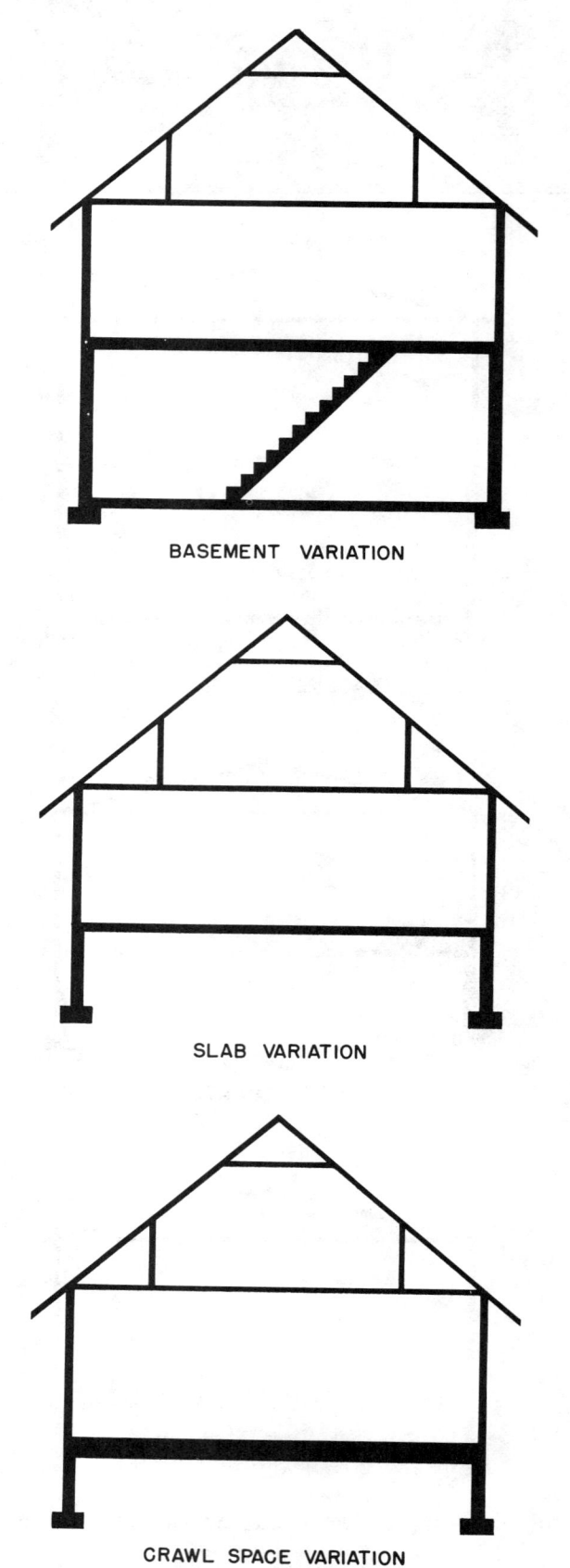

**Figure B–2** One-and-a-half story house variations.

SLAB VARIATION

BASEMENT VARIATION

CRAWL SPACE VARIATION

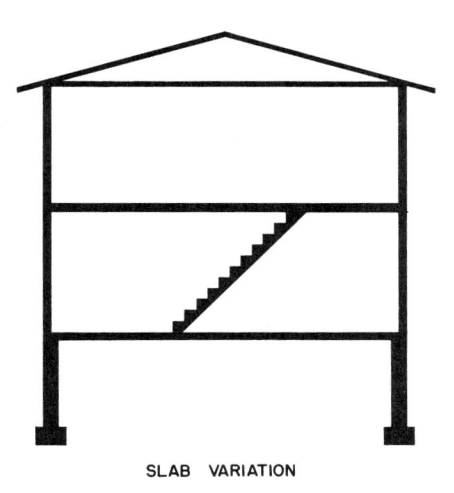

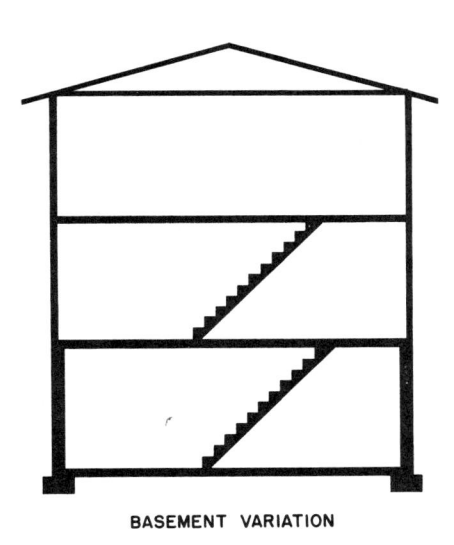

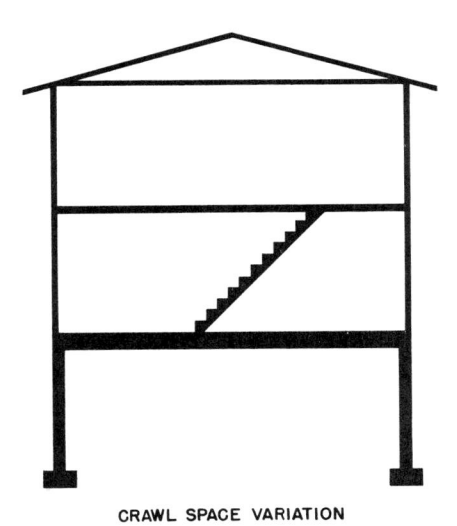

**Figure B-3** Two-story house variations.

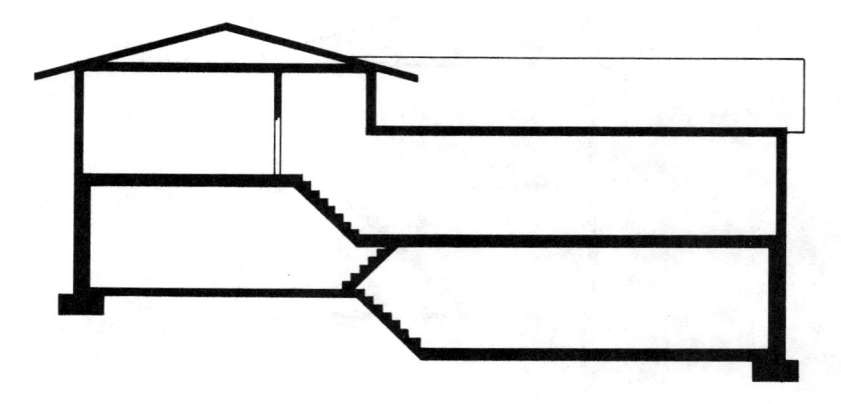

SIDE - BY - SIDE VARIATION

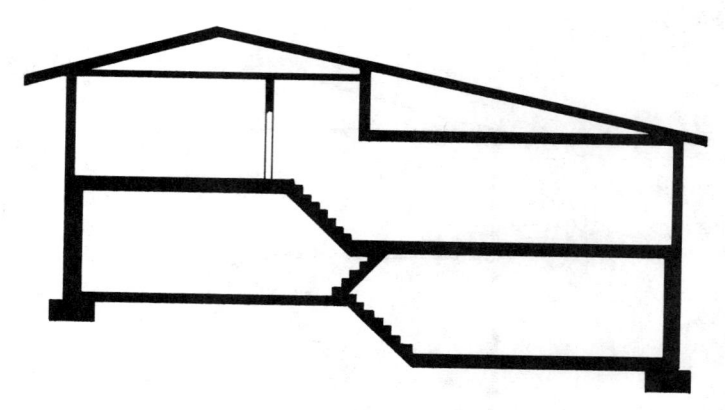

FRONT - TO - BACK VARIATION

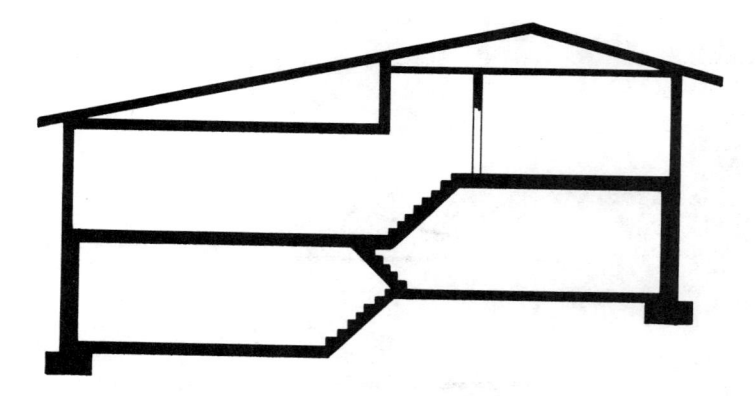

BACK - TO - FRONT VARIATION

**Figure B–4** Split-level house variations.

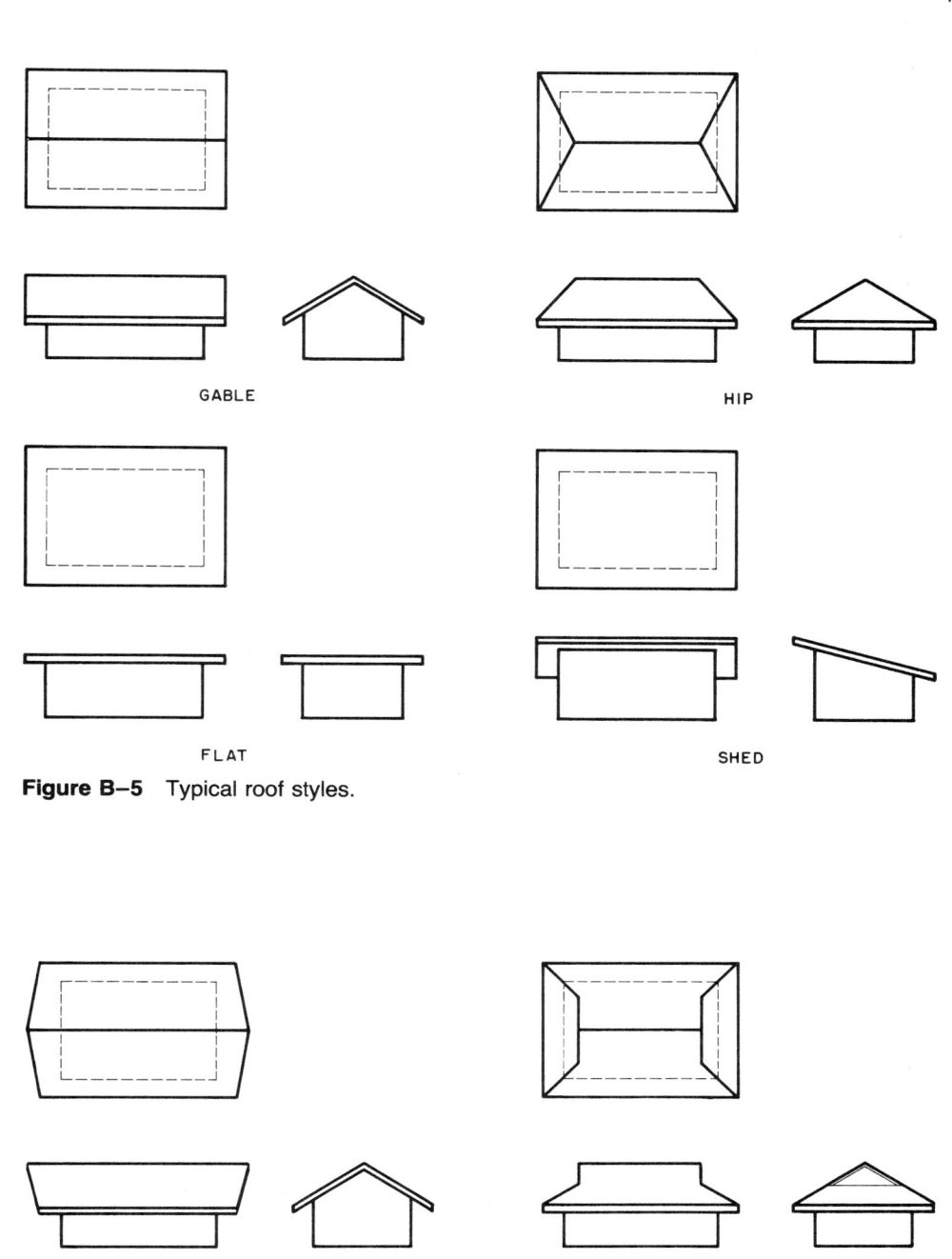

Appendix B Design Data | **187**

**Figure B-5** Typical roof styles.

**Figure B-6** Typical roof styles (continued).

RECTANGULAR DINING TABLE

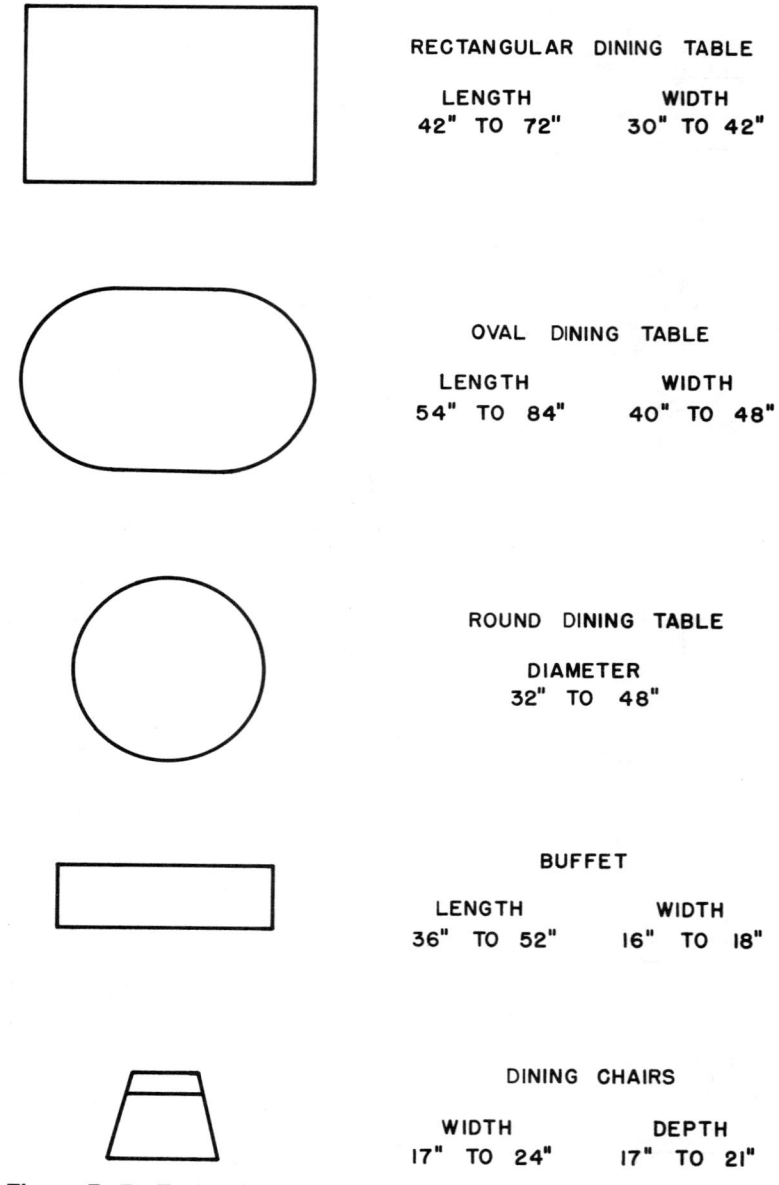

LENGTH     WIDTH
42" TO 72"     30" TO 42"

OVAL DINING TABLE

LENGTH     WIDTH
54" TO 84"     40" TO 48"

ROUND DINING TABLE

DIAMETER
32" TO 48"

BUFFET

LENGTH     WIDTH
36" TO 52"     16" TO 18"

DINING CHAIRS

WIDTH     DEPTH
17" TO 24"     17" TO 21"

**Figure B-7** Typical furnishing sizes.

Appendix B Design Data | **189**

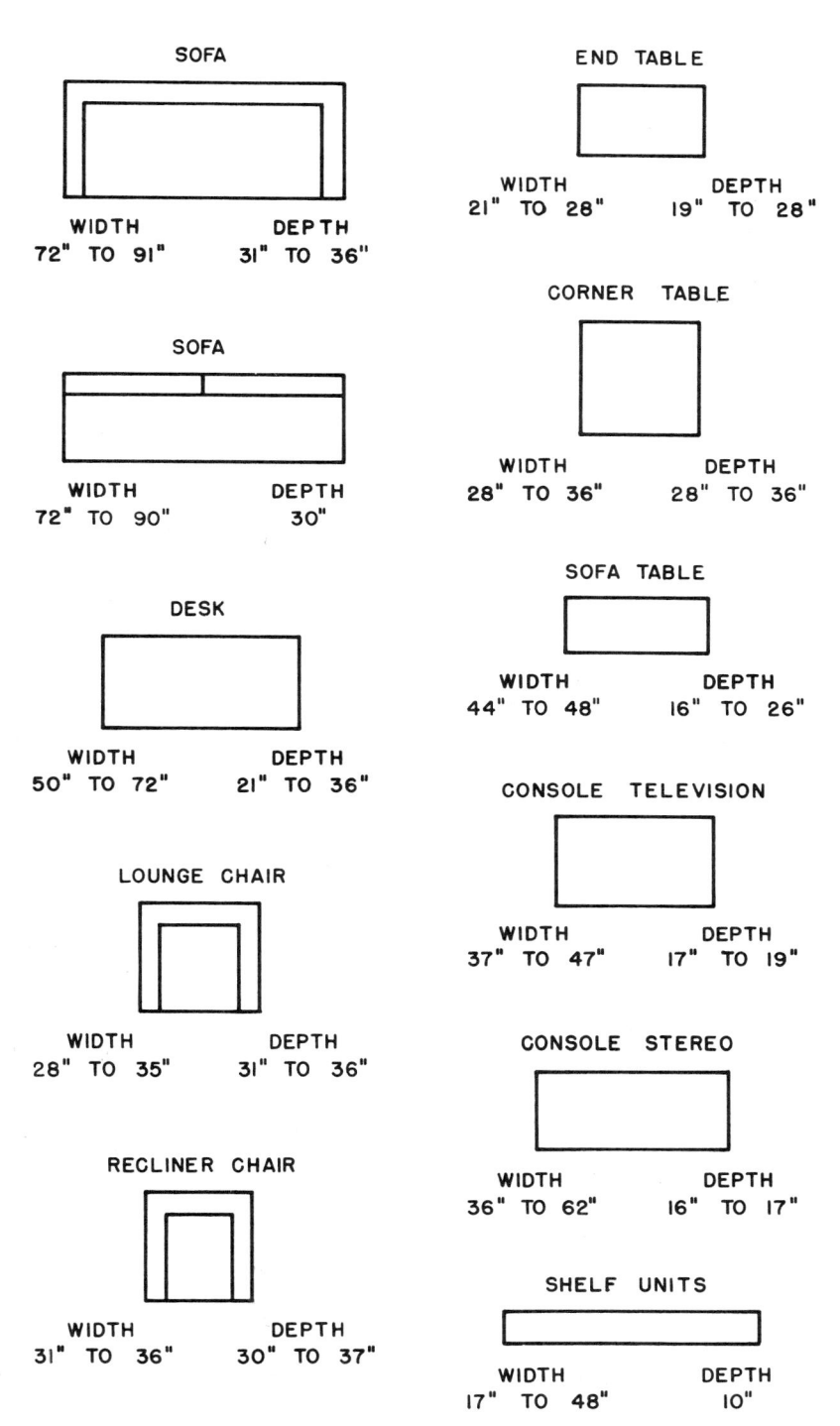

SOFA
WIDTH 72" TO 91"   DEPTH 31" TO 36"

SOFA
WIDTH 72" TO 90"   DEPTH 30"

DESK
WIDTH 50" TO 72"   DEPTH 21" TO 36"

LOUNGE CHAIR
WIDTH 28" TO 35"   DEPTH 31" TO 36"

RECLINER CHAIR
WIDTH 31" TO 36"   DEPTH 30" TO 37"

END TABLE
WIDTH 21" TO 28"   DEPTH 19" TO 28"

CORNER TABLE
WIDTH 28" TO 36"   DEPTH 28" TO 36"

SOFA TABLE
WIDTH 44" TO 48"   DEPTH 16" TO 26"

CONSOLE TELEVISION
WIDTH 37" TO 47"   DEPTH 17" TO 19"

CONSOLE STEREO
WIDTH 36" TO 62"   DEPTH 16" TO 17"

SHELF UNITS
WIDTH 17" TO 48"   DEPTH 10"

**Figure B-8** Typical furnishing sizes (continued).

# CAD Applications: Architectural

```
                DESK                                    CHEST OF DRAWERS
              WIDTH    DEPTH                          WIDTH       DEPTH
           33" TO 43"  16" TO 20"                  20" TO 36"   15" TO 18"

           NIGHT TABLE                                  DRESSER
                                                      WIDTH       DEPTH
                                            DOUBLE
                                            DRESSER  48" TO 50"     18"
              WIDTH    DEPTH                TRIPLE
           22" TO 24"  15" TO 22"           DRESSER  52" TO 60"   16" TO 18"

           SINGLE BED                              DOUBLE BED
```

|  | LENGTH | WIDTH |  | LENGTH | WIDTH |
|---|---|---|---|---|---|
| BUNK BED | 75" | 30" TO 33" | DOUBLE BED | 75" TO 84" | 54" |
| DORMITORY BED | 75" TO 80" | 33" TO 36" | QUEEN-SIZE BED | 80" TO 84" | 60" |
| TWIN BED | 75" TO 84" | 39" | KING-SIZE BED | 80" TO 84" | 72" TO 76" |
| THREE-QUARTER BED | 75" TO 80" | 48" |  |  |  |

**Figure B–9** Typical furnishing sizes (continued).

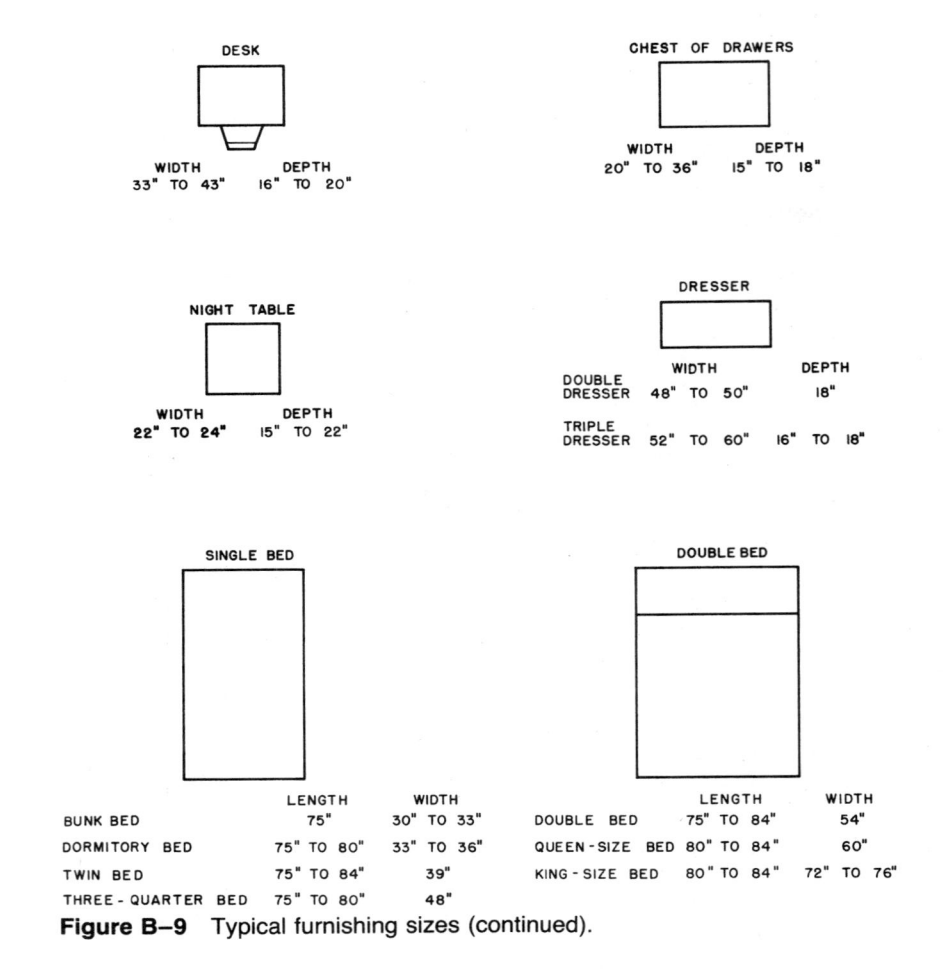

```
           STANDARD TUB
                                                  WALL HUNG SINK

             WIDTH       LENGTH                    WIDTH       DEPTH
         30" TO 31 1/2"  54" TO 72"             19" TO 24"   17" TO 20"

                            WATER CLOSET

                                                  WIDTH            DEPTH
         FLOOR MOUNTED ONE-PIECE               17" TO 21"    25 1/2" TO 26 3/4"
         FLOOR MOUNTED TWO-PIECE                 20 3/8"     27 3/4" TO 29 3/4"
```

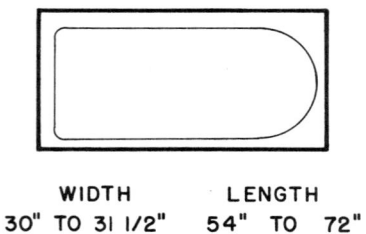

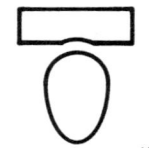

**Figure B–10** Typical fixture sizes.

REFRIGERATOR
WIDTH      DEPTH
24" TO 36"  24" TO 30"

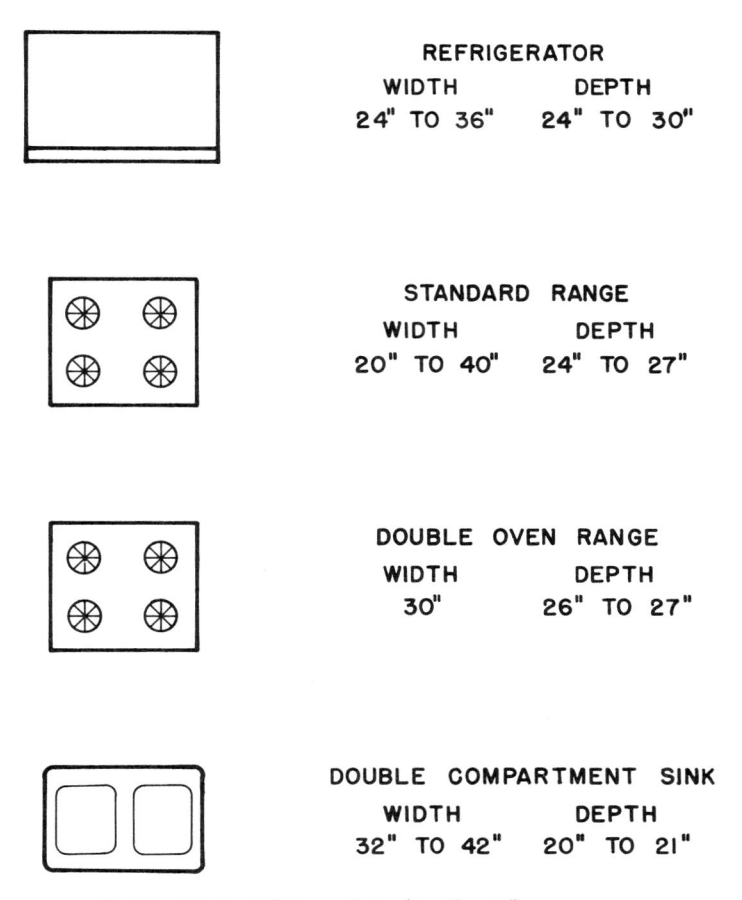

STANDARD RANGE
WIDTH      DEPTH
20" TO 40"  24" TO 27"

DOUBLE OVEN RANGE
WIDTH      DEPTH
30"        26" TO 27"

DOUBLE COMPARTMENT SINK
WIDTH      DEPTH
32" TO 42"  20" TO 21"

**Figure B-11** Typical fixture sizes (continued).

**192** | CAD Applications: Architectural

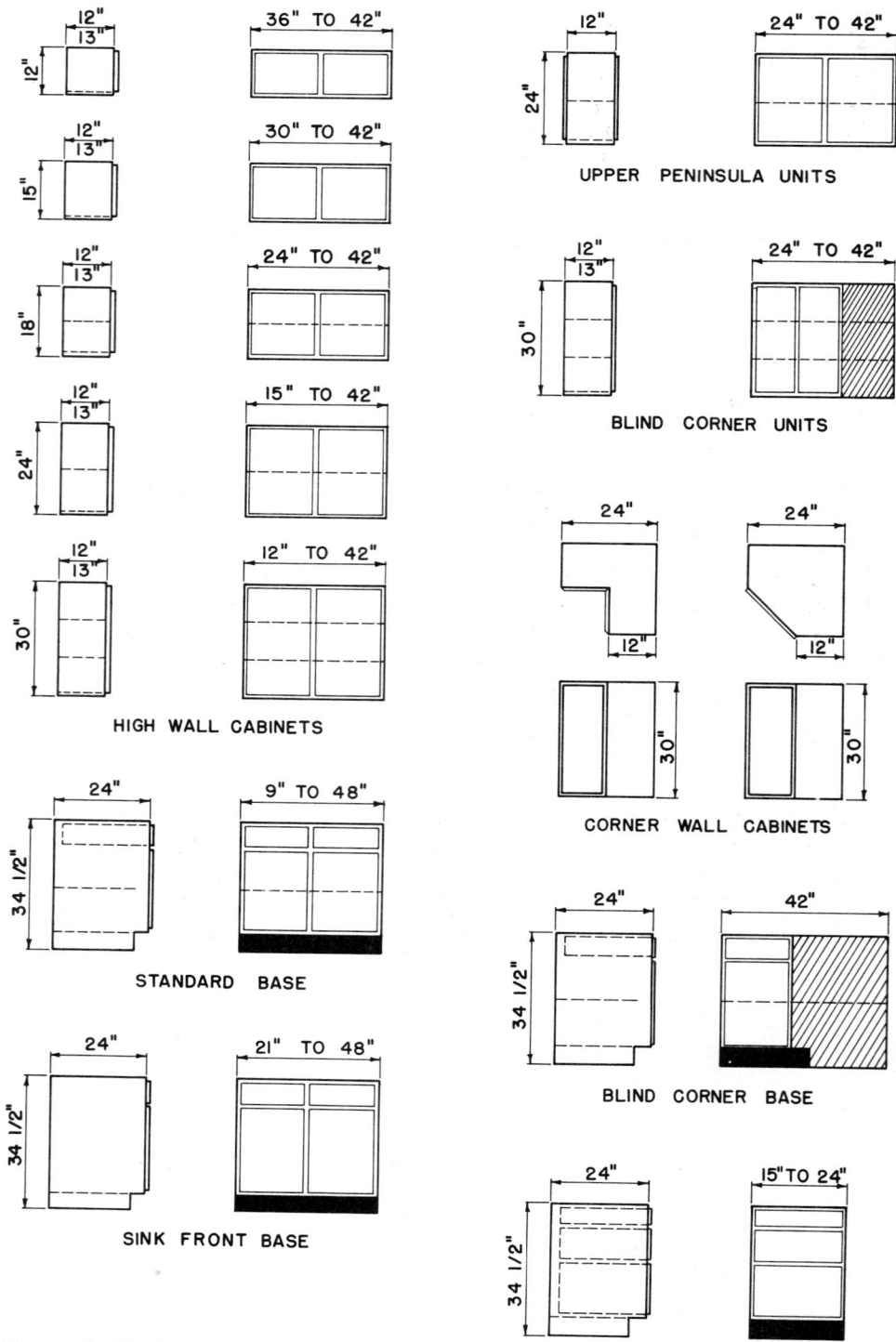

**Figure B-12** Typical cabinet sizes.

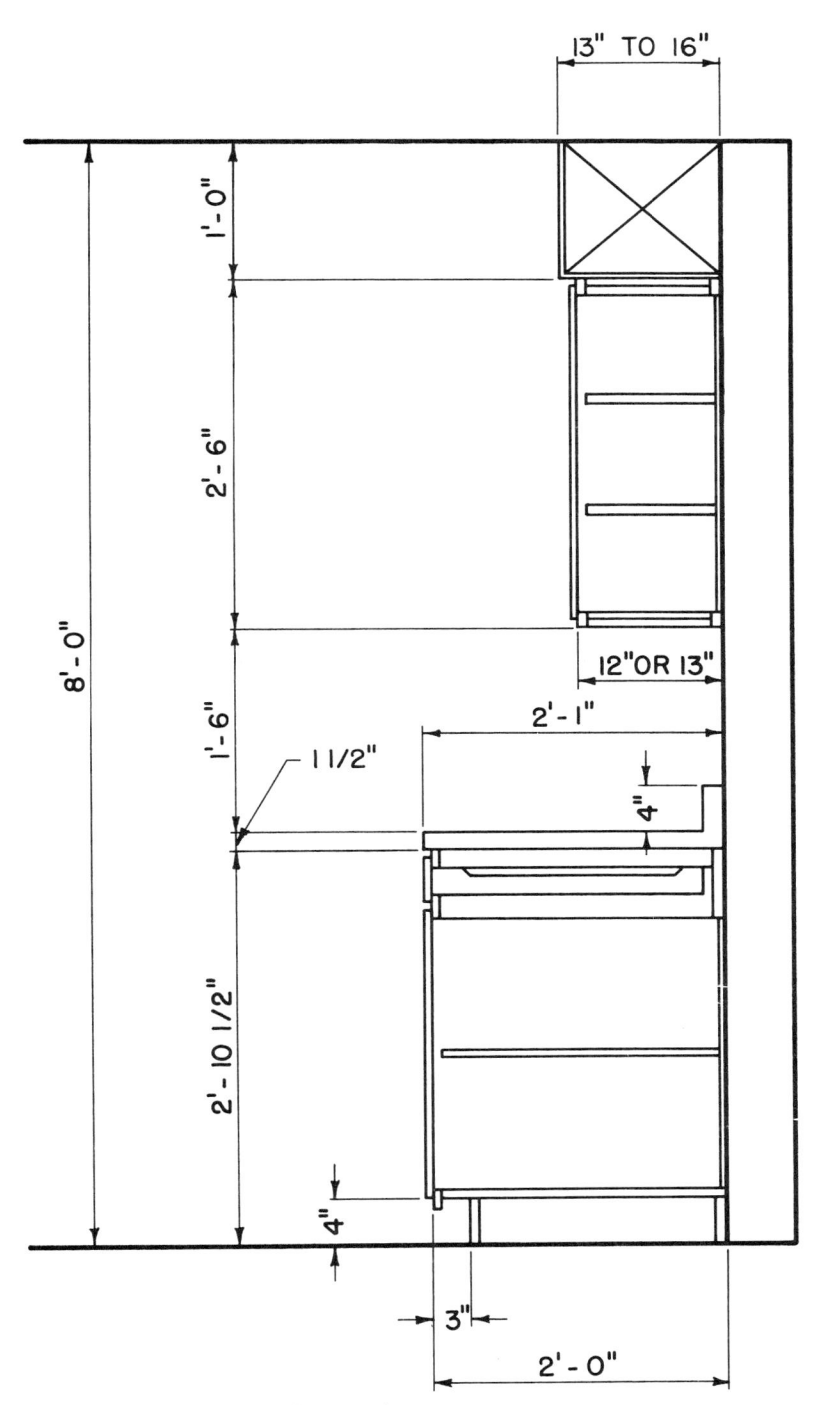

**Figure B–13** Typical cabinet section.

Fitz Memorial Library
Endicott College
Beverly, Massachusetts 01915

NA
2728
.G64
1986

DATE DUE

Nov 2, 2001

DISCARDED